DATE DUE

NO 15 04			

PETE
TOWNSHEND

Pete Townshend. Photograph courtesy of John S. Blonsick III. Used with permission.

PETE TOWNSHEND

The Minstrel's Dilemma

Larry David Smith

PRAEGER

Westport, Connecticut
London

Library of Congress Cataloging-in-Publication Data

Smith, Larry David.
    Pete Townshend : the minstrel's dilemma / Larry David Smith.
      p. cm.
    Includes bibliographical references (p.) and index.
    ISBN 0–275–96472–8 (alk. paper)
    1. Townshend, Pete. 2. Rock musicians—England—Biography.
    3. Townshend, Pete—Criticism and interpretation. I. Title.
    ML410.T69S65 1999
    782.42166′092—dc21
    [B]   98–35320

British Library Cataloguing in Publication Data is available.

Library of Congress Catalog Card Number: 98–35320
ISBN: 0–275–96472–8

First published in 1999

Praeger Publishers, 88 Post Road West, Westport, CT 06881
An imprint of Greenwood Publishing Group, Inc.

Printed in the United States of America

The paper used in this book complies with the
Permanent Paper Standard issued by the National
Information Standards Organization (Z39.48–1984).

10 9 8 7 6 5 4 3 2

COPYRIGHT ACKNOWLEDGMENTS

The author and publisher gratefully acknowledge permission for use of the following material:

Excerpts from *Horse's Neck* by Pete Townshend. Copyright © 1985 by Pete Townshend.
Reprinted by permission of Houghton Mifflin Company. All rights reserved.

Excerpts from *Before I Get Old: The Story of The Who* by Dave Marsh. Copyright © 1983 by
Dave Marsh. Reprinted by permission of St. Martin's Press, Inc.

Dedicated to

Jeptha Glenn Smith

"I know a man who's a man"

Contents

Preface

I'm a college professor. That means I have to go to a lot of meetings. A few years ago I attended a research presentation by a job applicant. During the show I noticed a colleague was reading a graduate student's Master's thesis. The paper's methodology section opened by paraphrasing John Lennon: "I don't believe in method, I believe in me." Trust the critic/theorist, such perspectives assert; all other considerations are, at most, secondary.

This book offers a different view.

This book is about commercial art, and it urges you to trust nothing—especially me. I encourage you to consider *everything* possible before rendering the slightest opinion about the commercial art world. That's a pretty tall order, so let's trust systematic argument to qualify our judgments and focus our claims. Simply, let's trust method.

Before exploring Pete Townshend's version of "the minstrel's dilemma," I must thank several people. First, I thank Reid Stephenson. Reid's battle with cancer inspired the commitment necessary to see this work through. Thanks to Kevin Brown, Diana Cable, Michael Holmes, Roland Kelts, and Brent Tebeau (along with everyone who contributed in any way). Thanks to John Blonsick for the frontispiece photograph. And thanks to the folks at Greenwood Publishing: Pamela St. Clair, Leanne Jisonna, and David Palmer.

A special thank you goes to Carol Latham, Nicola Joss, and Pete Townshend. Mr. Townshend makes this book possible in many ways. Ms. Joss makes this work possible PERIOD. Without Nicola Joss, there would be no *Minstrel's Dilemma*. She is the hero in *my* story.

Though I'm tempted to talk about my mamma playing the boogie-woogie on the church piano (my first musical recollection), and how I was raised on Elvis, gospel music, and Saturday night wrestling, good taste prevails. Instead, I'll just say that artistic vision is a powerful thing. Fighting for those visions, however,

xx
x PREFACE

can be hell.   So, as you read the following pages, focus on that vision, Townshend's persistence, and the results.   I'll try to stay out of the way.

PART I

The Minstrel's Dilemma

Introduction

Pete Townshend was disappointed by Nik Cohn's response to the demo tape of his first completed opera, *Tommy*. After years of outrageous histrionics (on and off stage), Townshend's band, The Who, was in financial trouble; moreover, the band's latest single, "I Can See For Miles," had failed to achieve its commercial projections (at least in Townshend's view). Townshend, therefore, faced a formidable artistic/commercial hurdle, and he hoped *Tommy* might meet that challenge. Cohn—a respected young music journalist with the *Manchester Guardian* (and later the *New York Times*)—met Townshend at a local pinball parlor to discuss the project. Cohn concluded that the "rock opera" innovation's emphasis on the protagonist's spiritual journey was tedious and boring. While they played pinball, Townshend inquired whether a shift in plot might help. A positive response sent the songwriter home, where he wrote the track "Pinball Wizard" that very evening. He also shifted *Tommy*'s story line by using the pinball metaphor to articulate his spiritual stance. The author's willingness to compromise his work for a favorable review (from a respected journalist/friend) demonstrated a tenacious commercial drive and its relationship to an equally ambitious artistic impulse. At this point in his career, Pete Townshend was not to be denied.

Music historian Henry Raynor's (1978) observations regarding his lack of "purely musical" (p. 6) evidence establishes a similar pattern. Raynor contends that the history of Western music involves an evolving series of negotiations between artists and auditors in which various institutions, industries, or individuals influence the musical trends of a given age. For instance, he writes that "Mozart's letters explain how he will contrive effects that will delight his audience" and that Haydn's and Beethoven's personal letters "show how publishers should be dealt with." Raynor maintains such tendencies continued beyond these legends in that "their successors are equally business-like and equally concerned not with aims but with practicalities." In other words, the history of Western music consists not of artists shaping sounds that communicate personal "aims" (i.e., a "purely musical" endeavor); rather, that history is a story of give and take, negotiation and compromise. Raynor argues:

> Our musical thinking has been so completely dominated by the nineteenth-century conceptions of art as pure activity, occupying only the higher strata of its creator's consciousness and unaffected by such lower strata as those which reckon up the bills and consider the possibility of paying them, that we do not consider the composer's relationship to the musical world in which he must, as employee no less than as freelance, secure performance and publication. (p. 11)

Further proof of Raynor's point resides in the "minstrel's" evolution. Attali (1985) reports that "it took centuries for music to enter commodity exchange" (p. 14) and describes how an early Western minstrel, the *jongleur*, was originally a social outcast. These musician/entertainers were condemned by the Church and relegated to an "itinerant life-style" that cast him (there were few "hers") as "a highly unrespectable figure, akin to the vagabond or the highwayman." Consequently, the jongleur roamed from place to place and rendered his services in private settings. During this phase of the musical world's evolution, the jongleur "was music" in that he "alone created it, carried it with him, and completely organized its circulation within society." Over time a new era of minstrelsy emerged, the jongleur's nomadic days ceased, and he "settled down, attached to a court, or [became] the resident of a town" (p. 15). To secure and sustain employment these musicians joined guilds, learned gimmicks (juggling, bird imitations, jumping through hoops, and storytelling were popular), built alliances (with other musicians and their guilds), and perfected local polemics. A successful minstrel was one who obtained a position in a court or municipality, mastered that audience's musical tastes, and restricted his style to that format. Attali concludes that "from that day forward" the musician was "economically bound to a machine of power, political or commercial," which in many instances subjugated artistic ideal to audience expectation.

No doubt this artistic climate induced varying levels of anxiety in its musical talent. Consider the case of the romantically inclined minstrel—wishing to sit quietly and recite his poetry to a light instrumental accompaniment—who must jump through hoops, juggle his instrument, sing tributes to his audience, and correspondingly suppress his amorous proclivities, in order to please his benefactors. Scenarios such as this represent an early version of what I call the *minstrel's dilemma*. Should this minstrel forsake his audience and play what he pleases, he could easily threaten his livelihood and invite destitution. As with the Townshend/*Tommy* example, the minstrel's choice between satisfying his audience and fulfilling his artistic impulses may require little, if any, deliberation.

The centuries passed, and the proverbial wisdom held: the more the musical environment changed, the more it remained the same. Sources of authority moved from the institutional decrees of the Church or State to the industrial pronouncements of corporate elite, but the *minstrel's dilemma* remained.

Throughout music history musicians have quarreled with one another, their management, and their audiences over artistic "aims" and commercial "practicalities" (among other things). Perhaps this is providence. Such conditions are conducive to the ebb and flow of a creative process in which conservative and liberal instincts clash, ideals and realities collide. In response, music industry operatives actively *negotiate* the style and substance of their commercial products. The exact nature of these negotiations varies with situational factors, professional roles, individual personalities, and an infinite number of other possibilities. Particulars aside, these negotiations are literally omnipresent: no single entity controls commercial art.

Here I examine this phenomenon as it unfolds throughout Pete Townshend's career. Simon Frith (1978) argues that rock music "is musical communication and its ideology as a mass culture derives not just from the organisation of its production, not just from the conditions of its consumption, but also from the artistic intentions of its musical creators and from the aesthetics of its musical forms" (pp. 14-15). In his discussion of "rock as art" Frith cites the presence of "the rock auteur" who "creates the music with his or her unique experience, skill and vision" (p. 201). Still, the "rock auteur" must reconcile a basic tension that Frith denotes as a "permanent contradiction between being an artist—responsible only to one's own creative impulses—and being a star—responsible to one's audience's perceived values and needs" (p. 202). Echoing Henry Raynor, Frith concludes that rock artists also actively negotiate the inherent conflict "between art idealism and commercial reality" (p. 163).

Frith explains that rock musicians differ from other artists in that they often have to achieve commercial success *first* and then gain license for creative freedom. Just as the early minstrel exercised restraint and suppressed his artistic aims, the aspiring rock musician may also have to subordinate creative ambitions to commercial objectives (unless, of course, the artist forsakes the commercial world). Frith maintains that many British musicians in the mid-1960s achieved the popularity that paved the way to artistic freedom through their ability to entertain. If a musician was playing Soho clubs and doing James Brown covers, his/her road to distinction was in the way s/he performed those songs and obtained the popularity required to persuade managers or record companies of his/her merits. Pete Townshend is one of those artists.

Townshend achieved commercial success through his innovative instrumental, performance, and songwriting techniques. What distinguishes him from his songwriting peers is the continuity and breadth of his writings. Townshend weaves a consistent story across a protracted period of time, through a variety of media. The final products are certainly compromises between "art idealism" and "commercial reality" (i.e., negotiated artifacts—as in the *Tommy* example); in spite of that, they provide evidence of "the auteur" and his creative impulse. A study of Pete Townshend's oeuvre, then, yields knowledge of his stylistic response to the various creative/commercial conflicts he endured and, in turn, exposes the negotiations that rendered that work.

"Auteur theory" appreciates the "power" of "individual authorship" and considers an artist's "output as an oeuvre, a repetition and enrichment of characteristic themes and stylistic choices" (Bordwell, 1989, p. 44). Establishing the conceptual foundation of what would become auteur theory, I. A. Richards (1924) discusses the various "impulses" (pp. 180-185) that guide the artist's "stylistic choices." Richards contends these "impulses" separate the "ordinary mind" from its artistic counterpart. He argues the "ordinary mind" must "suppress" the "greater part of the impulses" that a given situation "might arouse" in "order to keep any steadiness and clarity in his attitudes" (p. 184). Since the "ordinary mind" is "incapable of organising" those attitudes, "they have to be left out." Richards concludes that "the artist" may encounter the "same situation" but, unlike the "ordinary mind," the artist "is able to admit far more without confusion." From this point of view, the artist not only employs a series "stylistic choices" that suggest "individual authorship" but relies on skills unavailable to those without that *talent*. Auteur studies, therefore, support an "artist-centered conception of meaning" (Bordwell, p. 65). A song is a "vehicle for meanings" placed there by the artist "either as an act of deliberate *communication* or as an act of only partial, self-aware *expression*." Unlike the "autonomous object model" (p. 67), in which the critic searches for meaning without regard for authorship, this approach stresses the artist and attempts to discover implicit themes/structures that represent *artistic signatures*—stylistic tendencies that may also provide the organizing framework for interpretation.

Townshend's "stylistic tendencies" render an extended narrative that I deem, *The Seeker*. This composite text explores the individual's search for identity in intrapersonal, interpersonal, group, and societal contexts. A variety of supporting themes flow from that master plot: the search for beauty, anxieties over interpersonal and/or societal relationships, insecurities over personal appearance, and concerns for individual freedom and spiritual growth (and a corresponding fear of oppression). Many songs follow this story line directly, others more indirectly, others not at all. Yet when Townshend's lifework is considered in its totality, this narrative structure is dominant. The manner in which the story evolves from simplistic constructions of *The Seeker*'s quest to more complex versions is particularly revealing. In the end the evidence suggests Townshend faced—and eventually resolved—a contemporary minstrel's dilemma. That "dilemma" was no overnight phenomenon. Over a thirty-year period a young artist who initially subordinated his creative instincts to commercial agendas gained artistic freedom through commercial success, eventually grew frustrated with the limits imposed by that prosperity, withdrew from that situation in varying degrees, and later resolved that creative/commercial conflict. Across that time frame, Townshend's artistic impulse—a narrative impulse—subtly negotiated its way through an evolving entertainment industry.

Let me pause and take a moment to qualify this argument. Although I interpret the lyrical dimension of Townshend's lifework, I advance no claims with regard to the lyrics' superiority to other facets of the creative process (e.g., the lyric-music interplay, the engineering, or variations in performance, to name a few possible considerations). Townshend's lyrics are treated as a "species of script" (Booth, 1976, p. 242), and I pursue the narrative qualities of that script. Booth states, "A song is music and words, and music may be the better half.... The balance varies from song to song, and from one style or tradition to another: words may dominate, or fade to little more than musical sounds." Nevertheless, "the words must have an internal discipline to play their part in the interaction, a discipline conditioned to the cooperation and also the competition of the music." The following pages expose the narrative impulse that provided the "internal discipline" for this artist's lifework. In them I treat Townshend's writings as "artistic communication" and examine how his art evolved from stories designed for persuasive purposes (i.e., a rhetorical/instrumental application) toward more expressive narratives (i.e., a poetic application). Bloodworth (1975) maintains that "recent rock songs" (p. 306) offer "no way to distinguish whether or not a song was originally written with an expressive purpose or instrumental purpose or both." In many respects, this judgment can only be rendered by the artist, since he or she may be the only person who understands the intent behind that creative act. Subsequently, I label Townshend's writings "artistic communication" and plot them along a poetic-rhetoric continuum.

This is Part I of that study. I begin with Chapter One's overview of Townshend's biography, writing technique, artistic philosophy, and lifework. I continue with Part II ("The Minstrel's Struggle"), where Townshend's career with The Who is considered. Part II is divided into three chapters which examine early Who material (Chapter Two), Townshend's rock opera projects (Chapter Three), and the remaining Who albums (Chapter Four). The study concludes with Part III ("The Minstrel's Resolution"), where Townshend's solo albums and multimedia projects are discussed. The final chapter returns to my theoretical claims and *The Seeker*'s thematic development to close this study of a contemporary minstrel's dilemma.

Producer/critic Jon Landau contends that "the criteria of art in rock is the capacity of the musician to create a personal, almost private, universe and to express it fully" (Wicke, 1990, p. 23). My charge involves the explication of Townshend's writings in terms of the narrative impulse that appears to have sustained his art. *The Seeker* reflects a "personal, almost private, universe" that, somehow, endured the various conflicts and negotiations that constitute commercial art. Mozart labored to please his audience, Beethoven and Haydn their publishers. Pete Townshend did both and more. All the while, a creative impulse drove the auteur. This book is the story of that impulse's victory.

1

The Auteur, the Impulse, the Oeuvre

I begin our study of this contemporary minstrel's dilemma by visiting popular music history. Raynor (1978) writes that popular music's movement from East to West was "like [that of] goods and new ideas of all sorts" in that it traveled "along the main trade routes" (p. 45). Rowbotham (1895) reports that Provence—with its "combination of beauty and fertility rarely equalled in the earth" (p. 24)—provided our "musical" entry port. Provence became the "cradle" of popular music, as this lush Mediterranean region rendered an artistic environment in which the East's musical influences could evolve into a revised Western art (Rowbotham, p. 23; see also: Finney, 1935; Hughes, 1954; Pratt, 1907). As minstrelsy developed a social hierarchy and moved northward, "the first troubadour of world-wide celebrity" (Rowbotham, p. 45) led the way. William of Poitiers was not only the first troubadour (aristocratic minstrel/poet) to achieve this lofty status but also the grandfather of Eleanor, wife of Henry II and progenitor of the English line of kings (Abraham, 1979; Finney, 1935; Hughes, 1954; Pratt, 1907). Abraham notes that William achieved notoriety upon his return from the First Crusade by "entertaining noble audiences with...humorous accounts of his military misfortunes" (pp. 94-95). Yet William's subject matter extended beyond witty tales of war. Rowbotham contends that "his choice of subjects" (p. 47) exhibited "immaturity and rawness" and the "coarse and brutal terms in which he invariably alludes to women recall rather the bluff spirit of the precrusading baronage than speak of that delicate and over-refined timorousness of amorous sentiment which was to be the marked character of the troubadours." Complementing William's "coarse" writing style was his strong antagonism toward the Church. William "constantly opposed the

Church and churchmen throughout his dominions, turned the customs of the former into mockery and flouted openly the latter" (p. 48). This opposition to the Church was not unique to William; in fact, "this spirit" was "in a manner common more or less to all" of the celebrity's contemporaries.

Hence, from its inception Western minstrelsy involved a variety of tensions and conflicts. Raynor (1978) observes "like all the art which compresses expression within extremely rigid rules, much of its vigour was won from the tensions between the creator's determination to express himself and the formal regulations, limitations and inhibitions which he accepted" (p. 72). With these observations as our foundation, we now turn to the specifics of Pete Townshend's career. This chapter offers a biographical overview, a compilation of Townshend's comments on the songwriting process and his artistic philosophy, and concludes with a preview of the lifework. Like that of William and his contemporaries, Townshend's history reflects a "vigor" that is the direct product of his "determination to express himself" and the "limitations and inhibitions" he encountered.

THE AUTEUR

There is much in the popular press about the life and times of Peter Dennis Blanford Townshend. Born in London on May 19, 1945 to Betty and Cliff Townshend—two professional musicians (Betty, a singer; Cliff, a saxophonist)—Pete was indeed delivered into a musical family. Betty's father had performed in a minstrel act as a youngster and Cliff's parents shared a musical background (his mother a soubrette; his father a flutist and comic). As is true for everyone, Townshend's relationship with his parents and family lifestyle played a meaningful role in his development. Sources indicate that Townshend's musical parents appreciated his artistic inclinations and therefore supported his early music career and his enrollment in art college. Yet in 1968 when Jann Wenner (1981) asked Townshend to characterize his parents' influence on his work, he responded with confusion and doubt, in an "I can't place it...and yet I know it's there" (p. 38) reply.

Over the years Townshend's reflections on his parents' influence have expanded. In 1985 he told the *Chicago Tribune* that he derived his interest in the music business from his parents, since "I must have realized that [they] were getting something out of this music business that they weren't getting from me" (Kolson, 1985b). In 1989 Townshend went into greater detail for the *San Diego Union*. He described his relationship with Cliff Townshend as not "that intimate," since his father was "very busy," and yet he considered his father to be "very simple, very loving, very uncomplicated, very straightforward and immensely proud that I was successful at anything...he was an absolutely sterling supporter of anything I did" (Varga, 1989). Later in that interview, Townshend offered these thoughts about Betty Townshend: "I wrote about my mother and the relationship we had. I've continued to write about it, and it still hurts. She's still a very fiery, exciting, stimulating character, and she can hurt you very badly if she wants to. And I find myself doing the same thing back to her."

One portrayal of Townshend's youth appears in a 1993 *Rolling Stone* interview in which he described his parents as "two fiery people who split up when I was very young" and "dumped" him with his grandmother for "two years" (DeCurtis, 1993, p. 109). He continued: "I was very lonely, never heard from my father at all. My mother used to come down on the weekend for an hour to see me, dressed incredibly seductively." Young Townshend "*longed* to be with" his "beautiful" mother, but instead he "was with this bitter, crotchety, clinically insane grandmother." (He described his grandmother to David Letterman in this fashion: "She was clinically insane and it's kind of been the one ribbon that's run continually through my life" [*Late Night*, 1993].) This period was certainly traumatic; his grandmother required him to remain still for extended periods, and after allowing him to purchase toys with money from his father, forced him to put them away until a parent visited. The Townshends eventually reconciled, had two more children (after Pete was twelve years old), and his "life was fairly normal from then on." Townshend's (1997) reflections on this period are illuminating: "This is my caldron.... If I go too deeply into this...opening it up...my relationship with my grandmother is something—which to date—I've not been able to make any sense of whatsoever. It's the only bit of my life that I haven't been able to make any sense of and, in a sense, I feel that if I was able to go into regressive hypnosis and either find some terrible trauma or nothing at all, it would be equally damaging to me as an artist."

Joining these familial matters was the Townshends' influence on their son's artistic development. Regarding his father: "I just wanted to be like my dad; you know, I worshipped him. He was a magnificent player and a fantastic man" (Resnicoff, 1989a, p. 80). In radio interviews promoting his 1993 Broadway debut, Townshend probed further into his father's impact on his art and his music theater background:

What you have to remember is that...I don't feel at all uncomfortable in a Broadway theater, cause I actually was brought up in theaters. My father was a musician in a dance band, so I was brought up in two places. During the week we were in dance halls, so I know what to do when people start fighting....This is as young as two or three years old, I was running around dance halls. My mother used to sing with my dad's band, I was kind of on the loose with guys that drank. I was a real kind of rock and roll baby.... The other thing that they used to do at weekends was these Sunday concerts where there would be like variety shows. So there would be like girls, comedians, big stars from the USA.... But my father also took me a little bit further, he took me into the orchestral writing of Duke Ellington which was very very avant-garde in its time. He took me to see the Basie Band. You know, I did my chops there really and he also took me to my first rock and roll concert—which was kind of rock and roll in name alone probably it was more like kind of rockabilly because it was Bill Haley—when I was eleven and a half years old...and I remember once my friend Graham who came with me saying to him, "Do you like this music Cliff?" He said, "Graham, I like anything that swings." (*Rolling Stone's One*, 1993)

These experiences influenced the youngster's musical education: "And so I got exposed to the work of Irving Berlin and Cole Porter and the Gershwins and people like that and I think I can tell the difference between what's good and what's bad and I was very influenced by [the Sunday shows]" (WFBQ, 1993). To that end, he told Sheff (1994): "My family used to play music without boundaries. They would play Tchaikovsky, bebop, Stan Kenton, string quartets, Scottish folk music, anything. There was never any snobbery" (p. 56). Complementing these musical influences were Betty Townshend's burning ambitions for her son. Townshend (1997) affectionately recalls how his mother "worked damn hard" to "pretty much make sure that I was gonna get rich and famous." Mrs. Townshend obtained "critical auditions" for her son's early bands, supplied a van to transport the band to and from shows, and—in general—provided unwavering support for her musical son's career. Assuredly, Townshend's youth had a major impact on his art in terms of both his artistic orientation and thematic content; his lack of "snobbery" and commercial drive would have far-reaching consequences.

No life experience, it appears, had the developmental impact of Townshend's perceptions regarding his physical appearance. He may have been uncertain as to his parents' influence, but Pete Townshend clearly recalls how his physical appearance—specifically, his nose—affected his youth. In 1968, he told *Rolling Stone*: "It was huge. At the time, it was the reason I did everything. It's the reason I played guitar—because of my nose. The reason I wrote songs was because of my nose, everything, so much. I eventually admitted...what I wanted to do was distract attention from my nose to my body and make people look at my body, instead of at my face—turn my body into a machine" (Wenner, 1981, p. 42). Such anxieties surfaced in many media interviews, such as this session with Cameron Crowe (1974):

High school was very painful for me...I was very embarrassed and self-conscious about my nose for quite a while. I got obsessed with it. Music was my escape. My mother was no help, she seemed to think that anybody who wasn't beautiful couldn't be any good. She was gorgeous, of course. My father was very good-looking, too. How they spawned me I'll never know. Dad was kind to me about the nose, but in an unintentionally devastating manner. He used to say things like, "Don't worry. Arthur Miller married Marilyn Monroe, didn't he?" I didn't want to look like fucking Arthur Miller, I wanted to look like James Dean. (pp. 95-96)

Whereas he performed well in school, people viewed Townshend as "arrogant and hostile, too quick to fight" (Marsh, 1983, p. 19). His recollection of an encounter with a schoolmaster reinforces this perception. "I know why you leave egg stains on your jacket, milk dribbles in the lap of your gray flannels and tea stains on your shirt," the schoolmaster declared, "it's your perverted way of saying to the world, 'Look at me—I'm dangerous!'" (Townshend, 1983, p. 19). Supposedly, this "dangerous" personality once hit a band mate with his book bag, producing a concussion for his victim and peer rejection for himself.

Marsh's analysis of Townshend's youth is helpful: "It's hard to imagine a more miserable adolescence than this: a smart kid who fears that he's ugly, with irascible parents and newborn siblings."

Townshend's 1997 response to all this is instructive. First, he claims that there was no "concussion" involved in the fight with his schoolmate—although he was "sent to Coventry" (i.e., ostracized) by his classmates for an extended period of time—and that his childhood was basically a contented, happy period (despite all the reports to the contrary—his time with his grandmother is, of course, an exception). Second, he maintains he was never embarrassed over his physical appearance. The whole routine about his nose was a media game that was the result of a publicity photograph arranged by one of his managers, Chris Stamp. It appears Stamp and photographer Colin Jones used a "fisheye" lens (a lens that covers an 180 degree angle and produces a circular image with a barrel distortion) to shoot a cover photograph for a story on The Who's management team, Kit Lambert and Stamp. Although the former art school student understood that standing in front of the group for that photo would severely exaggerate the length of his nose (he realized he would look "absolutely grotesque"), he allowed it to happen anyway. He felt "incredibly betrayed" by Stamp and Jones, yet he admits, "I was really doing that art school thing.... I didn't care about the consequences.... I didn't care about the fact that I would see it written again and again and again for the rest of my life." Hence, when Townshend told *Rolling Stone* "it was huge," he meant that "it was huge in the photograph." Townshend concludes, "I wasn't ugly, I didn't have difficulties in my neighborhood, I had a really good childhood." Such are the negotiations associated with image building and the media games that may result from those commercial efforts.

Townshend's first public musical experiences "were ecclesiastical" (Sheff, 1994, p. 56); he joined a church choir when he was eight years old. His first band, "The Confederates" (DiPerna, 1994, p. 42), was formed in 1959. The Confederates were a Trad-jazz band (traditional American Dixieland jazz) that featured Townshend on banjo and schoolmate John Entwistle on horns. Entwistle and Townshend next formed "a Shadows-influenced rock band that they first called the Aristocrats and later, The Scorpions" (DiPerna, p. 43). Townshend then followed Entwistle into a rhythm and blues band named "The Detours," led by guitarist Roger Daltrey. The Detours evolved from a local (Shepherd's Bush) R&B band (managed by Bob Druce) to "The Who" to the "High Numbers"—a carefully packaged band managed by Helmut Gorden and Pete Meaden that catered to the musical and social taste of the British youth movement known as the Mods—back to The Who, managed by the aforementioned filmmakers Kit Lambert and Chris Stamp. The group's composition changed over time and eventually settled upon the foursome of Daltrey (singer), Entwistle (bassist, singer), Townshend, and drummer Keith Moon. (Richard Barnes [1982] and Dave Marsh [1983] offer the definitive accounts of "Who history." Readers are encouraged to consult those sources for additional biographical detail.)

Townshend's enrollment at Ealing Art College in the fall of 1961 was another pivotal point in his artistic development. The combination of classes and the school's social environment introduced the young artist to the bohemian lifestyle that gradually informed his instrumental, performance, and writing styles. Frith (1978) observes the English art school system was a virtual harbinger of rock talent, in that such future celebrities as David Bowie, Eric Clapton, Ray Davies, Bryan Ferry, John Lennon, Jimmy Page, and Keith Richards attended art schools in the late fifties and early sixties. Townshend's art studies transcended traditional definitions, promoted art theory (especially cybernetics), emphasized the technical and conceptual aspects of a variety of art forms, and elevated the importance of the audience-performer relationship. Although this educational approach appears to have offered little vocational utility for its students, it did have a compelling impact on their creativity.

While at Ealing Townshend was exposed to a variety of music through an American art student with a large record collection. The student, Tom Wright, was later deported, leaving that collection with Townshend and roommate Richard Barnes. Townshend (1970d) recalls his American friend, his vast record collection, and its impact on his life: "He had piles of Jimmy Reed, Howling Wolf, Little Walter, Chuck Berry, Mose Allison, Bo Diddley, Booker T., Lonnie Mack, Ray Charles, Jimmy Smith cuts and a few rather less obvious gems which none the less changed my head, the shape of my fingers, the way I walked and generally improved the appearance of the ladies I associated with" (p. 25). That musical education was accompanied by another Wright innovation, marijuana. Such conditions suggest the classic bohemian: an artistically inclined individual who pursues alternative lifestyles as a vehicle for creative inspiration.

A major development in Townshend's emerging stage act involved neither guitar heroes nor lifestyle matters but the auto-destruction art theories of Gustav Metzke that he encountered at Ealing. If Townshend denounced academic auto-destruction (Marsh, 1983), the idea must have impressed him. Consequently, when he accidentally rammed the neck of his Rickenbacker guitar into the Railway Tavern's ceiling during a performance (the club had low ceilings) and smashed the remaining pieces, he introduced a new dimension of musical performance. He later recounted that event to his former roommate:

I started to knock the guitar about a lot, hitting it on the amps to get banging noises and things like that and it had started to crack.... It banged against the ceiling and smashed a hole in the plaster and the guitar head actually poked through the ceiling plaster. When I brought it out the top of the neck was left behind. I couldn't believe what had happened. There were a couple of people from art school I knew at the front of the stage and they were laughing their heads off.... So I just got really angry and got what was left of the guitar and smashed it to smithereens...picked up [another Rickenbacker] plugged it in and gave them a sort of look and carried on playing, as if I'd meant to do it. (Barnes, 1982, p. 37)

The show-ending auto-destruction routine—in which Townshend smashed his guitar and attacked his amplifiers while Keith Moon destroyed his drum kit—

became The Who's trademark. Roger Daltrey recalled, "After two years, people were just coming to see us smash up all our gear. The music meant nothing" (Crowe, 1974, p. 96).

(Several 1993 interviews indicate that Townshend initiated his guitar-smashing career at a much earlier date. On *Late Night with David Letterman* he maintained that his "clinically insane" grandmother purchased his first guitar—the type that hangs "in a Spanish restaurant"—and that he broke it in an attempt to gain a new one from his father [*Late Night*, 1993]. In *Rolling Stone* Townshend claimed his father supplied him with an electric guitar and a small amplifier; as the story goes: "One day my grandmother ran into the room and said, 'Turn that fucking row down!' I did a Keith Moon—long before I'd ever met Keith Moon. 'You think that's a fucking row? Listen to this!' And I got my guitar and smashed it over the amplifier" [DeCurtis, 1993, p. 182]. There appears, then, to be a rather rich history of instrument smashing in Townshend's life.)

Townshend's instrumental approach had already achieved notoriety; therefore, the closing auto-destruction routine seemed a logical extension of that act. He exaggerated the playing style of Rolling Stone guitarist Keith Richards by whirling his arm in the air in a windmill motion and striking the strings (Richards has no recollection of performing this way, but Townshend extends credit to the guitarist in any event). He acknowledged that the technique is painful: "It is terribly painful. But I'm used to the fact that there will be pain. I know that I will take my nail off at the beginning of every tour.... The string gets under the fingernail and rips it off. It's part of the job...like a boxer in the middle of a fight" (Sheff, 1994, p. 53). Townshend's act was innovative, with its swinging arms, leaping athletics (e.g., flying scissor kicks), and "Birdman" poses (Swenson, 1979, p. 22—the "Birdman" routine, Diperna [1994] writes, was "a stage pose" [p. 44] in which Townshend stood "stock still with his limbs extended while feedback from his instrument swelled cataclysmically"). He elaborates on his stage presence in Jeff Stein's Who-produced documentary, *The Kids Are Alright*:

When I'm on the stage I'm not in control of myself at all. I don't even know who I am.... I'm not this rational person that can sit here now and talk to you. If you walked on stage with a microphone in the middle of a concert, I'd probably come close to killing you. I have come close to killing people that walked on the stage. Abbie Hoffman walked on the stage at Woodstock and I nearly killed him with my guitar.... A policeman came on when the bloody building at the Fillmore in New York was burning down and I kicked him in the balls and sent him off.... I'm just not there. It's not like being possessed, it's just, I do my job and I know I have to get into a certain state of mind to do it.

That "state of mind" is audience centered, as these early comments to Nick Jones (1965b) indicate: "I bang my guitar on my speaker because of the visual effect. It is very artistic. One gets a tremendous sound, and the effect is great.... But, if the audience isn't right I don't smash guitars. They wouldn't appreciate the full visual effect" (p. 11). These comments suggest a young artist in touch with his act *and* its publicity. (In fact, Townshend's 1997 views indicate the comments in Stein's film may involve more media posturing.)

Swenson (1983) describes The Who's inversion of instrumental roles and Townshend's part in that approach: "Moon and Entwistle were doing most of the soloing in a sense—Townshend was constructing contexts for them with his unique approach to chords and drone sounds. He would hold chords, stretching them out like platforms for the band's other voices, or he would strum heavily-syncopated rhythm patterns for an effect heard best on 'Magic Bus' and 'Pinball Wizard'" (p. 42). There Townshend acknowledged transferring these techniques from the banjo: "Those trad banjo solos always used a lot of syncopation and I took that over to guitar." Complementing that banjo background was manager/producer Kit Lambert's appreciation of classical music. Lambert—the son of composer/arranger Constant Lambert—introduced Townshend to "the harmonics of Henry Purcell, Archangelo Corelli, William Walton, and Darius Milhaud" (Moritz, 1983, p. 407) and, in all probability, reinforced a musical orientation inclined toward the "platforms" Swenson describes. Townshend discussed Lambert's influence in this *Guitar Player* interview: "Kit Lambert gave me an album by a 17th-century composer called Henry Purcell. It was full of Baroque suspensions, and I was deeply, deeply influenced by it.... Then I sat down and wrote all the demos for the Who's first album, and it's just covered in those suspensions" (Resnicoff, 1989b, p. 70). (Aledort [1994] contends that Townshend invented the famed guitar "power chord" through this technique.)

The Who's instrumental strategy complemented Townshend's visual diversions and his pioneering use of audio feedback to create a unique act. The Who was "the first band to stack amplifier speaker cabinets at the back of the stage to create an imposing effect," and as a result they "literally revolutionized rock and roll performances" (Swenson, 1983, p. 42). Swenson maintains that, once more, the speaker arrangement "was a purely visual move," because the band initially "just used giant cabinets with small speakers inside, then later used dummy cabinets on the bottom." Another stage innovation involved the lighting procedures instituted by Lambert and Stamp. Moritz (1983) reports The Who was "the first rock group to carry their own movie studio-style lighting rig" (p. 407); thus, when Lambert and Stamp made arrangements for concert lighting, theatrical makeup, and trendy stage clothes, they slowly but surely created a distinctive stage presence. All of these maneuvers stressed style over substance, or as Townshend often said, "We never let our music get in the way of our stage act" (Swenson, 1983, p. 42).

These performance tactics may have attracted a growing audience, but auto-destruction cost the band a considerable amount of money. As The Who moved through a series of management changes, built a following, and pursued a record company contract, the costs of auto-destruction grew immensely. In Stein's film an interviewer raises questions about the costs of auto-destruction and notes that in one week with three appearances, the band earned "370 pounds" and, during that same time period, spent "1,946 pounds" including "785 pounds" for new equipment. Such dire economic matters aside, this performance style led to a memorable stage act—an important trait for fledgling bands in the early-to-mid 1960s. Recall Frith's (1978) comments about mid-sixties bands and how they achieved commercial success, and eventually artistic freedom, through their ability to entertain. The Who most certainly followed this path—a trail beaten out by the dance steps of a surging youth movement, the Mods. Sociologist David Hebdige (1979) describes the Modernists, or Mods, and their "subcultural" style: the Mods wore "conservative suits in respectable colours...were fastidiously neat and tidy" with hair "generally short and clean...[in] the stylish contours of an impeccable 'French crew'" and pushed "neatness to the point of absurdity," as they "made themselves...into 'masterpieces'" (p. 52). Schaffner (1983) contends the Mods "represented the ultimate in trendiness" (p. 114), adding "style was substance; image was everything" (p. 115). Manager Pete Meaden's dedication to the Mod audience was complete: he changed the group's name to the "High Numbers" (a Mod reference), personally selected each band member's attire, and wrote Mod songs (the band's first single, "I'm the Face" and "Zoot Suit"). Later, under new managers Lambert and Stamp, a club of Who fans called the "100 Faces" was created to generate enthusiasm for shows and fill the band's venues (a "face" was Hebdige's "masterpiece"). Treasured venues were cleverly secured by Lambert and Stamp; a Tuesday night residence at the "Marquee" in West London was particularly significant. The band's new management team developed innovative ways to confirm attendance figures and assure proper remuneration. And a consuming market was carefully cultivated. Auto-destruction and the Mod façade drained the band's limited resources, yet the Mods' allegiance guaranteed record sales potential. The group dressed for the Mods, concocted and imitated Mod lifestyles and mannerisms, performed songs that appealed to the subculture's musical taste, and recorded singles tailored specifically to that audience. Like the wise minstrel from yesteryear, The Who understood its "patron" and performed accordingly.

And yet The Who was still one major ingredient away from commercial success: a songwriter. When The Beatles' popularity soared, the industry's control over lyrical content ebbed, as executives realized that musicians understood their audiences far better than record companies did. Hence, the new English groups featured their own songwriters, and The Who, if it was to achieve star status and the accompanying record company contract, needed a songwriter. To fulfill that need the band turned to its art school student, who penned a series of successful singles beginning with "I Can't Explain" and following with "Anyway, Anyhow, Anywhere" (the eventual theme song for the British pop music television program *Ready Steady Go!*) and "My Generation." Following the era's standard prescription for commercial success, The Who released singles first and foremost, and from those materials shaped albums.

The 1966 album *The Who Sings My Generation* (the U.S. release) is an uneven work, due to its mix of original material and blues covers. Furthermore, Lambert and Stamp's royalty deal with producer Shel Talmy was pitiful. Townshend's memories of that first album are unpleasant: "From my point of view that first album was just miserable. There was no fun at all" (Barnes, 1982, p. 42). Later—perhaps in response to the Talmy debacle—the songwriter sought other venues of expression and pursued his first "concept" project, *Quads*. *Quads* was to be the tale of a futuristic (in 1999) family who lived in a world where parents selected their children's sex. The parents requested four girls but received three girls and a boy instead. Not to be deterred, they raised the children as a group of girls and, predictably, much comedy followed. The project was never completed and yielded but one song, the single "I'm A Boy" (released in August 1966 in the U.K.).

After the U.K. release of *Ready, Steady, Who!* (an EP that featured the Townshend compositions "Circles" and "Disguises," Jan & Dean and Beach Boy covers, and the theme song from the *Batman* TV series), the band issued its second album, 1967's *A Quick One (Happy Jack)*, that also features a mix of covers and original material. The uneven qualities of this work were assured because the band signed a publishing contract that required each member to contribute two songs to the project. The album does represent another decisive moment in Townshend's songwriting through a commercially inspired happening, the "mini-opera" (a nine-minute track entitled "A Quick One While He's Away"). While we may view this innovation as yet another historical moment in rock's evolution, it was in fact motivated out of economic necessity. Realizing the band was running short on material, Lambert asked Townshend to write a long song to meet time requirements. He responded with a vague story that recast several ditties into a single track. Townshend "half-jokingly" called the results a "mini-opera," but that arrangement "made the Who's reputation" and placed the band "firmly in rock's avant-garde" (Marsh, 1980, p. 288).

The Who made its first appearance in the United States in 1967 as a participant in New York radio personality "Murray the K's" Easter weekend show. In mid-June The Who performed at the legendary Monterey International Pop Festival; in July it toured as the opening act for Herman's Hermits and the Blues Magoos; and later that year toured with Eric Burdon and the Animals, with an appearance on national television (the *Smothers Brothers Comedy Hour*). The Who's success in the States no doubt influenced *Rolling Stone*'s decision to name the band its "Rock & Roll Group of the Year."

The band's third album, 1967/68's *The Who Sell Out*, expanded the group's pop art, avant-garde image through its burlesque of commercial radio and its rejection of the psychedelic-concept LPs of that period (e.g., The Beatles' *Sgt. Pepper's Lonely Hearts Club Band*). *Sell Out* pursues a single concept, but not in the psychedelic rock genre, which uses abstract sound effects and disjointed mixes as vehicles for "mystical" renderings. *Sell Out* is classic camp. The album's cover art portrays various band members consuming the products satirized within: Townshend with a huge stick of deodorant, Daltrey in a bathtub of baked beans, Entwistle in Charles Atlas/caveman attire, and Moon with a giant tube of acne medication. The band contemplated selling advertising space on the album (only Coca-Cola seemed interested, so the idea was dropped). Whereas *Sell Out* foretold the future via instrumental/lyrical segments that would appear in later projects, 1968's *Magic Bus: The Who On Tour* revisited the past through its use of tracks from previous albums. During this period The Who's material was under the control of *two* record companies due to the legal problems with Shel Talmy: Decca, from the Talmy days, and Track, Lambert/Stamp's new label. That year Track issued an album entitled *Direct Hits* (a mix of singles), while Decca released *Magic Bus* under the guise of a concert album. Such was the late-1960s popular music industry.

As The Who's commercial status and pop art image prospered, the former art school student's personal maturation advanced. Townshend's commitment to his ideals—ideals grounded in a blossoming spirituality—fueled his determination to push his work to new heights. He describes his spiritual evolution toward Indian master Meher Baba in this fashion:

Much of my early spiritual focus, before I heard of Meher Baba, was tempered by my reading of the Spaceship sagas of George Adamski. He had said that on another planet in our system existed a race of people who were spiritually perfect. He claimed that he was in contact with them. While reading the books I believed this, somehow this man taught me to open my mind. In other words he taught me faith. The first few prayers to Meher Baba contained extracts from what he said he had been told by these spacemen. They talked of The Divine Presence, The Divine Intelligence, The Divine Awareness. Meher Baba talked of Infinite Power, Infinite Knowledge and Infinite Bliss. (Barnes & Townshend, 1977, p. 10)

The songwriter elaborates on Meher Baba in an article he prepared for *Rolling Stone*. There Townshend relates that Baba was born in India in 1894 and that while in college he "built up an affection for an old woman named Hazrat Babajan, who was in reality a Perfect Master" (Townshend, 1970d, p. 26). After being kissed on the forehead by this Perfect Master, Baba "neither ate nor slept for months, and spent the next seven years in study with the five Perfect Masters of the time." Later, Baba ascended to the role of Perfect Master and from "July 10th, 1925 until he died in 1969" Baba did not speak, "You have had enough of my words, now is the time to live by them."

Townshend's allegiance to Baba was an important development. Unlike other celebrities who withdrew from society after spiritual revelations, Townshend engaged the world through a combination of Baba's teachings and his personal philosophy. "Henceforth," Shaffner (1983) observes, "all of Townshend's writing was to be infused with a spiritual quality few of his peers have equaled" (p. 125), since he insisted "on fashioning his sermons and confessions in the context of gut-level rock music." Townshend supported Shaffner's point when he described Baba's influence: "I can talk for hours about Meher Baba the God Man.... But ultimately, I realize that I see it all through these two little slits labeled R & R" (Marsh, 1980, p. 290). Once again, we return to Townshend's *Rolling Stone* piece for insight:

From the peace of the original note, the single unmultiplied breath of life, the eternal silent singing that pervaded all, came this. Us. What are we supposed to be doing?

Here am I, in suburban Twickenham, skinny, vain, and obsessed by the word "forward"; how am I equipped to begin to understand Infinite Love.... The key is that knowledge of [Baba's] awesome power, awesome knowledge and bliss he enjoys; that flash, is the basis for the search for my true self. (Townshend, 1970d, p. 26)

That piece concludes: "As the river flows down outside my home, I look out and remember that eventually it will reach the sea. Each little stream that runs into the Thames feeding it and building it sustains the ocean. Retains the cycle of life that keeps our planet moist and airy. We too need sustaining, love is the only thing that can do it" (p. 27). Several themes appear here that become central organizing principles for Pete Townshend's work. The "peace" of an "original note" would be the centerpiece of a major project; the obsession with the word "forward" would be both a blessing (via creativity) and a curse (via personal sacrifice); the "river" metaphor would find countless applications in future songs; and most importantly, "the search" for a "true self" would become dominant. Townshend was evolving into more than a pop artist. An "auteur" was emerging whose creative vision involved a fusion of family background, education, spiritual orientation, and a firm commitment to his art form.

Having introduced America to auto-destruction and pop art fashion, The Who—in particular, Townshend—pushed for a new direction. With Lambert's support, Townshend pursued an "opera" concept based on his conclusion: "I thought we had to do something grand, almost daft...and possibly pompous" (Cocks, 1979, p. 93). His answer was *Tommy*. Initially entitled *The Amazing Journey* (among other working titles), Townshend built the tale of a "seeker" who "saw his life in reality and in a dream" (Barnes & Townshend, 1977, p. 112). That original concept involved a series of songs "that flashed between the point of view of reality and the point of view of illusion" as witnessed through "the eyes of someone on the spiritual path, a young boy" (p. 22). The writer abandoned that "two-pronged concept," because it was too "cumbersome," hence the central character "became deaf, dumb and blind" (p. 30) in order to communicate the reality/illusion duality (a direct application of Baba's teachings). After Townshend's lengthy description of the *Tommy* concept in his 1968 interview with Jann Wenner, the "grand, daft, and pompous" idea would now have to become a *reality*. The concept evolved into the tale of a deaf and blind child whose condition emerged after witnessing a murder through a mirror. Tommy endures dysfunctional familial relationships, becomes a celebrity pinball player and a cult leader.

Tommy reached number 2 on the U.K. charts and number 4 in *Billboard*, remaining in the U.S. charts for forty-seven weeks (Charlesworth, 1995). The project transformed The Who financially, and the band desperately needed financial transformation. After suffering through years of auto-destruction (both on stage and in hotel rooms, the latter venue perfected by Keith Moon) and expensive image building, The Who was in dire financial straits. The band also faced a substantial tax bill in England; in the absence of *Tommy*'s commercial success, it would have encountered serious legal difficulties (Crowe, 1974).

The Who followed *Tommy* with the 1970 concert album, *Live at Leeds*. Afterward, Townshend's obsession with artistic progress (always "forward") and the growing need to transcend *Tommy* crystallized into his most ambitious idea, the *LifeHouse* project. He announced the band was "investigating a new kind of theater" that involved "two thousand people" kept "in a theater...with us for six months" (Schaffner, 1983, p. 130). The intriguing story involves a futuristic account of an age when the government controls the polity via "experience suits" and television programming. The populace eventually revolts through music (the central character rediscovers rock & roll) and just as government troops invade a musical revival, the "rebels" disappear through the attainment of a single musical note that represents life's essence. Townshend described the plot as a "derivative of '1984' and 'Fahrenheit 451'" (Barnes, 1982, p. 99), and he endeavored to make that science fiction a "reality." The logistics eventually overwhelmed him (unmanageable audiences, lack of facilities, technical constraints), but the idea clearly reflects Townshend's Baba/rock philosophy and, again, that intense preoccupation with artistic progress.

The early 1970s were eventful for The Who: *LifeHouse*'s remnants became the successful album, *Who's Next*; the London Symphony Orchestra, Royal Canadian Ballet, and moviemaker Ken Russell all initiated their own versions of *Tommy*; another management debacle began to unfold, this time involving Lambert and Stamp's removal; and the band's attitude toward touring began to change. In 1973 The Who returned with Townshend's second opera, *Quadrophenia*. That project involves the story of a young Mod, Jimmy, who suffers from "double schizophrenia" (each of his four personalities represents a band member's persona). Using Richard Wagner's leitmotif system of associating a melodic passage with a recurring character, Townshend assembled the story of the young Mod's struggle for identity. The technical complexities conjure images of *LifeHouse*, as Barnes (1982) indicates: "Pete was trying to record the most ambitious and complex album of their careers in a studio that was still being built, without a producer and in quadrophonic sound, a medium that had not yet been perfected" (p. 103). Popular reports indicate that the rush to release the album moved the group to distribute a less than ideal version of the opera which, like *Tommy*, represented another triumph of economics over inspiration. *Quadrophenia* joined *Tommy* in terms of its appeal to filmmakers. Franc Roddam directed a Who-produced version of the concept several years later, and Entwistle produced a movie soundtrack that was considered to be an improvement over the original version.

The band entered the mid-1970s with an album of previously recorded material (the Entwistle-produced *Odds & Sods* in 1974), an album of new material (1975's *The Who By Numbers*), and the debut of Russell's *Tommy* film. That Roy Carr described *By Numbers* as "Townshend's suicide note" (Barnes, 1982, p. 119) effectively captures the album's thematic qualities. By 1977 the band had virtually stopped touring and apparently had accepted its role as "big business entertainment." Townshend now openly despised what had once been his principal source of inspiration: performance. He told the *Trouser Press*, "Bits of the Who's show are still rooted in tradition, and we go through the motions to a certain extent because people do wanna hear the old stuff...but what's annoying is when you realize that most of the gestures are used up and it's fucking difficult to come up with anything new" (Murray, 1980, pp. 18-19). A Who "show" had evolved into a Who "concert," and Townshend lamented the change. He complains about The Who's act in *The Kids Are Alright*: "What we have to do is, we have to decide whether or not we're going to remain the circus act...doing what everyone knows we can do and what we know we can do, right, until the band eventually turns into a cabaret, which is inevitable." Later in the film Townshend declares the band had "realized the end" of its "tether" and arrived at "the point when the [arms swinging wildly] nosebleeds and all that, you know, they're no good...it's beyond the beyond."

The Who had gained much from performance, and the decision to back off had consequences. The audience no longer joined the band in its rock-oriented search for self; rather it attended Who concerts to *confirm* its reality. A Who concert was now a nostalgic interlude. Subsequently Townshend lost sight of his narrative inspiration, backed away from the audience and its nostalgia (fearing he was imitating himself), and entered the "end of The Who" phase and its unique spin on *The Seeker* narrative. Townshend's "worst nightmare" had become a reality—the band became "enmeshed in the affairs of tax accountants, lawyers, and money issues" (Marsh, 1983, p. 462).

With the popular press chronicling the band's demise, The Who rendered 1978's *Who Are You*—an album based on a series of songs that extend the themes initiated in *By Numbers*. Keith Moon died from an overdose of antialcoholism medication on September 7, 1978, only a month after the album's release; he was but thirty-one years old. That was the end of that band. *The Kids Are Alright* film captures it for posterity. This was not the only Who-related death of the period: Pete Meaden committed suicide in August 1978, and in April 1981 Kit Lambert died from a fall down his mother's stairs. The Who hired Kenney Jones to replace Moon and released *Face Dances* in 1981 and its final studio album, 1982's *It's Hard*. Townshend assessed the band's condition just prior to *It's Hard*'s release:

Well, first, I don't see the Who going on for very much longer. I think that with this next album...we're really gonna throw ourselves into it 100 percent. And then we're gonna stop. I'm pretty sure of that. It's not because we want to, but because we've come to the point where we don't really want to go through all these periods when the public and our fans and the record company and even we don't know what the fuck's gonna happen next. The tension is just too much. (Loder, 1982a, p. 19)

After *It's Hard* the band staged a "Farewell Tour" in 1982 (sponsored by Schlitz Breweries, making The Who one of the first major acts to do sponsored tours) and, from its "last show" in Toronto, produced a concert video and album (the latter entitled *Who's Last*). The Who performed occasionally (1985's "Live Aid") and returned for a twenty-fifth anniversary tour in 1989 (without Jones and with a much larger band). That tour was sponsored by Miller Brewing or Budweiser—depending on the show in question—and once more produced a concert video featuring a star-studded version of *Tommy* and an album (*Join Together*). In 1991 Daltrey, Entwistle, and Townshend participated in a project dedicated to Bernie Taupin and Elton John (*Two Rooms*) and contributed the Taupin/John number "Saturday Night's All Right For Fighting." The 1993 Broadway production *The Who's Tommy: The Musical* presented another opportunity for a public reunion, as Daltrey and Entwistle attended Townshend's debut on New York's Great White Way. Daltrey celebrated his fiftieth birthday with a "tribute" to Townshend's songwriting at New York's Carnegie Hall in February 1994. There Entwistle and Townshend appeared (separately), along with a variety of artists and a sixty-five-piece orchestra. That two-night production was edited and distributed on pay-per-view television and a Daltrey album. The 1994 project *Thirty Years of Maximum R&B* (a four-CD set and a separate video of live performances/interviews) presents The Who's musical history in a comprehensive package. And lastly, The Who reissued its entire catalog with digitally remastered, extended versions of its original material—complete with expanded liner notes and essays on the respective projects.

With the end of The Who, Townshend was able to shed the cumbersome "knapsack" (Marcus, 1981, p. 406) that was the band and its history. Townshend's personal version of the "minstrel's dilemma" was a painful one—the "curse" that accompanied his "obsession" with artistic progress, as he conveyed to David Fricke (1987b): "I ultimately had to stop using the band as a vehicle for my songwriting.... Commercially, leaving the Who was the dumbest thing I've ever done in my life. But artistically, it was undeniably the most logical thing to do. It was the most important thing I've ever done for me—to allow me to have a new beginning, to actually grow" (p. 182).

That "growth" started in 1972 with his solo debut, *Who Came First*. *Who Came First*, dedicated to Meher Baba, was primarily a vehicle to praise his cause, since the album was distributed only among Baba followers; however, the project "was accorded a general release after bootleggers got into the act" (Shaffner, 1983, p. 136). Townshend followed that Baba tribute with a 1977 collaboration with fellow Baba devotee Ronnie Lane (*Rough Mix*). His first genuine solo album, 1980's *Empty Glass*, was yet another important transition in Townshend's artistic evolution. Music critics assumed the album probed into the author's drinking and drug problems. Townshend's media interviews assume various stances: most discuss the album's spiritual ramifications, others deny any meanings at all, and still others posit lifestyle themes. Barnes (1982) observes, "Pete's admission that his life was a mess, and the album's mixture of spirituality, carnal knowledge and boozing was a true reflection of what he was undergoing at that time" (p. 145).

By 1981, Townshend's financial holdings were extensive. He invested in a publishing company (Eel Pie), a bookstore (the Magic Bus Bookshop), a barge fleet that operated on the Thames River, a public address system rental company, and several Baba projects and recording ventures (Loder, 1982b; Marsh,

1983). Barnes (1982) remembers being "staggered at the stupidity of some of the people Pete had given key jobs" (p. 122) and Marsh (1983) claims Townshend had entrusted those operations to "cronies and amateurs" (p. 520), who proved incompetent. Eventually, Townshend discovered he was over a million dollars in debt. With financial problems, domestic strife, and substance abuse dominating his life, Pete Townshend was in trouble. After several flirtations with death, he sought therapy for his dependencies with Dr. Meg Patterson, overcame those conditions, and returned with the intensely personal 1982 release, *All The Best Cowboys Have Chinese Eyes* and a video of the same title. (See McAuliffe, 1983 for a fascinating account of Patterson's "NeuroElectric Therapy" [NET].)

With The Who's retirement and the resolution of these personal conflicts, 1985 witnessed a Townshend renaissance. A dual film-album concept, *White City: A Novel*, as well as a book of short stories, *Horse's Neck*, appeared that year. Between that burst of productivity and The Who's 1989 anniversary tour, Townshend performed for charitable causes (see Denselow, 1989), released a live album (*Deep End*) and corresponding feature-length video in 1986, wrote songs with Pink Floyd's David Gilmour for Gilmour's solo album *About Face*, attended to his publishing company (Eel Pie), worked as an editor at the publishing house Faber & Faber, and in 1989 released *The Iron Man: The Musical* (featuring a variety of artists and two tracks by The Who).

A story Townshend told Matt Resnicoff (1989b) seems to capture his professional life at that point in time. Townshend recounted the complaint of a park keeper who cleans a park next to his home: "Why don't you blokes do something fucking decent, like in the old days? You're fucking useless now. What are you doing in that big fucking house you've got 'ere? I'll bet you just sit up there and just do fucking nothing all fucking day" (p. 82). Amazed, Townshend remarked that this was "the guy that sweeps the park.... You know, I don't get any respect, as Rodney Dangerfield says." He explained the story's significance:

I can honestly say that I would trade places with the park keeper at the drop of a hat...because I can just see that he's happier than I am, and that he's been through less hassles than I have.... It's very difficult to respond to criticism like, "There you are, with a hundred thousand quid in the bank, moaning about how unhappy you are.... Don't give me your miserable songs. Cheer me up."... Artists have been elected by the public to be the happy people, to be entertainers, to be the constructive, positive force. And when they fail to do that, they're expected to disappear.

This is the minstrel's dilemma: a condition fostered through the complex relationships that exist between the artist, his/her artistic aims, the commercial art industry, and his/her audience. According to Townshend, the audience gives you stardom and demands that you do what it wants. Therefore, artists negotiate. If they are unwilling to enter into these negotiations, "disappearing" is a likely option.

The musical world saw little of Pete Townshend in the early 1990s. Suffering from tinnitus (a painful hearing disorder that Townshend claims was the result of playing his guitar through his headphones), he worked in the publishing business. In October 1992 Townshend wrote that he had an album featuring a "pure narrative" and several theatrical projects in progress. Just prior to that correspondence he suffered a bicycling accident that severely damaged his right wrist. Guitar playing, it seemed, was now in the past, and music theater opportunities assumed newfound importance. The artist who was "expected to disappear" because his band was "useless" was on the verge of another artistic renewal. In a December 1993 television program Townshend opens a segment on his "1993" with this statement: "I often wake in the morning and think that this year's been the greatest year of my life. It's just been bliss" (*Rolling Stone's 1993*, 1993). A second Townshend renaissance occurred that year: in April *The Who's Tommy* opened on Broadway, breaking box office records and winning five of eleven Tony Award nominations. Townshend's solo album *PsychoDerelict* (a radio play released in two versions, one with dialogue, one without) was issued in June and was followed by a tour (along with a pay-per-view broadcast of a New York show). Townshend and his Broadway collaborators wrote a book about "the making of" the New York production. Broadway *Tommy* opened across the United States that fall. And, in November, Townshend released a video of the pay-per-view *PsychoDerelict* concert. More importantly, his hearing "stopped deteriorating" (DeCurtis, 1993, p. 107), and Townshend reported that he was "really invigorated by spending so much time in New York" (*Late Show*, 1993). Of these various ventures from 1993, one is hard pressed to determine which was the more ambitious. The move toward musical theater in general—and Broadway, in particular—involved considerable risk. *PsychoDerelict* was an extremely unique, commercially hazardous endeavor and its tour, Townshend's first as a solo artist (at age forty-eight), initially provided much anxiety.

After the 1994 Daltrey "tribute" at Carnegie Hall, other ventures continued to unfold (European and London openings of *Tommy*). This trend advanced with the systematic reissue of The Who's catalog and several major happenings in 1996: Townshend released a "greatest hits" work entitled *The Best of Pete Townshend: Coolwalkingsmoothtalkingstraightsmokingfirestoking* (featuring one new track, "Uneasy Street"); conducted a small "supper club" tour in support of that record; and The Who returned with a stage production of the band's second opera, *Quadrophenia*. The latter project began with a single show in London for the Prince's Trust charity, traveled to New York's Madison Square Garden for a six-night stand, toured across the United States in the fall, returned to the United Kingdom for a series of shows that winter, and continued with an extensive spring/summer 1997 tour of Europe and the United States.

An active Pete Townshend remains married to his Ealing classmate and wife of almost thirty years, Karen Astley—a relationship he once described as a marriage "made in heaven" (Loder, 1982a, p. 19). The father of two girls (Emma & Aminta) and a boy (Joseph, born in 1989), Townshend remains torn over the need to balance his artistic inclinations with his private life, as these 1993 re-marks to *Rolling Stone* indicate:

The beginning of the year, I was very happy.... But toward May, June, I started to get uneasy, and I'm still in that place. I'm still not sure how I'm going to do the things I want to do without traveling an enormous amount—which is again something my wife and I find difficult. So there's a kind of feeling of dread which runs through me, my oldest daughter, my younger daughter and all my friends, including my wife, that we're heading for difficult times, because of the career I want, which is a show-business career, and show business is destructive. It's both disturbing and incredibly exciting. (DeCurtis, 1993, p. 182)

In other words, Townshend's version of the minstrel's dilemma persists in vari-ous ways. The auteur may aspire to push his trade "forward," but those aspira-tions are not without cost. While he may no longer have to argue with band members, rock journalists, or movie producers, an internal conflict continues. As Tannenbaum (1986) reports, "According to legend, Roger Daltrey once pre-dicted that Pete Townshend would be a great songwriter only as long as the guitarist had hellhounds on his trail" (p. 48). Perhaps this internal struggle—Townshend's personal "hellhounds"—represents the quintessence of his artistic impulse, our next topic.

THE IMPULSE

I now move from biographical matters to Townshend's extended commen-tary about his writing technique and his role as an artist. This is, after all, the crux of the auteur: the synthesis of biography, technical style, and artistic phi-losophy driven and sustained by the creative impulse—an instinct that serves as a lens through which that individual construes the world. First, however, a dis-claimer is warranted. Throughout this section Townshend's comments suggest a writer in a constant state of reevaluation. The way he envisions a work's "meaning" or rationale on Day One may be very different from Day Two—much less Day One Thousand. Perhaps this is further proof of an *artistic impulse*'s strength and its potential to operate beyond the artist's awareness.

With that in mind, we begin with Townshend's reflections on his early songwriting. At first, he "wasn't keen" on writing, since he "was very much into an image thing" ("I lived and breathed image"—Shaffner, 1983, p. 118). He told Carr (1975b), "I was trained in graphic design...to be an ideas man...to think up something new and different...like, let's give a lemon away with the next album" (p. 53). Townshend describes his earliest songwriting efforts in this manner:

Writing songs was something I ended up doing. When I was young I thought of myself as a Rock Star rather than a rock writer. I would dress in front of a mirror, standing with a guitar, legs apart, trying to look like one of "The Shadows." I wrote a couple of songs for The Who when they were call "The Detours" back around 1960. My first song to be published was called "It Was You" and was recorded by a Beatle-ish group called "The Naturals" in 1963. Needless to say it was a flop.... I just remember showing up at art college having visited the publisher, full of talk of "advances" and "really big money." (Barnes & Townshend, 1977, p. 6)

Originally, Townshend considered songwriting to be just another "one of the little experiments that I'd done" (Resnicoff, 1989a, p. 81). He explained: "I'd tried oil painting, I'd tried making a Super 8 film—you know, this was the kind of art-school dilettantism that I was involved in. And along the way I tried making a *song*.... And then I just thought, 'Well, that's songwriting; didn't enjoy that very much,' and *left* it." Townshend's views on his early writings are, to say the least, mixed and suggest the raw qualities of an emerging impulse. He told one interviewer, "I really like my first few songs, because they were an incredible surprise" (Marsh, 1983, p. 141); elsewhere, he reported his "early years...suffered" while he searched for his "niche" which is why his "first songs were so screwed-up and indecisive" (Crowe, 1974, p. 96). Sometime later, he contrasted his early writings with later ones and concluded his more recent work "is clumsier than it was in the early days," in that when he "wrote the first five or six hit songs for the Who" he "was completely and totally alone," with "no girlfriend, no friends, no nothing—it was me addressing the world" (Marcus, 1981, p. 408). Townshend harbors negative feelings about that era as well: "I think back now to the way I was when I wrote those [early] songs and I must admit that I don't really like myself in retrospect. I just don't like the person I remember" (Crowe, 1974, p. 98). That interview continues:

Through writing I discovered how to free my subconscious, in a way.... I wrote "I Can't Explain," and I thought it was about a boy who can't explain to a girl that he's falling in love with her. But two weeks later I looked at the lyrics, and they meant something completely different.... At that point I became the greatest rock critic in the world. I was two people—someone who sat down and wrote a song for some particular purpose, and then somebody who looked at it and saw something totally different.

An inexperienced instinct—Richards's (1924) artistic impulse—was quickly becoming a persuasive tool. Various audiences had to be satisfied, simultaneously. The Mods were one of Townshend's first challenges. The Mod desire for "original arrangements, not original songs" (Marsh, 1983, p. 137) was in direct conflict with the band's attempt to gain a recording contract with original material. The band quarreled intensely over its musical direction (occasionally to the point of fisticuffs), yet Townshend learned how to reconcile The Who's agenda, the industry's demands, and the Mods' expectations. To accommodate these audiences, Townshend became "obsessed with writing rock songs" and "concentrated far more on that than on any other single thing.... I just used to go back after gigs and write and write and write all the time" (Swenson, 1983, p. 42). He concluded that he once smashed "guitars because I just couldn't play them the way I wanted...now I smash words" (Garbarini, 1982a, p. 54).

Two factors were central to the development of his "word smashing." First, once again, was his experience at Ealing Art College, in general, and his exposure to Bob Dylan's early work, in particular. Townshend was drawn to Dylan's voice, humor, and content. He explained that Dylan was his teenage hero and that he "couldn't wait for the day when somebody would get to [Dylan] and do that in-depth interview where everybody would find out what really was in the back of his head" (Crowe, 1974, p. 97). When Townshend discovered there were no grandiose explanations for Dylan's songs he "was incredibly disappointed," and Dylan "ceased to be [his] hero." The "greatest rock critic in the world" was in his professional infancy and would soon emerge as Bob Dylan's opposite: a writer who could and would engage in lengthy discussions about his art's intentions and meanings (at times, to his own chagrin).

The second developmental factor in Townshend's songwriting involved his exposure to home recording. Musician Andy "Thunderclap" Newman introduced the young songwriter to the marvels of home recording. Townshend gradually accumulated the equipment necessary to tape his compositions and present "demos" to the band. Appreciating the value of such demos, Kit Lambert purchased equipment that advanced Townshend's home-studio capabilities. Townshend made demos that either had all the instrumentation included or indicated where they should be placed. This practice became standard operating procedure in the rock industry because of Western music notation's limits and, often, the musicians' inability to read music. As Jerry Leiber and Mike Stoller relate: "We didn't write songs, we wrote records.... Now that it was possible to manipulate the sound properties of both instruments and voice and reproduce them precisely, the focus of musical performance gradually shifted from the written parameters, pitch, dynamics and formal development, from the melodic and harmonic aspects, to the reproducible details of the expression of sound. Thus, sound became the central aesthetic category of rock music" (Wicke, 1990, p. 13). Subsequently, Townshend wrote and wrote and wrote AND recorded and recorded and recorded. The songwriter claimed that recording taught him how to write: "I learned to write because I was playing about with tape recorders. You know, I would lay down the bass part and then add the rhythm part and then play the lead, and I used to do shows by myself.... I would play that tape to my girl friend and say, 'That's all me' and she would go, 'aahhhhooo'" (Brooks, 1972, pp. 30, 32). Years later, Townshend concluded that the sophistication of his home equipment enabled him to grow as a musician and to function "more like a composer than a songwriter" (Resnicoff, 1989a, p. 77).

Kit Lambert's contributions to Townshend's home studio and his support for the songwriter's proclivity for detailed narratives cannot be minimized. If Townshend engaged in some of his Ealing theorizing to members of the band, he might very well receive blank stares in response. Lambert was different. Lambert would take Townshend's "college bull sessions and prod them toward reality" (Marsh, 1983, p. 119), and in so doing, "teach him a sense of proportion about his own intelligence" (p. 312). With experience and Lambert's help, Townshend eventually realized: "I need language. I need it not for specifics, I need it for the abstract stuff that I can't do musically.... I think of myself mainly as a writer of lyrics, a writer of words. The music is tacked on in a sense" (Gill, 1993a, p. 104). Evidence of that contention appears in his 1968 *Rolling Stone* interview, in which he described his writing/recording technique: "When I write a song, what I usually do is work the lyric out first from some basic idea that I had, and then I get an acoustic guitar and I sit by the tape recorder and I try to bang it out as it comes. Try to let the music come with the lyrics" (Wenner, 1981, p. 35). There are instances where this approach reaches extremes, such as the song "Sheraton Gibson" from Townshend's *Who Came First* tribute to Baba. Townshend told Timothy White (1990), "I turned on the tape machine, and I sang about twenty songs, with my Gibson acoustic guitar, off the top of my head, making the words up as I went along" (p. 222).

What comes "off the top" of Townshend's head tends to appear in "trains of thought for maybe up to two years, which means that anything I write from now to say two years from now will probably end up with a similar purpose" (Pollock, 1975, p. 83). He continued, "I'll start to write a song and I won't really know what it's got to do with, then two years from now I'll look back on it and then I'll know why I wrote it." In the *All The Best Cowboys Have Chinese Eyes* video, he reinforces that point: "I can't really explain what happens when I write songs.... I think writing is a mysterious process until you look back on it. And then like a critic—like a clever critic—you can see clearly where you went wrong or where you succeeded." Whereas Townshend once thought that he wrote "consciously," he eventually discovered that "the real meaning was coming from somewhere else that I had absolutely no control over.... I suppose I was surprised by how obviously observant I was, without ever really being conscious of it" (Pollock, p. 88). It appears that his narrative impulse organizes this mysterious process of invention, as Townshend relates: "Why I'm attracted to the idea of storytelling, as a songwriter, is because I think it enables me to get closer to people with my heart ideas.... I don't think that genius is a part of rock and roll, I think its an instinctive process. A bit like sport. If you can do it, you can do it. You don't often know why you can do it but you can do it" (*Good Morning*, 1993). Since Townshend's creative instincts occasionally follow impulsive inspirations, he relies on his home recordings to temper those "heart ideas":

One of the reasons I still find to this day the need to make a recording of a song myself, is that songwriting to me (and probably to everyone) is a very impulsive process and a very revealing process. One has to be very careful that one doesn't say anything that one is going to regret at a later date. Making tapes, complete tapes in fact, you don't just have an idea whether a song is good, you also know whether it is going to be possible to complete it. (Barnes & Townshend, 1977, p. 18)

Nowhere is there stronger support for Richards's (1924) observations regarding the artistic "impulse" and how that instinct separates the "artist" and the "layperson." To that end, Townshend admits that he often does not have a clue what his work means or where it is going: "But it's such a peculiar working process. Like often I pretend to everybody that I know what I'm doing when a lot of the time I really don't. I seem to think I do but I don't really...until things come together. That's why *Tommy* and *Quadrophenia* haven't got properly conceived endings...because they were never properly conceived in front.... Rather than something that was scripted in front and made to happen, it was allowed to happen" (Pollock, 1975, p. 84).

The spontaneous qualities of Townshend's approach provide a context for interpretive flexibility. His interview with Vic Garbarini (1982a) discusses several examples of this trait. He said the song "I Can See For Miles" was originally about "jealousy" but, with time, it came to be about "the immense power of aspiration" (p. 57). "Behind Blue Eyes" was originally about a character from *LifeHouse*—a character that was "accused of being a liar and a cheat, when in fact his motives are absolutely pure." Townshend later realized that the song is "about a part of me that I hadn't considered: the inability to be taken literally because of the way people take you to be." When asked if the political implications of the song "Won't Get Fooled Again" were intentional, he replied, "No, it's grace, I'm afraid.... It sort of happens out of the sky.... And I think you have to be fairly unconscious, you have to be naive, to some extent" (p. 56). Elsewhere, he was emphatic about that particular track: "It's the dumbest song I've ever written" (Fricke, 1987b, p. 180).

Not only do his meanings change or evolve, Townshend also uses word games, opaque metaphors and other camouflaging techniques: "I still have a tendency to get very wordy, and as it gets easier to write the longer you write, the easier it gets to veil what you're really trying to say behind clever words" (Murray, 1980, p. 17). Once more, we turn to Barnes and Townshend (1977) for insight into this writing style:

I get really irritated today that if in a rock song you actually mention anything specifically.... You know, hitting something head on. You're supposed to skirt round it and flirt round it in a way say that a Stones lyric would, and maybe mention it in a sort of double-meaning, double-edged vague way. I've always been very frustrated with this aspect of rock, I don't get anything from that type of song.... Like if you sit down and listen to a piece of Debussy, one person can see the Arctic and another can see the Russian Revolution, you can see anything you like because there's nothing suggested by it other than in a musical way. When you've got words, "I walked into the room and I picked up my spade, and I work for the Revolution" type of thing...I mean that is enough to kill anything stone-dead. (pp. 113-114)

In a 1993 radio interview the writer embellished his point: "I don't think you draw conclusions in rock and roll. What you actually do is you share ideas and you share feelings and you talk about transitory emotions and one of the smart things to do in rock and roll is to play dumb. You don't tell people what to think, EVER" (*Rolling Stone's One*, 1993). Townshend reiterates that point in this discussion about *Tommy*'s ending—or lack thereof: "What I was doing at the time was attending to the fact that in rock and roll what you don't do is make people's decisions for them, you share their ideas and you share their difficulties and you share their period of frustration, but you don't say 'the thing that you have to do now is get yourself a job, get a pension scheme.' You don't do that stuff, you say 'let's go get drunk and talk about it'" (*The Who's Tommy*, 1993). And Townshend conveys the strength of that conviction in this simple statement: "Drawing a conclusion is just not my job!" (Townshend, 1997). Finally, as we will discover, whether his intentions involve a vague or direct expression (and Townshend employs both strategies, despite his comments), the writer's temperament plays a role in the writing process: "I think if you're miserable, you write about things that are close to you. And if you're okay, you look a bit wider afield for subject matter. There's always plenty to get miserable about temporally" (Loder, 1982b, p. 20).

Joining Townshend's temperament and writing style is another significant aspect of the composing process—the audience. His dedication to his audience is intense: Ealing stressed it, commercial success demanded it, and during The Who's final days, his narrative impulse temporarily succumbed to it. For Pete Townshend, the audience makes, maintains, and controls its celebrities; therefore, these "stars" have a *responsibility* to that audience. This process is reciprocal; as he explained, "You've got to discover what makes that audience tick to discover what makes you tick" (Crowe, 1974, p. 97). This "discovery" is also complex, as indicated by these comments about the rock audiences' "two poles" and how these two distinct orientations influence songwriting:

One [pole] is very intimate and very private and very much like reading a book. You sit at home with your earphones on, completely private, listening to a record, listening to statements and feelings and moods. Then there's the concert, which is the shared, celebratory experience—the affirmation of rock, where you all get together.... So as those poles get wider apart, the use of both the extremes is what fascinates me. And that's why...I try to use both of those extremes. In other words, have moments in the lyrics which can only really be effective when I'm talking directly to somebody and they're all alone, but also when there's a load of kids sitting around at a party.... And also a couple of songs which would be great on a stadium stage in front of 20,000 people. (Garbarini, 1982b, p. 49)

This commentary suggests that Townshend's writing is a two-dimensional process (at least): on the one hand, it is a strategic activity inspired by a specific train of thought that is shaped on the basis of its appeal to certain audiences or situations; on the other, it is an unconscious activity that may follow some train of thought or temperament but also involves vacillating meanings, word games, and idiosyncratic tendencies. Such a process of invention is merely *the starting point* of an industry-wide phenomenon and, in turn, reveals how an artist may maintain an awareness of and commitment to both the instrumental *and* expressive aspects of commercial art as his/her impulse operates on varying levels of consciousness. Moreover, Townshend's narrative impulse seems to require a variety of media forms; he has written screenplays, musicals, record reviews, music commentaries, and a book of short stories (*Horse's Neck*). The oeuvre's breadth is one of its most distinctive characteristics.

Having established Townshend's approach to writing, I now focus more specifically on the artistic philosophy that guides these stylistic tendencies. The writer's statements of artistic philosophy are plentiful; hence, my charge is to lay out those statements as they unfold. First, Townshend maintains that "rock" is *the* vehicle for the individual's search for identity and fulfillment, as he told the *San Diego Union*: "Rock has all the ingredients for being probably the most eloquent art form of this century. You can be very specific and at the same time be entertaining and produce music which freezes time and takes an emotional snapshot" (Varga, 1989). In a 1993 television interview he reinforces that perspective when he declares "rock and roll is the most powerful cultural artistic force that exists" (*Rolling Stone's 1993*, 1993); afterwards, he proclaims: "Breaking down boundaries and introducing new ideas into rock and roll is my absolute mission in life." Townshend actually introduced this philosophical orientation in the 1968 Wenner interview: "Rock and roll is one of the keys, one of the many, many keys to a very complex life. Don't get fucked up with all the many keys. Groove to rock and roll, and then you'll probably find one of the best keys of all" (Wenner, 1981, p. 43). These very early sentiments (he was but twenty-three years old) establish two major themes: first, the presence of multiple alternatives—there are "many keys" available; second, the absence of any guarantees ("you'll *probably* find one of the best keys"), which suggests that perseverance is a virtue. This philosophy has never been repudiated, only modified. Almost twenty years later *Rolling Stone* asked Townshend if his views had changed: "At the time, rock & roll to me was another word for 'life.' What I was saying was it doesn't matter what you do or how you do it.... If I went back to that age, knowing what I would go through in the next twenty years, I'd probably say the same thing again" (Fricke, 1987b, p. 183).

Meher Baba's teachings and Townshend's spiritual worldview provide the foundation for this artistic philosophy: "A lot of people equate finding a spiritual master with discovering the escape clause in life. Actually it's just the opposite. All that happens is that, for the first time in your life, you acknowledge the fact that you've got problems instead of futilely trying to solve them" (Crowe, 1974, p. 97). The consistency of Townshend's argument is evident six years later: "I don't know what religion is. It's a machine that surrounds spiritual need. Spirituality is the need, and religion is the junk food, really.... Spirituality to me is about the asking, not the answers" (Murray, 1980, p. 20). And in 1994 Townshend's position remains unchanged:

I don't know if it is important to me whether Meher Baba is *a* one or *the* one or what. But if I focus on him I actually feel a kind of—I'm trying to think of a word that personalizes the idea of pilgrimage, because that is what I feel: that I'm attending to my inner pilgrimage. It's the idea that one's time on earth is about more than just getting through the time allotted. It is the idea that the main purpose of the human animal is to try to rise, to stand taller. It is the energy to aspire to more, to create, to discover or to invent.

Meher Baba gives me an idea of what the target is. It is very simple: Thinking of him makes me aspire to more for myself and my family and the planet. It is not a religion, which often has more to do with guilt than anything inspired. (Sheff, 1994, p. 55)

Later Townshend (1997) discovered the "word that personalizes the idea of pilgrimage," and that word is "epiphany." That is, his "acquaintances with Meher Baba are more about the epiphanies or the pauses in the spiritual path" than anything else. Baba "is like a mirror" for Townshend and he uses that spiritual reflection "to look after" himself—not others; therefore he concludes, "I don't have any message to carry...I don't want to proselytize in any sense, particularly not about the subject of Meher Baba."

Such sentiments constitute the heart of Townshend's artistic philosophy and the thrust of *The Seeker*'s value orientation: the importance of "the search" and its superiority to "answers." Echoing Baba's plea "Don't worry, be happy, and leave the rest to God," Townshend's philosophy is anything but dogmatic. He consistently states there are "many keys to life" (some, however, resemble "junk food") and that music has a capacity to initiate and sustain the spiritual quest for "the" key to "your" life. There is no escaping life's problems, but rock allows the auditor to, as Townshend prescribed, deal with "this crazy world" and "not run away from the problems that are there but to face up to 'em and at the same time to sort of dance all over 'em" (Swenson, 1979, p. 9). In 1993, Townshend once again demonstrated the consistency of his perspective: "What I've always felt is so great about rock and roll is that you confront the issues and then you give people the juice to dance all over them. There's a purity and fundamentalism that is necessary to create the poetry that is required, so when I tell you what I want to tell you, it won't hurt you" (Gill, 1993a, p. 110). This is his art's function, and Townshend abhors its misuse: "I don't like to see rock and roll abused, I don't like to see it used as some pawn in some political argument or as some freak's weapon. It does what it does, because it is what it is" (Brooks, 1972, p. 40).

What "rock does" for its audiences is quite clear to Pete Townshend. "Rock" addresses a specific moment in our *individual* lives and provides a means for our *individual* search for identity, as this passage indicates:

I think the function started to be about the fact that we needed music which was about escape. That we weren't really sure of our function, I don't think. My generation, I was two years away from conscription, I didn't have to go into the army. We didn't know what we were supposed to do, you know, we really didn't know what our function was gonna be. And when it actually came to the moment that we brought that confrontation to our families, what it turned into was the fact that we're alone from that moment on. I think that's what rock and roll is all about. This is a clever, fancy way of putting it, but I think rock and roll can be defined now like this: it's the dynamic between confrontation and escape. I mean that domestically. The moment when you confront your family or whoever's brought you up...you confront those people and you release yourself. You become free and there's a moment of freedom which then turns into acute loneliness because you are alone and we had no culture of our own, we had no music, no style, no fashion. So we had to concoct it all and I think that's what rock and roll did is it just said listen we're alone, there's no system here, there's no progress here for us. We understand now. And I think in England, what we did in the early sixties was appropriated R & B because it was so plaintive in a sense, it spoke so eloquently about the loneliness that we felt, as individuals I mean. I don't mean as a group of people. (*Rolling Stone's One*, 1993)

On another occasion Townshend used the movie *East of Eden* to pinpoint the specific moment in a teenager's life when he or she faces this break away from the family: "I think [the moment] tends to happen to most boys around sixteen or seventeen and for some girls as early as twelve or thirteen" (*In the Studio*, 1993). He advanced his point in an interview with WXRT-Radio Chicago in which he compared "rock" to "pop" music:

Pop music is wonderful, it's essential, it makes the day go by, it makes us happy, it makes us sad, it's good stuff. There's never been anything wrong with it.... But rock always set itself a slightly higher target which was to try to share big ideas, big problems, *deep* stuff. Particularly the problems that you tend to carry with you from your teenage years. Now listen hard, because I think we carry a lot of teenage stuff with us to our deathbed. I don't think we let it go and I think we're formed in our teenage years to some extent. The person that leaves home is the person that becomes an adult whether they're ready for it or not. (WXRT, 1994)

Townshend extended this argument in 1997 by introducing another level to the discussion: the psychological notion of "introjection." Introjection, as Townshend employs the term, involves the genetic imprinting of emotions from generation to generation—what he denotes as psychological "generational echos." Each generation confronts the next with the embedded anxieties associated with that generation's adolescence. "Maturity," then, involves the resolution of the emotional echoes that are buried deep within the individual. Townshend explains, "As young people going through an extended...rite of passage, we introject the emotions that are caused by the loss of our adolescence...the loss of our relationship with our adolescent peers...and the feelings that other people feel about us at the time [we move] into our adulthood." He continues: "We've understood this for a long time. What we haven't understood is why we have allowed one form of storytelling and entertainment to completely monopolize all of the emotions to deal with that process; which is rock and roll." These "introjected psychological disorders" are "pathological," but they are "medicated" by rock and roll, even though "advertising reinforces" the problem: "It's an addictive process, we want to keep people fucked up...we don't want them to mature, that's why I use this mischievous term, 'I'm suffering from maturity,' it means that you're no longer subject to somebody putting a beautiful blonde next to a Harley Davidson, you're not gonna buy it.... I think I'll have a Volvo, I can get my golf clubs in the back." Hence, Townshend aspires to provide "hope and optimism" through work that probes the introjected fears of his generation as he offers audiences the opportunity to "dance" with those anxieties and, from there, seek a *personal* resolution to their situations.

There is no shortage of Townshend's rock philosophy commentary. Whereas Keith Richards once told Townshend "Pete, you think too much. Get down and play your guitar" (Fricke, 1987b, p. 180), Townshend's philosophical expositions are a vital element of his perceived artistic role (quite a contrast to the Dylan example cited earlier). That he described himself as a "journalist" is evidence of this orientation: "I'm very much a journalist in a sense; I see what I see, and I talk about it, and sometimes I see things which, just because of that capacity to observe, and probably just because of the privilege of my position and the freedom I have to move about...I tend to see things that are to become trends a little before the average guy would" (Resnicoff, 1989a, p. 74). (Shades of I. A. Richards.) Townshend-the-journalist perceives a *responsibility* to stay informed, to use stardom for access, and to communicate his views—often via media interviews. Since he may be impressionistic with his art—a notion he described as abiding by "the old set of rules" and refraining from interjecting "your idea of the month" (Gill, 1993a, p. 102)—he looks to other venues for his commentary: "I do that in interviews. I take an interview as a chance to say, 'Let's talk about Bosnia or Amnesty International.' Interviews are a good place to explore these things because journalists are well-read, they're activists, they're smart, and they know what you're talking about."

From all of this emerges a clear view of Townshend's perspective regarding his artistic role. That role is "always to challenge," but one must first obtain the public's attention; hence, *the artistic responsibility* involves "entertaining first, challenging and inviting debate later" (McKenna, 1986, p. 50). To be sure, Townshend's songs are inspired by and predicated on a responsibility to enlighten through entertainment—his philosophy of "rock." That duty may involve unpleasant references to life's darker sides as well as happy-go-lucky scenes. In either case, his purpose is clear: a "song is a message, a song is a letter, nothing more, nothing less" (White, 1990, p. 218). For further insight into these "letters," let us turn to their manifestation, the oeuvre.

THE OEUVRE

I have to this point presented the artist and his career as well as his writing/recording approach and artistic philosophy. I have, then, established the auteur and his mission. When these elements are joined with the lifework, we have the "oeuvre"—the subject of this section. Townshend's oeuvre consists of 207 songs, thirteen short stories and poems, several essays, a video EP, a film, a musical, a Broadway production, and a staged radio play. That there is more to his lifework than is reported here is certain. First, the project does not use "unofficial" materials or the "outtakes" featured on the reissues of The Who's original catalog (the original U.S. releases provide our subject matter). Second, there could easily be ten more *Scoop* projects (home demo tape compilations) and countless unpublished short stories. Be that as it may, the works cited here

are sufficient for the purposes at hand, in that they are a representative accounting of thirty years of commercial art. This section organizes those writings in
terms of five phases.

The Singles Period

That portion of Townshend's work designated as "the singles period" involves The Who's first four albums as well as songs that were written during
this time frame but appear on greatest hits or other compilations (again, the
demo tape collections released as Townshend's *Scoop* and *Another Scoop* albums). This group, ranging from 1963 to *Tommy*'s release in 1969, consists of
forty songs of varying lengths and styles. In fact, when considered in its totality
this portion of the oeuvre contains the greatest stylistic diversity, with its mix of
blues and surf covers (e.g., "Please, Please, Please" and "Bucket T"), "Moon
and June" pop music love songs (e.g., "The Good's Gone," "Our Love Was, Is"
and "So Sad About Us"), innovative narrative vignettes (e.g., "Happy Jack,"
"Pictures of Lily" and "Little Billy"), and the emergence of the concept-based
writing style (e.g., "A Quick One While He's Away" and "Rael").

The Who's first album, 1966's *The Who Sings My Generation*, was produced by Shel Talmy. The remaining albums—1967's *A Quick One (Happy
Jack)*, 1968's *The Who Sell Out*, and 1968's *Magic Bus: The Who On Tour*—
were produced by Kit Lambert and "executive producer" Chris Stamp. There
are several important songs from this era, and they serve different purposes. "I
Can't Explain," "The Kids Are Alright," "My Generation," "Happy Jack," "I
Can See For Miles," "Pictures of Lily," and others are significant for their
commercial achievements. Songs such as "My Generation" and "The Kids Are
Alright" are important statements for the Mod movement. And others are interesting glimpses of an emerging *The Seeker* story line. "The Search" is, at this
point in Townshend's writings, unclear and unfocused, but such songs as "Tattoo," "Substitute," and "I'm A Boy" introduce questions regarding individual
identities and appearances.

This portion of the oeuvre contains some of The Who's most acclaimed material; correspondingly, it represents the springboard for commercial success
and, eventually, artistic independence. But this era was also the band's most
combative, as The Who endured internal struggles over musical direction, intense personality conflicts, and legal problems with management. Without
question, "the singles period" involved an artistic and commercial climate
totally unlike that of any other portion of the oeuvre.

The Opera Period

That segment of Townshend's writings designated as "the opera period"
contains three double-album, multimedia projects (one of which was never realized in its original form), a collection of old material, and songs that were
written during this time frame but appear on greatest hits or other compilations.

This phase, ranging from *Tommy* (1969) through *Odds & Sods* (1974), comprises fifty-two songs of varying lengths, but with a far more even style than their predecessors because of this group's emphasis on "opera" as an organizing framework.

Tommy was produced, once again, by Lambert/Stamp—the last Who studio album to be produced by that team. *Tommy* was followed by a live album entitled *Live at Leeds,* which received strong reviews but contains no new material. Townshend then initiated the huge, albeit never realized, multimedia project *LifeHouse.* The band used material from that project and, together with engineer/producer Glyn Johns, compiled the 1971 single album release *Who's Next* (with assistance from "executive producers" Lambert, Stamp, and Pete Kameron). The second opera project, 1973's *Quadrophenia,* credits "The Who" as producers (actually Townshend), with engineering assistance from Johns and Ron Nevison (the album credits cite Stamp, Kameron, and Lambert as "executive producers"). The last album from this phase, 1974's *Odds & Sods,* was produced by John Entwistle. This collection contains yet more remnants from *LifeHouse* and assorted cuts from various points in time (several of which were composed during The Who's singles period).

One important change from this period involved The Who's—and the rest of the industry's—shift with regard to the importance of albums. Instead of singles resulting in albums, album concepts now rendered singles. Consequently, there is a more even quality to these albums which improves their narrative continuity (with the exception of *Odds & Sods* or *Meaty Beaty Big and Bouncy,* yet another singles collection). This period did yield several singles of varying degrees of success which led to the commercial demand for "greatest hits" compilations, such as the long-awaited *Meaty Beaty.* The Who was a thriving business operation during this phase. Much money was made (and spent), and the seeds of fragmentation were sown. Those complications aside, Townshend's narrative impulse enjoyed one of its most prosperous periods, if not its finest with The Who. But the strains from *LifeHouse*'s failure, the dominant nature of the *Tommy* concept and its various spin-offs, and the pressures to move beyond *Tommy* (always "forward") joined or created personal anxieties that assured that this period of prosperity would be short-lived.

The End of The Who

The segment of Townshend's writings that constitutes "the end of The Who" contains four studio albums—two with drummer Keith Moon, two with replacement Kenney Jones—and eight songs from Townshend's *Scoop* compilations. This period, ranging from *The Who By Numbers* release in 1975 through the band's final studio album, 1982's *It's Hard,* consists of thirty-nine songs of varying lengths and styles (not unlike the early Who songs). Although this portion of the oeuvre is not as disjointed as early Who material (there are no covers, for instance), songs vacillate between a variety of topics or spin-offs of *The*

Seeker's plot. None of these works displays the self-evident continuity of the opera period's original material.

The period's first album, *The Who By Numbers*, was produced by Glyn Johns and features nine songs by Townshend (the tenth was by Entwistle). It was this album that music critic Roy Carr deemed "Townshend's suicide note." The Who's 1978 release *Who Are You* also assumes a dark tone. Produced by Glyn Johns and Jon Astley (Townshend's brother-in-law), this nine-song album (with six Townshend compositions) was the band's last with Keith Moon. The New Who's first studio effort, 1981's *Face Dances*, was produced by Bill Szymczyk and contains nine numbers (seven by Townshend). Finally, the band's last studio album, 1982's *It's Hard*, was produced by Glyn Johns and features twelve songs (nine by Townshend). This phase of Townshend's writings reflects a combination of traits from earlier segments, albeit with a distinctive spin. It shares the fragmentary nature of early Who material because of the albums' formats. These are not operas or soundtracks; on the contrary, they represent an assemblage of songs that are not necessarily thematically related. This phase also introduces an introspective turn in *The Seeker*'s plot. In every respect, the "end of The Who" phase transforms the raw optimism of youth into a deep-seated adult cynicism.

The Solo Career: Parts One and Two

This segment involves Townshend's solo projects, which range from his tribute to Baba, 1972's *Who Came First*, through his most recent original work, 1993's *PsychoDerelict*. The period is divided into two phases that feature six solo albums, one collaboration (1977's *Rough Mix* with Ronnie Lane), material from the *Scoop* projects not attributed to an earlier songwriting period, a video EP (*Chinese Eyes*), a film (*White City*), several essays, and a book (*Horse's Neck*). Thus, this segment contains seventy-six songs of considerable diversity, along with the multimedia ventures. Due to *Empty Glass*'s and *Chinese Eyes*'s overlap with The Who's existence, these albums display styles and tones distinct from post-Who work. The *Chinese Eyes* album/video and *Horse's Neck* represent major transitional statements. The three post-Who albums also involve extended narratives: one is part of a conjoint album-movie project (*White City: A Novel*), another is a musical based on a children's story (written by Ted Hughes) and features a cast of voices playing recurrent roles (*Iron Man*), and the third is a radio play (*PsychoDerelict*) complete with actors, dialogue, and extended musical interludes.

These albums do not feature a hodgepodge of producers and musicians; instead, they involve a fairly consistent cast. Setting aside *Who Came First* and *Rough Mix*, Townshend's solo ventures were produced either by Chris Thomas (1980's *Empty Glass*, 1982's *Chinese Eyes*, 1985's *White City*) or Townshend (1989's *Iron Man*, 1993's *PsychoDerelict*). They also regularly feature artists such as John "Rabbit" Bundrick (keyboards), Peter Hope-Evans (harmonica), Billy Nicholls (vocals), and Simon Phillips (drums). *The Seeker*'s quest is renewed and turns in a new direction during this segment (especially the post-Who phase). Stories about the search for individual identity move to interpersonal or societal settings as opposed to the opera phase's emphasis on social structures, peer groups, and isolated identity crises. Here tales of internal and interpersonal conflict join searches for beauty, lifelong dreams, spiritual bliss, and love. Gone are statements of distrust and themes of self-destruction as central organizing principles (though they do appear from time to time) in favor of a more positive outlook. If productivity and perseverance are tests of an auteur's vision, this portion of the oeuvre unveils the power of Pete Townshend's narrative impulse.

THE MINSTREL'S DILEMMA: CONCLUSION

I have covered much ground since the introduction of the minstrel's dilemma. We have discussed auteur theory, reviewed the subject's career, considered his artistic philosophy, and previewed his lifework. In all of this a complicated art form operating in a complex field of action has been exposed. Any given song is the offspring of an industry consisting of many different roles and agendas; yet somehow those diverse interests negotiate, compromise, and deliver. The chapters that follow present a study of one artist whose longevity, level of success and innovation, and artistic style lend themselves to an examination of something much larger than one artist and his work. A study of rock auteur Pete Townshend sheds light on the entire artistic communication continuum, reveals the negotiation processes that constitute commercial art, and presents a compelling example of the power of artistic vision.

PART II
The Minstrel's Struggle

2

The Singles Period

As minstrelsy evolved throughout Europe in the middle ages, it gradually assumed Western society's hierarchical structure. The aristocratic singer-poet who exemplified the Provençal tradition, the troubadour, occupied the top of that musical food chain. Serving the troubadours were the jongleurs, who, as noted in Part I, performed services much like the court jesters of later times. These were men "who emphatically lived by their wits" (Rowbotham, 1895, p. 154) and displayed considerable vocal and instrumental skills. Grout (1960) maintains that the jongleurs "were neither poets nor composers; they sang and danced to the songs that others had created" (p. 59). Consequently, a jongleur experienced strong inducements to "overdo" rather than "underdo" his act in the hope that the "performance might be striking, and that the lords and ladies who heard him sing or play might speak with admiration or surprise at his graphic delineations of character or incident" (Rowbotham, p. 155). In pursuit of distinction, the jongleur dressed in a fashion "specially designed to strike the vulgar" (p. 167), achieved excellence on a variety of instruments, and acquired memorable performance skills. There was no shortage of ambition for the jongleurs—this role provided an avenue to a better life.

This process of "discovery" involved considerable competition. Occasionally, an aspiring jongleur challenged an established troubadour in an attempt to unseat the veteran and obtain his station. Rowbotham (1895) describes one such situation in which "Arnaud Daniel"—a troubadour in the service of the king of England—was confronted by a young jongleur with a talent for "constructing difficult rhymes" (p. 71). A "match" was proposed, and the king ordered the men into seclusion for fifteen days, after which the "tenson" was to be performed in his presence. The veteran suddenly "became quite dumb" (p. 72) and lost all inspiration, whereas the aspiring jongleur readily composed and practiced his lines. Unfortunately for the aspirant, the seasoned Daniel was blessed with a strong memory, and as the jongleur continued to practice his lines in his strong, "jubilant" voice, Daniel mastered his opponent's material. When the two men faced the king, the veteran performed first, and to his challenger's astonishment Daniel sang the jongleur's song. The jongleur decried the infringement, the king ignored him, and in his frustration the youngster forgot his own verse. In time, Daniel admitted his duplicity; nevertheless, the king "was so pleased with the piece of merriment that he divided the stakes between them" (p. 73).

While contemporary musicians rarely compete for the affections of political monarchs, they most certainly vie for the rewards distributed by a variety of musical kings and queens. The modern "jongleur" may work as a studio musician, serve as the opening act for an established performer, or write memorable tunes (songs that may suffer a fate similar to the young jongleur's work), all in pursuit of prosperity. This chapter charts how Pete Townshend's band, The Who, achieved success in the volatile music industry of the 1960s. The process of musical discovery was as rich with tension in the 1960s as at any time in Western music history and—like the jongleurs that preceded them—The Who used instrumental and performance innovations, controversial clothing, and celebrity histrionics to achieve its goal.

THE SINGLES PERIOD

If it is possible to characterize The Who's "singles period" in one term, that word would have to be *aggression*. Intense conflicts between assertive personalities, a violent performance style, ambitious marketing and promotional tactics, and enterprising songwriting typified this era of the band's history. The Who sought commercial success over all else and readily made whatever artistic adjustment was necessary to reach that goal. That is, The Who endured a process of discovery not unlike that of an aspiring jongleur. In order to be discovered, The Who would "overdo" its act, engage in celebrity tomfoolery, and challenge the status quo. This portion of Townshend's oeuvre, then, reflects an instrumental-persuasive orientation that rendered more rhetorically based art than any other phase. Artistic expression was not ignored, but Townshend's narrative impulse accommodated commercial necessity in order to meet the various challenges before the group.

THE WHO SINGS MY GENERATION

Before the first single, the first television appearance, or the first trip abroad—before anything in the history of The Who—was the band's concern for its *image*. Christgau (1969) asserts that until Townshend "met his first manager, Peter Meaden, he never thought in terms of image, and until he hooked up with his present advisers, Kit Lambert and Chris Stamp, he didn't try to extend the images musically" (p. 36), but Townshend's biography indicates otherwise.

Recall his comment that he "lived and breathed image" in art school and that he spent as much time posing with his guitar as he did playing it. (Maybe posing with the guitar *was* playing it.) The clothes, haircuts, music selection, and demeanor all reflect a carefully contrived image that originated with the band and changed in response to commercial motivations.

This image, according to Townshend, was uniquely British and sharply contrasted the American bands and their "hippy" outlook; as he told David Fricke (1987b), "when you look back at the [American] flower-power era, it all looks daft" (p. 179). Townshend related that he has always felt "particularly cynical" about the hippy movement, "because I thought it was daft at the time." Support for that contention exists in a 1968 *Rolling Stone* interview:

I think the hippie thing compares favorably [to the Mod phenomenon], but it's a different motivation...[the hippies] dig other people. They dig the way the room looks. The way the flowers look, the way the music sounds, the way the group performs, and how good the Beatles are. "How nice that is." They never say, "How fantastic am I".... The acceptance of what one already has is the thing. Whereas the mod thing was the rejection of everything one already had. (Wenner, 1981, p. 39)

Townshend reinforced that view twenty-five years later on *Rolling Stone's 1993 Year in Review*: "You don't have to save the world, save yourself." This was the foundation of The Who's image and, interestingly, of Townshend's artistic orientation (i.e., Chapter One's statements regarding the "individual" aspects of "rock"). *The Seeker* composite text is about the individual's search for that individual's "answer." Characters may turn to groups or other social structures to search for answers, but *the story* always returns to the individual's quest. That story line originates not in the singles-period song content but in the band's commercial image and its appeal to the Mods—a movement that valued individual competition ("How fantastic am I") over group solidarity.

The Who's image was designed to ensnare the music press as well. *Melody Maker*'s Nick Jones was among the first to "cover" The Who, and his comments offer insight into "music journalism" at that point in time. Jones (1965a) reports:

"The Who"...should be billed not only as "Maximum R & B" but as "Far-out R & B." These four young musicians present their own brand of powerful, stinging rhythm-and-blues which, last Tuesday, quickly stimulated an enthusiastic audience.... This performance demonstrated the weird and effective techniques of guitarist Paul Townshend, who expertly uses speaker feedback to accompany many of his solos. "The Who"... must surely be one of the trendsetting groups of 1965.

While Jones may have missed the "guitarist's" name, he did not miss the image. Later that year he chronicled Townshend's alleged "expenses" and contributed to the band's damn-the-costs image: "The real wrecker of the group, guitarist Peter Townshend, owns nine guitars, all on HP [on credit]. Five of them cost 170 [pounds] each, four of which are already smashed to bits" (Jones, 1965c,

p. 9). The article goes on to detail the costs of guitars and amplifiers, Townshend's home "studio" ("Peter records many singles for the group and other artists in his own studio which cost 1,000 [pounds] to set up"), and his sartorial habits ("clothes wise, Pete spends about 20 [pounds] a week on a jacket"). Two years later, Jones (1967b) contends the band was "largely responsible for introducing fashion to pop" and describes the group's original demeanor: "As a group the Who were untouchable hardnuts. They were feared by all and sundry.... Loping through crushing crowds they would maul and tear with the best of them, throwing off clinging teenagers with the same venom they display on stage. The Who would insult, blaspheme, and send-up like they owned the world" (p. 7). To be sure, one could not purchase better publicity for The Who's aggressive image.

Aspiring filmmakers Kit Lambert and Chris Stamp understood the importance of image and, once they obtained control of the band, improved the strategic qualities of The Who's image building. Their aggressive managerial style focused on three areas: money, promotion, and performance. Lambert's financial dealings were clever to the point of recklessness as he first secured an office at a prominent address for credibility with banks. Lambert would then write a bad check at one bank to cover a bounced check at another. He also bounced checks at casinos to cover debts at banks, music shops, or wherever. Barnes (1982) indicates that Lambert used his "upper class accent" (p. 40) to con the banks and casinos so well that he could go back and repeat the same stunt. What a fascinating story of image manipulation in service of image manipulation!

The management team used an advertising philosophy they called "WOMP," for "word of mouth publicity," to promote Who shows (Barnes, 1982, p. 38). If a Thursday night performance was booked on Monday, Lambert and Stamp turned to their "100 Faces" to promote the show within the Mod community. The plan worked. The show was expensive, with its violence and innovative staging, yet it effectively reinforced the band's image. As Stokes (1974) observes years later, "Though the Who's violence seemed almost involuntary...it was also an artifact, a fully controlled creation of conscious artists" (p. 62).

The band's first recording session occurred in 1964 when the group was known as the "High Numbers." Manager Pete Meaden produced the first single, "I Am the Face"/"Zoot Suit," which he wrote for the Mod audience. The record flopped. Fontana records pressed a mere thousand copies, 250 of which Meaden claimed to have purchased (Barnes, 1982, p. 11). The Who's first three singles also pursued persuasive ends. Townshend wrote "I Can't Explain" in the style of a Kinks song in an attempt to persuade the Kinks' producer, Shel Talmy, to produce the group. Townshend told Vic Garbarini (1982b) that in order to get Talmy "more interested" in The Who he composed a song "similar to a Kinks song, hoping he'd think, 'Well, this is going to be easy to produce so I'll take them on'" (p. 50). He did, and the "I Can't Explain" session typified the pop music industry of that era. Talmy had a singing trio (the Ivy League) on hand for backing vocals and a session guitarist (Jimmy Page) ready to replace

Townshend. Townshend fought for the right to play *his* guitar on *his* song (refusing to loan Page his twelve-string guitar), and the two hour session inspired much acrimony. The number's flip side (the "B-side") offered a song written by Talmy ("Bald Headed Woman") that featured Page on the guitar.

The recording session aside, "I Can't Explain" (issued in January, 1965 in the United Kingdom, February in the United States) is a straightforward account of a young man's inability to articulate his feelings to a girl:

> Gotta feeling inside, can't explain
> Certain kind, can't explain
> I feel hot 'n' cold, can't explain
> Yeah down in my soul yeah, can't explain
> Said, can't explain
> I'm feeling good now yeah, but can't explain
> Dizzy in the head now I'm feeling blue
> Things you say well maybe they're true
> I'm getting funny dreams, again and again
> I know what it means but
> Can't explain, I think it's love
> Try to say it to you, when I feel blue, but I can't explain
> Yeah hear what I say girl.

At first, the character expresses positive feelings ("I'm feeling good now") even though he "can't explain" why, but the song quickly introduces uncertainty, as he starts to feel "blue." He thinks "it's love," although his "funny dreams" raise doubts. The girlfriend says "things" that upset him ("Things you say got me real mad") and apparently give rise to insecurity. The song ends with a statement of affection ("you drive me out of my mind"), his admission of insecurity ("I'm the worrying kind babe"), and his frustrating predicament, "I can't explain."

Townshend's second single—"Anyway, Anyhow, Anywhere"—is another matter completely (released May, U.K./June, U.S.). The song's central character declares:

> I can go anyway, way I choose
> I can live anyhow, win or lose
> I can go anywhere, for something new
> Anyway, anyhow, anywhere I choose
> I can do anything, right or wrong
> I can talk anyhow and get along
> Don't care anyway, I never lose
> Anyway, anyhow, anywhere I choose
> Nothing gets in my way
> Not even locked doors
> Gonna follow the lines that been laid before
> I get along anyway I dare
> Anyway, anyhow, anywhere.

The song continues by repeating the opening stanza and closes with rising instrumental action as the character barks out: "Do myself/Do myself yeah.... Way I choose/Way I choose." The song's use of feedback, rebellious lyrics, and Daltrey's aggressive vocals create the quintessential "angry young man" message in which the character does whatever he pleases through sheer force of will. That the pop music television program *Ready Steady Go!* used the number as its theme song suggests the track's youthful appeal.

Townshend's third single, "My Generation" (released in November), builds on this angry-rebellion theme with a slight shift toward a generational stance. Townshend writes:

> People try to put us down, talkin' 'bout my generation
> Just because we get around, talkin' 'bout my generation
> Things they do look awful cold, talkin' 'bout my generation
> Hope I die before I get old, talkin' 'bout my generation
> This is my generation
> This is my generation baby
> Why don't you all f-f-f-fade away, talkin' 'bout my generation
> Don't try and dig what we all s-s-s-say, talkin' 'bout my generation
> I'm not trying to cause a big sensation, talkin' 'bout my generation
> I'm just talkin' 'bout my g-g-g-generation, talkin' 'bout my generation
> My generation
> This is my generation baby.

The narrator's forceful stutter deploys the invective—"Why don't you all f-f-f-fade away"—and demands "Don't try and dig what we all say." After a brief instrumental, the song recycles the first two stanzas and closes with the "This is my generation" refrain.

These three "teen anthems" offer evidence of Townshend's impulsive writing style, as he explains: "There is little to say about how I wrote ['Can't Explain']. It came off the top of my head when I was 18 and a half. It seems to be about the frustration of a young person who is so incoherent and uneducated that he can't state his case to the bourgeois intellectual blah blah blah. Or, of course, it might be about drugs" (Townshend, 1971e, p. 37). Later in that article he admits that "My Generation" yielded an important songwriting lesson: "that spontaneous words that come out of the top of your head are always the best," because he had "written the lines of 'Generation' without thinking, hurrying them, scribbling on a piece of paper in the back of a car." Although he says he penned the words to "Generation" off the top of his head, Lambert and Stamp had considerable input into the song's style. The original "Generation" demo used a "walking blues" format that Townshend says "sounded like... Jimmy Reed at ten years old suffering from nervous indigestion." A subsequent version introduced the "stutter" (an imitation of the Mods and their habit of stuttering while consuming amphetamines) and another featured "several key changes, pinched, again, from the Kinks." The end result was a "Mod anthem" that articulates youthful rebellion through a carefully packaged style.

The powerful delivery complemented The Who's image, and the lyrical content appealed to the song's target audience.

When these three songs are considered together, an interesting trend emerges. The relatively polite young man who "can't explain" himself quickly turns into a bragging, barking bully. The aggressive, inarticulate kids who are the central characters of "Anyway" and "Generation" display a form of arrogant ignorance: nobody can "go anywhere...do anything, right or wrong...[or] live anyhow, win or lose," and most assuredly, nobody "hopes" they "die before" they "get old." *Image* drove these songs and that image was violent. Stokes (1974) elaborates:

Violence was not an affectation for the Who, it was survival. They were trapped within the perpetual shabby gentility of the aspiring British middle class, and their musical assault—the full volume feedback, the reckless smashing of instruments, the speed stuttering *hatred* of "Why don't you all just f-f-fade away?"—was terrifyingly analogous to the hordes of ritually costumed youths who boarded weekend trains to Brighton in the hope that they could use their fashionably pointed Winklepickers to kick the eyes out of young men who dressed differently. (p. 62)

The Who reinforced its violent image through the words of a songwriter who could instinctively articulate *individual* cries of frustration and rebellion (the song stresses "my"—not "our"—generation). Moreover, Townshend was quite willing to cultivate those instincts to accommodate commercial objectives.

From these image-conscious singles came one of the most persistent lyrics in all of popular music history: "I hope I die before I get old." Marsh (1983) named his book after it and virtually every Townshend interview mentions it. Townshend (1971e) quipped that "for years" he waited "for the day someone says, 'I thought you said you hoped you'd die when you got old.... Well, you are old. What now?'" (p. 37). Over the years he was haunted by the remark. For instance, when Robinson (1982b) asked if he regretted the phrase, he replied in this detailed statement:

Not really. I still believe it. That very self-destructive streak that I was on definitely had to do with me being old and acting old—being defeated. And infuriating everybody around me with my sense of futility. Like somebody who won't get out of bed in the morning when the sun's shining. You just feel like kicking them. If life isn't worth living, you might as well die. And if life isn't worth living, you're old, you're finished. Life is worth living. Very much so. When I first wrote those words I was thinking that if I ever started acting in a pattern that had been laid down by time immemorial, that's when I'd give up, because I'd rather be dead. I still feel that way. I'd rather be dead than allow status to rule my life, and I'd rather be dead than to allow race or class, or category to rule my life.

In a 1989 interview Townshend's response demonstrated less conviction: "It's a masterpiece of a statement and there's nothing more to be said. I certainly don't have to live by it. It will end up in one of the future editions of the Oxford

Dictionary of Quotations, and that's all I care about at this stage. It's got a life of its own" (Harrington, 1989). (In 1997, Townshend proudly reports the lyric made it into the Oxford Dictionary.) Perhaps a response offered during a 1993 radio interview sums the author's attitude best:

I think that the thing I feel now is that I still carry the kid who wrote that. I still carry the anger of it and the threat of it...and I think that that kid is pissed off that he didn't turn into James Dean...but you know, I think I'm afraid of it now—I'm not afraid of death, I'm not afraid of not being here—but I think I'm afraid of the idea that I might die and not be remembered...it was an angry statement. I was living a good life at the time, but I wasn't accepted by the establishment in which I lived. Rock and roll and people like me were not considered to be worthy of living really.... I used to live in Belgravia at the time because it's where Kit used to live...with the aristocracy of England's establishment and I'd go to Harrod's to do my shopping and women in fur coats would literally just shove me out of the way...when are they gonna accept that what I'm doing is art? So, a lot of that anger was directed at them...I don't want to be old like you are old, I don't want to ever become like you. (*Rolling Stone's One*, 1993)

Few popular music lyrics have attained the mythical status of that one, simple line.

Throughout this initial wave of singles, Lambert's and Stamp's persistent pursuit of publicity intensified, the fights between band members escalated (literal fights, Daltrey punching people out!), and Townshend's unique relationship with his audience advanced. The Talmy singles also expanded the publicity The Who received for its auto-destruction act. Since the contemporary music press resembled a "fan magazine" more than anything else, Lambert and Stamp used the newfound attention to their advantage. Consider Lambert's efforts with the *Daily Mirror* in which he invited reporter Virginia Ironside to a Who show with the promise of a guitar-smashing story. Marsh (1983) writes that Townshend was "reluctant" (p. 159) to smash his *last* guitar, yet he relented upon Lambert's instruction. When Lambert and Ironside missed the smash-up (they were in the bar), Lambert was furious over both his failed publicity plan and the guitar's cost. Such were the risks of auto-destruction as a publicity ploy.

There were less expensive publicity devises. For example, *Melody Maker*'s "Pop Think In" featured "articles" by musicians. Townshend (1966) offers opinions about Vietnam, "Sunday Colour Supplements," "Wimpy Bars," the "Chinese" ("I only know Chinese Jamaicans and I like 'em very much"), and more. Keith Moon (1966) deliberates on money ("I think you need a certain amount. And the rest, spend like dust!"—p. 7), "plaster," "Walt Disney," sex, Townshend, and more. Joining these publicity efforts were Chris Stamp's attempts to secure stories in more prestigious, mainstream print media. Stamp "pulled off a major publicity coup" (Barnes, 1982, p. 43) when he obtained space in one of the "respectable Sunday newspaper colour supplements." Stamp's success in getting The Who's picture on the cover elevated the publicity's value (the infamous "fisheye" shot from Chapter One). That one article took "about four or five months' work" to secure. Stamp's persistence paid dividends since the record companies were far more impressed with the "respectable" papers than the "fan" publications. The Who aggressively pursued every opportunity for any type of publicity.

All the while The Who's publicity machine gained momentum, the internal disputes intensified. Roger Daltrey was particularly committed to the band's success; he did not want to return to his job as a sheet metal worker. Perhaps the most serious problem for Daltrey involved the other three members' drug habits and their corresponding attitudes. Daltrey despised the amphetamines (the foundation of a Mod's diet) and marijuana, and he used his fists to enforce his position. There were also battles over musical direction, with Townshend pushing for a stronger pop art orientation, Moon arguing for California surf music, and Daltrey demanding a continuation of the R&B, Mod style. Eventually Moon, Entwistle, and Townshend kicked Daltrey out of the band. With Lambert and Stamp's intervention, Daltrey rejoined the group with a promise to act as "Peaceful Perce" (Barnes, 1982, p. 41; Marsh, 1983, p. 185).

Until late 1965 The Who was a "singles" band; as Townshend (1971e) writes in *Rolling Stone*, "we believed only in singles" because "in England albums were what you got for Christmas, singles were what you bought for prestige" (p. 37). Sure enough, The Who's first album was released in the United Kingdom in December 1965. The album was delayed due to internal fights over musical direction, but compromise prevailed. The *My Generation* session must have been dreadful. Conflicts between Lambert and Talmy, between Lambert and Talmy's engineer (Glyn Johns), and within the band itself dominated the endeavor. Barnes (1982) and Marsh (1983) agree that the most time-consuming aspect of this first album involved the selection of tracks from Townshend's demos. Lambert subtly selected the songs and Talmy recorded them. Lambert's input into this process joined his work on the "My Generation" single to initiate the Lambert-Townshend creative team that would guide The Who well into the opera period. Despite the pain of working with Talmy, Kit Lambert emerged from this first album session with a new, vitally important role.

The U.S. release, *The Who Sing My Generation* (issued in April 1966), contains twelve songs of considerable diversity (running 35:49). There are two blues covers (James Brown's "I Don't Mind" and Brown/Terry's "Please, Please, Please"), three "Mod anthems" (Townshend's "Out in the Street," "My Generation," and "The Kids Are Alright"), three songs about romantic break-ups (Townshend's "The Good's Gone," "Much Too Much," and "A Legal Matter"), one instrumental (Townshend/Moon/Entwistle/Hopkins's "The Ox"), two songs about lying (Townshend's "La La La Lies" and "It's Not True"), and one song that could be about anything (Townshend's "Instant Party (Circles)"). Evidence of the band's compromise over musical direction is found in the inclusion of the blues covers, the Mod anthems, the love songs, and the instrumental (a California surf sound). That Townshend penned the ten original compositions indicates his initial control over The Who's material.

The Mod anthems about street life ("Out in the Street" is a "look out 'woman' here I come" story), peer identification ("My Generation"), and group solidarity ("The Kids Are Alright") are predictable in light of the band's following. Consider the opening tune, "Out in the Street": "Out/Out in the street/ A car drives slowly/A light turns red/Woman you don't know me/Yeah, you don't know me no/Know me no/Know me no/Yeah, but I'm a gonna know you." The song's tone—both instrumentally and thematically—communicates the street-tough Mod's attitude toward women. The character barks, "Hey listen woman/Ya just can't throw me/I won't stand it/You don't know me," as he tells her that he understands that she's "in need" but not to worry, "you're gonna know me now." The number emphasizes the band's instrumental style over the song's lyrics (complete with Townshend's guitar feedback and Moon's furious drumming).

From scenes of Mod street life and peer group identification we turn to one of The Who's future singles, "The Kids Are Alright." Here we notice the Mod's complete dedication to his peers as he confronts his feelings of wanderlust. The lyrics are forthright:

> I don't mind other guys dancing with my girl
> That's fine, I know them all pretty well
> But I know sometimes I must get out in the light
> Better leave her behind where the kids are alright
> The kids are alright
> Sometimes I feel I gotta get away
> Bells chime, I know I gotta get away
> And I know if I don't I'll go out of my mind
> Better leave her behind where the kids are alright
> The kids are alright
> I know if I go things'd be a lot better for her
> I had things planned but her folks wouldn't let her
> [Repeat opening stanza].

The song evokes traditional teen angst themes through the character's deep frustrations over his plans for his girl and his belief that the "grass is greener" elsewhere. Nevertheless, the character understands that if he must move on, his girl will remain in good company (the song celebrates the narrator's peers). That aside, the song's emphasis on a "search" for an uncertain entity is revealing. Townshend's character perceives the need to "get out in the light" or else he'll "go out of [his] mind," but we do not have a clue as to what "the light" represents.

Whereas the Mod/teen angst themes are predictable, Townshend's songs about lying ("La La La Lies" and "It's Not True") are a surprise. The songs appear to address anxieties over media misrepresentations, although one cannot be certain. For example, "La La La Lies" opens:

> If I'm so lost without a friend

Tell me who's this by my side
This girl with eyes like gems
And cool reactions to your lies
Lies, la la la la la la lies
You can't repeat what you put round
All the things that made me cry
You kicked me when I was down
And they hurt me, all those lies
Lies, la la la la la la lies.

The narrator takes considerable pride in his "girl with eyes like gems" and uses that relationship to discredit the sources of the "lies" (a friend? a reporter?). The character merely argues, "why would a girl as beautiful as this stand by my side if your lies were true?" After declaring his pain over these "lies" the narrator forgives the source: "I don't insist that you feel bad/I just want to see you smile/Don't ever think you made me mad/I didn't listen to your lies/Lies, la la la la la la lies." The song's internal contradictions elevate the message's mysterious qualities.

From "La La La Lies" general complaint I move to "It's Not True" and its more specific, albeit adolescent, refutation:

It's not true.
You say I've been in prison
You say I've got a wife
You say I had help doin' everything throughout my life
[chorus] It's not true, it's not true
          I'm telling you
          Cuz I'm up here and you're nowhere
          It's not true, so there
I haven't got eleven kids
I weren't born in Baghdad
I'm not half Chinese either
And I didn't kill my dad
[chorus]
If you hear more rumors you can just forget them too
Fools start the rumors, none of them are true
[chorus].

This song objects to specific misrepresentations by way of an adolescent "Cuz I'm up here and you're nowhere/It's not true, so there" retort. Just as "La La La Lies" uses the character's girlfriend as the basis of credibility, this character uses the stage/star status to that end. In other words, you may print all the lies you want, but "I'm a star" and "you're nowhere"—"So There." Consistent with Townshend's emerging style, the details (i.e., "who's lying and why") are left to the auditor. The presence of two songs on the same—relatively obscure—topic stands out amongst the typical tunes about breaking up, street life, and machismo.

Townshend's three "break-up" songs are exemplars of the 1960s pop music heartache genre. The first entry, "The Good's Gone," merely reiterates that line throughout the song after such statements as: "I know when I've had enough/ When I think your love is rough," "Once we used to get along/Now each time we kiss it's wrong," and "Now it ain't no fun/And the good's gone now/We used to love as one/But we have forgotten how." The complaint is simple, direct, and dominant. This principle also appears in the album's fifth track, "Much Too Much." This time the central character laments that "your love is too heavy on me" and "it's much too much too bad." Townshend sums up the situation via a classic stanza: "There was a time I could give all I have to you/ But my enthusiasm waned and I can't bear the pain/Of doin' what I don't wanna do/Much too much too bad." "The Good's Gone" and "Much Too Much" are standard romance-gone-bad pop songs that employ simple narrative structures which lend themselves to heavy repetition. This principle holds true for "A Legal Matter" as well:

> I told you why I changed my mind
> I got bored by playin' with time
> I know you thought you had me nailed
> But I've freed my head from your garden rails
> Now it's a legal matter baby
> You got me on the run
> It's a legal matter baby
> A legal matter from now on
> My mind's lost in a household fog
> Wedding gowns and catalogs
> Kitchen furnishings and houses
> Maternity clothes and baby's trousers
> It's a legal matter baby
> Marrying's no fun
> It's a legal matter baby
> A legal matter from now on.

Townshend's love complaint shifts context from a "love gone bad" to a "love gone legal" and the complications of married life. The character returns to a macho, streetwise stance in the closing stanza:

> You ain't the first and you ain't the last
> I gain and lose my women fast
> I never want to make them cry
> I just get bored don't ask me why
> Just wanna keep doin' all the dirty little things I do
> Not work all day in an office just to bring my money back to you
> Sorry baby.

Townshend's message is without mystery. If a relationship manages to survive to the point of marriage, this is what "guys" have to look forward to: wedding gowns, kitchen furnishings, and baby clothes. He explains: "What this song was screaming from behind the lines like, 'It's a legal matter baby, marrying's not fun, it's a legal matter baby, you got me on the run,' was 'I'm lonely, I'm hungry, and the bed needs making.' I wanted a maid I suppose. It's terrible feeling like an eligible bachelor but with no women seeming to agree with you" (Townshend, 1971e, p. 38).

My Generation's mystery song, "Instant Party (Circles)" (U.S. title), is significant for two reasons: this is the track that will be used in future legal confrontations with Shel Talmy, and it offers a strong example of Townshend's emerging impressionism. The song could be about a lover always returning to his/her love, a spiritual master, drugs, patriotism—anything. The track opens with a complaint:

> Circles, my head's goin' round in circles
> My mind is caught up in a whirlpool
> Draggin' me down
> Time will tell if I'll take the homeward track
> Dizziness will make my feet walk back
> Walk right back to you.
> Everything I do, I think of you
> No matter how I try, I can't get by
> These circles, leading me back to you
> Round and around and around and around and around
> And around and around and around
> And round and round like a fool I go...Draggin' me down.

"Dizziness," "guilt," and "dreams" bring the narrator "back to you." The question here, of course, is the "you." Townshend leaves that up to the audience and provides the initial evidence of an impressionistic writing style that persists in varying degrees throughout the oeuvre. Without question, The Who's first album—complete with its Mod anthems, moon and June love songs, humor, and cryptic characterizations—establish the commercial, and creative, foundation for a career that would at times be as uneven as *My Generation*'s contents.

Critical responses to this first album fall into two camps. The music press of 1966 stressed the sensational, publicity-based commentary that typified fan magazines. Years later, however, music critics searched for the album's significance; for example, Malamut (1976) labels The Who as the Rolling Stones' "bastard child" (p. 76) and declares: "They take the blues less seriously, seem to enjoy to rock a little harder and accept the ultimate truth that purists are copyists.... The Who laugh as much at their roots as they love them.... So rock is no longer merely light entertainment. It shows more than one face—like art should; like theater does. It is not ironic that the Who, therefore, are theatrical. Not always for your pleasure, but certainly for shock." Swenson (1979) claims *Generation* is "certainly the most explosive, energetic recording of its time" (p. 36). And Marsh (1983) adds, "whatever complaints one may have about details,

My Generation is a great rock album and one of the most influential ever recorded" (p. 193).

Townshend's (1971e) recollections are mixed. On one hand he maintains
that The Who's "first few albums are among our best" (p. 37); on the other he
notes that "they were the least fun to make." He sarcastically concludes: "However, dear Shel got us our first single hits. So he was as close to being God for a
week as any other unworthy soul has been." Such thoughts are intriguing in that
The Who managed to render quality work in spite of the intense turmoil that
surrounded the band. While this level of conflict may have stimulated creativity, it most certainly could not advance indefinitely.

A QUICK ONE (HAPPY JACK)

The post-*My Generation* period advanced the aggressive qualities of the previous time frame, albeit in somewhat different directions. Lambert and Stamp
now focused on a legal confrontation with Shel Talmy and the United States
market. Townshend's enterprising songwriting turned away from the Mod anthem genre, and the aggressive reciprocity of the Townshend-audience relationship expanded. As The Who moved away from Talmy—and the Mods for that
matter—the Lambert-Townshend creative team flourished, internal tensions
gradually relaxed, and Townshend assumed firm control over the group's creative direction.

Barnes (1982) cites three reasons why Lambert and Stamp wanted to break
the contract with Talmy: it was a bad deal financially, it reduced the opportunity to break into the American market (apparently, U.S. Decca—Talmy's
American affiliation—was not very innovative), and the band wanted creative
freedom in the studio (no more Ivy League/Jimmy Page situations). Talmy
"adamantly refused" to release The Who; therefore, the band sought legal counsel in order to break the contract (Barnes, p. 42). The Who selected the B-side
of the single "Substitute" as its battleground. There the band placed the song
"Circles" (labeled "Instant Party" on the U.K. *My Generation*) and released the
single on Robert Stigwood's newly formed label, Reaction (Talmy's U.K. label
was Brunswick). Since "Circles" *was* "Instant Party," and since Talmy had produced the original version (thereby establishing a copyright on that sound),
Talmy easily obtained an injunction preventing further distribution. Correspondingly, Talmy's Brunswick label issued the single "A Legal Matter" (cute)
with its version of "Instant Party" on the B-side. The fight was on.

Initially, Lambert and Stamp sought alliances with The Beatles' management (Brian Epstein), and the Rolling Stones' manager (Andrew Loog Oldham)
conveyed an interest in obtaining The Who. The plot thickened quickly. Talmy
insisted that the Rolling Stones' American business manager, Allan Klein, handle the negotiations. By this time, Stamp was in charge of The Who's American
business, and Lambert focused on England and Europe. Thus Stamp and Townshend traveled to New York to meet Klein. Here is where Stamp's aggressive
nature spawned entrepreneurial genius. The Who signed a deal with Klein that

gave him twenty days to arrange and sign a formal contract. Lambert and Stamp simply confused the matter for twenty days (Klein never realized what had happened), and Lambert and Stamp retained The Who. The Talmy settlement granted him five percent of all Who recordings for five years; a period that included the very successful *Tommy* and *Who's Next* albums. As Stamp told Marsh (1983), "We were left with Shel Talmy on paper...but we were not left with Shel Talmy in the studio" (p. 207). These legal debates may appear to have little relevance to Townshend's artistic development; however, they were central to his art's evolution. With Talmy "in the studio" the Lambert-Townshend team would have been severely restricted. Moreover, The Who's entry into the United States provided a source of financial support that eventually allowed Townshend to emphasize his creative pursuits. In every respect, this was a pivotal moment in the songwriter's history.

Several Who singles were released by both Brunswick and Reaction during this period. Evidence of Townshend's emerging thematic orientation may be seen in two of those releases: "Substitute" and "I'm A Boy." Both of these songs deal with questions of identity, and neither one positively. The overriding message is "I'm not OK." The central character is either a deception ("Substitute") or a delusion ("I'm A Boy"). The stories, while full of anxiety over identity, are somewhat superficial, as Townshend (1971e) indicates: "'Substitute' makes me recall writing a song to fit a clever and rhythmic sounding title. A play on words. Again it could mean a lot more to me now than it did when I wrote it" (p. 37). "Substitute" (the first song produced by Townshend) is open to a variety of readings. The song opens:

> You think we look pretty good together
> You think my shoes are made of leather,
> But I'm a substitute for another guy
> I look pretty tall, but my heels are high
> The simple things you see are all complicated
> I look pretty young, but I'm just back dated, yeah.
> Substitute, your lies for fact
> I can see right through your plastic mac
> I look all white but my dad was black
> My fine looking suit's really made out of sack.

Townshend may be talking about a lot of different things, such as "The Who" being a substitute for the "Rolling Stones" (he does admit imitating Mick Jagger's accent and the song "Nineteenth Nervous Breakdown" on his demo—see Townshend, 1971e), the origins of the band's music ("I look all white but my dad was black"—see Willis, 1969, p. 65), or his frustrations with women ("Substitute/You for my mum/At least I'll get my washing done"). The one clear reference is the identity theme—"I look pretty tall but my heels are high.... Look pretty young but I'm just back dated.... My fine looking suit's really made out of sack"—and its emphasis, once more, on lying ("Substitute, your lies for fact/I see right through your plastic mac"). Townshend's working-class characterization ("I was born with a plastic spoon in my mouth" on the wrong side of town) and the identity theme reflect both an understanding of his audience and an emerging narrative orientation through which he effectively discusses the adolescent insecurities that engulfed Mod life.   Mods worked desperately to outdo one another (usually to no avail), and "Substitute" addresses that condition.   Furthermore, Townshend's line—"The simple things you see are all complicated"—subtly advances the theme introduced in "The Kids Are Alright" in which he intimates that there is more happening here than meets the eye.   That Townshend claims "Substitute" is a "play on words" designed to "fit a clever and rhythmic title" suggests an emerging narrative impulse that may very well operate on multiple levels of consciousness.

"I'm A Boy"—the first single produced by Kit Lambert—is equally insightful. Townshend writes:

> One girl was called Jean Marie
> Another little girl was called Felicity
> Another little girl was Sally Joy
> The other was me and I'm a boy
> My name is Bill and I'm a head case
> They practice making up on my face
> Yeah, I feel lucky if I get trousers to wear
> Spend evenings taking hair-pins from my hair
> I'm a boy, I'm a boy
> But my ma won't admit it
> I'm a boy, I'm a boy
> But if I say I am I get it.

"Bill" longs to "play cricket on the green," ride his "bike across the stream," and "cut myself and see my blood/I wanna come home all covered in mud." Yet his mother treats him as one of four girls. Remember, this song is from the aborted *Quads* project. *Quads* never materialized, but the urge for a more extensive storytelling format and the identity theme most certainly portend Townshend's songwriting future. Both "Substitute" and "I'm A Boy" foreshadow a role confusion narrative that will at times dominate the songwriter's pen. Townshend's "generation" is unsure of itself and its role in society—an insecurity that originates in domestic gender identities and social role taking.

The Who was a hot commercial property in 1966. Multiple television appearances, tours of Europe, large festival shows, and much publicity typified that year. Once more, the holiday season offered an album, *A Quick One (Happy Jack)* (the U.K. and U.S. titles differ). While *My Generation* offers evidence of the band's musical compromises, *A Quick One* extends the uneven nature of that arrangement; a publishing contract stipulated that each band member compose two songs. Consequently, the work features a blend of Moon's instrumentals, Townshend's love songs, and Entwistle's odd stories. Lambert and Stamp produced promotional films to accompany songs such as "Cobwebs and Strange" and "Happy Jack," and Lambert worried about overexposure for the first time. Barnes (1982) recalls: "Kit Lambert, who would have done anything, who would have pestered, bribed, bullied, promised and pleaded for any TV spot or press story, Kit, whose famous catchphrase in the trade was, 'If you print a picture you can have the story exclusive,' was actually keeping his carefully nurtured creation off the nation's TV screens" (p. 44). Lambert was aggressive, yet savvy.

The Who's second album contains eleven songs (running 34:20): three Townshend compositions about boy-girl relationships ("Run Run Run," "Don't Look Away," and "So Sad About Us"), two Entwistle songs ("Boris the Spider" and "Whiskey Man"), one cover (Holland/Dozier/Holland's "Heat Wave"), one Daltrey number ("See My Way"), two Moon songs (one a brief ditty entitled "I Need You," the other an outrageous instrumental, "Cobwebs and Strange"), and two Townshend stories (the mini-opera "A Quick One While He's Away" and the single "Happy Jack"). The album's most significant artistic contribution is the commercially inspired mini-opera that Townshend pieced together in order to meet the required album length.

The mini-opera's principal contribution to the oeuvre lies not in its thematic content but in its transitions and continuity. The movement between the number's "nine different tunes and fragments" (Landau, 1967, p. 47) suggest a writer capable of longer concept pieces. The story—about a "wife," her tardy husband, and her subsequent anxieties—appears in six parts: "Her Man's Been Gone," "Crying Town," "We Have A Remedy," "Ivor the Engine Driver," "Soon Be Home," and "You Are Forgiven." The story begins with this a cappella announcement: "Her man's been gone/For nearly a year/He was due home yesterday/But he ain't here/Her man's been gone/For nigh on a year/He was due home yesterday/But he ain't here." From there we move to part two, "Crying Town": "Down your street your crying is a well known sound/Your street is very well known throughout your town/Your town is very famous for the little girl/Whose crying can be heard all around the world." Suddenly, "a remedy" is proposed by an unknown source (presumably potential suitors):

Fa la la la la la [repeated several times]
We have a remedy, you'll appreciate
No need to be so sad, he's only late
We'll bring you flowers and things, help pass the time
We'll give him eagle's wings, then he can fly to you
Fa la la la la [repeated]
[Spoken] We have a remedy. We have!
        Little girl, why don't you stop your crying?
        I'm gonna make you feel alright.

A tempo shift and furious drumming introduce "Ivor" the "engine driver," who offers comfort ("I know why you feel blue/Just 'cause he's late/Don't mean he'll never get through"), requests a "smile" in return, and encourages her to "take a walk" back to his "place" where they will "sort" everything out ("better be nice to an old engine driver"). After the interlude "Soon Be Home" ("We'll soon be home.... We'll soon soon soon be home"), and an "instrumental" (actually the band singing "cello cello cello..."—supposedly Lambert was too cheap to hire the real thing), the woman's lover returns:

> Do my eyes deceive me?
> Am I back in your arms, away from all harm?
> It's like a dream to be with you again,
> Can't believe that I'm with you again.
> I missed you, and I must admit I've kissed a few,
> And once did sit on Ivor the engine driver's lap,
> And later with him had a nap.

The lover forgives her with his only words, "you are forgiven." These scenes unfold via a variety of musical styles: the opening a cappella vocals, a "cowboy song" transition ("Soon Be Home"), and closes "in a brilliant burst of semi-operatic counterpoint, a coda of falsetto voices singing 'you are forgiven'" (Marsh, 1983, p. 228). "A Quick One While He's Away" is silly, lighthearted entertainment. There is little metaphorical mischief in this straightforward yarn about the lonely woman's adventures. The Monterey International Pop Festival film features The Who performing the mini-opera and conveys the irony of a Who performance from this period: dressed in outrageous clothes, smashing their gear, and singing soft, elaborate tunes such as "A Quick One."

This narrative trend appears in "Happy Jack" as well. There Townshend describes how mean-spirited school kids torment a happy-go-lucky seaside hermit:

> Happy Jack wasn't old, but he was a man
> He lived in the sand at the Isle of Man
> The kids would all sing, he would take the wrong key
> So they rode on his head, on their furry donkey
> The kids couldn't hurt Jack, they tried and tried and tried
> They dropped things on his back, and lied and lied and lied
>   and lied and lied
> But they couldn't stop Jack, or the waters lapping
> And they couldn't prevent Jack from feeling happy.

This light, adolescent storytelling style is a major Townshend signature from this period. The art school student's talent for constructing simple stories about youth experiences joined his pop art philosophy to produce these initial stylistic trends.

All the while Townshend refined that narrative style, he did not forsake the pop music "boy-girl" genre. From the raw driving beat of "Run Run Run" (and its bragging, macho central character—"Out in the Street" revisited) to the remorseful tale about love lost in "Don't Look Away" to the forthright elegy in "So Sad About Us" Townshend sings of adolescent romance and its volatile qualities. Consider the opening of "So Sad About Us":

La la la la la la la la [repeated]
So sad about us [repeat]
Sad, that the news is out now
Sad, suppose we can't turn back now
Sad, about us
So bad about us [repeat]
Bad, never meant to break up
Bad, suppose we'll never make up
Bad, about us
Apologies mean nothing
When the damage is done
But I can't switch off my lovin'
Like you can't switch off the sun
La la la la la la la [repeated].

The song's moon and June style was the industry's songwriting prescription of the period, and assuredly Townshend paid his dues. In every respect *A Quick One* offers a compelling snapshot of a songwriter forging a style that is thematically flexible and, therefore, commercially viable.

This period also introduced a more sophisticated music press in which a new breed of "music critic" *used* music reviews to establish a professional reputation. Many pop artists dismissed these occasionally mean-spirited commentaries; others took them to heart. While "fan magazines" continued to compromise between public relations, rumor, and facts, the new critics became sources of inspiration and consternation for Pete Townshend. Several reviews of *A Quick One* reflect this journalistic turning point. *Melody Maker*'s Chris Welch (1966) follows tradition as he notes that The Who has been "bedeviled" by "schemes that haven't always worked out" and proceeds with a superficial overview of the various cuts. "I Need You" ("Is it a Beatle song?" Welch asks) and the "miniature pop opera" ("It's fun, and a new departure for any pop group") are mentioned briefly. The review is short, snappy, and sensational. That approach contrasts Landau's (1967) extended treatment for *Crawdaddy* and Willis's (1969) commentary in the *New Yorker* magazine. Willis opens with Who history—"As funny as the Beatles, as arrogant as the Stones, the Who specialized in an unbohemian youth-prole defiance that was much closer to the spirit of fifties rock" (p. 62)—before assessing the state-of-the-band: "The Who's music had grown more complex and subtle; the violence was balanced by playfulness, and the suggestion of the fifties was gone. Generational polemics had given way to narratives and character sketches, often infused with whimsy. I missed the crude energy but liked what had replaced it." Landau (1967) follows a similar logic and concludes The Who's "humor" and "sense of the real" are the "two factors" that create "their dynamism and their ethos," since "They aren't earnest or 'serious.' They aren't proselytizers, even when they proselytize" (p. 47). With regard to the album, Landau writes: "*Happy Jack* is an almost arty, and for the Who, restrained affair. It emphasizes the group's rare talents, in the areas of self-editing (a lost art if ever there was one), humor, lyricism, and other things which one doesn't generally expect to find in the wilder groups. The more extroverted side of the group is, in fact, played down" (p. 44). Whether one agrees with these points is irrelevant. What matters is that Landau and Willis advance *arguments* regarding their observations and, in turn, extend the popular music critic's role. In America this journalistic style appeared in magazines (from *Time* to *Playboy*) and the major daily newspapers to produce a diversity of coverage popular music had never before known. The Who's sophisticated image manipulation now had to accommodate this new element, and Townshend expanded his audience to include "the critics."

The post-*A Quick One* period was an exciting one. The Who had a strong European following and spent considerable time there in early 1967. Barnes (1982) reports the band toured Germany, France, and Sweden (where it had a number-one single) and in general enjoyed strong sales on the Continent. In February 1967 Townshend announced that he was working on a "big pop opera" (Barnes, p. 44) that would contain twenty-five acts and appear in a double album set. And in March 1967 The Who came to America. Once again, Chris Stamp's clever management was responsible. Stamp wanted to improve the Decca situation and obtain an American booking agent. His choice for the latter was Premier Talent, managed by Frank Barsalona and Dick Freedberg (Barsalona secured the talent; Freedberg was responsible for financial matters). Barsalona rejected Stamp because of his apparent relationship with Allan Klein. Not to be deterred, when Barsalona left New York City for a West Coast business trip Stamp persuaded Freedberg to sign The Who. Barsalona had to honor the deal due to musician union rules; thus, "Stamp had achieved the impossible. The Who now had an incompetent American record company and a booking agent who hated them" (Marsh, 1983, p. 239).

The Who's U.S. breakthrough was just as weird. New York radio personality "Murray the K"—widely known as the self-proclaimed fifth Beatle and a very influential radio personality—sponsored an annual Easter show in New York City. The shows were marathons featuring five performances each day for a week; nevertheless, Murray usually had his pick of performers (being a fifth Beatle had its rewards). Murray wanted Mitch Ryder—one of Barsalona's clients—for the 1967 shows, but Ryder wanted no part of the five-shows-a-day booking. Consequently, Barsalona made outrageous demands of Murray in order to keep Ryder out of the show (a high fee, painting his dressing room a particular shade of blue, and the inclusion of this obscure English act, The Who). Much to Barsalona's chagrin, Murray accepted. Barsalona then demanded an unusually high price for The Who, which Murray accepted. After further negotiations between Barsalona, Robert Stigwood (the band's U.K. booking agent), and Murray, the deal was complete.

To wager that American audiences (including Barsalona and Murray) had never seen anything quite like The Who's act is a safe bet. The *Village Voice* opines: "But their's is a toy music, with massive drumming and a vocal that sounds as though someone's batteries need charging. There are bleeps and crashes, falsetto and absurd bass effects, all merging into a screeching tunelessness...it is all for laughs" (Goldstein, 1967, p. 23). The Who used smoke bombs ("disgruntled, the go-go girl holds her nose and mutters: 'I smell the Who'"—Goldstein, p. 23) and destroyed the set during every single performance. The price of auto-destruction was high, as Shaffner (1983) conveys: "Over the course of their twenty-one mini-concerts, The Who utterly demolished five guitars, four speaker cabinets, twenty-two microphones, and sixteen individual pieces of percussion" (p. 113). In response Townshend developed a penchant for guitar repair, and Stamp's entrepreneurial skills expanded to coaxing equipment from American sources. As a result of the Easter shows, Murray promoted "Happy Jack," the song reached the U.S. Top Forty, Barsalona convinced Decca to hire independent promotional personnel to push The Who (the label released the second album), and—in general—the band boldly entered the American market. Barnes (1982) reports that The Who was scheduled to appear on *The Ed Sullivan Show* but had to honor a "newsreader's strike" (p. 45) and could not perform.

The next single, "Pictures of Lily"—the band's first record on Lambert and Stamp's new label, Track—extends the narrative style Townshend introduced in "I'm A Boy" and "Happy Jack." Here Townshend describes a teenage boy's sleepless nights and his father's successful intervention:

> I used to wake up in the morning, I used to feel so bad
> I got so sick of having sleepless nights, I went and told my dad
> He said, "Son, now here's some little somethings" and stuck them
>   on my wall
> And now my nights ain't quite so lonely, in fact I, I don't feel bad at all
> I don't feel bad at all
> Pictures of Lily, made my life so wonderful
> Pictures of Lily, helped me sleep at night
> Pictures of Lily, solved my childhood problems
> Pictures of Lily, made me feel alright.

Townshend offers a clever insight into adolescent reasoning, as the youngster falls in love with "Lily" and seeks counsel from his father who explains that "Lily" has been "dead since Nineteen Twenty Nine." The boy's response—"If only I'd been born in Lily's time/It would have been alright"—demonstrates Townshend's understanding of adolescent fantasy and its novel, idiosyncratic reasoning.

Media responses to "Lily" were predictable, considering its contents. The masturbation genre was as yet underdeveloped; however, Townshend dodged the issue by saying the song is about every boy's "pin-up period" (Barnes, 1982, p. 45). Later, Townshend (1971e) tells the truth: "Merely a ditty about masturbation and the importance of it to a young man. I was really digging at my folks who, when catching me at it, would talk in loud voices in the corridor outside my room. 'Why can't he go with girls like *other* boys'" (p. 38). Those details aside, Townshend's adolescent perspicacity is impressive. His ability to weave stories with sharp, poignant insights was maturing and when coupled with his desire for longer, more detailed projects suggests his future.

The Who returned to America in mid-June 1967 for the Monterey International Pop Festival. Since the festival provided considerable publicity but no revenue, Stamp booked performances in Detroit, Chicago, and San Francisco to help pay for air fare and equipment (always a concern for a band specializing in auto-destruction). Later that year, Frank Barsalona demonstrated his new-found faith in the band by booking The Who on an American tour with one of his top acts, Herman's Hermits. Here The Who was introduced to the American "flower-power" movement and a completely different approach to perform-ance—the longer "concert," as opposed to the brief English "show." During this period The Who also perfected another forum for auto-destruction, the hotel room, and solidified its reputation for violence. Keith Moon's systematic de-struction of hotel rooms quickly became legendary. Townshend described the drummer's approach:

He was a hotel-room-wrecking artist. It wasn't about violence or hedonism. It was art. Quite seriously. It was part of the statement against materialism, against neatness, against order, values, role models, against all that shit. He'd come into a freshly made-up room and look at it intently and study it. Then he'd rearrange it. Afterward, he would always go to warn the maid. "A slight problem in room 1308," he'd say. (Sheff, 1994, p. 53)

Using Moon's "art" to its advantage, The Who's aggressive publicity machine marched onward. Townshend (1967b) penned a series of letters to *Melody Maker* offering his reflections on America and on one occasion wrote: "We're all looking forward to the tour in general excepting a few crisis points we would rather avoid, like Dallas and Houston, etc. The New York groups have told us such amazing tales of the effect long hair has on shotgun carrying farmers there!" In 1968 Townshend made a radio commercial for the United States Air Force and Moon promoted the U.S. Navy. Barnes (1982) reports the "Airforce" spot opened with "a few bars of *Happy Jack*" and Townshend's voice-over, "Hi, this is Pete Townshend of the Who, I just want to say the United States Air Force is a great place to be" (p. 48). During this same period Townshend wrote a spot for the American Cancer Society ("Little Billy"), and Townshend/Moon sang a "jingle for Great Shakes Milkshakes." Townshend's recollections are revealing: "Young Americans were concerned about being blown to bits in Vietnam, and I, as a naive English twit, came prancing over, hot on the heels of the Beatles and Herman's Hermits, to make my fortune and bring it back to Britain. And I didn't really give a fuck about what was happening to the American young men. I really didn't!" (Denselow, 1989, p. 108).

These publicity moves suggest more than The Who's promotional style; they also provide another view of the band's—and Townshend's—artistic philoso-phy. The Who was not political. Therefore, why not cut an advertisement for the government? It was just another promotion. (The band was appearing on an

Air Force base, and according to Denselow, Townshend was told the spot would be used to promote the U.S. space program.) The fact that the group reissued "Substitute" in the United States—changing the lyric from "I look all white but my dad was black" to "I try walking forward but my feet walk back" (Barnes, 1982; Marsh, 1983)—indicates a preference for the commercial realm. Correspondingly, The Who did not care for the American "hippy scene," with its long concerts where audiences sat and stared at psychedelic acts, consumed powerful hallucinogenic drugs, and preached political activism. The Who was a rebel-rousing act that promoted (actually required) rugged individualism ("How fantastic am I") through shows that stressed individual involvement. As time passed, this fundamental distinction between The Who's notion of rock performance and the flower-power-inspired concert format emerged as a serious source of contention. American audiences would come to *watch* The Who, and Townshend would lose interest in the proceedings.

The *Quick One* portion of The Who's singles period was among the most dynamic in the band's history. The legal confrontations, Townshend's emerging narrative style, the aggressive reciprocity between the band and its audience, and the group's emergence in the United States worked together to transform The Who from a Mod-oriented domestic happening into an international act without peer. Through it all, the art school "ideas man" slowly faced his obsession with artistic progress as projects such as the twenty-five act "pop opera" festered inside him. In his January 1967 *Melody Maker* "Pop Think In" piece, Townshend (1967a) writes about his "need" for security and explains: "I need it to work and I need it to be happy. I'm like most people, I work to be secure. I never am, so I have to go on working" (p. 7). That work would now involve longer, detailed concept pieces that respond to his narrative impulse's inclinations, although providing little comfort for his insecurities. As early as April 1967 Townshend told *Melody Maker*'s Nick Jones that he was "working on an opera" (1967a, p. 9). While the next album would fall short of that goal, it most certainly represents a significant artistic innovation.

THE WHO SELL OUT

The Who would never completely turn away from "singles" as a musical outlet, but the band—and the industry—of this period discovered a new use for the long-playing record. Instead of compiling a number of singles (and B-sides) to be sold at Christmas, albums were now being used to articulate "concepts" to various audiences. The 1967 music scene featured a variety of concept albums, which occasionally used strange sound effects and disjointed mixes as avenues for "mystical" experiences. In fact, an entire genre of music emerged from this era of sound and lyrical experimentation. The *New York Times* cites Townshend's rejection of "the growing formalism" (Nelson, 1968, p. 20) and notes the songwriter's complaint, "there's no bloody youth in music today." In response Townshend co-opted the new trend to his ends, as he related to Nelson:

[The Who's new record's] got a slight formalism because we thought we needed a form throughout the album to make it stand up within the terms of the other albums coming out today. Having a form for an album seems to be what is happening, and we wanted a form for ours which would be...humoristic.... We've got commercials on the album which we composed about genuine products like Heinz Beans, Medac, Odorono, and stuff like that. We've written songs about them and stuck them in. And that led to another idea: that of making the whole album into a radio program.

Townshend's decision to write *The Who Sell Out* in this fashion not only reflects his interest in pirate radio (radio stations located on ships offshore that provided competition for government-managed British radio) but directly integrates his Ealing Art College education as well as Kit Lambert's love of camp. As a result, The Who could have it both ways: the band could keep up with the times by producing a concept album and hang on to its youthful identity through humor—a humor that also advanced the rebellious, anti-establishment themes associated with The Who's image.

    The Who Sell Out (released in December 1967, U.K.; January 1968, U.S.) contains twelve songs (running 39:38) that are more thematically focused than any previous Who album. Nine of the twelve songs are Townshend compositions ("Mary-Anne with the Shaky Hand," "Odorono," "Tattoo," "Our Love Was, Is," "I Can See For Miles," "I Can't Reach You," "Relax," "Sunrise," and "Rael"), three are by Entwistle ("Heinz Baked Beans," the second part of the opening number, "Medac," and "Silas Stingy"), and one track was written by the band's driver, John "Speedy" Keene (the first part of the first track, "Armenia City in the Sky"). The album opens with an electronically enhanced voice citing the days of the week (Monnddaaay, Tuuuessday ...) as per late-1960s Top Forty radio and slides into Keene's "Armenia" with its heavy emphasis on the psychedelic genre that The Who purported to reject. After the segue—"Wonderful Radio London, whoopeee"—Entwistle's "Heinz" jingle appears prior to yet another radio segue ("more music more music more music more music") into Townshend's "Mary-Anne" (a track that Charlesworth [1995] denotes as either a second tribute to masturbation or "a tasteless ode to an afflicted unfortunate" [p. 17]). That opening reveals the entire album's flow: a mix of tracks tied together with samples of radio jingles or Who-created advertisements. The radio samples feature classic '60s material such as "It's smooth sailing with the highly successful sounds of wonderful Radio London," "Radio London reminds you: go to the church of your choice," and "You're a pussy cat, you're where it's at...The in sound." These samples cease with the album's sixth cut ("I Can See For Miles") in favor of Who-generated "ads" (e.g., the "Charles Atlas" ad) that sustain the piece's continuity. (As a quick aside, of the various reissues of Who material, the *Sell Out* entry actually extends and concludes the original concept.)

    The album's internal coherence is enhanced by three factors: the emphasis on Townshend compositions as opposed to a song or two from each band member, the various radio segues, and Entwistle's songs, which serve the album's concept (Entwistle was establishing his own, unique narrative style). Townshend continues to expound on relationship themes ("Our Love Was, Is" and "I Can See For Miles"); however, that trend is somewhat constrained in favor of narrative vignettes that serve the album's format and the songwriter's subtle spiritual messages.

Two examples of the former are "Odorono" and "Tattoo." "Odorono" is a "commercial" that explores the vicissitudes of inadequate hygiene. The central character—a female singer—had performed well on stage ("She'd sang the best she'd ever sang/She couldn't ever sing any better"), and yet she understood that her ambitions with "Mr. Davidson" were in peril ("But she knew she'd failed the test/She knew he would forget her"). Suddenly, she felt "triumphant" as "she acknowledged the applause" from her audience and traveled backstage only to find "him at the dressing room door." Our character was "happier than she'd ever been" but unfortunately Mr. Davidson's "expression changed" when "he leant to kiss her face"; thus, "he claimed a late appointment." Townshend's character "quickly turned" in order to "hide her disappointment" as she realized her "deodorant had let her down/She should have used Odorono."

Our second example—"Tattoo"—involves two brothers' search for manhood, the discovery of the answer, the subsequent celebration, the parents' response, more celebrations, and a resolution. The track opens:

> Me and my brother were talking to each other 'bout what makes
> a man a man
> Was it brain or brawn or the month you were born? We just couldn't
> understand
> Our old man didn't like our pairs, he said that only women wear long hair
> So me and my brother borrowed money from mother, we knew what we
> had to do
> We went downstairs, past the barber and gymnasium, and got our arms
> tattooed.
> [chorus] Welcome to my life tattoo!
> I'm a man now thanks to you
> I expect I'll regret you
> But the skin-graft man won't get you
> You'll be there when I die
> Tattoo
> My dad beat me 'cause mine said, "Mother," but my mother naturally liked it and
> beat my brother
> 'Cause his tattoo was of a lady in the nude and my mother thought that was
> extremely rude
> [chorus] Welcome to my life tattoo!
> We've a long time together, me and you
> I expect I'll regret you
> But the skin graft man won't get you
> You'll be there when I die
> Tattoo
> Now I'm older, I'm tattooed all over

My wife is tattooed too
A rooty toot too, rooty tooty toot too...To you!

These two songs demonstrate Townshend's ability to weave simple, colorful tales that offer potentially probing insights into everyday problems. In the first case, we observe the lady's dilemma over her selection of deodorants in a song that fits nicely within the context of a "radio program." "Odorono" displays tragic qualities, in that the central character fails to achieve her aspirations because of a simple yet fatal flaw. In classic advertising logic, the story introduces the product and its capacity to avert such a dilemma. "Tattoo," on the other hand, probes the adolescent psyche as two brothers search for masculine identity through very superficial means. Here again we note Townshend's sense of humor as he depicts the parents' response and the boys' never-ending commitment to their tattoo-inspired identities. "Tattoo" joins such songs as "I'm A Boy," "Pictures of Lily," and "Happy Jack" as examples of Townshend's penchant for lighthearted stories based on adolescent characterizations. The songwriter's ability to take a teen dilemma (personal identity, sexual frustrations, the search for manhood) or a personality trait (hounding a seaside hermit) and present that scenario from the adolescent's perspective is impressive. This narrative signature is one of the striking trends in Townshend's early songwriting.

Perhaps the most significant thematic development on *The Who Sell Out* involves Townshend's "spiritual" songs. I exercise care when I suggest these cloudy expressions are "spiritual"; they could be about anything. "I Can't Reach You," "Relax," and "Sunrise" all appear to describe the bliss that accompanies the spiritual search (or they could just as easily be about relationships, drugs, or gardening). For example, "I Can't Reach You" opens with what appear to be mystical metaphors ("I'm a billion ages past you/A million years behind you too/A thousand miles up in the air/A trillion times I've seen you there") and describes "your" golden hair, how "you walk on grass, it turns to hay," and how the narrator just "can't reach you." Townshend's line, "Once I caught a glimpse of your unguarded, untouched heart/Our fingertips touched and then my mind tore us apart," suggests the narrator's struggle between romantic/spiritual longings and intellectual inclinations. (I think this song is the first glimpse of a story line that appears in a lengthy poem, "The Amazing Journey," which provides the narrative foundation for the *Tommy* project.) Townshend's characterological ambiguity leaves the auditor free to make of the song what he/she wishes; that is, is the song about your lover, your god, or a scary airplane ride? (Marsh [1983] and Charlesworth [1995] claim that Townshend penned this song during a particularly hazardous airplane trip, thus the references to "a thousand miles up in the air" and the inability to "reach you.")

"Relax" and "Sunrise" are more direct statements. "Relax" urges: "Relax and settle down/Let your mind go round/Lay down on the ground/And listen to the sound/Of the band, hold my hand/Relax." Here Townshend encourages the auditor to "let your mind go roam" and to "open all your problems" as you "relax" and listen to the band. The song encourages patience as the path to peace of mind: "We try harder and harder trying to get away/But it's a long long wait til judgement day/So settle your prayers and take your time/Cause everything in the world is yours and mine/Yours and mine." Such lines fit nicely within the late-1960s psychedelic genre, since the audience is encouraged to meditate, face "your" problems, and gain comfort from "the band." Interestingly, while Townshend's pen cleverly packaged those views in contemporary terms, his lyrics foreshadow his forthcoming spiritual writings, his belief in music's healing powers, and his philosophical stance that one must face one's problems and use rock to "dance all over them."

"Sunrise" features Townshend unaccompanied on his guitar in the "prayer" style that would typify later projects. "Sunrise" also contains a guitar bridge that reappears in *Tommy* and introduces elements of the "Amazing Journey" poem:

> You take away the breath I was keeping for sunrise
> You appear and the morning looks drab in my eyes
> And then again I'll turn down love
> Having seen you again
> Once more you'll disappear
> My morning put to shame
> [tempo shift, repeat stanza]
> Sometimes I fear that this will go on my life through
> Each day I spend in an echoed vision of you
> And then again I'll turn down love
> Remembering your smile
> My every day is spent
> Thinking of you all the while
> The times I've let myself down
> My head's spinning round
> My eyes see only you
> The chances I've lost
> Opportunities tossed
> Away and into the blue.

These songs represent a marked departure from the narrative style that rendered "My Generation," "A Quick One," and "So Sad About Us." While Townshend's tendency for witty characterizations remains, his choice in subject matter is shifting from tight adolescent/romantic stories toward impressionistic spiritual statements. In both cases he refuses to "hit" his audience "over the head" with prescriptive commentary and either exploits the humorous qualities of daily events—as in the radio commercials and the adolescent stories—or urges spiritual and emotional reflection. These songs also introduce a trend in which Townshend pursues spiritual worth through a narrative style that raises the value of the spiritual quest without imposing any particular answer. Here again we note a manifestation of Townshend's artistic philosophy in that he encourages his audience to face their problems and address their situations on their own terms. The songs' narrative strength exists in their plots' ambiguity which, in turn, facilitates individual interpretation.

The album's final cut, "Rael," also foreshadows *Tommy* and represents the twenty-five-act "opera" Townshend mentioned in February, as he explains:

"Rael" was politically based thematically, perhaps that's why it flopped even before it began.... The story was about the year 1999 (not as cliched as 2000 you see) and the emergence of the Red Chinese (The Redchins) as world leaders. The only spiritual note was that the Redchins were regarded as being fairly evil because they were crushing the old established religions as they conquered.... Basically the story was running into about twenty scenes when Kit Lambert reminded me that while I was pretending to be Wagner, the Who needed a single.... No-one will ever know what it means, it has been squeezed up too tightly to make sense. Musically it is interesting because it contains a theme which I later used in *Tommy* for "Sparks" and the "Underture." That music was written in 1966. (Barnes & Townshend, 1977, pp. 11, 18)

Several important points emerge from Townshend's remarks. First, we note that "Rael" is "squeezed up" so "tightly" that a thematic interpretation becomes problematic; the lyrics are disjointed, but the instrumentals and transitions demonstrate Townshend's longing for expansive formats. "Rael" contains at least six tempo shifts, which indeed appear to be "squeezed" together. Townshend writes:

> The Redchins in their millions
> Will overspill their boarders
> And chaos then will rain in my Rael
> Rael the home of my religion
> To me the center of the Earth
> [repeat first three lines]
> My heritage is threatened
> My roots are torn and cornered
> And so to do my best I'll homeward sail
> Now captain listen to my instructions
> Return to this spot on Christmas Day
> Look toward the shore for my signal
> And then you'll know in Rael I'll stay.

The "story" continues with more "instructions." Should the character signal with a "yellow flag" (which indicates his "courage has ended"), the "captain" is to "send your boat ashore"; if a "red flag" flies, the character has decided to stay and his "yacht" belongs to the "captain." There is no evident ending. How interesting that Townshend's first "mini-opera" is stretched out to meet time requirements and his second "mini-opera" reflects just the opposite trait. In both cases, the instrumental bridges that serve as narrative transitions are impressive and indicate Townshend's willingness to sacrifice lyrical directness for musical coherence. My second point involves the accuracy of Townshend's claim that his writings follow trains of thought over extended periods of time.

Instrumental elements of *Tommy* appear in two *Sell Out* songs, and the album's spiritual themes provide the foundation for the *Tommy* plot. Once more, such characteristics offer serious evidence of the writer's narrative impulse and its power over his pen. Years later Townshend claims that he has a script and a score for "Rael" that, in his opinion, make "more sense than *Tommy*" (Townshend, 1997).

The most significant commercial happening on the *Sell Out* album is the single "I Can See For Miles." Townshend was certain that this track would be The Who's biggest single ever, and when the song did not chart as well as he predicted he was devastated. The song features powerful Who instrumentals as Townshend weaves what was initially a tale of deception:

> I know you've deceived me, now here's a surprise
> I know that you have 'cos there's magic in my eyes
> I can see for miles and miles and miles and miles and miles
> Oh yeah
> If you think that I don't know about the little tricks you play
> And never see you when delib'rately you put things in my way
> Well here's a poke at you, you're gonna choke on it too
> You're gonna lose that smile, because all the while
> I could see for miles and miles.

Whereas Townshend (1971e) jokes, "The words, which aging senators have called 'Drug Oriented,' are about a jealous man with exceptionally good eyesight. Honest." (p. 38), he vacillates between a couple of possible interpretations (recall Chapter One). In any event, the song's significance lies in the turning point it represents for the aspiring songwriter. Townshend told the *Los Angeles Times*: "When 'I Can See For Miles' didn't get in the charts I was extremely irate. Also, we needed bread and water so I started writing other stuff. That's when my values as a rock 'n' roller dropped. I discovered you could reach a vast amount of people by playing a slightly wider range of music" (Mills, 1977, p. 70). Townshend's disappointment may have moved him toward "other stuff," but that material was surely an extension of themes initiated in *The Who Sell Out*.

Critiques of *Sell Out* range in accordance with the source's format. *Time* concludes the "album is The Who's imaginative antidote to the greatest danger they see in rock today: its solemnity" ("The what and why," 1968, p. 86). *Rolling Stone* maintains the "album is fantastic, it has an exquisite sense of humor (songs of the humbly homespun) and consummate musicianship" and continues with comments about the various cuts (*The Who Sell Out*, 1968, p. 20). And the *New Yorker* places the album in a broader context with an emphasis on its songwriting style: "'The Who Sell Out' emphasized the tender aspect of Pop—its humanity, rather that its aggressive vulgarity. The characters in the songs were all more or less unworldly—misfits in some way—but nonetheless the kind of people who eat Heinz baked beans and sign up for instruction from Charles Atlas.... Townshend's message seemed to be that people's foibles made

them worthy of love" (Willis, 1969, p. 63). Willis's observations about Townshend's propensity to write songs that help people deal with their looks, weight,
or whatever and the lighter (she claims "tender") aspects of his songs are right
on the mark. Once again, as we proceed through this study, we witness more of
this style of criticism (for good or ill) and less of the publicity-oriented commentaries observed to this point.

The *Sell Out* period was one of the more tranquil phases in Who history.
The band achieved a state of internal harmony that it had never before experienced as individual members accepted their respective roles.   Townshend
explained this change to Nick Jones (1967a): "We've learnt how to get on with
each other, we've forgotten immature feelings—like 'who's getting all the
limelight' and silly things like that.... If Keith cuts his hand now, I worry and so
does Roger and so does John" (p. 9). This newfound internal harmony proved
to be one of the most valuable features of the *Sell Out* and *Tommy* sessions. The
Who now had genuine confidence in Townshend's creative energies, and that
confidence would help the songwriter's work to flourish.

The post-*Sell Out* period was not without its legal problems, or at least the
results of previous legal controversy. U.S. Decca's release of *Magic Bus: The
Who On Tour* coincided with Track's U.K. release *Direct Hits* and, once more,
demonstrated the music industry's preference for the commercial over the artistic. Greil Marcus's (1968) review articulates the extent of Decca's arrogance—
"This is not so much a review as a complaint" (p. 21)—and continues with a
strong attack on Decca for the "inattention they have lavished on the Who, such
as their forgetting to send review copies of some of the group's singles to Billboard and Cashbox." Marcus points out the "dozen fantastic cuts by the Who
that have never been released on American LPs" would make a strong album,
but instead Decca offers a "random collection of tracks." Marcus concludes by
urging his audience to write "angry letters" to Decca in protest of this ill-
advised, deceptive piece of commercialism.

Magic Bus is everything Marcus says it is. The album's eleven tracks contain one cover (Altfeld/Christian/Torrence's "Bucket T."), three previously
released Townshend compositions ("Run Run Run," "I Can't Reach You," and
"Our Love Was, Is"), three Entwistle songs ("Dr. Jekyll & Mr. Hyde," "Someone's Coming," and "Doctor, Doctor"), and four "new" Townshend songs
("Disguises," "Call Me Lightning," "Magic Bus," and "Pictures of Lily"). The
album is uneven and omits, as Marcus complains, many Who singles from this
period. A thematic interpretation of *Magic Bus* is, well, useless. "Disguises"
and "Call Me Lightning" return to portrayals of boy-girl relations. In the former, the "girl" wears "wigs" and "shoes" too big for her feet as "disguises"—a
clear reference to the identity/deception theme; in the latter, the chase is on as
the hip boy with his "XKE" sets his sights on that "little girl who's dancing so
lightly." Townshend's (1971e) reflections on the "Magic Bus" track capture the
album's essence:

The words...are garbage, again loaded with heavy drug inference. For example, "thruppence and sixpence every way, trying to get to my baby." Obviously a hint at the ever rising prices of LSD. When I wrote "Magic Bus" LSD wasn't even invented as far as I knew. Drug songs and veiled references to drugs were not part of the Who image.... We very soon got bored with drugs. No publicity value. Buses, however! [the album cover features The Who hanging on a multi-colored, flower-printed bus—an interesting sight for a band that purported to reject "flower power"].... Also a swindle as far as insinuating that the record was live. Bastards. They have lived to regret it, but not to delete it. (p. 38)

Such was the nature of the music industry during The Who's singles period (note Townshend's reference to The Who's *image* and its maintenance). Marcus's (1968) point about the number of Who singles that failed to reach American audiences is well taken. Evidence exists in the number of songs available for compilation albums, such as 1971's *Meaty Beaty Big and Bouncy*, 1974's *Odds & Sods*, 1985's *Who's Missing*, 1987's *Two's Missing*, Townshend's demo tape album releases, and other outlets (e.g., *Hooligans*, *The Kids Are Alright* movie soundtrack). It is surely impossible to discuss all of those songs, but three tracks from the *Odds & Sods* album capture specific facets of Townshend's work during the singles period and, as a result, merit brief mention here.

"Little Billy," "Glow Girl," and "Faith in Something Bigger" make unique contributions to the oeuvre. "Little Billy"—written for the American Cancer Society—demonstrates Townshend's penchant for adolescent based narrative vignettes:

Little Billy was the fattest kid in his class
Always the last in line
All the other little kids would laugh at him
Said he'd die before his time
Ha ha ha ha ha ha ha ha
But little Billy didn't mind
Most of the kids smoked cigarettes
To prove that they were cool
The teacher didn't know about the children's games
And Billy always followed the rules
Ha ha ha ha ha ha ha ha
And little Billy didn't mind
Billy was big on the outside
And there's an even bigger man inside
Ten million cigarettes burn every day
And Billy's still doing fine
Now Billy and his classmates are middle aged
With children of their own
Old smoking games are reality now
And cancer's seed is sown
Ha ha ha ha ha ha ha ha
Little Billy's doing fine
Most of them smoked maybe forty a day

A habit Billy doesn't share
One by one they're passing away
Leaving orphans to Billy's care
Ha ha ha ha ha ha ha ha....
Little Billy's doing fine.

Here again, notice Townshend's ability to weave insightful adolescent tales through a "commercial" narrative style. He effectively communicates the kids' mean-spirited attitude toward Billy, Billy's pleasant response in spite of his classmates' cruelty (shades of "Happy Jack"), and the moral of the story. That resolution is more complex than a mere antismoking statement in that Townshend cleverly suggests that "today's goat" may easily emerge as "tomorrow's hero." That irony does not overcome the song's surface reading (the antismoking message) which, once more, indicates the writer's capacity to negotiate a product.

Our second tune, "Glow Girl," was written during the Herman's Hermits tour when Townshend was on board an airplane that he was certain would crash. He told Charlesworth (1995), "I thought that if I was a chick and I was in a plane that was diving for the ground and I had my boyfriend next to me and we were on our honeymoon or we were about to get married, I know what I'd think of. I'd think about him and I'd think about what I am going to be missing" (p. 61). The woman goes through her purse (finding "separates," shoes, makeup, and "sentimental photographs") and the man comforts her about their life in heaven. Townshend writes:

The wing of the airplane
Has just caught on fire
I say without reservation
We ain't gettin' no higher
All you wanted from me
All I had to give
Nothing matters, you'll see
When in paradise you live.
The plane is diving faster
We're getting near the ground
Nobody is screaming
No one makes a sound.

The plane crashes (rising guitar feedback signals the explosion), a soft tune emerges from the flames ("It's a girl, Mrs. Walker, it's a girl"—lines that appear again in *Tommy*, with a gender shift), and the couple is instantly reincarnated as this little girl (of which Townshend added, "that was supposed to be the end of the thing" [Charlesworth, p. 61]). The third song, "Faith in Something Bigger," is a spiritual song that stresses life's transitions:

It may be warm, but the snow is going to fall
Enough to cover us all

> We've gotta be strong, man, and follow the path again
> We've got to have faith in something bigger, faith in something bigger
> Faith in something big inside ourselves.
> It might be cold, but the heat of our love will melt
> The snow we never felt
> We're young and hardy again
> We can bow to weaker men.

Next the song emphasizes the need for spiritual perseverance ("The more we learn, the less we believe to be true/The more we grew, the more remains to be moved") and concludes that "we've gotta be strong, man, and follow the path again" and, no matter what, we must maintain "faith in something bigger."

These three simple songs represent the wave of Townshend's songwriting future. Townshend's ability to articulate life's ironies (as in "Little Billy"), his belief in a musical essence (the "tune" that emerges from the crash in "Glow Girl"), and his commitment to human spirituality would guide his pen through the *Tommy*, *LifeHouse*, and *Quadrophenia* projects. These themes may mix and match within these works, but they consistently reappear as central organizing features over the next five years.

This phase of Townshend's oeuvre reflects an aggressively marketed product in search of a consuming public. First, the band achieved distinction via its performance style as The Who chose to "overdo" its act in order to attract attention. The band's management aggressively pursued every possible avenue for publicity and so reinforced the group's rowdy image. And The Who followed industry prescriptions and produced singles that served a variety of persuasive functions. Just like the aspiring jongleur from days gone by, The Who challenged the status quo as an avenue for discovery, all the while operating within the industry's established framework. In fact, The Who always seemed to respond to a given situation's needs. Townshend wrote "I Can't Explain" to secure a producer, Lambert-Stamp-Townshend modified "My Generation" to appeal to the Mods, Townshend penned "A Quick One While He's Away" to satisfy industry album length requirements—and as a result embellished a new format for his narrative impulse—and the "radio program" concept album both competed with the contemporary works of other major acts and reinforced The Who's commitment to pop art. Townshend may be writing for "the market," yet his lyrical inclinations slowly move toward more extensive songwriting formats, more expressive themes (in his case, spiritual messages), and more detailed characterizations. All of these culminate in the next phase of his career, the "opera period."

3

The Opera Period

From Chapter Two's treatment of The Who's ascension to an internationally recognized band we move to the second phase of the group's history. For insight into this portion of Townshend's work we once again visit music history. Just as Chapter Two's aspiring jongleur relied on ambition and creativity to secure independence and security, the accomplished troubadour extended those traits as he encountered the *expectations* that accompanied that role. The English troubadour, for example, faced demanding social standards in that he was expected to entertain friends in an extravagant manner and to "give numerous *fetes* of originality" (Rowbotham, 1895, p. 96). This occasionally led to ruin as troubadours attempted to outdo one another "for the sake of useless display and extravagant ostentation." (Rowbotham observes that men who lost their fortunes in attempts to preserve their status either joined the Crusades and died in combat or became jongleurs.) Joining these social prospects were performance expectations that required the troubadour to "'go through the world'…and give the aristocratic public at large a specimen of his powers, and a means of judging his proficiency" (p. 98). Consequently, the troubadour traveled "the world" with his jongleurs each spring to share the artistic innovations of the winter months. His social standing depended on these duties, and failure most certainly meant ruin. Predictably, troubadours unable to advance their art quickly turned to social extravagance as a diversion; hence, artistic tensions arise once more. The pressure to prolong creativity in musical form and content joined the demands of celebrity to produce serious expectations for the troubadours. Whether the troubadour achieved his status through his aristocratic birth and talent or through sheer talent alone, once that station was obtained far-reaching demands followed. We have, therefore, yet another dimension of the minstrel's dilemma: how established artists meet their role expectations and simultaneously pursue artistic innovation (again, the "entertainer versus artist" conflict).

Here I pursue this scenario as it appears in Pete Townshend's career with The Who. The Who achieved popularity—and some measure of financial success—in its "singles period." Still, the group's stage act and pop art façade were expensive ploys, and Townshend sought some vehicle to place the band over the top. His answer was the rock opera. While this innovation propelled The Who to new levels of financial success, it also introduced the various pressures the successful troubadours endured. How the band, and its songwriter, handled the expectations that accompanied prosperity is the subject of the following pages.

THE OPERA PERIOD

The aggressive management of The Who's singles period transformed the band into one of the leading acts of the highly touted "British Invasion." The price of discovery was high. Auto-destruction, publicity antics, and bad business deals left the band in desperate financial straits. The Who could tour and tour and, eventually, make ends meet (perhaps). Yet Pete Townshend would never be satisfied with that approach. Townshend was intuitively committed to his craft, and that commitment would be the driving force in The Who's response to the artistic/commercial turning point before the band.

A *Time* article relates the commercial crossroads The Who faced after its singles period. With a photo caption proclaiming, "The Who breaking them up on U.S. tour. Better known for the put-on than output" (the photo features a glimpse of auto-destruction in progress—"The what and why," 1968, p. 86), *Time* describes the band's act and announces: "Last week in London, the boys prepared to follow up *The Who Sell Out* with what they hope will be an equally inventive recording. They need to. It is the only way they will convince serious listeners that they can break through more than just their instruments." Indeed, The Who had to move beyond smashing its gear, singing adolescent ditties, and wrecking hotel rooms. In response, the band turned to its creative team— Townshend and Lambert—to devise a way to extend The Who's image (*always* image) without forsaking its past. The results changed *everything*.

TOMMY

Tommy is certainly the most enduring project of The Who's career. As a result, Townshend's first completed opera is examined in terms of its artistic plan, its commercial aspirations, its production, Kit Lambert's role, the opera's contents, the critics' responses, its impact on the band, and its impact on Townshend. In *The Who's Tommy: The Musical* (Townshend, 1993b) Ira Robbins relates the project's evolutionary qualities. Robbins cites the lines from "Glow Girl" ("It's a girl, Mrs. Walker"), the lyrics from "I Can't Reach You" ("see, feel or hear from ya"), and the instrumental bridge in "Rael" as evidence of *Tommy*'s slow incubation. Townshend maintains that the story that inspired *Tommy* was a product of his spontaneous writing, but as Robbins indicates, several songs within the piece were either long in the making, revisions of previously existing materials, or responses to specific requests. *Tommy* is not the single stroke of one writer's pen; it is an at times raw mixture of a variety of independent ideas.

The complexity of the opera's plot reveals the extent to which the *Tommy* project departs from the narrative vignettes of the singles period. That plot varies significantly between productions—the movie differs from the album, and the Broadway production differs from the previous two. The album omits much background material, a point Ken Russell notes in his description of the original story: "There were huge gaps in the story.... You never knew exactly who his father was, why the father was killed or why the boy went blind, deaf and dumb. It's almost as though [Townshend's] album started almost halfway through the story and the first half was in his mind but had never been written" (*The Who's Tommy*, 1993). The album version opens in World War I and the announcement that Captain Walker is missing in action. Mrs. Walker then gives birth to his son, Tommy. Afterward, Mrs. Walker becomes involved with another man (identified only as "lover"). In 1921, Captain Walker miraculously returns to find his wife with the "lover" and kills him as Tommy watches in a mirror. The parents panic, rage at Tommy, and the boy enters an autistic state, constantly staring into the mirror. Tommy endures a series of dysfunctional relationships with an uncle (Ernie) who rapes him and a cousin (Kevin) who physically abuses him. All the while his parents try every possible cure. Suddenly, the boy displays a propensity for pinball; he becomes a pinball champion and a cult figure. After a failed visit to a medical "specialist" Captain Walker believes holds the answer to Tommy's autism, Mrs. Walker smashes Tommy's mirror in anger. The boy's senses return, he forms a holiday camp for his followers, and his "disciples" reject him. The album ending is unclear, as Tommy's disciples denounce him and he is left, presumably, alone.

Through *Tommy* Townshend revises and extends the narrative tendencies evidenced thus far. His use of oddball characters (Uncle Ernie, the Acid Queen) and spiritual themes extend signatures from the singles period, whereas the movement toward nebulous narratives that *stress* characterization over story development is an emerging trend. Sanders and Dalton (1969) cite Townshend's explanation of the story's spiritual foundation:

There had to be a loophole so I could show this. The boy has closed himself up completely as a result of the murder and his parents' pressures, and the only thing he can see is his reflection in the mirror. This reflection—his illusory self—turns out to be his eventual salvation. In general terms, man is regarded as living in an unreal world of illusory values that he's imposed on himself. He's feeling his way by evolution back to God-realisation and the illusion is broken away, bit by bit. You need the illusions until you reach very pure saintly states. When you lose all contact with your illusory state, you become totally dead—but totally aware. You've died for the last time. You don't incarnate again, you don't do anything again—you just *blend*.... Tommy's real self represents the aim—God—and the illusory self is the teacher; life, the way, the path and all this. The coming together of these are what make him aware. They make him see and hear and speak so he becomes a saint who everybody flocks to.... He gets everything in a very pure, [un]filtered, unadulterated, unfucked-up manner. Like when his uncle rapes him—he is incredibly elated, not disgusted, at being homosexually raped. He takes it as a move of total affection, not feeling the reasons why. Lust is a lower form of love, like atomic attraction is a lower form of love. He gets an incredible spiritual push from it where most people would get a spiritual retardment, constantly thinking about this terrible thing that's happened to him. In Tommy's mind everything is incredible, meaningless beauty. (p. 16)

From this detailed description we note Townshend's reliance on the "Glow Girl" reincarnation story and his growing interest in life's essence—seen here in his reduction of human emotions to a pure physical condition, "atomic attraction." Through Tommy and his predicament, Townshend initiates a search for life's "pure state" and attempts to separate that quality from the artificial values imposed by society and its institutions (religions, media, governments). This search—Townshend's "Amazing Journey"—provides *Tommy*'s narrative foundation.

Townshend acknowledged that point in a 1993 interview: "I think 'Amazing Journey' was the song and is the song that in a sense tells the story of Tommy in a kind of synopsis.... And that was the first song that I wrote, the very first" (*In the Studio*, 1993; also see *The Who's Tommy*, 1993). Actually, "Amazing Journey" first appeared as a poem which Townshend presents in *The Story of Tommy* (Barnes & Townshend, 1977). The 237-line work, Townshend claims, is "all stream of consciousness stuff" (p. 30) and expresses "a story that I could never have dreamed of myself let alone put to music." He recalls: "I just lived with the story, invented a name for my hero, Tommy, and started to write songs. I got Tommy's name from mid-air, but it suited. The middle letters were OM which was aptly mystical, and it was an English name associated with the war and heroism. It was also fairly close to To-Me, again you can see the obvious spiritual bent." Once he recognized the difficulty of communicating "our ignorance of reality," Townshend turned to the "deaf, dumb and blind" characterization. Eventually, he realized an appealing "parallel" to that notion in an autistic child and the therapeutic goal of bringing autistic children "out of their 'dream' through a combination of love and music."

The "Amazing Journey" poem represents more than the starting point for the *Tommy* project. That work may very well be the founding statement for *The Seeker* composite text as the singles period's "urge" now matures and unfolds. Throughout this study you will see ideas from this original work reappear in a variety of forms. The poem opens with these lines:

I awoke on Tuesday morning
My illness much improved
In fact I felt fantastic,
My spirits ache removed.
And so I tried to move again,
At first it was a strain,
And so I fell back on my bed,

My head and heart in pain.
At twelve my mum brought dinner,
At four my mum brought tea,
At eight my mum brought supper
And ten o'clock brought sleep
And sleep brought moods and yearning
To travel just once more,
That one amazing journey
I slept through once before.
Sickness will surely take the mind
Where minds can't usually go
Come on the amazing journey
And learn all you should know.

Those lines initiate a spiritual journey of pleasure and pain as the narrator, a seeker, rotates between the beauty of a journey with his "Master" and the harsh realities of daily life. Townshend next describes the Master:

A vague haze of delirium creeps up on me.
Then at once a tall stranger I suddenly see
He's dressed in a silver sparked glittering gown
And his golden beard flows nearly down to the ground
His eyes are the eyes that transmit all they know
And sparkle warm crystalline glances to show
That he is your leader and he is your guide,
On the amazing journey together you'll ride.

The narrator realizes, "The dream that I'm dreaming is a vision it seems/For now reality itself appears in dreams/I know that here's my Master, my guide and saviour." The work continues with more descriptions of the Master before the journey begins—"The illness is gone and my Master's ahead, calling me on./We walk through the city, the streets I know well." Suddenly, they enter a new "place":

The grass seems to relish our toes and our heels,
And the flowers the wind and the pollen the bees
Fishes lay writhing in shrinking puddles of silver.
The tall trees, golden leafed, joined hands overhead
Making a shadowed avenue. No shafts of sunlight
But lines of nodding seekers, clothed in the robes
Of their order. And pointing the way to us.
They pointed within and my Master decided
That at least they were faced the right way

After seeing a "light far off in the distance" the seeker and Master approach their journey's end, when a "shock wave" separates them. The seeker suddenly exits the journey/dream and is thrust into a state of loneliness and ignorance (the Masterless reality). He feels trapped in the "womb-like darkness" of the material world, where he places "labels on each friend, article and emotion/That appears" (the "unreal world of illusory values that he's imposed on himself"). That pain is relieved as the journey resumes; our seeker standing "A little taller at his [the Master's] side" as a result of the "first lesson"—"I had learnt that whatever situation my Master prescribed/I should accept without question. Not immediately reverting/To the illusory plan and skating on the ice of life's pleasure."

The second part of the journey is more beautiful than the first as he comes to more fully understand his Master's patient power ("By his very existence that I am forgiven"). Yet, once more, he suddenly finds himself off the path:

I am lost. An eternity must have passed since I felt enlightenment.
Eons must have passed since I made any progress towards my Lord.
I am perpetually praying to him for guidance, but he never answers.
I am beginning to believe that he has carried on without me.
One life is all I know. The present life.
And yet because of my ignorance of the infinite
I cannot enjoy it. I am sad, poor, wrapped in indignity
The narrator proclaims his "pathetic cry for reward falls on hardened ears"
    until his Master's return:
And again, like a flash I see the vision of my Master.
Ever patient. Totally forgiving. All knowing, waiting
At the exact spot I left him. I quickly run towards him
Bringing my wife and family, bringing my business partners
And odd acquaintances who had shown interest in my Amazing Journey.
I know the ground so well, and we hurry along, occasionally
Waiting while some of our party absorb an amazing sight.
There is no real rush, we are again aware of eternity.

This time the dreamer is "even taller" than before, enriched by his experience with pain and loneliness. He leaves his family and friends behind in order to pursue further knowledge: "To teach them all more I had to learn more myself/And so with the Master I set off once more." The renewed journey is more dangerous than previously, as the seeker struggles to maintain his "balance" while he marvels at his Master's strength and agility. Here the poem reaches its turning point and the moment of realization:

Then one morning as the sun's mellow warmth awoke me
I realized my position. Here was the tallest mountain in
The whole of the universe, and yet when I climbed it
What did I find? Only myself. If I had climbed a mountain
Any higher I would still only find myself. Maybe if I
Searched every jungle in the cosmos I would find the throne of the LORD.
Perhaps if I ransacked the Ocean floors on every planet
In every galaxy, in every universe in the infinite cosmos
I would find him. The Master gravely shook his head and I
Knew that despite his infinite wisdom, infinite power, infinite awareness

That he would not, could not tell me where to look.
Or even what to look for. I had to find the answer myself.

Without warning, the seeker finds himself in "the dark" once more, dominated by confusion, and asking anyone for answers. He laments, "When the wind blows, I am chilled, even though I am the wind/When the midday sun shines, I sweat, even though I am the sun." Everywhere he searches for answers and suffers in his futility. At this point the poem elaborates on life's ebb and flow ("Mothers gave birth to children and Undertakers collected the dead") and the seeker's frustration over his inability to discover "the answer." A vicious circle engulfs Townshend's character as he tries to find those who can "give, take, and love" without having to "justify" giving, taking and loving: "As one man attained these merits./Another man was conceived without them, as one child was born divine,/Another was born mortal./As one man found within himself the truth, another began to look." Eventually, the seeker returns to the dream and the Master:

I was delighted and warmly greeted him and caressed him as though
We had not seen each other for years, but the Master
Acted as though I had never been away. As though I hadn't been
Through countless reincarnations since I first slept.
I knew yet another truth.

The seeker's elation over rejoining his Master inspires him to hope "for the day when my Master and I could be as one"; however, that "very longing threw me back [down the spiritual path], but this time not too far." Our characters review all of the lessons from the "Amazing Journey" as a preface to the final vision. There the Master opens the door to all of the cosmos:

When I gazed in awe at all I already knew the Master
Showed me the creatures from all over the cosmos.
Each one more confounding than the next, but all with the same aim.
Each one amazed me and many were completely beyond
Anything I had ever imagined. Many existed on planes and spheres
Beyond my imagination. Many lived in terms of existence that
Defied explanation, many had to be viewed through the body of
One of their kind in order to utilise their radically different senses.
And see them at all.

With that line, the poem stops (apparently). The work does not end with the seeker achieving his ambition (*the* answer) but with an understanding that all "the creatures" are searching as well ("all with the same aim"). The lesson has been learned: the goal is not a state of exclusivity with the Master but an intense identification with all of the "creatures" in the "cosmos" and, from there, an acceptance of the *search* for *individual* spiritual bliss. Remember, whenever the seeker longed for the privileged state with the Master, he was sent back to a previous point in order to correct his error and learn his "lesson." An appreciation of "the search" was the prize, not a superior spiritual status. This elaborate, stream of consciousness poem—foreshadowed in *Sell Out*'s "I Can't Reach Yóu"—firmly establishes the connection between George Adamski's science fiction and Baba's teachings featured in Chapter One, and it provides the narrative foundation for the songwriter's most enduring project.

Townshend's spiritual revelations would now have to negotiate with The Who's commercial agenda—which brings us to the second area of activity and *Tommy*'s "commercial plan." Evidently, prior to *Tommy* Townshend was lost, as he explained to Roy Carr (1975b): "I really got lost after 'Happy Jack' and then when 'I Can See For Miles' bombed-out in Britain I thought 'what the hell am I gonna do now?' The pressures were really on me and I had to come up with something very quick and that's how *Tommy* emerged from a few rough ideas I'd been messing about with" (pp. 53-54). Townshend's frustrations over "I Can See For Miles" were intense, as evidenced in these recollections about *Tommy*'s commercial motivations:

I went to Kit Lambert and I said I'm never, ever, ever, going to be able to top this song ["I Can See For Miles"].... What am I gonna do, what are we gonna do? And I don't know who's idea it was, I don't know whether it was Kit's—I've forgotten now—or mine or whether it came out in conversation or whatever, but we decided to do an opera...it felt not only a dangerous thing to do, but did actually feel like...an exception to the rule and I actually felt like I was stepping outside my job. I was abandoning my rock and roll legion...I was leaving my boys behind and writing this thing which was actually very much trying to address what had happened around me in the late 60s; which was a drug revolution, a psychedelic drug revolution. Which was producing something that people called...peace and love. You know, I'm so cynical about that stuff.... I had some nice times, but...so to some extent it was a desperate, desperate act and to some extent a cynical act...a confused act...I didn't really know what I was doing and I didn't really know it was gonna work. (*In the Studio*, 1993)

Townshend's commercial desperation led him to accept the risk, the "danger," of being labeled "pretentious": "It really was a last gasp.... And I just felt like my God I've got to be honest now. What am I? I'm a writer. I'm an ideas man. I'm a simple soul. Address that. Do it. If people think it's shit, fine, at least it's you. So *Tommy* was a very very kind of honest, direct piece of work. It...came out of an adversity which was partly financial, but also partly emotional."

In response, Townshend married his "Amazing Journey" spiritual vision to a musical device he had by now mastered, the single. He felt constrained by the three-minute single and "wanted to find a way to 'stretch' it a bit more, without making it pretentious or pompous and without making it sound too much like classical music" (Marsh, 1983, p. 310). He assembled a series of singles that could stand on their own, yet when heard consecutively told a story. His fear of pretension faded, and with Lambert's help he embraced the single as his storytelling tool. Townshend later reported that this was his artistic goal: "When I sat down to write *Tommy*...my prime objective was to...say listen, the three minute rock song is so effective that if you string a bunch of them together you can deal with a much bigger idea, a spiritual idea, perhaps the idea that we are all living in a dream" (*Rolling Stone's 1993*, 1993).

While the "Amazing Journey" poem provides a narrative baseline for the spiritual aspects of Townshend's oeuvre, the *Tommy* project itself was a raw, impulsive manifestation of that original concept. The 1968 interview with *Rolling Stone's* Jann Wenner actually provided the "blueprint" for *Tommy*, as Townshend explains: "When I actually really put the whole thing together...was in a conversation—a long, long, long conversation—after a Fillmore show in San Francisco with Jann Wenner...he printed the whole article, the whole conversation, it was a two or three hour conversation. He printed it absolutely verbatim.... And that became my blueprint.... The book for *Tommy* is that *Rolling Stone* article" (*In the Studio*, 1993). Elsewhere he describes that conversation as his first articulation of his "vision" (Barnes & Townshend, 1977, p. 6); however, that "vision" was substantially different from either the "Amazing Journey" poem or *Tommy*. The *Rolling Stone* interview features a Tommy who is *born* "deaf, dumb and blind," and it emphasizes the parents' frustrations over their dilemma. That version does use the "Uncle Ernie" rape scene and stresses the "musical vibrations" that constitute Tommy's autistic world, but many "Amazing Journey" details are omitted, as are references to "Cousin Kevin," pinball, cult figures, and holiday camps. Whereas Townshend may view the Wenner conversation as a "blueprint," its actual significance may be elsewhere. He told Bruce Pollock (1975): "What I do is force myself to do [projects] by announcing things up front...I said so much [about *Tommy*] that it just *had* to be finished—I had to get it done" (p. 84).

All of which takes us to the "production process" and three more factors Townshend had to consider: The Who's image, the band's response, and the audience. Townshend was fully aware of The Who's image as a performing act, and *Tommy* was designed to accommodate that image:

I think that in a sense everything that I did always had—if it was written for The Who—it was obviously gonna be a stage piece, we were a performing band. We weren't a studio band like the Beatles had become and so that was the distinction I would make to myself is that we can't do a *Sgt. Pepper* type thing, we can't do a *Pet Sounds* type thing, we can't do a studio masterpiece, we have to do something that we can play. That's why *Tommy* is so simple, that's why its so unorchestrated, so...unscrewed around with in the studio.... We kept it really simple because we wanted to play it. So in a sense—although it was recorded—it was recorded and composed for the stage. It had to work live. (*In the Studio*, 1993)

In another Broadway *Tommy* interview, Townshend notes he "was aiming at... a stage work" and how the piece "grew on stage" (WFBQ, 1993). Part of that growth was attributable to the band's cooperative attitude. Townshend did not work in isolation on *Tommy*; in fact, it was a group project unlike any other in

Who history. He elaborated on Daltrey, Entwistle, and Moon's contributions to Sanders and Dalton (1969):

It was approached in exactly the way anti-intellectual rock people would hate. We went into it in depth before we worked out the plot; we worked out the sociological implications, the religious implications, the rock implications. We made sure every bit was...solid. When we'd done that we went into the studio, got smashed out of our brains and made it. Then we listened, pruned and edited very carefully, then got smashed and did it all again.... I mean, what other three musicians would have put up with all my bullshit in order to get this album out? (p. 18)

Roger Daltrey supports that view: "We used to talk for hours, literally. We probably did as much talking as we did recording" (Barnes, 1982, p. 50). Uncharacteristically, Townshend brought unfinished demos to the studio in order to solicit the band's input. Twenty-four years later, he recalls "a general feeling of being amazed at how supportive everybody in the band was" because of the "silly" qualities of the songs preceding *Tommy* (*In the Studio*, 1993). After writing "songs about dog racing or whatever" Townshend anticipated skepticism. He was wrong.

Throughout *Tommy*'s planning sessions The Who focused on its audience. Townshend wanted *Tommy* to appeal to as broad an audience as possible: "The thing was we wanted it to work on lots of levels...we just want to turn on the whole gang" (Cott, 1970, p. 34). One part of that "gang" involved the music press. Townshend may have been driven by a spiritual impulse to tell the "Amazing Journey" tale, but his willingness to compromise that story to suit his audience is most evident in the inclusion of *Tommy*'s first single, "Pinball Wizard." He explains:

["Pinball Wizard"] was a fairly spontaneous piece which I think is why it's so good.... We delivered the album for review, preview, to a friend of ours, called Nick Cohn, who was a writer for the *Manchester Guardian*. He was very young...he was the youngest pop writer in England at the time, working for a conventional newspaper. And he hadn't really liked *Tommy* and I was very disappointed, I expected him to like it and he said it's OK. We went out and we were shooting pinball in some arcade somewhere...and I said to him "If Tommy was a pinball player, would you...be more receptive to the idea?" And he turned to me and said "yeah." So I went home and I wrote the song. And I [rewrote] the piece with all of the references to Tommy rather than just being a spiritual leader, being a pinball player. So the pinball became a metaphor for the life of a rock star or even the life of a guru. And Nick said it's great, it works. It's not just great because you've done this for me and I will give it a good review, what it's actually done is it's added some color and some real pop to this otherwise really quite boring idea about...the spiritual life. (*In the Studio*, 1993)

Townshend shifted the entire plot in order to satisfy a friend, and correspondingly, to obtain a positive review. Since he was prepared to move from "the sublime to the ridiculous" (Cott, 1970, p. 34), that move is understandable. The spiritual metaphor remained intact; the author merely changed his expression to accommodate the project's commercial potential. This willingness to compromise would eventually aggravate Townshend, a point he expressed to David Fricke (1987b):

> I suppose the mistake I made in *Tommy* was instead of having the guts to take what Meher Baba said—which was "Don't worry, be happy, leave the results to God"—and repeating that to people, I decided the people weren't capable of hearing that directly. They've got to have it served in this entertainment package. And I gave them *Tommy* instead, in which some of Meher Baba's wonderfully explicit truths were presented to them half-baked in lyric form and diluted as a result. (p. 180)

These commercial compromises led Townshend to claim several years after the album's release that "the definitive *Tommy* album is still in my head" (Carr, 1975b, p. 53).

Another important aspect of the *Tommy* project involves our fourth area of inquiry, Kit Lambert's role. *Tommy* represents the high point of Lambert's work with The Who, and sources suggest that he would forever feel short-changed regarding the credit he received for his contributions (Barnes, 1982; Barnes & Townshend, 1977; Marsh, 1983). Whether or not that is the case, only Townshend played a larger role in *Tommy*'s development in that Lambert functioned as both a co-author and a producer. Lambert understood Townshend's intellect, the tensions within the band, how the band operated in the studio, and The Who's image to a point where he—and he alone—was capable of orchestrating the *Tommy* sessions. Lambert's role as co-author is most evident in his commitment to the project's opera format. Barnes and Townshend (1977) report that Lambert tried to remain detached from the album's spiritual themes in order to be objective about its presentation, preferring that the finished product represent a "Rock Opera" more than a "God Opera" (p. 30). Thus, it was Lambert who insisted the project have a formal overture to tie everything together. Although various band members contributed to *Tommy*'s development in individual ways—Entwistle writing "Fiddle About" and "Cousin Kevin," Moon inventing the "holiday camp" idea (and Townshend extending authorship to the drummer, even though he wrote the song), and Daltrey acquiescing to Townshend's authorship—it was *Lambert*'s script that pulled the project together (Barnes, 1982). Barnes cites Chris Stamp's observation that the project "was falling all over the place, it was just not coming together and that's when Kit wrote a script" (p. 50). Stamp recalled that Lambert worked diligently on the script, completed it, and had it "printed up as a script to impress the group." Townshend supplied the spiritual inspiration and the band supported his artistic intuition, but Kit Lambert was the force that held the project together.

Lambert's technical contributions to the *Tommy* recording were not as impressive. Lambert's studio strength was in his understanding of the band's temperament more than in engineering matters. Marsh (1983) presents Townshend's recollections regarding Lambert's studio style:

Kit...knew the value of burning studio time.... He knew the value of saying, "Right, there's too many takes, they're getting worse; everybody over to the pub." Pick everybody up and take them out and perhaps not go back into the studio all night. You'd go home feeling terrible, and you'd think, "Oh, we've had a terrible day and why did Kit take us out," but the next day you go in and do that track straight away because you've built up to do it overnight and you get this great recording. He knew about techniques like that; he knew human nature and he knew about the Who. (p. 223)

This approach required even more studio time and contributed to the recording's expense, cited at the "previously unthinkable $36,000" (Pareles, 1993a, p. 18; Walker, 1993). With all the effort that went into the *Tommy* sessions, it is surprising that the final recording received so much criticism for its technical qualities. Townshend thought the sound quality was "passable" (Barnes, 1982, p. 50), and Entwistle observed, "The drums always seemed to sound like biscuit tins" (Marsh, 1983, p. 325). Entwistle also felt Lambert rushed the band by limiting the opportunity for overdubs (perhaps an April 1969 tour hurried the process). Barnes maintains these opinions "hurt" Lambert and notes Stamp's conclusion: "Kit was never a great ears producer. He wasn't into getting a perfect sound, he didn't know about the best place to position the mikes and all that. He was a creative and intuitive 'ideas' producer" (p. 90).

Having established *Tommy*'s artistic and commercial goals as well as the band's and Lambert's roles in the production process, let us now turn to the opera itself. *Tommy* (running 74:45) contains twenty-one songs of considerable diversity, ranging from extended instrumentals and songs (an "Overture" [5:58], an "Underture" [9:59], and the song "Amazing Journey/Sparks" [7:09]), to three-minute "singles" ("Pinball Wizard" [3:00], "The Acid Queen" [3:33]), brief segues ("There's A Doctor I've Found" [:23], "Miracle Cure" [:11]), and featuring one cover (Sonny Boy Williamson's "Eyesight to the Blind"). Two songs were composed by John Entwistle ("Cousin Kevin" and "Fiddle About") and one is attributed to Keith Moon ("Tommy's Holiday Camp"). The story begins with an interlude in the "Overture" in which Captain Walker's demise is announced: "Captain Walker/Didn't come home/His unborn child/Will never know him/Believe him missing/With a couple of men/Don't expect/To see him again." Mrs. Walker then gives birth to Tommy by way of "It's a Boy" ("A son! A son! A son!"). The "Overture" gives way to the opera's first pivotal scene in which Captain Walker returns home to find his wife with her lover celebrating "1921" and anticipating "a good year":

Lover: I've got a feeling twenty one
            Is gonna be a good year.
            Especially if you and me
            See it in together.

Father: So you think 21 is gonna be a good year.
            It could be good for me and her,
            But you and her—no never!

> I had no reason to be over optimistic,
> But somehow when you smiled
> I could brave bad weather.

Captain Walker kills the lover and the parents confront Tommy: "You didn't hear it/You didn't see it/You won't say nothing to no one/Ever in your life/Oh how absurd it/All seems without any proof/You didn't hear it/You didn't see it/You never heard it not a word of it/You won't say nothing to no one/Never tell a soul/What you know is the truth." With that, Tommy's "Amazing Journey" begins:

> Deaf dumb and blind boy
> He's in a quiet vibration land
> Strange as it seems his musical dreams
> Ain't quite so bad.
> Ten years old
> With thoughts as old as thought can be
> Loving life and becoming wise
> In simplicity.
> [chorus] Sickness will surely take the mind
>   Where minds can't usually go,
>   Come on the amazing journey
>   And learn all you should know.
> A vague haze of delirium creeps up on me
> All at once a tall stranger I suddenly see
> He's dressed in a silver sparked
> Glittering gown
> And His golden beard flows
> Nearly down to the ground.
> Nothing to say and nothing to hear
> And nothing to see.
> Each sensation makes a note in my symphony
> [chorus]
> His eyes are the eyes that
> Transmit all they know.
> Sparkle warm crystalline glances to show
> That he is your leader
> And he is your guide
> On the amazing journey together you'll ride.

After the instrumental "Sparks," the story features the "Eyesight to the Blind" cover (with "the Hawker" raving about his "woman" and her ability to inspire the blind to see, the "dumb" to talk, and the deaf to hear) and "Christmas"—a song about children frolicking on Christmas morning expressing worry about Tommy's understanding of that religious holiday. "Father" states:

> Did you ever see the faces of the children
> They get so excited.

Waking up on Christmas morning
Hours before the winter sun's ignited.
They believe in dreams and all they mean
Including heaven's generosity.
Peeping round the door
To see what parcels are for free
In curiosity.
Tommy doesn't know what day it is.
He doesn't know who Jesus was or what praying is.
How can he be saved?
From the eternal grave.

"Christmas" continues with a thorough description of Tommy's condition (he plays "poxy pin ball," "picks his nose," and "pokes his tongue at everything"), the father's plea "Tommy can you hear me?" and the boy's internal response, "See me, feel me/Touch me, heal me."

Next the opera introduces Entwistle's "Cousin Kevin" ("I'm the school bully!/The classroom cheat/The nastiest play friend/You ever could meet/I'll stick pins in your fingers/And tread on your feet") and his torture of Tommy (ducking his head underwater in the bath, burning him with cigarettes, and dragging him around by his hair). The first act closes with the "Acid Queen" and the "Underture." In the "Acid Queen," the "Gypsy" declares:

If your child ain't all he should be now
This girl can put him right
I'll show him what he could be now
Just give me one night.
[chorus] I'm the Gypsy—the acid queen.
            Pay before we start.
            The Gypsy—I'm guaranteed
            To tear your soul apart.
Give us a room and close the door
Leave us for a while.
Your boy won't be a boy no more
Young, but not a child.
[chorus]
Gather your wits and hold on fast.
Your mind must learn to roam.
Just as the Gypsy Queen must do
You're gonna hit the road.
My work is done now look at him
He's never been more alive.
His head it shakes his fingers clutch.
Watch his body writhe.
I'm the Gypsy—the acid queen
Pay before we start.
I'm the Gypsy—I'm guaranteed.
To break your little heart.

The second act begins with "Do You Think It's Alright" (a brief track featuring the Walkers debating leaving Tommy with Uncle Ernie, who has had a bit too much to drink) and Entwistle's "Fiddle About" depicting Tommy's sexual abuse by his uncle ("Down with the bedclothes/Up with the nightshirt!"). Suddenly, "Pinball Wizard" appears and the story shifts to Tommy's mastery of pinball. A "local lad" declares:

> Ever since I was a young boy
> I've played the silver ball
> From Soho down to Brighton
> I must have played them all.
> But I ain't seen nothing like him
> In any amusement hall
> That deaf dumb and blind kid
> Sure plays a mean pinball!
> He stands like a statue
> Becomes part of the machine.
> Feeling all the bumpers
> Always playing clean.
> He plays by intuition
> The digit counters fall.
> That deaf dumb and blind kid
> Sure plays a mean pinball!

Tommy, without the "distractions" that "buzzers, bells, and lights" bring, "always gets a replay," never "tilts at all," and even defeats the "local lad" on his "favorite" (or "usual") table. Here we have the story's first reference to Tommy's "disciples," who lead him to the pinball machine "and he just does the rest."

From tales of pinball mastery the story shifts to Captain Walker's announcement that he has discovered a doctor who "could cure the boy" and Tommy's visit with that physician. The scene unfolds in this fashion:

> Doctor: He seems to be completely unreceptive.
>   The test I gave him showed no sense at all.
>   His eyes react to light the dials detect it.
>   He hears but cannot answer to your call.
>
> Tommy: See me, feel me, touch me, heal me.
>   See me, feel me, touch me, heal me.
>
> Doctor: There is no chance no untried operation.
>   All hope lies with him and none with me.
>   Imagine though the shock from isolation.
>   When he suddenly can hear and speak and see.

A conversation between the doctor and the Walkers ensues, with the parents expressing an anxious curiosity about Tommy's condition ("What is happening in his head?"). All the while, Tommy's autistic journey continues:

> Listening to you I get the music
> Gazing at you I get the heat
> Following you I climb the mountain
> I get excitement at your feet
> Right behind you I see the millions
> On you I see the glory
> From you I get opinions
> From you I get the story.

From Tommy's private "Amazing Journey" vision we experience a brief segue ("Tommy Can You Hear Me?") to the opera's second pivotal scene—"Smash the Mirror"—in which an angry Mrs. Walker smashes Tommy's mirror and releases him from his autistic state (remember, Tommy had witnessed the murder in that mirror). Here we hear Tommy's first words—the song "Sensation"—and his surprising proclamation:

> I overwhelm as I approach you
> Make your lungs hold breath inside!
> Lovers break caresses for me
> Love enhanced when I've gone by.
> [chorus] You'll feel me coming,
>   A new vibration
>   From afar you'll see me
>   I'm a sensation.
> They worship me and all I touch
> Hazy eyed they catch my glance,
> Pleasant shudders shake their senses
> My warm momentum throws their stance
> [chorus]
> Soon you'll see me can't you feel me
> I'm coming
> Send your troubles dancing I know the answer
> I'm coming
> I'm a sensation.
> I leave a trail of rooted people
> Mesmerised by just the sight
> The few I touched now are disciples
> Love as One I Am the Light.

"Sensation" (a Townshend song written during the band's only trip to Australia years before—Townshend, 1993b, p. 10) is followed by the brief segue "Miracle Cure" ("Extra! Extra!/Read all about it/Pin Ball Wizard in a miracle cure!/ Extra Extra read all about it/EXTRA!") and a series of songs celebrating the Tommy Cult. That segment opens with "Sally Simpson"—a lyrically dense song about a young girl who disobeys her parents, attends a Tommy Rally, and receives a serious facial scar by attempting to touch Tommy—and moves to "I'm Free" – where Tommy announces his spiritual prowess:

I'M FREE—I'm free,
And freedom tastes of reality,
I'm free—I'm free,
And I'm waiting for you to follow me.
If I told you what it takes
To reach the highest high,
You'd laugh and say "nothing's that simple"
But you've been told many times before
Messiahs pointed to the door
And no one had the guts to leave the temple!

After repeating the "I'm free" lines (featuring instrumentals from "Pinball Wizard"), a "chorus" rejoins: "How can we follow? How can we follow?" The story continues with "Welcome" and its invitation for all to come to Tommy's house—"Come to my house/Be one of the comfortable people...We're drinking all night/Never sleeping." Here Tommy invites everyone to visit (the "milkman," "baker," and "shoe maker" included) before he decides that more room is required ("There's more at the door," Tommy is told). Next we travel to "Tommy's Holiday Camp" and a brief ditty featuring none other than Uncle Ernie as he welcomes everyone to "Tommy's" ("The camp with a difference/Never mind the weather/When you come to Tommy's, the holiday's forever!").

The opera ends with "We're Not Gonna Take It" in which Tommy welcomes his followers by telling them that in order to "follow" they must wear eye "shades," ear plugs, and place a cork in their mouths before playing pinball; denounces drinking alcohol and smoking marijuana; and is rejected by his "followers": "We're not gonna take it [repeated]/Never did and never will,/We don't have to take it./Gonna break it!/Gonna shake it!/Let's forget it better still!" The turnabout is sudden. Tommy refuses to acknowledge the rejection and announces that Uncle Ernie will guide each follower to "your very own" pinball machine. Again, the followers denounce Tommy ("We forsake you!/Gonna rape you!/Let's forget you better still!"). *Tommy* closes with the cult leader apparently returning to his previous condition (the ending is ambiguous) and repeating his autistic plea ("See me, feel me, touch me, heal me.... Listening to you I get the music/Gazing at you I get the heat/Following you I climb the mountain"). Where Tommy ends up is unclear.

Interpreting *Tommy*—like much of Townshend's oeuvre—is risky business. I suspect the "Amazing Journey" poem yields insight as to the opera's turning point and sudden ending. Recall in the poem that the seeker endeavors to "become one" with the Master and that each time he reaches for that goal he is sent back down "the path" in order to correct his error (his "lessons"). Perhaps *Tommy*'s "Sensation" represents that crucial mistake. There Tommy proclaims himself to be "the Light" and, correspondingly, "the Answer." The song "I'm

Free" reinforces that point. From that moment on, the search is over. Tommy welcomes his followers to his "holiday camp" and preaches the constricting doctrine common to so many organized religions. Tommy is no longer a seeker. He no longer shares the "aim" of all the "creatures" in the "cosmos." He is rejected and left to ponder his "lesson" and, perhaps, renew his search for "the story." This approach is standard Townshend. Although he claims the original *Tommy* has no "proper ending," Townshend's style of writing *around* his point—here, the error of forsaking the "search" for false "answers"—is evident in *Tommy*'s closing scenes. Townshend may lament that he compromised Baba's teachings for an entertainment package; however, his use of vague story structures is not only a prominent stylistic signature but a direct manifestation of his artistic philosophy.

There are two other points to be addressed before leaving the original *Tommy*. First, Townshend claims in his 1993 Broadway *Tommy* interviews that he wrote many more songs than were used in the original opera (e.g., "Kevin's a Model Child"—*In the Studio*, 1993) and he omitted those tunes in favor of the more ambiguous ending. He explains:

There were [instances]...in *Tommy*'s later incarnations in the film and in the [Broadway] show where I've written new songs to serve particular functions that have been required to help tell the story better, I already had anticipated that and there are songs that were supposed to serve those functions. But really when we put the album together we realized that the story shouldn't be too complete, for rock and roll.... There should be mystery in it and loose ends.

The second point involves the autobiographical qualities of several of *Tommy*'s songs. While Entwistle wrote "Cousin Kevin," Townshend says that the song, which to him is about "bullying," reflects several of his own childhood experiences (*In the Studio*, 1993). Elsewhere, he elaborates:

There was a period of darkness in my life; a bit that I don't remember. My mom and dad split up for awhile. Now this is not something that I knew when I wrote *Tommy*. It's only something that I found out recently.... But in a sense it amounted to me to a kind of abuse because the person that they farmed me out to was my mother's mother who turned out to be clinically insane and treated me very strangely. (*The Who's Tommy*, 1993)

Similarly, "Acid Queen" evokes the Townshend family's gypsy heritage: "My family has got some gypsy blood, my mother's mother was born of a gypsy girl" (*In the Studio*, 1993). "Sally Simpson" involves Townshend's response to a similar incident that he witnessed at a Doors concert (Marsh, 1983) and speaks to his anxieties over the "star-audience" relationship (*In the Studio*, 1993). Hence, *Tommy* may follow the "Amazing Journey" poem's spiritual themes, but the opera also employs stories that involve Townshend's youth, his experiences with rock celebrities, and a variety of other sources (including Nick Cohn, Lambert, and band members).

From this discussion of *Tommy*'s contents we turn to our final areas of interest, the various responses to *Tommy*, and the opera's impact on the band and Townshend. *Tommy*'s debut once again demonstrated The Who's understanding of rhetoric. Just as Townshend used pinball to please Nick Cohn, Lambert and Stamp made special arrangements for the opera's presentation to the music press. "Pinball Wizard" was issued as a single prior to the album's release (March 1969) and received considerable condemnation as a "sick" story. Townshend used this response to explain the story and gain publicity from the exposure (Townshend, by the way, refused to back down from the "sick" themes and affirmed that the opera addresses a variety of dysfunctional behaviors). Lambert and Stamp manipulated the situation to The Who's advantage, as Townshend relates:

Because of the way that we'd handled it, because we'd had the salutary lesson of "Pinball Wizard" being attacked for being sick, what we did is we pandered, absolutely, to the main spice of the journalist's life, we hired a club and we gave them free booze and we entertained them so the reviews were ecstatic...generally, there were a few exceptions. There were people that found it pretentious. There were people that found the whole thing distasteful, but it was all spectacular news, whatever it was...some people hated it, some people loved it, but everybody spoke very loudly about it. (*In the Studio*, 1993)

Once more we observe The Who's aggressive publicity machine in action. Barnes (1982) offers an overview of the British media's reactions, which ranged from the BBC's and *New Music Express*'s views that the work was "sick" to *Disc* magazine's praise, "WHO'S TOMMY—A MASTERPIECE" (p. 96). Once the band took *Tommy* on tour, the praise increased, as Barnes recalls: "Listening to *Tommy* the album is one thing, seeing the Who perform it live is a whole new ball game."

Tommy's reviews vary with the source. Pop fan magazines pursued their agendas, while more serious reviewers probed for the opera's artistic significance. An example of the latter is Ellen Willis's (1969) review, in which she contends *Tommy* displays a "quiet, melodic lyricism that represents spirituality" which renders "a dramatic—even operatic—tension, expressed as noise vs. music, between the outside world's destructiveness toward Tommy and his inner peace and growth" (p. 64). Walley's (1969) review for *Jazz & Pop* magazine seeks definitional clarity as a starting point for a dramatic reading of the story:

Before I proceed further, one thing I must clarify. *Tommy* is NOT an opera. A real opera is acted as well as sung; it has well-defined parts and *recitative* and many other characteristics. *Tommy* is a rock cantata: in other words, a piece of music which is primarily vocal—a sung piece...although *Tommy* could be easily called a "Passion" in the traditional sense. In many senses, Tommy's journey to realization is very like Christ's, and his eventual densification (Tommy, at the end, is "crucified" by an angry crowd and returns to his deaf, dumb and blind state). One can go overboard, however, with such an analogy and it would be foolish indeed to do a step-by-step comparison. *Tommy* is far better treated as the unique entity it is. (p. 44)

(Ken Russell concurs, "He's a modern Messiah, all you gotta do is look at the words and you see what Townshend's about"—*The Who's Tommy*, 1993.) Walley closes by proclaiming *Tommy* to be a "real and thoroughly valuable piece of music" that constitutes "a rare experiment" which "needs to be heard, not analyzed."

Such "analysis" aside, *Tommy* produced a new balance within The Who. Daltrey, Entwistle, and Moon accepted the songwriter's direction, and that co-operation facilitated Townshend's creativity. If Townshend had difficulty with any aspect of the story, he turned to the band or Lambert for assistance. Never before had Townshend received this level of creative input. Furthermore, Daltrey's portrayal of the Tommy role elevated his presence as the group's "front man" and restored his balance with regard to Townshend's creative leadership. Daltrey explains: "You have to understand for me *Tommy* was an absolute dream...and when the whole piece came together and we started performing it on stage all of a sudden I almost found myself within it. It was an amazing catalyst for me" (*The Who's Tommy*, 1993). Townshend may conceive the project and write the songs, but Daltrey delivered them, and this artistic balance saved a band bent on self-destruction. Swenson (1974) contends that The Who represented "the best observable example of the rock band *gestalt*, the strange magic that enables very ordinary people sometimes to form a whole that is not only greater than the sum of its parts but actually supports each one" (p. 48). That "rock gestalt" reached its creative peak with *Tommy*.

Tommy was a mixed blessing for its principal author. Recall the pressures Townshend described, how he referred to *Tommy* as a "desperate act" and how he realized that he "had to do something" but feared that he "would never, ever, ever top" the single, "I Can See For Miles." That intensity did not subside with *Tommy*, it grew. The inspiration for "Pinball Wizard," Nick Cohn (1970), captures Townshend's state of mind for the *New York Times*:

[T]his problem has always existed: Townshend is intelligent, creative, highly complex and much given to mystic ponderings, but the things that he values most in rock are its basic explosions, its noise and flash and image.... So he writes stuff like "Tommy," so-phisticated as it is, and he can see that it's good but, at the same time, he feels that it's a cop-out from all the things that rock lives off, almost a betrayal. And he goes out on stage and he smashes his guitar, simple, mindless release. But then he gets his breath back and he knows that that's not it either, to deny his own brain. And so it goes on, round and round with no end. (p. 2)

A post-*Tommy* interview reinforces Cohn's point. Townshend complained that "it's a bit difficult, writing heavy when you really want to write light or when you really want to write devotional" and expressed his realization "that if you want to get anything done you've got to actually do it, you know, with a capital D, and not wait" (Cott, 1970, p. 32). His internal conflict was intense, so intense that *he* perceived that *he* gets in the way of *his* own art, "I think that the self is an enemy that's got to be kicked out the fucking way so that you can really get down to it" (pp. 32-33). There Townshend asserted that "rock...[is] the ultimate vehicle for everything," including "self-destruction" (p. 34). He concluded: "You just can't be as effectively self-destructive if you're a writer, for example, or a painter, you just can't make sure that you're never going to fucking raise your head again; whereas if you're a rock star you really can." The post-*Tommy* Townshend was in a confused state of mind. Not only was he confused about his artistic direction (to write for himself—as in "Amazing Journey"—or to write for the market—as with "Pinball Wizard"), but he appeared to advocate an artistic self-sacrifice with no worldly resolution. Also citing Cohn's views, Marsh (1983) maintains that this perspective would represent the Pete Townshend of the 1970s. Townshend would now establish "rules only he saw, leaping over hurdles he had set up for himself, desperately trying to top himself over and over again" (p. 360) to the extent that "each success was meaningless because it only caused more anxiety over what came next." This state of mind was now the driving tension in Townshend's evolving version of the minstrel's dilemma.

In *The Who's Tommy* (1993) Barnes, Daltrey, Entwistle, and Townshend elaborate on *Tommy*'s impact. Barnes opines: "There was a whole period in Pete's life where he really was trying to live down *Tommy* and distance himself from it because I think he felt that it was overtaking The Who and their work and him." Daltrey's views are insightful as well:

We'd had a similar thing happen to us with "My Generation." We had this huge kind of cult pop song which at the end of it we used to smash our equipment. And of course we did that for like two years and it became expected and the same thing happened with *Tommy*. We played it for four or five years and people were expecting it. And once they start to expect it and you're stuck in that, you stop doing what you want to do and you're startin' to do what everybody wants you to do and that's fatal as an artist.

As The Who toured with *Tommy*, Lambert and Stamp skillfully managed to book some of the world's most prestigious venues: Champs Elysees Theatre in Paris, the Royal Theatre of Copenhagen, the Cologne Opera House, the Hamburg State Opera House, the Berlin Opera House, the Amsterdam Concertgebouw, and New York's Metropolitan Opera House, among others (Barnes, 1982). Stamp told Barnes that he and Lambert worked to secure a booking in Moscow in the hopes of obtaining the headline, "ROCK BREAKS THE IRON CURTAIN" (p. 97), but to no avail (they were, however, offered a date in Leningrad). The appearance at New York's Metropolitan Opera House allowed the Big Apple's opera critics a view of the rock spectacle. The *New York Times* interprets *Tommy*'s message in this fashion: "Many young people today firmly believe they have been traumatized into something figuratively akin to autism, and it has left them functionally blind, deaf and dumb to the values of the gerontocracy that rules them and us all. So they are evolving what they hope

are their own 'miracle cures,' among which pop music is one of the more potent" (Henahan, 1970, p. 42). Phillips (1970), also writing for the *Times*, observes that "for five hours yesterday the Metropolitan Opera House became the
Fillmore North" and cites the Met's assistant manager's view that *Tommy* is, in
fact, opera: "It's a story told with music and words.... It uses the methods and
the means of opera. It's opera in a new language. Is it an opera that we'll have
in our repertory.... I don't know. Not right away. Perhaps in the future" (p.
42). (Interestingly, the piece features one usher's view that "these kids are
much more polite than their parents.") Townshend was accurate when he said
that people may like or dislike *Tommy*, but *everybody* had something to say.

The Who also appeared at the legendary Woodstock and Isle of Wight festivals and performed large portions of the opera. Marsh (1983) offers a fascinating description of how The Who was persuaded to appear at Woodstock and
how the band hated that show. The group waited sixteen hours to perform,
and the water was spiked with psychedelic drugs. Still, The Who's Woodstock
performance produced two of rock history's more memorable moments: Townshend kicking activist Abbie Hoffman off the stage—an act he later proclaimed
to be the "most political thing I ever did" (p. 350)—and the band's performance
of "We're Not Gonna Take It" as the sun rose over the horizon. Townshend's
recollections are unpleasant: "I immediately got into an incredible state and I
rejected everyone.... Woodstock wasn't what rock's about, not as far as I'm
concerned" (Cott, 1970, p. 35). Years later, he recalls *Tommy*'s Woodstock
resurgence:

We just kind of kept playing *Tommy* and playing *Tommy* and playing *Tommy* and playing *Tommy* and then reviving *Tommy*.... And then just as when *Tommy* was about to go
to sleep and we were gonna get on to our next project, Woodstock came along and it
went back to number one.... It was another nine months of walking *Tommy* around, this
time with Roger in his Woodstock incarnation. Chest [Townshend sticks his chest
out]...that was even tougher 'cause by then I was really fed up with *Tommy*; and extremely fed up with Roger's chest. (*The Who's Tommy*, 1993)

To be sure, *Tommy* changed everything. *Tommy* represents the high point for
The Who in terms of the band's internal harmony and its relationship with Lambert and Stamp. The project transformed The Who financially, solidified its
standing with the music industry, and opened the door to new audiences. Everything would be different from now on, and Townshend's version of the minstrel's dilemma would assume a new form. He surpassed his audience's
expectations, yet his obsession with artistic progress created personal demands
that would prove to be overwhelming. There is little doubt that if Townshend
had lived with the English troubadours of yesteryear, he would have gladly
packed it in and headed for the Crusades. An external battle would have surely
been a relief when compared to the internal war he was about to experience.

LIFEHOUSE

The period of *Tommy*'s release was eventful for Pete Townshend. The Townshends' first child, Emma, was born just prior to the record's debut (Barnes, 1982). The Townshend-produced band "Thunderclap Newman" released the single "Something in the Air," which charted well in both the United Kingdom and United States. And the aforementioned Woodstock and Isle of Wight festivals, European opera house and U.S. *Tommy* tours kept Townshend on the road for extended periods. Through it all, another project was brewing. Townshend conveyed his creative restlessness to Michael Cott (1970): "I think a film would be the ideal thing...a rock film which is not a documentary and not a story and not a comedy either but a fucking rock film. A film which is the equivalent of a rock song, only lasting an hour or longer" (p. 35). The Who's next single, "The Seeker," also reflects the creative anxieties that engulfed Townshend:

```
I looked under chairs
I looked under tables
I tried to find the key
To fifty million fables
[chorus] They call me the seeker
        I've been searching low and high
        I won't get to get what I'm after
        Till the day I die
I asked Bobby Dylan
I asked The Beatles
I asked Timothy Leary
But he couldn't help me either
[chorus]
People tend to hate me
Cause I never smile
As I ransack their homes
They want to shake my hand
Focusin' on nowhere investigating miles
I'm a seeker
I'm a really desperate man
[guitar solo, partial chorus]
I learned to raise my voice in anger, YEAH
But look at my face ain't this a smile
I'm happy when life's good
And when it's bad I cry
I got values but I don't know how or why
I'm looking for me
You're looking for you
We're looking at each other
And we don't know what to do
[chorus].
```

That "The Seeker" contributes to *The Seeker* is certain. Townshend described the song's central character—and his spiritual dilemma—in the aforementioned *Rolling Stone* interview: "He's just like a whirling dervish. It started off as being very much me, and then stopped being very much me. It's very personal, but then the whole thing is that, as soon as you discover that songs are personal, you reject them.... Quite loosely, 'The Seeker' was just a thing about what I call Divine Desperation, or just Desperation. And what it does to people" (Cott, 1970, p. 33).

The internal battle we first observed with "I Can See For Miles" has now blossomed into a war. When Townshend tries to express himself, he pushes "himself" away in favor of his perceived responsibilities. The music industry's commercial demands join his commitment to The Who and its fans to create an artist with an intense desire to express his spiritual longings but unable to do so. His message—articulated in the "Amazing Journey" poem—must be transformed into an entertainment package that inevitably fails to satisfy Townshend's artistic urges. Therefore, all the while he believes rock to be the ultimate artistic form, he assumes a self-destructive stance and becomes hellbent on achieving that end.

While this creative struggle festered, The Who's commercial machine advanced. The band followed *Tommy* with its first live album, *Live at Leeds* (unlike *Magic Bus*, this one was actually recorded live). That album was to be recorded during The Who's U.S. *Tommy* tour. Townshend claimed the band recorded "80 performances" in an attempt to capture a "good show" (Cott, 1970, p. 34), he recalled: "Suddenly someone realizes there are 240 hours of tape to be listened to. You know, now who's going to do this?... So we just fucking scrapped the lot, and to reduce the risk of pirating we put the lot on a bonfire and just watched it all go." The band recorded a performance at Leeds University, as Townshend explained: "We went to Leeds and it just happened to be a good show and it just happened to be like one of the greatest audiences we've ever played to in our whole career, just by chance." Notice the insistence that "the audience" inspired a performance that Cohn (1970) refers to as, "Quite simply, it is the best live rock album ever made" (p. 2).

Years later, Townshend provides the rationale behind the *Leeds* project: "The feeling of power in the band at the time was just extraordinary and that was really all we had. That power had been rehearsed, practiced, refined on the road in America and around Europe and around the world playing *Tommy*.... God, we got good; we were really good and it was looking at what have we got to put out now.... And I think it was obvious that what we had to do was to get on record this extraordinary moment in our careers" (*In the Studio*, 1994).

Returning to creative matters, Townshend's *sincere* belief in rock's artistic power would now lead to the *LifeHouse* project, in which we revisit the "Amazing Journey" and the songwriter's musical pursuit of the human's physical essence. But first, in typical Townshend style, he must leak his plans to his audience, and once again he relies on a journalistic format for that task. Beginning in August 1970 Townshend served as a guest columnist for *Melody Maker*.

The monthly "Pete Townshend Page" synthesizes the pop music fan magazine "what I love/hate" genre, with Townshend's propensity to counterattack journalists and to float ideas. For instance, his August entry (Townshend, 1970a) features light talk about his vacation in "Osea" and his opinions about Joe Walsh's guitar playing. His September (Townshend, 1970b) column describes his travels in his "motor caravan" and, in an interesting twist, introduces the "idea" for the *LifeHouse* project:

Here's the idea, there's a note, a musical note, that builds the basis of existence somehow. Mystics would agree, saying that of course it is OM, but I am talking about a MUSICAL note. There is air that we breathe, we swim in it all our lives, we love it with our physical being and we watch it sustain the world around us. We seem adaptable and receptive to almost everything it produces; but most of all, and this has little to do with the essence of survival, most of us enjoy music. I've never been able to quite get to grips with how it all comes about, but artists and writers outside music have noticed it too. (p. 19)

The seeker from the "Amazing Journey" is about to learn another "lesson" regarding his impetuous search for The Answer. Townshend is certainly thinking out loud; nevertheless, this statement represents the first glimpse of an idea that an obsessive Pete Townshend would actually try to *prove*.

Other "Pete Townshend Page" entries address how The Who is changing its stage act to reserve energy for the finale (Townshend, 1970c), a long piece attacking music television shows in general and reporter Tony Blackburn in particular (Townshend, 1970e), another column on British media (this time, radio) and Blackburn (Townshend, 1971a), a piece on the need for touring in order to gain feedback from audiences (Townshend, 1971c), and an insightful comparison of U.S. and U.K. audiences (Townshend, 1971d).

The February 1971 entry announces the *LifeHouse* project: "Change. Is it really possible to change anything with music, or to even ease society into a position where what they listen to can change what they feel? Rock is capable of doing amazing things" (Townshend, 1971b, p. 14). From there, Townshend launches into a detailed explanation of how The Who must lead this "change"; he proclaims, "The music we play has to be tomorrow's, the things we say have to be today, and the reason for bothering is yesterday." The project aspires to "make the first real superstar" and that "star would be us all." Thus, London's Young Vic Theatre must become "the 'Life House,' the Who become musicians and the audience become part of a fantasy." That fantasy, Townshend states, has been invented by the band, "and now we want to make it happen for real." Only through this Rock Endeavor, he reasons, can the required "change" come about. Townshend follows this introduction with a message from "Bobby," the "mystic-cum-roadie" who represents the "superstar" inside us all:

Music and vibration are at the basis of all. They pervade everything, even human consciousness is reflected by music. Atoms are, at their simplest, vibrations between positive and negative. Even the most subtle vibrations detectable can effect us, as ESP, or "vibes." Man must let go his control over music as art, or media fodder and allow it freedom. Allow it to become the mirror of a mass rather than the tool of an individual. Natural balance is the key. I will make music that will start off this process, my compositions will not be my thoughts, however, they will be the thoughts of others, the thoughts of the young, and the thoughts of the masses. Each man will become a piece of music, he will hear it for himself, see every aspect of his life reflected in terms of those around him, in terms of the Infinite Scheme. When he becomes aware of the natural harmony that exists between himself as a man and himself as part of creation he will find it simple to adjust and LIVE in harmony.... We can live in harmony only when Nature is allowed to incorporate us into her symphony. Listen hard, for your note is here. It might be a chord, or a dischord. Maybe a hiss or a pulse. High or low; sharp or soft, fast or slow. One thing is certain. If it is truly your own, your own song, it will fit into the scheme. Mine will fit yours, and yours will fit his, his will fit others. You are what you are, and where you are, because that is what IS. To realise the harmony, that RIGHTNESS about your own note; even your own life, however you feel it could be improved by change, it has to be revealed. It can only be revealed by your own efforts.

This "message from Bobby"—presented through a pop music magazine's celebrity column—articulates a potential resolution to Townshend's creative-commercial struggle. Townshend does not undermine his work to suit external restrictions; to the contrary, he uses "Bobby" to confront his situation in various ways. First, he announces his thesis: music and vibration are "at the basis of all." Second, commercial influences must release their controls over music—"allow it freedom"—so that the necessary *changes* may occur. If that "freedom" is granted, music will emerge as a societal "mirror" through which each of us may pursue our individual "harmony" with nature's "Infinite Scheme" and, in turn, play our respective parts in "Nature's symphony." Most importantly, we, the audience, must work to get there ("it can only be revealed by your own efforts"). Townshend has certainly not cast himself aside so that he can "get down to doing" his work. Instead, he embraces his ideals about music, rejects its commercialism, and renews his spiritual commitments and belief in the performer-audience reciprocity.

Townshend, believing he had secured a million-dollar advance from Universal Pictures for the project (Marsh, 1983; Barnes, 1982), prepared the Young Vic Theatre for concerts which would be filmed. A *Penthouse* magazine interview details the technical aspects of the *LifeHouse* project. After citing how the plot followed the "Sufic notion that all life and all nature...[are] based on harmony or disharmony of a very physical variety" (McAuliffe, 1983, p. 169), Townshend turned to the technical specifics:

While I was working on "The Lifehouse" script I actually did a lot of experiments with sounds that were produced from natural body rhythms. I was working with the musical bursar of Cambridge University at the time. What we did was ask some individuals a lot of questions about themselves and then subject them to the sort of test a G.P. might undertake. We measured their heartbeat and the alpha and beta rhythms of the brain; we even took down astrological details and other kinds of shit. Then we took all the data we'd collected on paper or charts and converted them into music, and the end result was sometimes quite amazing. In fact, one of the pulse-modulated frequencies we generated was eventually used as the background beat to "Won't Get Fooled Again." Later I used another one of the pulse-modulated frequencies as the foundation for "Baba O'Riley." (pp. 169-70)

Through his experiments with "pulse-modulated frequencies" Townshend refined the synthesizer as a musical instrument (directly complementing Stevie Wonder's work in that area). As Atkins (1995) explains:

Emphasis was put on computers and electronics, and the ways in which a theatrical workshop environment could harness the untapped creative energy within a responsive young audience.... The plan, inasmuch as there was such a thing, was for The Who to take over the theatre with a regular audience, develop the new material onstage and allow the communal activity to influence the songs and performances. Individuals would emerge from the audience and find a role in the music and the film. When the concerts became strong enough, they would be filmed along with other peripheral activity from the theatre. A storyline would also evolve alongside the music. Although the finished film was to have many fictitious and scripted elements, the concert footage was to be authentic, and would provide the impetus for the whole production. Townshend wanted to get to know each member of the audience and provide them each with a personal musical theme, generated from a synthesizer fed with computerised biographical data. Ultimately, these thematic components would merge to create a "universal chord," representing the audience and musicians as a unified entity. This would form the climax of the film.

While he experimented with the technology, Townshend worked out the details of the *LifeHouse* "storyline." He described that plot to John Swenson (1971) in an extremely long statement that conveys the project's complexity: "It's an age when overpopulation and pollution and all that kind of stuff has forced man into a totally artificial existence. He lives out his experience in his life in a cocoon—it's a very stock science fiction idea called an experience suit. You put on a suit and you live programs, if you like, for your experience" (p. 30). The story features societal elite who control "the scum" ("hippies" and "farmers") who dwell on the polluted surface through experience suit programming. Townshend continued:

The heroes of the thing are the scum on the surface which is meant to be the lower classes and the people in the experience suits. The Festival Hall in London is taken over and various experiences take place like...orgies and football matches and everything you can conceive of. But this has become a kind of theatre—like an art form in itself—to provide good experiences for people on the experience suits. Art is taken way, way beyond what it is now, that is, something to be appreciated, for it *is* life, it's what you *get*.

Next the author introduced his hero, Bobby ("an old rock and roll musician"), who "put on a six month concert event" protected by a "force field." Bobby's "concerts" grow to the point that they threaten the government and its use of experience-suit programming as a tool for controlling the public. The story concludes in this fashion:

It ends up, basically, with an amazing day. Bobby gets everybody's pieces of music together and.... The pitch gets bigger and bigger and bigger and bigger...the force field goes down at a given moment, the government troops come in and as they walk in, Bobby is up on the platform and he gets shot by the government official and he falls off the balcony. As he hits the ground, all the kids rush in to catch him and as he hits the ground they all disappear, and that was just gonna [be] the end of it, right? But the way it's written is that everybody that was taking part in the rock concert disappears but nobody else does and they're just standing there, looking, and they don't know what has happened to the people, right? They've gone. And that's when "Song is Over" starts.... The whole point is that the hardware that is used, that they use in the theatre, is the hardware that was used to program the experience suits, so everyone in the experience suits is dead because they've had no experience, no food, no nothing. The kids have disappeared, and the only people left are the farmers and the government official and a few scattered individuals, and its just like a wasteland sort of thing.

Years later, Townshend relates that he was looking for a "metaphor" (*The One That*, 1996) as "satisfactory" as *Tommy*'s "to explain the degree of marginalization and isolation that we would be living in at the time of the millennium." There he explains how futuristic "peace barons" will bridge the gap between "entertainment" and "spiritual longing" in a fashion that controls the polity through its "life of pleasure"—channeled, of course, through experience-suit programming (the functional equivalent of virtual reality programs). The plan was massive, as Atkins (1995) relates: "*Lifehouse* was to be a sprawling concept work of multiple dimensions: big-budget feature film, theatre event, double-album, song-cycle, concert performance piece and general purpose statement about youth, modern society, spiritual harmony and the future of rock and roll.... Pete wanted to create a much more all-encompassing work of Art than a mere double-album or 'rock opera': he wanted an active, ongoing, tangible, participatory event." Barnes (1982) reports that Townshend produced four scripts and around forty songs for the project. Despite his intensity, the project failed, and according to Marsh (1983), Townshend never recovered. He recounted the experience to his former roommate:

In the end it got to the point where people were saying "It won't work. It won't work." I said, "Listen, not only will it work but I'll fucking do the film, I'll show you how it works. I'll actually put a concert together where people actually do start to transcend themselves." A lot of the things I was talking about and claiming were pretty wild then, but now they're common knowledge—the fact that each individual, has a particular kind of electronic frequency, that music is healing, and all that kind of stuff. And everybody has just been treating me as if I was some kind of loony and I think for a while I lost touch with reality. The self-control required to prevent my total nervous disintegration was absolutely unbelievable. I had the first nervous breakdown of my life. (Barnes, p. 99)

At first the band was supportive, but the technical demands were simply too great. Townshend tried to make a film, change (always *change*) the band's artistic orientation, move music in new directions, and introduce quadrophonic sound. Townshend, and his ideal, collapsed. He recalled: "It fell apart and I had the first nervous breakdown of my life. And I'm just not the sort to have nervous breakdowns. What'd happen is I'd spend a week explaining something to somebody and it'd be all very clear to me, then they'd go, 'Right, that's OK—now can you just explain it again?' There were about 50 people involved and I didn't have the stamina to see it through" (Collins, 1974, p. 20). On another occasion, he states: "It was like being in a group of people in the middle of the desert and saying 'All we have to do is go over there and there's a tap and we can drink' and them saying 'What? A tap? He's mad! A tap? I can't see a tap!'... Please let's go over there.... But nobody would move. And this started to affect my sense of my own sanity.... I had the good sense at that time to let the whole thing go" (*The One That*, 1996).

Townshend later dismissed his efforts as fancy: "It was a silly story. It gets sillier by the day. I'm no Ray Bradbury. It was my attempt at science fiction. The important thing was that it produced the songs" (Fricke, 1987b, p. 180). Even so, *LifeHouse* reflects Townshend's firm commitment to *push* his art form, as these comments indicate: "Rock is an accelerating medium.... But if it doesn't keep accelerating, it's not reflecting the changes in kids, because the kids are still accelerating, life accelerates.... And when Rock levels off and starts to rest on its laurels, that's when I start to feel pain" (Swenson, 1971, p. 30). *LifeHouse* was neither a filler designed to meet the required record length (as was the mini-opera), a compromise between the psychedelic sounds of the times and Townshend/Lambert's love of camp (as was *Sell Out*), nor a hodge-podge of ideas organized around a loose theme that was more than subject to compromise (as was *Tommy*). *LifeHouse* was *Pete Townshend's* idea—a response to his "pain" and a potential resolution to this minstrel's internal conflicts.

There was one other development of note from the *LifeHouse* project, Kit Lambert's absence. Barnes (1982) and Marsh (1983) report that Lambert attempted to shift some of the money Townshend received from Universal for the *LifeHouse* film to make a *Tommy* film. A *Tommy* film was rapidly becoming Lambert's obsession, and Townshend wanted no part of that venture. In the reissue of *Who's Next*, Townshend's (1995) liner note essay describes a pivotal meeting with Lambert and Stamp, his rejection of their *Tommy* film plans, and his conclusion, "I lost Kit...his response was dejection, frustration and a sense that I was being disloyal and ungrateful and he eventually moved to New York." Lambert's departure certainly affected the *LifeHouse* project. Lambert and Townshend had operated as a creative team, as Townshend notes: "Separately we were merely babbling ad-men, together we were serene Wagnerian genius. I probably carried on writing believing he would function as he always had, and help me explain to the willing but befuddled people around me what I was on about. He had done it with *Tommy*, and I expected him to do it again with *Life-House*." That never happened.

With Lambert gone, The Who turned to one of his old rivals, Glyn Johns, to produce its next record. The Who was excited about Johns and the role he played in the studio, as John Entwistle noted: "We've got our own engineer now. Glyn Johns. He's sort of signed to us, we don't need a producer, we need a sort of producer-engineer who can just sit in the box and give us the sound we want while we're outside, since we can't sit in the control booth and play at the same time" (Swenson, 1971, p. 28). The Who was prepared to move on without Lambert; therefore, the band turned to a *professional* engineer to help it mold Townshend's and Entwistle's ideas into the desired musical form.

The *LifeHouse* remnants rendered the commercially successful *Who's Next* (complete with cover art featuring band members zipping up their jeans after urinating on a monument from the set of Stanley Kubrick's movie, *2001*; Townshend admitted that the cover was a response to Kubrick's rejection of a *Tommy* film proposal—Rothman, 1979). The album (running 43:23) contains nine songs that, on the surface, have little or no relationship to one another. Eight of the songs are Townshend compositions ("Baba O'Riley," "Bargain," "Love Ain't For Keepin'," "The Song Is Over," "Gettin' In Tune," "Goin' Mobile," "Behind Blue Eyes," and "Won't Get Fooled Again") with the ninth penned by Entwistle ("My Wife"). The album omits several strong *LifeHouse* compositions (e.g., "Pure and Easy" and "Join Together") that find their way onto compilation albums such as *Odds & Sods*, the band's "greatest hits" records, or Townshend's demo collections. Several *Who's Next* songs were released as singles, and the album joined *Tommy* as two of The Who's most successful commercial works (much to Shel Talmy's glee).

The *LifeHouse* plot directly addresses the seeker's quest through its "musical essence" theme. The search, then, focuses on that one note that constitutes the individual's "song," and from there the one note that ties us all together with Nature's Symphony. *Who's Next*'s portrayal of that spiritual/musical quest is, well, cloudy. Several songs—although powerfully presented—actually say little, once out of the *LifeHouse* context. For instance, "Baba O'Riley" (named after Meher Baba and electronic inspiration Terry Riley) features Townshend's driving synthesizer, Moon's brilliant drum work, and some of Daltrey's most powerful vocals. Yet, the lyrics lack any narrative development if one is unaware of the *LifeHouse* context: "Out here in the fields/I fight for my meals/I get my back into my living/I don't need to fight/To prove I'm right/I don't need to be forgiven." While the bridge ("Don't cry/Don't raise your eye/It's only teenage wasteland") is a show-stopper in live performances, this song joins "Goin' Mobile" (a *LifeHouse* song about the "scum" cruising around in a big air-conditioned car on the "surface") and "Love Ain't For Keepin'" as three of the work's more nebulous numbers. Engineer Glyn Johns concurs: "The lyrics—if you don't understand the story 'cause I never did—if you listen to the lyrics of all the songs you don't really know what the hell he's going on about, but it doesn't matter. There's enough content in each of the lyrics for you to grab on...you can make it whatever you want" (*The One That*, 1996).

"Bargain," "Gettin' In Tune," and "The Song Is Over" also revisit Townshend's penchant for characterological ambiguity: that is, these songs may evoke romantic or spiritual themes (if the song is construed outside of the *Life-House* context). "Bargain" is a powerful number in which the character declares a willingness to "pay any price just to get to you" and offers self-sacrifice to achieve that goal ("I'd gladly lose me to find you/Gladly give up all I got/To catch you, I'm gonna run and never stop"). No matter the price, "you" remain a "bargain" (whatever or whoever "you" may be). Charlesworth (1995) addresses Townshend's use of "you" in this particular song: "Most songs addressed to 'you' are sentimental love songs but Pete's 'yous' are almost always addressed to Meher Baba, and...they are actually not-so-cunningly disguised prayers soliciting forgiveness for his early foibles and unworthiness, seeking advice on spiritual advancement or simply offering thanks for his avatar's bountiful virtue" (pp. 42-43).

In "Gettin' In Tune" the character sings a song that fits the "chords I'm playing" and urges us not to "pretend there's any meaning hidden in the things I'm saying." In fact, "words" may interfere with the "harmony" the character sees "in your eyes" and the "symphony" that exists "in your heart." Townshend's character endeavors to get "in tune to the straight and narrow" as a pathway to "you." Lastly, in "The Song Is Over" (the *LifeHouse* finale, placed in the middle of *Who's Next*) the character acknowledges "our love is over" but insists on "singing out" anyway: "I'll sing my song to the wide-open spaces/I'll sing my heart out to the infinite sea/I'll sing my visions to the sky-high mountains/I'll sing my song to the free, to the free." The number laments that the "song is over," samples the song "Pure and Easy" ("The song is over, excepting one note, pure and easy/Playing so free, like a breath rippling by"), and closes with an instrumental flourish. Townshend may be striving to point to music's spiritual value by proclaiming that he would do anything to obtain that state of bliss ("Bargain"), that the words do not matter ("Gettin' In Tune"), and that the discovery of that musical essence—that one note—can transcend the loss of any individual love ("The Song Is Over"). Yet without the *LifeHouse* superstructure to anchor those sentiments, they assume an open-ended quality that leaves the song's interpretation to the auditor's imagination, as in Glyn Johns's remarks.

That writing style appears in two of the album's successful singles as well, "Behind Blue Eyes" and "Won't Get Fooled Again." Recall from Chapter One that Townshend insists that these two songs' meanings have changed considerably over time: "Behind Blue Eyes" was originally about a *LifeHouse* villain and then became autobiographical; "Won't Get Fooled" rotates between a political anthem, an anti-revolutionary song, and a "stupid song"—depending, apparently, upon Townshend's mood. When taken as an autobiographical statement, "Behind Blue Eyes" is revealing. The song opens with a light acoustic guitar and these lines:

No one knows what it's like
To be the bad man
To be the sad man
Behind blue eyes
No one knows what it's like
To be hated
To be fated
To telling only lies
But my dreams, they aren't as empty
As my conscience seems to be
I have hours only lonely
My love is vengeance that's never free
No one knows what it's like
To feel these feelings
Like I do
And I blame you
No one bites back as hard on their anger
None of my pain and woe can show through
But my dreams, they aren't as empty
As my conscience seems to be
I have hours only lonely
My love is vengeance that's never free.

The song's instrumentals shift into an Entwistle/Moon/Townshend tour de force as Daltrey barks: "If my fist clinches, crack it open/Before I use it and lose my cool/When I smile, tell me some bad news/Before I laugh and act like a fool." After a few more lines pleading for help if the character "swallows anything evil" or "shivers" from the cold, the song ends softly: "No one knows what it's like/To be the bad man/To be the sad man/Behind blue eyes." Where "Behind Blue Eyes" fits into the *LifeHouse* plot is uncertain (the "villain's" role is unclear), yet its autobiographical connotations may be compelling (one just cannot be sure). Perhaps Townshend is feeling alone, misunderstood, and confused; only his belief in his dreams sustains him. Maybe he realizes that he has hurt people and that his love is costly; nevertheless, he reaches for help, because "no one knows what it's like" to be lost, all alone, in your dreams. "Behind Blue Eyes" introduces three potentially important points: the author's personal anxieties, his advancing autobiographical style (more than likely, a *blend* of fact and fiction), and his concern for his "dreams" and their possible deterioration.

"Won't Get Fooled Again" is open to a variety of interpretations as well (Barnes [1982] asserts the song is "We're Not Gonna Take It" revisited). The track starts with rebellion: "We'll be fighting in the street/With our children at our feet/And the morals that they worshipped will be gone/And the men who spurred us on/Sit in judgement of all wrong/They decided and the shotgun sings the song." The chorus suggests the futility of that rebellion as the character "smile[s] and grin[s] at the change all around," quickly realizes that nothing has really changed, and bemoans: "Then I'll get on my knees and pray/We won't get fooled again." The song advances images of despair over the uselessness of rebellion whether that "change" is inspired by the "left" or the "right." After a rousing instrumental interlude featuring Townshend's synthesizer work and Moon's powerful drumming, the final lines. are unequivocal: "Meet the new boss/Same as the old boss." This song is a direct manifestation of "Bobby's message" and Townshend's plea for "change" that we first observed in the "Pete Townshend Page" column. "A change it had to come/We knew it all along" the lyrics pronounce, but that "change" is not political. The Who, according to Townshend, "consciously kept out of politics...'cos it's all a lot of nonsense" (Denselow, 1989, p. 97). Years later, Townshend regretted that trait: "I would gladly give up a lot of the great moments of entertainment, and great events in my theatrical career, in order that I could put my hand on my heart and feel I'd done society some good!" In every respect, "Won't Get Fooled" stands out as a classic Pete Townshend composition: devotional, evasive, compromised.

Critical responses to *Who's Next* depend upon the writer's awareness of the *LifeHouse* project and the context of the various songs' creation. Mendelsohn (1971) maintains the album is "neither the soundtrack to the realization of Pete Townshend's apparently-aborted Hollywood dream...nor a, shudder, rock opera, but rather an old-fashioned long-player containing intelligently-conceived, superbly-performed, brilliantly-produced, and sometimes even exciting rock and roll" (p. 42). Noting the change in the band's style (the "need to demonstrate themselves Serious Artists instead of gimmick-mongering punks"), Mendelsohn praises Glyn Johns's studio work and The Who's return to "rock records." *Creem*'s Dave Marsh (1971) takes a different tack as he rejects certain parts of the album (the synthesizer work and "fiddle interlude" [p. 68] on "Baba O'Reilly" [*sic*]) and focuses on a "State of The Who" message. In the style that would soon dominate popular music criticism, Marsh moves away from an emphasis on the album's internal workings, with asides regarding the "state of the artist," toward reviews that focus on the artist, with asides about the work. Such is the nature of pop culture journalism and its synthesis of gossip, thoughtful analysis, and trendy commentary.

With *Who's Next*'s release, The Who toured with a series of powerful new songs. And yet the audience-band chemistry began to change during the *Who's Next* tour. Townshend told Swenson (1971) that the band had "developed a sixth sense about where the audience's heads are at a certain time" (p. 31) but that those "senses suddenly seem to be working in different ways," which, to the songwriter, "indicates that the group are facing audiences much more as individuals at the moment, and much less as a group." Townshend's fear that the audience was losing sight of the rock experience that "the band" facilitates was rapidly becoming a reality.

Another deteriorating situation, once again, involved Kit Lambert's post-*Who's Next* activities. Once Shel Talmy's rights to The Who's music expired, the band released *Meaty Beaty Big and Bouncy*: the much-anticipated "Who's Greatest Flops" album, featuring virtually all of the band's singles from "I Can't Explain" through "The Seeker," but no new material. Marsh (1983) writes that Lambert was in the United States during the album's release and upon his return attempted to stop the record's distribution due to his dissatisfaction over its contents and arrangement (he failed). To be sure, Lambert's utility was diminishing. His principal value had always been his uncanny creativity with financial, promotional, and studio matters. As The Who became an internationally successful business, Lambert's entrepreneurial skills were in less demand. Moreover, Townshend's lack of interest in a *Tommy* film, the band's reliance on Glyn Johns for the *Who's Next* sessions (remember, Johns and Lambert had had serious disagreements during The Who's first recording sessions with Shel Talmy), Daltrey's examinations of The Who's finances (Lambert was careless there), and—interestingly—The Who's *lack of concern for image* (see Marsh, 1983, p. 395) all added up to the end of the Lambert-Who era.

This was a critical time in Who history. Townshend's paranoia over his artistic inclinations induced a creative uncertainty. Lambert's absence damaged the band's chemistry, and the growing detachment from the audience influenced Townshend's performance standards. In response the band once again debated its artistic direction: Daltrey, Entwistle, and Moon preferring to satisfy the audience (play more of the same); Townshend aspiring to change rock and challenge that audience. All of these factors meant that The Who faced yet another important decision point. Marsh (1983) describes The Who's situation as a "classic artist-versus-entertainer syndrome" (p. 426), with no simple solution: "No challenge was worth much if it wasn't amusing to masses of people, and no mass audience was worth much if it only accepted what it came for." This was The Who's—and Townshend's—version of "the minstrel's dilemma." Townshend won, and the result was yet another opera.

QUADROPHENIA

The Who's initial response to its post-*Who's Next* situation was to return to the studio and produce another single album. Townshend told Robin Denselow (1972) that the subsequent material was cast aside (sounding too much like "shades" of *Who's Next*) in favor of a new approach. He described his plans for a second opera: "The theme is a mixture of the history of the group and the story of a kid who's going through adolescence, and then becoming very spiritually desperate and then finding the secret to life. When he's a child he doesn't suffer from schizophrenia but from quadrophonia. The album will be quadrophonic and each different part of the guy's character will be a reflection of one member of the group" (p. 52).

Here again, Townshend relied on a journalistic context to introduce his next "idea of the month." Notice that he continues to cling to themes from days gone by—the discovery of "the secret to life," teen angst, complicated characterizations—while he simultaneously pursues another technological innovation (the still raw notion of quadrophonic recording). Townshend modified various elements of the story, nevertheless, after announcing the project in *Rolling Stone*, *he now had to do it.*

Quadrophenia's central character, "Jimmy," is a Mod. Townshend told Perry and Bailey (1974) that he "was moved emotionally by Mods" (p. 13) because he identified with the social movement's emphasis on "fashion and haircuts" ("it was one thing that held me together, gave me a feeling of belonging"). Consequently, he used *Quadrophenia* to depict the Mod phenomenon, The Who's role in that movement, and Jimmy's unique form of teen angst (what I call "Mod angst"). In order to tell his story, Townshend again established technological hurdles that would be difficult to clear, and as in *LifeHouse*, his technological failures would contribute to another artistic compromise. Not only was the quadrophonic sound idea unrealistic (the music industry had not yet agreed upon a standard approach to quadrophonic equipment, which would make distribution extremely difficult) but as Perry and Bailey report, the band used a new studio (an old church) that was still under renovation. Thus, the group used a mobile studio with the control unit deployed outside on the sidewalk. Townshend also produced the project. Daltrey claimed Townshend had written "enough for five double albums" (Swenson, 1974, p. 49), and Townshend presented that material to the band in the form of incomplete demos. Just as in the *Tommy* sessions, Townshend hoped the various band members would assume responsibility for their individual parts. Even though they liked the idea, Daltrey, Entwistle, and Moon had little to offer creatively, and there was no Kit Lambert to spur everybody onward. Townshend operated without creative assistance in an unfinished studio as he attempted to shape a huge amount of material through an unrefined musical technology.

The result was a double album (running 82:15) of which all seventeen songs were Pete Townshend compositions (the first Who album composed by a single author). Unlike *Tommy*'s "Amazing Journey" poem or *LifeHouse*'s "message from Bobby" introductions, there was no independent guide to *Quadrophenia*'s story. Instead, Townshend penned an essay (printed with the liner notes and lyrics) that outlines the story from the young Mod's point of view. That essay begins:

I had to go to this psychiatrist every week. Every Monday. He never really knew what was wrong with me. He said I wasn't mad or anything. He said there's no such thing as madness. I told him he should try standing in a queue at Brentford football ground on a Saturday morning, I thought it might change his mind. My dad put it another way. He said I changed like the weather. One minute I'd be a tearaway, next minute all soppy and swoony over some bird. Schizophrenia, he called it. Nutty, my mum called it.

From there Jimmy describes his home life, with an emphasis on his parents' drinking and his propensity for "leapers" (amphetamines—"Each to his own sewage" he concludes). Jimmy offers a detailed account of his "paranoia," his on-going struggle with his amphetamine habit, his life in the streets, and his experiences with the Mod band, The Who. The youngster is dominated by deep-seated frustrations. He obtained a job but quit after two days. He simply could not understand his fellow workers' acquiescence to the "system." In fact, Jimmy just dislikes people:

There's a part of me that hates people. Not the actual people but how useless they are, how stupid. They sit and stew while the whole world gets worse and worse. Wars and battles. People dying of starvation. Old people dying because their kids have got their own kids and they ain't got time. That's what makes me smash things up. My shrink says I ain't mad. He should see me when I'm pissed.

Jimmy's frustrations peak after sleeping out in the rain for two nights (consuming vast amounts of "leapers"), seeing an old girlfriend with another guy, and wrecking his most prized possession, his "GS" (motor scooter). To deal with his plight, he eats "about twenty leapers" at one time and takes the train to Brighton, the seaside resort once frequented by Mods. There Jimmy copes with his Mod nostalgia, goes to the beach to explore his personal metaphysics, recounts his experiences with an Ace Face (a Mod leader), and—eventually—confronts his reality as he steals a boat, consumes more leapers, and takes a bottle of gin out to sea: "Me folks had let me down, Rock had let me down, women had let me down, work wasn't worth the effort, school isn't even worth mentioning. But I never ever thought I'd feel let down by 'eing a mod." Hallucinating to the sound of the boat's engine (Townshend experienced a similar event as a child), he arrives at his destination—a rock out in the ocean—climbs out on the rock (as his boat drifts away), and is stranded there in the rain. That introductory essay ends:

A tough guy, a helpless dancer.
A romantic, is it me for a moment?
A bloody lunatic, I'll even carry your bags.
A beggar, a hypocrite, love reign over me.
Schizophrenic? I'm bleeding Quadrophenic.

Quadrophenia begins where Townshend's essay ends, with the four parts of Jimmy's personality: according to Marsh (1983), one part is "violent and determined, aggressive and unshakable" (Roger Daltrey), another is "quiet and romantic, tender and doubting" (John Entwistle), another is "insane and devil-may-care, unreasoning and bravado" (Keith Moon), and another is "insecure and spiritually desperate, searching and questioning" (Pete Townshend—p. 420). The album opens with sound effects of the ocean crashing upon the shore with intermittent musical incarnations of Jimmy's four personalities (Townshend relies on Wagner's leitmotif system to announce the appearance of the various personalities): "Helpless Dancer" (Daltrey), "Is It Me?" (Entwistle), "Bell Boy" (Moon), and "Love Reign O'er Me" (Townshend). The first song, "The Real Me," conveys Jimmy's psychological state:

I went back to the doctor
To get another shrink.

I sit and tell him about my weekend
But he never betrays what he thinks.
Can you see the real me,
Doctor, Doctor?
Can you see the real me,
Doctor?
I went back to my mother.
I said "I'm crazy, ma, help me!"
She said, "I know how it feels, son
'cause it runs in the family."
Can you see the real me,
Mother, Mother?
Can you see the real me,
Mother?
The cracks between the paving stones
Like rivers of flowing veins.
Strange people who know me
Peeping from behind every window pane.
The girl I used to love
Lives in this yellow house.
Yesterday she passed me by.
She doesn't want to know me now.
Can you see the real me
Can you, can you?
Can you see the real me
Can you, can you?
I ended up with the preacher
Full of lies and hate.
I seemed to scare him a little,
So he showed me to the golden gate.
Can you see the real me,
Preacher, Preacher?
Can you see the real me,
Preacher?

"The Real Me" is followed by the instrumental "Quadrophenia" (6:15) and its protracted presentation of the opera's four themes. The next number, "Cut My Hair," takes us to the crux of Jimmy's conflict, his "Mod angst." Jimmy appears to appreciate his family (with all of their faults) and understands that they want him to follow "their way." He must reject his parents, however, "move with the fashion" of the Mods or "be outcast." He follows the Mods, dresses in the proper fashion and cuts his hair, yet he is haunted by "that uncertain feeling" that remains in his "brain" (shades of "I Can't Explain"). Jimmy struggles to keep up with the fashion, consumes the appropriate drugs (which his parents find and, he fears, will result in his expulsion), and "works himself to death just to fit in" with a "crowd of kids that hardly notice" his presence. Mods struggle for individual recognition ("How fantastic am I") all the while most of them merely blend into the crowd. They work and work to purchase splendidly tailored new clothes and learn new dance steps that go out of fashion before week's end. This is the heart of "Mod angst." This is Jimmy's dilemma: to follow a group that ignores him, to follow his parents' "way," or to strike out on his own.

Jimmy's plight gains intensity when he encounters one of his music heroes (one presumes from Townshend's essay a member of The Who, probably Townshend) and confronts him for "copying" the Mods, in "The Punk Meets The Godfather." Jimmy, the punk, announces:

> You declared you would be three inches taller
> You only became what we made you.
> Thought you were chasing a destiny calling
> You only earned what we gave you.
> You fell and cried as our people were starving,
> Now you know that we blame you.
> You tried to walk on the trail we were carving.
> Now you know that we framed you.

The Godfather replies, "I'm the guy in the sky/Flying high, Flashing eyes/No surprise I told lies/*I'm* the punk in the gutter." He insists: "I'm the punk with the stutter. My my my my my mmmm my my my GGGGG-g-g-g-g generation." The punk advances his assault, claiming the Godfather "could only repeat what we told you" and how "you only see what we show you." This time the Godfather reiterates his "I'm the guy in the sky" lines, but softly adds:

> I have to be careful not to preach
> I can't pretend that I can teach,
> And yet I've lived your future out
> By pounding stages like a clown.
> And on the dance floor broken glass,
> The bloody faces slowly pass,
> The broken seats in empty rows,
> It all belongs to me you know.

The song ends without resolution. Jimmy is angry because he feels he has been used by his rock idol, and his frustrations increase. Everyone is abusing Jimmy: his rock idols merely copy his group's fashion and lifestyle (and become rich in the process), the Mods demand so much from him but yield so little, and his closest support groups (parents, doctor, preacher, ex-girlfriend) turn their backs on him. Jimmy feels he is alone in a world of betrayal.

To convey that sentiment, the opera moves to the soft, reflective song "I'm One." Here Jimmy laments that he is "a loser—no chance to win" as his "loneliness starts sinking in." Still, he remains amazed by his fellow Mods' perfection ("Where do you get those blue blue jeans/Faded patched secrets so tight/Where do you get/That walk *oh* so lean?/Your shoes and your shirts/All just right") and his inability to obtain that "look" ("Ill fitting clothes/I blend in the crowd/Fingers so clumsy/Voice too loud"). Nevertheless, with all of his perceived flaws, Jimmy still believes that he will yet emerge from the pack and become an Ace Face ("You'll all see/I'm the one"). After Jimmy's confrontations in "Cut My Hair" and "The Punk Meets The Godfather," "I'm One" features a more introspective adolescent wavering between accepting his individualism (simply being "one" in a crowd and at peace with himself) and pursuing his Mod delusions of grandeur (being "The One").

From this meditative moment, we move to another series of confrontational scenes in which Jimmy decries working life ("Dirty Jobs") and society ("Helpless Dancer"), questions himself once more ("Is It In My Head"), declares "I've Had Enough," and travels to Brighton. In "Dirty Jobs" Jimmy—as a "young man"—identifies with the "pig keeper" and the "bus driver" as they all get "put down," "pushed round," and "beaten every day." Jimmy, in contrast, vows to fight back ("I'm not gonna sit and weep again") and chastises the workers: "My karma tells me/You've been screwed again/If you let them do it to you/You've got yourself to blame/It's you who feels the pain/It's you who takes the shame." After an interlude of circus sound effects, the story moves to a broader context, via "Helpless Dancer," in which Jimmy transcends the working-class struggle and addresses society as a whole. The song contains minimal instrumentation and emphasizes a forceful, angry vocal style:

> When a man is running from his boss
> Who hold a gun that fires "cost"
> And people die from being old
> Or left alone because they're cold
> And bombs are dropped on fighting cats
> And children's dreams are run with rats
> If you complain you disappear
> Just like the lesbians and queers
> No one can love without the grace
> Of some unseen and distant face
> And you get beaten up by blacks
> Who though they worked still got the sack
> And when your soul tells you to hide
> Your very right to die's denied
> And in the battle on the streets
> You fight computers and receipts
> And when a man is trying to change
> But only causes further pain
> You realize that all along
> Something in us is going wrong
> You stop dancing.

These powerful lines take us beyond Jimmy's Mod anxieties into what Townshend described as the character's "spiritual desperation" stage. The song's message is clear: when you acknowledge all of these societal problems and their implications, you must seek spiritual relief ("No one can love without the grace/Of some unseen and distant face"), and *stop dancing.* Jimmy recognizes that these are serious problems that cannot be ignored; just the same, he is torn by his Mod loyalties and the movement's disregard for society in favor of an emphasis on the self. In "Is It In My Head," Jimmy probes deeper into these apparent contradictions:

> I see a man without a problem.
> I see a country always starved.
> I hear the music of a heartbeat.
> I walk and people turn and laugh.
> [chorus]Is it in my head?
>   Is it in my head?
>   Is it in my head, here at the start?
>   Is it in my head?
>   Is it in my head?
>   Is it in my head or in my heart?
> I pick up phones and hear my history.
> I dream of all the calls I've missed.
> I try to number those who love me.
> Find out exactly what the trouble is.
> [chorus]
> I feel I'm being followed.
> My head is empty.
> Yet every word I say turns out a sentence.
> Statements to a stranger,
> Asking for directions,
> Turn from being help to questions.
> I see a man without a problem.

Jimmy is confused. Is his conflict in his "head" or in his "heart"? And where does he turn for relief? Is he capable of helping people, or must he merely resign himself to hate? Finally, Jimmy has "had enough" ("I've Had Enough"), faces life's contradictions ("You were under the impression/That when you were walking forward/You'd end up further onward/But things ain't quite that simple"), revisits his Mod allegiances ("My jacket's gonna be cut slim and checked,/Maybe a touch of seersucker, with an open neck/I ride a G S scooter with my hair cut neat,/Wear my wartime coat in the wind and sleet"), cries out "Love reign o'er me" (Townshend's theme: "a beggar, a hypocrite"), and decides to escape:

> I've had enough of dance halls
> I've had enough of pills
> I've had enough of street fights
> I've seen my share of kills
> I'm finished with the fashions
> And acting like I'm tough
> I'm bored with hate and passion
> I've had enough of trying to love.

Predictably, Jimmy's version of "escaping" is "returning" to Brighton. As the liner note essay previewed, he consumes vast amounts of amphetamines, hallucinates, reconsiders his plight on the train to Brighton (the song "5:15"—"Out of my brain on the train"), and develops a "Why should I care?" attitude toward the whole situation.

The song "Sea and Sand" again reviews all of Jimmy's problems: his parents (who have thrown him out), his anxieties over his girl (who is a "perfect dresser"), his Mod angst (over his clothes and scooter) and his frustrations over everyone else's superior attire, and his lone source of joy—"thank God I ain't old." Jimmy is, indeed, engulfed by his problems and briefly contemplates suicide in "Drowned" ("I am not the actor/This can't be the scene/But I am in the water,/As far as I can see.... I wanna drown in cold water"). He rebounds via "Bell Boy" (Moon's theme) in which he discovers the Ace Face from days gone by is now a bellhop at a resort hotel the Mods once rampaged. The beach clears Jimmy's thinking ("The beach is a place where a man can feel/He's the only soul in the world that's real") and he spots the bellboy/Ace Face:

> But I see a face coming through the haze,
> I remember him from those crazy days.
> Ain't you the guy who used to set the paces
> Riding up in front of a hundred faces?
> I don't suppose you would remember me,
> But I used to follow you back in sixty three.

The song seems to emphasize the acceptance of one's role in life and its inherent contradictions, as the bellboy responds:

> I got a good job and I'm newly born,
> You should see me dressed up in my uniform.
> I work in a hotel all gilt and flash.
> Remember the gaff where the doors we smashed?
> Bell Boy! I gotta get running now.
> Bell Boy! Keep my lip buttoned down.
> Bell Boy! Carry the bloody baggage out.
> Bell Boy! Always running at someone's heel.
> You know how I feel, always running at someone's heel.

The "Bell Boy" has to hustle to please everyone else, all the while, his alter ego "Ace Face" is the consummate Mod leader who sets the fashion, invents the latest dance steps, and wins all of his fights. Ultimately, the bellboy accepts his fate: "People often change/But when I look in your eyes/You could learn a lot from a life like mine/The secret to me isn't flown like a flag/I carry it behind this little badge/It says/Bell Boy!"

Jimmy's confusion, once more, leads to arrogance. In "Dr. Jimmy" we observe the inner struggle between "Dr. Jimmy" and "Mr. Jim," introduced through the "Is It Me?" theme (Entwistle's). One side of Jimmy is extremely

aggressive ("What is it? I'll take it/Who is she? I'll rape it/Get a bet there? I'll
meet it/Getting high? You can't beat it") while the other is longing for something better ("Is it me? For a moment/The stars are falling/The heat is rising/
The past is calling"). Jimmy's psychological struggle reaches an instrumental
climax in "The Rock," in which all four themes merge into one final, crashing
sound (shades of *LifeHouse*), which is followed by "Love Reign O'er Me"
(Townshend's theme and the album's final song):

> Only love can make it rain
> The way the beach is kissed by the sea.
> Only love can make it rain
> Like the sweat of lovers'
> Laying in the fields.
> [chorus]Love, reign o'er me
>   Love, reign o'er me, reign o'er me.
> Only love can bring the rain
> That makes you yearn to the sky.
> Only love can bring the rain
> That falls like tears from on high.
> [chorus]
> On the dry and dusty road
> The nights we spent apart alone.
> I need to get back home
> To cool, cool rain
> I can't sleep and I can't think
> The nights are hot and black as ink
> Oh God, I need a drink
> Of cool, cool rain.

Jimmy sits in the rain on the rock. Like *Tommy*, the story just stops. Jimmy has
endured several intense experiences, but his resolution is uncertain.

In his interview with Perry and Bailey (1974), Townshend explained that
Jimmy "feels" he is a "failure" (p. 13) because he is unable to keep up with the
older Mods and all their fashion, scooters, and girlfriends:

In a sense he's a failed Mod, because he's made the ultimate Mod mistake, bad timing.
This is 1965 and the Mod scene is already falling apart and what does he do but go to
Brighton *just to remember*. The crazy days when 300,000 Mod kids from London de-
scended on that little beach town were only three weeks ago, but already he's living in
the past.... He's damaging himself so badly so that he can get to the point where he's so
desperate that he'll take a closer look at himself. All he knows is that things aren't right
in the world and he blames everything else.... He ends up with the sum total of frustrated
toughness, romanticism, religion, daredevil—desperation, but a starting point for anybody. He goes through a suicide crisis. He surrenders to the inevitable, and you know,
you *know*, when it's over and he goes back to town he'll be going through the same shit,
being in the same terrible family situation and so on, but he's moved up a level. He's
weak still, but there's a strength in that weakness. He's in danger of maturing.

Townshend elaborated on Jimmy's character to Cameron Crowe (1974): "He's a workshop figure. An invention.... Jimmy, on the surface, looks like a simple kid with straightforward hang-ups, but he's far more surrealistic" (p. 97). When Crowe inquired as to the author's identification with his central character, Townshend replied: "I feel closest to Jimmy when he's reached the stage...of being stuck on the Rock. He's surrendered himself to the inevitable, whatever that is, and has put all his problems behind him."

These comments, Townshend's introductory essay, and *Quadrophenia*'s contents offer several compelling insights into the writer's state of mind and, unfortunately, his future. Townshend's work is taking a decidedly autobiographical turn. He effectively uses the "Mod angst" theme as an entry point for a discussion of several of his teen anxieties. Through Jimmy, Townshend revisits his family problems and his torn loyalties (he loved his parents, longed for their attention, and coped with his grandmother), discusses the powerful anxieties that emerge from the threat of peer group exclusion (as a young teen Townshend was ostracized by his peers for an extended period of time), and recounts various adolescent insecurities. He also massages his views regarding The Who-Mod audience reciprocity and his conclusion that he was labeled a "genius" for merely copying what he observed in that audience. And finally, Townshend's remarks concerning how Jimmy was "damaging himself so badly so that he can get to the point where he's so desperate that he'll take a closer look at himself" represent a powerful piece of foreshadowing in that he would follow this path himself in the late 1970s.

Quadrophenia also employs two themes that are now regularly featured in Townshend's writings. The instrumental "The Rock" invokes the *LifeHouse* notion of a "single note" capturing the essence of a given situation. In *Life-House*, everyone's musical essence eventually converges into one note in Nature's Symphony; in *Quadrophenia*, the four personalities and their corresponding music merge into one note once Jimmy reaches "the rock" (a symbol that is also open to a variety of interpretations). Second, Jimmy learns a lesson that takes him to the next "level" of his spiritual journey—a theme that clearly revisits Townshend's "Amazing Journey" poem. Herein lies *Quadrophenia*'s value to the oeuvre and *The Seeker* composite text. Jimmy's "search for identity" places a spin that is decidedly English on rock and roll's traditional "teen angst" theme ("Mod angst"). He searches himself and deals with conflicts involving his family, self image, romantic interest, peer group identification, society, and spirituality. He in no way discovers an *answer* to his search but instead gains an appreciation for the *question*. Subsequently, Jimmy moves "up a level" in his quest for identity. Townshend may have failed to develop the quadrophrenic personality and their qualities on a microscopic level; however, the story displays considerable coherence and continuity on a macroscopic level.

The music critics' responses to *Quadrophenia*, of course, vary in style. John Swenson (1974) endorses an autobiographical approach and argues the album is a "sociologically valid treatment of the mods from a historical vantage point" (p. 54). *Rolling Stone*'s Lenny Kaye (1973) notes the difficulty American audiences may experience with the Mod story line and compares that problem with an English reading of *American Graffiti*. That review concludes: "But on its own terms, *Quadrophenia* falls short of the mark. Jimmy Livingston Seagull, adrift on a stormless sea, with only his shattered wings and sharded memories to keep him company—so close, and yet so far" (p. 73). Little doubt, Townshend is increasingly willing to confront commercial expectations for the sake of self-expression. Unlike *Tommy*'s "pinball" compromise or *LifeHouse*'s total abdication, *Quadrophenia* is unadulterated Townshend—he wrote, produced, and packaged the album (the album credits Ron Nevison as engineer). Always the rock philosopher, Townshend (1977) describes his use of Jimmy's character to communicate his rock ideals in a piece he prepared for *Rolling Stone*:

> Mixed up in *Quadrophenia* was a study of the divine desperation that is at the root of every punk's scream for blood and vengeance. I can elaborate. It is really a fantastic conceit on the part of the Establishment to imagine that any particular fragment of society is ever the true subject of a rock & roll song. Even in the famous, folk-oriented, political complaining songs of the very early Sixties, a thread of upward groping for truth came through strongly. The definition of rock & roll lies here for me. If it screams for truth rather than help, if it commits itself with a courage it can't be sure it really has, if it stands up and admits something is wrong but doesn't insist on blood, then it's rock and roll. We shed our own blood. We don't need to shed anyone else's. (p. 56)

To express that sentiment Townshend focused on characterization. His characterizations now surpass his story lines to the extent that Stokes (1974) compares his style with Henry James's writing: "Yet unlike bands whose energy is the sole (and insufficient) resource, the Who are deliberately narrative. Townshend's lyrics, when they are successful, reveal a Jamesian obsession with detail. The emotions he portrays are circumscribed by white jackets with side vents five inches long, by hidden boxes of blue pills.... Yet nothing happens. Ever...it is literally mere sound and fury...the fusion of rage and boogie" (p. 62). Kaye (1973) concurs: "Pete, for better or worse, is possessed of a logic riveting in its linearity, and if in effect we are being placed in the mind of an emotionally distressed adolescent, neither the texture of the music nor the album's outlook is able to rise to this challenge of portraiture" (p. 73). *Quadrophenia* may fail to reach that "challenge of portraiture" and its various technological aspirations; nevertheless, the album represents yet another turning point for Townshend's writing for The Who, a point to which I now turn.

The post-*Quadrophenia* Who was not the same band that entered the group's opera phase. Entwistle told Swenson (1979): "I liked *Quadrophenia* at the time it was released.... But looking back on it I think the reason it didn't work was because it was more of a Townshend solo album with The Who as a backup band...[it] wasn't as much of a group effort as *Tommy* was" (pp. 121-122). At this point Entwistle attained new status through his emergence as an associate producer. Entwistle dedicated hours to refining *Quadrophenia*'s horn mixes and other qualities. Consequently, he produced the compilation album *Odds &*

Sods (the album that followed *Quadrophenia* in 1974) and the movie soundtrack for the *Quadrophenia* film. His studio work supported The Who's commercial viability through a troubled time. Moon, in contrast, continued his physical and emotional downward trend and as a result contributed less to the band's creativity. For the next few years, Moon would use his *Tommy* persona ("Uncle Ernie") to sustain his celebrity status. And Townshend and Daltrey renewed their battles of old. Just prior to the *Quadrophenia* tour, Townshend hit Daltrey with his guitar during rehearsals and Daltrey responded with a single blow that rendered Townshend unconscious. Years later, Townshend described the event to Mills (1978): "Roger caught me up proper, bang on the jaw. I went back like a board. I was out for about four hours. They took me to the hospital. It was then, in my coma, that I realized that really Roger was all right. He was a killer, but lovely with it" (p. 28). Despite Townshend's sense of humor, from that moment on, Townshend and Daltrey would struggle and fight (often via the media) until The Who disbanded. *Quadrophenia*—despite all of its promise—was simply not a "group" effort. Without Lambert to hold the group together, a prominent role for Daltrey (as in *Tommy*), and some institutional restraint on Townshend's control (who readily assumed all responsibility for any problem with the recording and browbeat himself incessantly), the group returned to its old combative ways.

The changing nature of Who concerts reinforced that disintegration. Edwards's (1974) piece for the *New York Times* captures the various "layers" (p. 3) of audience that attended contemporary Who concerts: "There is an original hard core group now essentially middle class and in its twenties.... Joining them are large numbers of younger followers added five years ago when the Who became superstars with the creation of 'Tommy'.... The latest addition is an even younger generation of adolescents who see the Who as a venerable classic" (p. 3). This diverse audience was prone to sitting in "near silence" (Perry & Bailey, 1974, p. 16) during *Quadrophenia* performances which, when combined with the show's technical problems (synchronizing the taped sound effects), Townshend was, once more, led to question his innovation's worth. For Townshend, Who audiences were now "very much like the kids in Tommy's Holiday Camp, they want something without working for it" (Barnes, 1982, p. 118). His growing distaste for rock audiences and the larger stadium venues slowly distanced him from his inspirational source and led to his narrative impulse's dark age.

Tommy and *Quadrophenia* provide the bookends for this portion of the oeuvre. Townshend hoped that *Quadrophenia* would distance the group from *Tommy*, but he was wrong: "So, thinking I was getting myself off the hook, I was really fooling myself because now I've got the biggest problem ahead of me as a writer, and I think the band has got the biggest problem ahead of them as a group" (Swenson, 1979, p. 117). That "problem" involved "not knowing the general sense of direction" for the future. Instead of pushing forward, *Quadrophenia* had, in Townshend's words, "wound up" the past ("to go on with that rock & roll adolescent stuff would be so stupid"). How Townshend's creative

instincts would respond to this challenge would truly test his artistic perseverance.

While The Who faced its directional uncertainty, the commercial machine
that surrounded the band had to be fed—hence, the compilation album *Odds &
Sods* was released in 1974. Fearing the mass distribution of Who outtakes by
bootleggers, The Who turned to Entwistle to organize and refine the various cuts
for the album. The album contains Pete Meaden's original High Numbers record ("I'm the Face"), a 1969 Entwistle tune ("Postcard"), Townshend's American Cancer Society promotion ("Little Billy"), two Kit Lambert productions
from 1968 ("Glow Girl" and "Faith in Something Bigger"), two Townshend
songs from 1969 ("Now I'm a Farmer" and "Naked Eye"), and four *LifeHouse*
era songs produced by The Who and Glyn Johns ("Put The Money Down,"
"Too Much of Anything," "Pure and Easy," and "Long Live Rock"). Townshend's liner notes suggest his views about the record's contents: "All of these
tracks have been part of bigger ideas, or at least grand dreams that didn't see the
light of day."

Miller's (1974) review offers an insightful interpretation of this snapshot of
The Who's past. The *Rolling Stone* review describes the "11 outtakes" as "an
uneven lot," yet Miller maintains that "the fumbling is almost as illuminating
as the flashes of inspiration dotting this album" (p. 73). Miller argues the project is "far from exploiting a random set of discards" in that it offers a "fascinating glimpse" of a band "caught in the process of forging a style." The review
contends Townshend is not so much "the grand architect" of The Who but rather
"the ingenious artisan." The writer elaborates: "He deals in cliches, but they
are his own cliches, so deftly assembled that they've become a bold musical
signature. Townshend's stylistic units function best in brief doses or in formats
where he can move quickly from theme to theme...whereas Townshend's
longer works...occasionally falter." Whether or not the operas "faltered," *Odds
& Sods* contrasts *Quadrophenia* for the reasons Miller suggests. The singles
compilation and the rock opera are quite distinct manifestations of Townshend's
narrative style. And, as Childs's (1973) review indicates, there were those who
preferred the old days: "The nicest thing about *Odds & Sods* is that it gives us a
chance to hear The Who working in the various versions of their evolving style
sans Townshend's superstructure for the first time since *Happy Jack*" (p. 82).

Townshend's "superstructures" would now give way, and the singles-era
style of album construction would return. The *expectations* of the opera period
now yield to the commercial/social *obligations* of the band's final years. As for
the troubadour of old, Townshend's commitment to meet—and surpass—the
musical world's artistic *expectations* was impressive during the opera period (as
was his capacity to endure the social trappings that accompanied his celebrity
status). He endeavored to push (and, therefore, change) his art form, its commercial industry, his audience, his band, and himself. To achieve that end he set
up goals that he could not meet; consequently, his commitment twice turned
toward the pathological. Townshend's creative impulse thrived, but his technical ambitions faltered. Without the support his narrative drive required, that too

would soon fade. For the time being, this was Townshend's version of the minstrel's dilemma, and his response would model young Jimmy: he would now damage "himself so badly so that he" will "get to the point where he's so desperate that he'll take a closer look at himself." Once more, it is too bad for this minstrel that the Crusades were no longer an option.

4

The End of The Who

Throughout music history successful commercial artists have struggled with the demands and expectations that accompany that standing. For the accomplished musician, the artistic expectations of a fledgling career may quickly evolve into the professional obligations of celebrity and as a result prove damaging to the creative impulse that supported the initial success. In order to maintain creative equilibrium, artists enter into various forms of negotiation (with collaborators, management, industry, and others) that may very well determine that individual's professional future.

Once more, English minstrelsy yields an interesting case in point. Consider the aspiring jongleur who obtains a position in a troubadour's gallery, a nobleman's court, or as a town musician and, once that job is secured, suffers a lapse of creativity. That is, role expectations and artistic obligations lead to inspirational and creative voids. Although our jongleur may be pleased with his steady employment (and receive a handsome salary), the institutional constraints that accompany his position could easily limit his ambitions and stifle his creative instincts. The advent of the "Guild of Minstrels" contributed to this potential problem. Like most trades, English minstrelsy developed a network of guilds. These guilds devised rules for the membership's welfare, collected dues, and provided health and legal assistance. English cities, towns, and counties formed guilds of minstrels, selected a "King of the Minstrels and his Court" (Rowbotham, 1895, p. 178), and devised codes of conduct, called the "Charter to the Minstrels" (p. 180). The good news involved the protection these guilds afforded their members; the bad news involved the limits they placed on their members' activities and the rewards they could collect for their services. Raynor (1978) writes that "the guild rules maintained standards, expelled the inefficient or the dishonest, who were thus deprived of any regular means of earning their living, and drew up the tests which governed promotion from grade to grade" (p. 56). The guild's fee structure also protected members against the "encroachments of amateurs, of wandering players or of unofficially organised bands which were prepared to undercut their prices" (p. 57). Raynor reports that the guild member who "behaved himself was secure for life."

"Security," however, is not always the harbinger of creativity. A state of mindless obligation may quickly overcome the artistic impulse that originally supported the artist. As he or she suffers through the institutional pronouncement of "give them what they want," the art may begin to lose quality, and the artist may begin to deteriorate. We now witness these happenings as they manifest in Pete Townshend's career with The Who. The expectations of the opera period now turn to the obligations of the band's final years. Commercial success may continue, but its toll may threaten more than the artist's professional demise.

THE END OF THE WHO

We are about to embark on a rather sad but intriguing journey. The "end of The Who" phase of Pete Townshend's career is full of somber tales of despair, exasperation, and grief. Townshend's cherished "rock ideals"—his commitment to artistic progress and his belief in a performer-audience reciprocity—now abandon him in a dramatic fashion. (That Townshend physically survived this period is, in and of itself, noteworthy.) Many of the tensions that characterized the first two portions of The Who's history now dissipate or disappear—conditions that have considerable consequences for the band's future. For insight into the "state of The Who" I turn to the October 1974 edition of *Creem* magazine and Dave Marsh's article celebrating the band's tenth anniversary. Marsh (1974) acknowledges that "it would be deliberately provocative to label any band the greatest live rock act in the world"; nevertheless, he maintains, The Who represents the "truth behind the rhetoric" (pp. 47-48). According to Marsh, rock and roll "demands excess," and "the Who simply understand the correct proportions." After 1974 that "understanding" fades. The exaggerated performance style that once thrived on audience participation drifts into the nostalgic atmosphere that engulfed the times. In the absence of "understanding," predictably, the "excesses" assume control.

During this portion of the oeuvre, Townshend's spiritual search (thus far, the foundation of *The Seeker* text) wanes while the songwriter struggles with questions of self-worth, relational identity, loyalty, friendship, and musical direction. As Townshend articulates these sentiments, the band merely goes through the creative motions and accepts virtually anything he offers. The "rock gestalt" that once typified The Who falls apart: Daltrey's film career, Entwistle's solo endeavors, Moon's move to California, and Townshend's detachment contribute to that disintegration. On other levels of activity, the band's management enters another round of legal confrontations as Lambert and Stamp officially exit in favor of Bill Curbishley and end the creative alliance upon which Townshend once thrived. The music industry completely yields to the band and its management (it will sell anything). And the audience has little to offer Townshend since Who "concerts" occur in huge venues before distant audiences who come to "hear" the band and celebrate history. The struggle to advance the art—and simultaneously inspire the audience, the music industry, Lambert and Stamp, and the band—vanishes and Townshend's words focus on its passing.

Evidence of Townshend's state of mind may be found in an article he prepared for *Rolling Stone* several years later: "If I try to imagine where my head was two years ago, it's a strange vision. Paranoia does not adequately describe my feelings, though I suppose all of the Who were to a degree paranoid toward one another. But my trouble was also manifestly spiritual. I felt I had let myself down morally and artistically; I felt quite genuinely to be a hypocrite" (Townshend, 1977, p. 54). The *Quadrophenia* project was a major source of Townshend's anxieties. He recalls that while he was busy writing and recording The Who's final rock opera trouble was brewing:

Kit Lambert had helped a certain amount while I was writing, and had promised to produce the album. He didn't make out very well, and argued with Daltrey. I felt let down and took over.... When the album was completed, it took only a few days for Roger to express his disgust at the result. I had spent my summer vacation mixing it, and he had popped in once to hear mixes, making a couple of negative comments about the sound but seeming quite keen to let me "have my head," as it were, in production. Fundamentally, I had taken on too much, as always, and couldn't handle the strain when things went wrong and people blamed me. I felt I was perfectly entitled to gamble and lose, as no one else seemed prepared to, either with *Quadrophenia* or even the Who's career.

Notice the striking similarity between the *Quadrophenia* and *LifeHouse* projects. Lambert's absence, the band's indifference (until the end), the failed technical ambitions, and Townshend's response all follow the *LifeHouse* pattern. Having gone down that "path" twice, to be sure, Pete Townshend had learned his "lesson."

Where would Townshend and The Who go from here? Like *Quadrophenia*'s Jimmy, to go forward, The Who revisited its past. The long-awaited *Tommy* film emerged as the dominant Who project of the mid-1970s. Townshend debuted as a solo act on April 14, 1974, and the pressures surrounding the show contributed to his troubles (his appearance was successful, however). Marsh (1983) notes that Townshend's hair fell out and his hearing deteriorated during this time. These physical afflictions were complicated by drinking cycles in which Townshend "was subject to raging fits of anger, hostility and irrational violence, both of word and deed, and *then*, as he came to his senses, equally ruthless rounds of painful self-absorption and depression as he tried to comes to terms with his drunken behavior" (p. 444).

A four-night engagement at New York's Madison Square Garden, scheduled during a break in the *Tommy* filming, provided a critical moment for Townshend's shifting attitude toward performance, his audience, and—most importantly—his writing for The Who. A series of articles in the *New York Times* document those events in considerable detail. One focuses on Townshend's personality and depicts the songwriter as "nervous, intense, full of repressed violence and quick small smiles, and above all capable of a level of analytical speculation rare in the world of rock 'n' roll" (Rockwell, 1974b, p. 53). The thrust of that personality, John Rockwell reasons, involves Townshend's "creative contradictions," which feature "his belief in the quiescent teachings of Meher Baba...and his simultaneous propensity for violence." Contributing to his internal turmoil was Townshend's growing distaste for performance, which he described to Rockwell: "For the first 80 times I did 'Listening to You,' from 'Tommy,' I got a terrific spiritual high. But now it's a ritual, and the last thing in the world I want to get into is ritual. I hate religions." To escape those rituals, Townshend perceived the need to strike out on his own:

Everything that I've written so far has been given to the Who for first refusal. What I'm saying is that that's going to stop, and that I'm going to get first refusal.... The basic idea is that I have to get my teeth into something that liberates me from the band.... The Who is a very difficult band to write for. It is very tied to tradition and to its audiences, and very slow to change. It's like swimming in your own wake. I'd like to do something crazy, explosive. I want to confront the spiritual issue head on. I don't even know if it will be rock 'n' roll.... People talk about classical music having limitations. But rock has the greatest limitations of all. The great unwritten rule of rock is that you can achieve amazing things by transcending its limitations. But if you allow yourself an open check, you're in big trouble.

After the *LifeHouse* and *Quadrophenia* debacles Townshend learned neither to issue himself "an open check" nor to follow his blind allegiance to The Who. Nevertheless, he remained obsessed with "changing" rock by pushing its limitations through, in his case, spiritual messages. Exacerbating those feelings was *the* major development from the New York shows. Whereas Rockwell (1974a) reports the band's "lack of preparation" for the opening show "constituted its own kind of rebellion against rock's own conventions" (p. 38), Townshend (1977), Barnes (1982), and Marsh (1983) present an alternative account. During the first of the four Garden shows, Townshend suddenly lost his performance instincts:

In all the years that I had been with the Who, I'd never once had to force myself. All the leaping and guitar smashing even. I'd done it a thousand times, it was totally natural. And then on the first night at the Garden, I suddenly lost it. I didn't know what I was doing there, stuck on stage in front of all those people. I had no instinct left; I had to make every move from memory. So I looked down into the front row and there were all these kids squealing, "Jump, Pete, jump, jump, jump." As if I was Pavlov's dog or some performing seal. And I panicked and I was lost. It was the most incredible feeling, after twenty years or whatever, more than half my life, to suddenly go blank. The other three shows I was terrified, I got smashed, or I couldn't have gone on. (Barnes, p. 106)

To cope with his performance anxieties, his decision to keep his best work for himself, and his distaste for touring, Townshend returned home to work on the *Tommy* movie soundtrack—a project that used quintaphonic sound (quadrophonic plus one speaker for voices) and required hours upon hours of tedious mixing throughout the production process.

When Pete Townshend faced uncertainty in the musical world, he returned to his one place of comfort: the studio. Marsh (1983) contends the artist was another "sort of rock star" (p. 454) in his studio. There he was "idealist, coherent, mature, principled, thoughtful, confident, articulate, a perfect specimen of what was right with rock as music and as a social institution." Once Townshend left his studio, Marsh argues, he faced a "world that taunted, tormented and further tempted him" as well as colleagues who could not understand his carefully conceived plans. Townshend "felt incredible pressure to make each album a giant step...to act out what was Expected of a Rock Star—though he had created much of the pressure and almost all of the ballyhoo himself and though he was fully capable of changing the definition of what was Expected any time he chose" (pp. 454-55). This was Townshend's version of the minstrel's dilemma. He consistently set up conceptual and technological expectations that were difficult to attain, announced his plans in the media (thereby placing pressure upon himself), succumbed to that pressure, and compromised the original idea. This was a vicious cycle of his own creation.

This chapter explores Townshend's evolution from a world of artistic "expectations" toward one of professional "obligations" in which he abandons his artistic impulse, enters a creative void, abdicates his "Amazing Journey" spiritual message, and suffers through the worst period of his professional life. Hence, I characterize "the end of The Who" phase of the oeuvre as "Pete Townshend's Complaint." The four albums that constitute this period represent a marked departure from the two previous phases in that Townshend's nebulous, open-ended plot structures now yield to direct complaint. Gone are brief narratives stressing oddball characters over plot development or lengthy tales emphasizing portraiture; in fact, this phase features minimal characterization, as Townshend's stories stress *values* over characters or plot progression. The four parts of "Pete Townshend's Complaint" are: the internal anxiety (or "confessional") period (*The Who By Numbers*), a "musician's elegy" period (*Who Are You*), the interpersonal angst (or "confrontational") period (*Face Dances*), and a "life complaint" period (*It's Hard*). This portion of the oeuvre offers a different version of *The Seeker* text in that "the search" now focuses on worldly matters and, on occasion, Townshend's concerns for masculine identity. Unlike previous phases, this search is not dominant. Each of the four albums makes a passing reference to this "journey," as the focus remains on the "complaint." Here Townshend's writings enter the "womb-like darkness" of the "Amazing Journey" poem's material world where he places "labels on each friend, article and emotion/That appears." I now turn to "Pete Townshend's Complaint," as we consider a period that involves Keith Moon's and Kit Lambert's deaths, a disillusioned artist, and the end of The Who.

THE WHO BY NUMBERS

I begin with the turning point that keeps on turning—*Tommy*. The early 1970s witnessed two more versions of Townshend's opera, and each displayed important consequences. The first involved Lou Reizner's adaptation featuring the London Symphony Orchestra (directed by David Measham), a host of guest stars playing various roles (Sandy Denny, Steve Winwood, Richie Havens, Ringo Starr, Rod Stewart and others [see: Hilburn, 1972b], along with Daltrey and Moon playing Tommy and Uncle Ernie, respectively). This project rendered a double album that Hilburn (1972b) describes as "a sort of Broadway, pop-rock middle ground" piece "that gives the work a texture more in line with, say, 'Jesus Christ Superstar' than the original Who album" (p. 66). Part of the Reizner venture included a charity benefit performance at London's Rainbow theatre. Townshend was selected to be the show's narrator, and the results were disastrous. Marsh (1983) and Barnes (1982) note that Townshend was apprehensive about the show; therefore, he got intoxicated, insulted almost everybody, and at the end of the show "wiped his ass with the libretto and staggered off the stage" (Marsh, p. 402).

The second *Tommy* revision was long in the making. For years, a *Tommy* film was the apple of Kit Lambert's eye, as Townshend explained to John Swenson (1971): "They [Lambert/Stamp] started with The Who for the sole purpose of makin' a movie. And it's something that I think Kit Lambert desperately wants to do before he's ready to die, I think this is probably what keeps him alive" (p. 32). The *Tommy* film project was first submitted to Universal Pictures for legal reasons (Universal was associated with the band's American record label, MCA). Barnes and Townshend (1977) describe the situation in this fashion: "There was a three-sided row going between Pete, Universal and Kit Lambert. Universal hated Lambert's screenplay, and there was no way they'd put up the money for his film of 'Tommy.' Pete was frustrated and blaming Lambert for the film not getting made" (p. 34). Townshend claims "our relationship never really recovered," and Lambert's dream was left unfulfilled (which sealed his departure—Townshend's essay in the *Who's Next* reissue corroborates these observations). After several years of negotiations with a variety of Hollywood producers, Chris Stamp and Bill Curbishley reached a deal with Robert Stigwood, who then secured backing from Columbia Pictures and hired Ken Russell to write and direct the film. Townshend wanted the film to represent an extension of the original concept; thus, he granted Russell considerable creative freedom. Russell changed *Tommy* in several fundamental ways: Mrs. Walker's lover—"Frank"—kills Captain Walker, leaving Tommy to fantasize about his father; the parents' reactions to Tommy are stressed over the youngster's spiritual journey; the parents exploit Tommy's disciples; and more. Major film stars (Ann-Margret, Jack Nicholson, Oliver Reed, and Tina Turner) were signed for key roles, and Daltrey made his cinematic debut as Tommy (of course, Moon played Uncle Ernie). By now, Townshend was sick of *Tommy*. He told *Rolling Stone* that he could no longer "raise the enthusiasm to raise the energy to do any more work on *Tommy*" (Collins, 1974, p. 20). Still, he praised Russell's revisions and raised a compelling point: "It's great working under somebody rather than always having to do the pushing and leading." Perhaps the author was not as burdened with all of his perceived responsibilities as he claimed; maybe he was simply tired of working alone. While Townshend now viewed *Tommy* as "rock's 'Pirates of Penzance'" and considered the work to be a form of "light entertainment," he was no doubt happy to have the film out of the way (he received an Oscar nomination for best musical score).

In the midst of all these happenings the writer who penned the line "I hope I die before I get old" turned thirty years of age. To capture that moment, Townshend granted several media interviews and, with those publications, initiated a "media war" with Roger Daltrey. He complained about the music business, the passive qualities of contemporary audiences, and pretentious rock stars. He also conveyed his confusion about his songwriting for the band: "So long as the Who exists, I'll never get the pick of my own material...and that's what I dream of. But if the Who ever broke up because the material was sub-standard then I'd really kick myself" (Carr, 1975a, p. 39). (Such remarks represent a considerable departure from Townshend's comments to the *New York Times* cited earlier.) Daltrey's response was sharp and concise. He distanced himself from Townshend's comments in every respect and blamed the guitarist for The Who's recent stage problems (citing the New York Madison Square Garden shows). The exchange—a confrontation carried out through the music press—established the tone for The Who's final years in which Townshend and Daltrey constantly fought from a distance, all the while somehow managing to coexist in recording sessions.

With Glyn Johns back at the helm, The Who regrouped for 1975's *The Who By Numbers*. The album (running 37:30) contains ten songs: nine by Townshend, the other by Entwistle. The Entwistle contribution, "Success Story," is an intense attack on the commercial music business (discussing celebrity frustrations and production hassles) and joins Townshend's "confessional" tales to present an extremely negative work. "Squeeze Box" (featuring Townshend on banjo) and "Blue Red and Grey" (featuring Townshend on ukulele) provide a brief flash to the past and the songwriter's penchant for light, silly stories. The other seven songs—"Slip Kid," "However Much I Booze," "Dreaming from the Waist," "Imagine A Man," "They Are All In Love," "How Many Friends," and "In A Hand Or A Face"—display varying versions of the "Pete Townshend's Complaint" story line.

This initial installment of "Pete Townshend's Complaint" is a two-pronged tale in which the author explores his life. In the first portion of the story Townshend complains that there is "no easy way to be free" ("Slip Kid"), that there "ain't no way out" of his endless cycle of frustration ("However Much I Booze"), that he does not trust his relationships ("How Many Friends"), and that he dreams of escape—"the day I can control myself" ("Dreaming from the Waist"). The second portion of the story is brief, but important. There Townshend acknowledges the new wave/punk music scene ("They Are All In Love") and introduces this phase's version of "the search" ("Imagine A Man"). I begin with the album's the most profound expression, "However Much I Booze" (so profound that Daltrey refused to sing it; Barnes, 1982). The song's message is dark and personal:

> I see myself on TV, I'm a faker, a paper clown
> It's clear to all my friends that I habitually lie—I just bring them down
> I claim proneness to exaggeration but the truth lies in my frustration
> The children of the night, they all pass me by
> Got to dress myself in brandy, in sleep I'll hide
> But however much I booze
> There ain't no way out, there ain't no way out
> I don't care what you say, boy, there ain't no way out
> I lose so many nights of sleep worrying about my responsibility
> Are all the problems that screw me up really down to him or me
> My ego will just confuse me
> Some day it's gonna up and use me
> Dish me out another tailor-made compliment
> Tell me about some destiny I can't prevent
> And however much I squirm,
> There ain't no way out, there ain't no way out
> I don't care what you say, boy, there ain't no way out.

Townshend's character pleads, "Won't somebody tell me how to get out of this place," with its "walls" that are "clawed and scratched like by some soul insane." The narrator laments, "I just can't face my failure/I'm nothing but a well-fucked sailor," and asks the audience for its judgment: "You at home can easily decide what's right/By glancing very briefly at the songs I write." The song closes with the refrain, "There ain't no way out." Townshend's character—a "habitual" liar and alcoholic dominated by his perceived "responsibilities"—is trapped in a personal cul de sac of his/her own creation. Little doubt the line "Are all the problems that screw me up really down to him or me" is a direct reference to the Townshend-Daltrey battles.

This complaint is introduced in the album's opening cut, "Slip Kid," with the character's realization that "it's a hard, hard world" and there is "no easy way to be free." Townshend writes:

> I've got my clipboard and textbooks
> Lead me to the station
> Yeah, I'm off to the civil war
> I've got my kitbag, my heavy boots
> I'm running in the rain
> Gonna run 'til my feet are raw.
> Slip kid, slip kid, second generation
> I'm a soldier at thirteen
> Slip kid, slip kid, realization
> There's no easy way to be free, no easy way to be free.

After discussing a "sixty-three-year-old soldier's" "doctor's prescriptions" and a "vacuum flask full of hot tea and sugar," Townshend's character barks: "Keep away old man, you won't fool me/You and your history won't rule me/You might've been a fighter/But admit you failed/I'm not affected by your black-mail/You won't blackmail me." These references to one generation's confrontation with another and the "war veteran" theme extend the "My Generation" segregationist angst and in so doing foreshadow a future thematic trend. The next song, "However Much I Booze," joins "Slip Kid" to seal the complaint on both the individual and societal levels. The brief respite provided by "Squeeze Box" (a humorous song about "daddy," "Mamma's squeeze box," and sleepless nights) lightens the tone prior to another round of intense complaint. "Dream-ing from the Waist" opens with an aggressive sexual fantasy:

> I feel like I want to break out of the house
> My heart is a pumpin', I got sand in my mouth
> I feel like I'm headin' up to a cardiac arrest
> I want to scream in the night, I want to manifest
> I got the hots for the sluts in the well-worn pages of a magazine
> I want to try, I want to slide like I do in the dreams I've never really been in
> I want to hump, I want to jump
> Want to heat up and cool down in a dream machine.

Afterward, the character acknowledges: "I'm dreaming from the waist on down/I'm dreaming but I feel tired and bound/I'm dreaming of the day that a cold shower helps my health/I'm dreaming, dreaming of the day I can control myself, I can control myself, yeah." The song continues with intense com-plaints—"I'm too old to give up but too young to rest"—and concludes: "I'm dreaming, but I know it's all hot air/I'm dreaming, I'll get back to that rocking chair/I'm dreaming, of the day when I can share the wealth/I'm dreaming, dreaming of the day I can control myself." While several of Townshend's metaphors are difficult to unravel, the general thrust of the message leaves little doubt as to the author's point.

After the powerful, self-evident aggression of "Dreaming" the album's pace shifts radically to the soft, reflective sound of "Imagine A Man" and its brief variation on *The Seeker* plot: "Imagine a man/Not a child of any revolt/But a plain man tied up in life/Imagine the sand/Running out as he struts/Parading and fading, ignoring his wife/Imagine a road/So long, looking backwards you can't see where it really began/Imagine a load/So large and so smooth/That against it a man is an ant/And you will see the end/You will see the end." The song con-tinues by asking "imagine events" that "occur every day" ("a shooting, a raping, or a simple act of deceit"), "imagine a fence" ("Around you as high as Pruden-tial/Casting shadows, you can't see your feet"), a girl ("With long flowing hair/And a body of chalky perfection and truth"), and the past ("That you wished you had lived/Full of heroes and villains and fools"). From there, we are again told that "you will see the end" as a preface to the final stanza: "Imagine a man/Not a child of any revolt/But a man of today feeling you/Imagine a soul/So old it is broken/And you know your invention is new/And you will see the end/You will see the end." The track's mixture of images—a "plain man" who ignores his wife and fails to grasp love, dark "daily events," and nostalgia ("the past" that "you wished you had lived")—appears to set up the conclusion: "You will see the end." The song stresses images (a "plain man," a "smooth load," violence, beauty, and a "broken soul") without references to story or character development. We are simply left with the understanding that if you can imagine these things, the "end" is visible. Swenson's (1996) views are helpful: "The lyrics speak to a past too full to remember where it began, and burdens so heavy they make a man feel like an ant, references all relating to the weight Townshend felt he shouldered in The Who. When he started out Townshend knew what he wanted, but here he no longer remembers, longing instead for resolution."

Preceding a closing round of complaint are "They Are All In Love" and "Blue Red and Grey." The album's seventh song, "They Are All In Love," offers an interesting juxtaposition of instrumentation and lyrics. This cut opens with a light, happy piano instrumental with pleasant vocals asking: "Where do you walk on sunny times/When the rivers gleam and the buildings shine/How do you feel when the pollen falls and the summer clothes brighten gloomy halls?" The song's lighthearted tone moves through a piano solo and into the crux of the story's message: "Hey, good bye all you punks, stay young and stay high/Hand me my checkbook, and I'll crawl off to die/Like a woman in childbirth grown ugly in a flash/I've seen magic and pain, now I'm recycling trash." The number closes with the "And they're all in love, they're all in love" chorus. This song appears to represent Townshend's tribute to the new wave musical trend and its more extreme form, punk rock. The number's wistful sound contrasts with its at times biting lyrics and cynical outlook. Charlesworth (1995) concurs, "One of the distinctive aspects of 'Who By Numbers' is that songs of personal anguish are couched in pleasant, almost cheerful melodies" (p. 69). Townshend's lament that he's "recycling trash" suggests his frustrations with The Who's lack of innovation and the growing nostalgia that engulfs the band. Whether that "trash" pertains to the band's performance, instrumentals, or lyrical themes is basically irrelevant. Townshend feels trapped by a situation in which no one endeavors to push his trade. This lack of innovation induces stagnation for the writer and signals a lyrical trend that controls this phase of the oeuvre.

The track "Blue Red and Grey" returns to the singles period writing style in which Townshend uses ambiguous characterizations to camouflage what appears to be a personal statement. He writes:

Some people seem so obsessed with the morning
Get up early just to watch the sun rise
Some people like it more when there's fire in the sky
Worship the sun when it's high

Some people go for those sultry evenings
Sipping cocktails in the blue, red and grey
But I like every minute of the day.
I like every second so long as you are on my mind
Every moment has its special charm, it's all right when you're around rain or shine
I know a crowd who only live after midnight
Their faces always seem so pale
And then there's friends of mine who must have sunlight
They say a sun tan never fails
I know a man who works the night shift
Feels lucky to get a job and some pay
And I like every minute of the day.
I dig every second I can laugh in the snow and rain
I get a buzz from being cold and wet
The pleasure seems to balance out the pain
And so you see that I'm completely crazy
I even shun the south of France
The people on the hill, they say I'm lazy
But when they sleep, I sing and dance.
Some people have to have those sultry evenings, cocktails in the blue, red and grey
But I like every minute of the day
I like every minute of the day.

The number's light, pensive sound (mostly, Townshend on ukulele) conjures images of "Sunrise" and other singles period pieces in which he sings of romantic/spiritual bliss in various contexts. This stylistic trend ends with *By Number*'s "Squeeze Box" and "Blue Red and Grey." Never again will Pete Townshend express himself in such a simplistic, folksy fashion as a member of The Who.

The songs "How Many Friends" and "In A Hand Or A Face" return to the introspective, confessional themes established in "However Much I Booze" and "Slip Kid" to close the record. "How Many Friends" is a straightforward elegy of considerable urgency:

I'm feeling so good right now, as a handsome boy tells me how I changed his past
He buys me a brandy, or could it be he's really just after my ass
He likes the clothes I wear, he says he likes a man who dresses in season
But no one else ever stares, he's being so kind—what's the reason?
How many friends have I really got, you could count 'em on one hand
How many friends have I really got
How many friends have I really got that love me, that want me, that'll take me
    as I am.

The song advances a dark curiosity about romantic relationships ("how do I rate?") and conveys Townshend's distrust ("Then you know that no one will ever speak the truth about you") as a preface to the final complaint:

When I first signed the contract it was more than a handshake then
I know it still is, but there's a plain fact

We talk so much shit behind each others' backs, I get the willies
People know nothing about their own soft gut
So how come they can sum us up without ever suffering all the hype we've known
How come they bum us up
How many friends have I really got, well you can count 'em on your one hand
How many friends have I really got
How many friends have I really got that love me, that want me, that'll take me
   as I am.

Here we observe direct references to music business deceit, media misrepresentations, and Townshend's obsession with lying. Recall that Townshend's complaints about reporters and the lying theme extend as far back as The Who's first album. Those views now expand into one of the dominant themes in "Pete Townshend's Complaint." The point is reinforced by the album's final song, "In A Hand Or A Face"—a simple number that posits the central observation: "Ain't it funny how they fire a pistol/At the wrong end of the race" (a line often cited as a suicide reference). After a dreadful scene depicting a "man" rummaging through "your dustbin" in search of "food" and the narrator's identification with his plight, the song drifts into a constant cycle of "I am going round and round" (with powerful, and seemingly forced, instrumentals: Marsh [1983] and Barnes [1982] both suggest The Who may have been copying its own style).

Townshend's responses to *The Who By Numbers* are mixed. On the one hand, he praises the producer, Glyn Johns: "Glyn worked harder...than I've ever seen him. He had to, not because the tracks were weak or the music poor (though I'll admit it's not a definitive Who album), but because the group was so useless. We played cricket between takes or went to the pub.... I felt detached from my own songs, from the whole record" (Townshend, 1977, p. 58). Townshend "felt empty" about his work, "All the songs were different, some more aggressive than others, but they were all somehow negative in direction." On the other hand, he stated, "the weird thing is that *Who By Numbers* was an extremely effective record in putting across what was in my head at the time and I think to some extent really what was happening to the band at the time" (Schulps, 1978, p. 16). Swenson's (1996) liner notes from the record's reissue may sum up Townshend's writing best when he says: "The songs here are very personal, a looking forward to Townshend's solo songwriting style dealing with the contradictions of becoming an adult while still attempting to live out the rock and roller's lifestyle.... Townshend was enduring a genuine spiritual crisis and working it out through his songwriting."

The music press agreed and focused on Townshend's preoccupation with age as well as the perceived dearth in his songwriting. *Creem*'s Lester Bangs (1975) suggests that although "The Who may be painfully aware of their elder statesmanship" (p. 62) the band has refrained from selling out. After describing Townshend as "a rock *auteur* of supreme discipline," Bangs divides the songwriter's "new compositions" into three "general categories (wimp, rave, world-weariness)" and concludes, "P. T.'s preoccupation with his own aging is by turns eloquent, self-indulgent, and plain syrupy." The *New York Times* concurs: "The Who is not only old; it is obsessed with age—or at least Mr. Townshend, its chief song writer and guru, is so obsessed" (Rockwell, 1975, p. 40). The *Los Angeles Times* review cuts to the crux of the situation: "The album's main problem is its lack of conviction...the band seems undecided about its own stance and, one might speculate, its future.... The frustrations of youth—once the band's chief theme—has been shifted in the main to the frustrations of the artist" (Hilburn, 1975, p. 9). The *Washington Post* contends the album is "more thoughtful and subdued than anything" the band "has ever done," which to the *Post* indicates that "Townshend seems intent on becoming a pop philosopher" (Rohter, 1975, p. E16). *Rolling Stone*'s Dave Marsh (1975) pursues a different approach:

> *The Who By Numbers* isn't what it seems. Without broadcasting it, in fact while denying it, Townshend has written a series of songs which hang together as well as separately. The time is somewhere in the middle of the night, the setting a disheveled room with a TV set that seems to show only rock programs. The protagonist is an aging, still success-ful rock star, staring drunkenly at the tube with a bottle of gin perched on his head, con-templating his career, his love for the music and his fear that it's all slipping away. Every song here, even the one non-Townshend composition...fits in. Always a sort of musical practical joker, Townshend has now pulled the fastest one of all, disguising his best concept album as a mere ten-track throwaway.... But there is an ominous quality even in the midst of the jokes.... As angry as it is desperate, the album moves from song to song on pure bitterness, disillusionment and hopelessness. (pp. 63-65)

Marsh's creative interpretation does appear to capture the author's emotional state. Townshend is a "musical practical joker," and that makes thematic criti-cism of his writings risky business. But *By Numbers* departs from that trend. Townshend is suffering, and the degree to which The Who allows him to "have his head" in creative matters is contributing to his decline. This reached the point that when Moon and Entwistle appeared on the BBC to introduce the new album, they did not know the song titles. Gambaccini (1975) reports that during a show with the BBC's John Peel, Moon admitted that "he had not even heard most of Daltrey's vocals and that the record was as new to him as it was to Peel" (p. 12). When Entwistle appeared the next evening to introduce the album's second side, Gambaccini continues, he said that Townshend had "changed the titles of a couple of tracks...so he wasn't sure of what he was introducing" and that "the songs were so personal to Townshend that nobody else could really discuss them."

The tensions that once surrounded The Who in creative matters had by now vanished. Townshend, much to his chagrin, was granted complete creative control by his colleagues, and the results were predictable. His writing turned from nebulous songs that refused to "hit his audience over the head" with spiri-tual messages toward intense expressions of personal angst that bludgeoned his audience with his anxieties. Townshend's rich characterizations depart in favor of shallow plots that drive home despondent, value-laden tales of distrust and

fear. And "The Who" (the band, Glyn Johns, Bill Curbishley, and the music industry) dutifully reported to the studio and recorded those sentiments.

WHO ARE YOU

With the *Tommy* film playing in theaters around the world and a fresh album
rising on the U.S. and U.K. sales charts, The Who toured in the fall of 1975.
Townshend, having just returned from a trip to the United States in which he
visited a Baba center in South Carolina and a Sufi group in California, was in
much better condition, and apparently, prepared for an extensive tour. The
Who's financial problems with Lambert and Stamp established the need for a
protracted tour; therefore, the band traveled through the United States, Europe,
and England for an extended period of time (Barnes, 1982; Marsh, 1983).
Throughout this long and elaborate tour—featuring lasers, state-of-the-art staging, and a huge entourage—The Who embraced its past by playing large portions of *Tommy* (clearly promoting the film) as well as popular songs from its
singles period and *Who's Next*. These shows also publicized the band's latest
album (especially the single "Squeeze Box"), but *The Who By Numbers* simply
lacked the power audiences associated with the group's performance and its
gloomy outlook did not lend itself to the "celebration" that a Who concert now
represented.

Keith Moon was in no shape for this tour. During a concert in Boston, the
drummer collapsed at the end of the show's *second* song (Barnes, 1982; Marsh,
1983). Later in the tour he severely cut his foot while in the midst of a hotel
auto-destruction routine—a ritual Moon was enacting by himself. The personality Swenson (1974) refers to as "a presence—the closest thing I've ever witnessed to a true Star quality" (p. 53) was changing. That flamboyant character
was in a serious, and extremely dangerous, condition. A tour—with all of its
now legendary antics—was the worst possible prescription for the drummer's
health.

The Who toured into 1976, and individual members pursued their various
solo projects: Daltrey acting and recording another album, Townshend working
with Ronnie Lane on the *Rough Mix* album. In March 1977 Townshend, The
Who, Lambert and Stamp, and Allen Klein (once again) negotiated a settlement
of a long-standing disagreement regarding the band's finances (in particular,
Townshend's U.S. royalties). Armed with a million-dollar check and frustrated
by the whole episode, Townshend and Chris Stamp retired to a Soho pub, where
Townshend got intoxicated (Barnes, 1982; Marsh, 1983). While at the pub,
Townshend saw two musicians that Stamp identified as members of a punk rock
group, the Sex Pistols. Townshend, thinking one of the two must be Johnny
Rotten (the band's front man), seized the moment to praise the punk movement
and condemn The Who. Much to his dismay, the two Sex Pistols—Rotten was
not present—were disappointed by the thought that The Who might disband.
Townshend declared his own disappointment, tore up his check, staggered down
the street, and passed out in a doorway. Later, a policeman awakened him and

offered him a chance to get up and go home. That episode—a definite indicator of Townshend's state of mind—provides a scene in the title song of the next album, *Who Are You*. The real significance of that story lies elsewhere. Townshend was deeply moved, and partially liberated, by the punk rock scene. He articulates his views in an article he prepared for *Rolling Stone*:

I'm sure I invented [punk], and yet it's left me behind. If anything was ever a refutation of time, my constant self-inflicted adolescence must be.... Damage, damage, damage. It's a great way to shake society's value system. It makes mothers drown their children. It makes schoolteachers puke.... The crucifixion is what these people stand for. They humiliate themselves and their peers and care nothing for any accolade. These stars are true stars, they are part of an audience of stars.... I am with them. I want nothing more than to go with them to their desperate hell, because that loneliness they suffer is soon to be over. Deep inside, they know. I prayed for it and yet it's too late for me to truly participate. I feel like an engineer. Just let me...watch. (Townshend, 1977, p. 56)

Here not only does Townshend identify with the punk movement but his description revisits "Bobby" and the *LifeHouse* project. He labels punk rockers as "true stars" that reflect an "audience of stars," and he admires their commitment to their craft (they "care nothing for any accolade"). In addition, punk audiences—like Who audiences of yesteryear—WORKED during shows and enacted the audience-performer reciprocity Townshend idolizes. Little doubt, Townshend *prayed* for the punk movement and its challenge to the nostalgic rock music industry that he so deeply abhorred. When that "prayer" was answered, Townshend's infamous burden—his responsibility to push rock—was lightened considerably.

With the punk explosion invigorating the music scene and liberating Townshend from his perceived duties, he was now prepared to address his own situation. The following sources outline Townshend's anxieties over Who concerts, touring, his domestic life, and his spiritual fears as they relate to his art. The lengthy tours from 1975 through 1976 no doubt contributed to Townshend's road anxieties, a point he expressed to Dave Schulps (1978):

All that seemed to work was a couple of the old singles, the stuff from *Tommy*, a few rock 'n' roll numbers and finish. That was the act we went out and did again and again and again. That was the act that we were acclaimed for. That was the list. And really it wasn't a list, it wasn't a act, it wasn't a group, it wasn't anything. It was a fuckin' celebration of our history. I'm fed up of doing it.... I don't think there's anything as exciting as going into "My Generation" and seeing people go crazy, but after awhile it's automatic, it's like being the Queen. People wave and shout just because you're there, they don't really care what you're doing...to actually go and hawk your body on the road for six weeks at a stretch twice a year in the USA, I don't think it really gets the right results anymore. (p. 16)

Complementing Townshend's attitude toward The Who's celebratory concerts and the mindless obligation to "do the list" was his growing concern for his family. In a *Los Angeles Times* interview, Townshend elaborated on his new-found professional orientation and its implications for The Who:

What I've done is slightly shift my priorities. I've put my family first and the band sec-ond. Up to now, I put the band first. The new arrangement makes life more difficult in terms of the group, but I feel the priorities are in order for the first time. What happened was my family life was damaged by all those years of touring. I've had to work hard at rebuilding it. I don't think I could do anything again to threaten that relationship, I don't think I could carry on if the band decided to resume extensive touring.... When I re-turned home [after the 1976 tour], I realized [that] over a period of 10 years I had com-pletely destroyed the relationship I had with my wife. She was feeling very little for me, very little sympathy because I had used it all up. I suddenly realized how much I needed her and the stability of a home. I had never felt that before. I always felt pretty much a free wheel. So, I've spent the last three years in a very formal, family existence. I work pretty much Monday to Friday in an office, writing songs or working on film projects. (Hilburn, 1978, p. 70)

Townshend's renewed dedication to his family was reinforced by his spiritual observations. He describes his "spiritual crisis" for *Rolling Stone*:

When you hold out an empty cup to God and demand that He fill it with wine, He fills it faster than you can ever drink. Then you know that the fault is your own incapacity to receive His infinite love, rather than His capacity to give it. I loosely quote Hafiz here, of course, but this is what I felt was happening.... My crisis was simply that I felt I was failing rock & roll. And for me this was a crime. For in doing this, I was failing friends and family, history, the future, and most important of all, I was failing God. No one less could have invented this sublime music. (Townshend, 1977, p. 59)

This was Townshend's evolving version of the minstrel's dilemma (we return to the "empty glass" analogy in Chapter Five). The mindless obligation of concert tours, his aspirations for his family, and his commitment to his art created artis-tic tensions that were gradually overwhelming the songwriter. The "punk ex-plosion" may have soothed his fears about his creative responsibilities; however, The Who's commercial machine still demanded attention, and Townshend seri-ously questioned his capacity to respond.

   That financial enterprise grew even more diversified in 1977. Sources indi-cate that The Who did virtually nothing together in 1977 for the first time in over a decade (not even a Christmas album). Everyone worked on individual projects (Entwistle writing a science fiction piece, Daltrey recording another solo album, Moon deteriorating, wherever), while the business invested its re-sources. The Who purchased the Shepperton Film Studios, signed nineteen-year-old American Who fan Jeff Stein to produce a documentary film about the band's history, negotiated the *Quadrophenia* film rights and hired Franc Rod-dam as the director, and remarkably, contemplated reviving the *LifeHouse* proj-ect. When asked about the band's future, Townshend replied: "It would be easy pickings to stick out an album which would sell a couple of million dollars in the States and then we'd bring the money into Britain through some tax dodge. I prefer to make a film, even though me hair fell out when we did the last one" (Mills, 1978, p. 28). When these projects are joined with Townshend's rapidly deteriorating hearing, Moon's disability, and Daltrey's film commitments, they signal the end of Who tours.

In December 1977 Townshend assembled enough demo tapes to warrant The Who's return to the studio. (In fact, Resnicoff [1996] describes Townshend's *Who Are You* demos as "extraordinary" in quality, often "so developed" as to require little input from others.) Glyn Johns's stellar performance during the *By Numbers* recording sessions was surpassed by an even stronger effort in the *Who Are You* sessions. By now, The Who was a difficult band to record. Early in the sessions Entwistle, Moon, and Townshend ignored the studio technicians and simply drank the day away; as a result, Johns left the studio in disgust and Daltrey did not bother to appear. These delays were exacerbated by two injuries: Townshend—attempting to break up an argument between his parents—broke a window and ground his right hand in the shattered glass, making guitar playing impossible, and John "Rabbit" Bundrick (a studio musician and future band member) broke his arm (Marsh, 1983). Johns was also struggling with Moon and Daltrey. Moon's drumming was in shambles; Daltrey and Entwistle were ready to kick him out of the band. With Johns and Townshend's help, Moon recovered to the point of completing the album, although several songs have limited drum work. Johns also had a serious disagreement with Daltrey (which resulted in violence). As we observed in *By Numbers*, The Who had a tendency to copy itself, and Johns worked to move the band away from its old style and into new directions. The tensions between a band resting on its laurels and a producer pushing for new sounds were the dominating characteristics of the *Who Are You* sessions. The sessions took so long that Johns eventually left and turned the project over to his associate Jon Astley (Townshend's brother-in-law).

Who Are You was released in August 1978. The album (running 42:21) contains nine compositions (six by Townshend, three by Entwistle). The Townshend songs—"New Song," "Sister Disco," "Music Must Change," "Guitar and Pen," "Love Is Coming Down," and "Who Are You"—place new spins on the unfolding "Pete Townshend's Complaint" story. The Entwistle numbers—"Had Enough," "905," and "Trick Of The Light"—also involve tales of complaint ("Had Enough") and insecurity ("Trick Of The Light"). The song "905" is a clever version of Entwistle's science fiction story about cloning that depicts the anxieties "test tube" babies face in their programmable worlds.

The Townshend compositions advance the "Complaint" by shifting its context from an "individual" to an "industry." Townshend continues his move away from ambiguous stories that stress detailed characterizations toward direct expressions about the music scene, and to a lesser extent, his relationships. Whereas songs such as "Sister Disco" and "Who Are You" feature the author's penchant for skirting around the subject in idiosyncratic ways, the bulk of the work is a straightforward complaint of one form or another. The search for "manhood" initiated in *By Numbers'* "Imagine A Man" is virtually absent.

There is one song of hope, "Guitar and Pen," where we are told to hang in there, never "spend your guitar and your pen," and believe in your work. The song is literally a songwriter's anthem, presented through Townshend's signature instrumental style.

The album opens with Townshend's attack on the music business. The writer's relief over punk rock's emergence did not preclude an attack on the "old guard" and its tendency to recycle the same material over and over. "New Song" wastes little time getting to Townshend's point:

> You need a new song
> I set the words up
> So they tear right at your soul
> Don't take me too long
> But there's a danger
> That I'll plagiarize something old
> My fingers kill me as I play my guitar
> Cos I've been chewing down at my nails
> My hairline ain't exactly superstar
> But there's one thing that never fails
> It never fails
> I write the same old songs
> With a few new lines
> Everybody wants to cheer it
> I write the same old songs
> You've heard a few few times
> Admit you really want to hear it.

Townshend's argument is without mystery: he recasts the same material time after time and "everybody" wants more. Apparently, he views the problem as a breakdown in performer-audience communication ("Whenever I see you/You always treat me like I'm some/Kind of perfect man/Just cos I feed you/You explain but you don't think/I can understand") that is aggravated by his lifestyle ("My head is spinning as I scroll with my pen/Cos I've been pouring vodka in my soul"). Townshend summarizes the situation by way of a revealing metaphor ("We took the same old wine from a brand new jar/We get hung over but we always survive it") prior to ending with the refrain, "We sing the same old song." (Sure enough, Townshend uses a line from *Quadrophenia*—"Let it rain, let it rain, let it rain"—as a segue into a standard instrumental thereby demonstrating his point. Or, as Resnicoff [1996] observes, "One theme that may have been made redundant through repetition was, oddly, a recurrent motif about the artist's temptation to be repetitious.")

From this opening statement, we move to Townshend's answer: the "Music Must Change." The song begins: "Deep in the back of my mind is an unrealized sound/Every feeling I get from the streets says it soon could be found/When I hear the cold lines of the pusher/I know it exists/It's confirmed in the eyes of the kids emphasized with their fists." Here Townshend revisits his belief in an as yet "unrealized sound" and its relationship to adolescence. His inability to achieve musical aspirations such as the *LifeHouse* experiment joins the industry's tendency to recycle material to add urgency to his complaint. This "unrealized sound" that exists "in the back" of the narrator's "mind" must be brought forward: "The music must change/For we're chewing a bone/We soared like the sparrow hawk flies/Then we dropped like a stone/Like the tide and the waves/Growing slowly in rage/Crushing mountains as old as the earth/ So the music must change." Notice Townshend's reference to his career's ebb and flow as "we soared" to new heights only to "drop like a stone" and, through that failure, induced a "rage." After raising the need to "change" the music, the narrator's insecurities remain: "But is this song different/Am I doing it all again/It may have been done before/But music's an open door." This is the one aspect of Townshend's dilemma that never fades completely. The commitment to artistic progress is ever-present, only its intensity varies.

"Sister Disco" appears to be a denunciation of "club life" and its "tramps" although Marsh (1983) and Charlesworth (1995) contend the song has nothing to do with "disco" but addresses Townshend's sentiments about audiences. Maybe so; the lyrics are evasive. The character's "dancing" (this could be anything, even though Townshend occasionally uses "dancing" as a metaphor for "lifestyle"—as per *Quadrophenia*) has left "sister disco" behind, thus, s/he now goes "where the music fits my soul" (in this case the "dancing-lifestyle" metaphor works). Townshend's character insists on staying "beside you" and comforting "your soul/When you are lonely and broken and old" although we never really know what/who "you" represents (the music? the audience? Karen Townshend?). The song seems to evoke images of *Tommy* in the chorus—"Goodbye sister disco/My dancing left you behind/Now you're going solo/Black plastic deaf, dumb and blind"—which could reinforce Marsh's point that Townshend is complaining about the audience. Equally possible is a deliberate attempt to recycle lyrics as part of the "Music Must Change" theme (the lines could also be gibberish). The writer's impressionism now deploys a metaphorical mischief that is difficult to unpack without imposing order on the song's intentional chaos.

Portions of "Who Are You" contain vague references to a source of unconditional love as well. The track opens with a synthesizer segment from the *LifeHouse* experiment, the aforementioned Sex Pistols story, and turns to the unconditional love question. The song begins with the "Who are you? (who who who who)" chorus repeated several times and continues:

> I woke up in a Soho doorway
> A policeman knew my name
> He said "you can go sleep at home tonight
> If you can get up and walk away"
> I staggered back to the underground
> And the breeze blew back my hair
> I remember throwin' punches around

And preachin' from my chair.
[chorus]Well, who are you?
      Who are are you? (who who who who)
      I really wanna know
      Who are you? (who who who who)
      Tell me who are you
      Who are you? (who who who who)
      Cuz I really wanna know
      Who are you? (who who who who)
I took the tube back out of town
Back to the rollin' pin
I felt a little like a dying clown
With a streak of Rin Tin Tin
I stretched back and I hiccuped
And looked back on my busy day
Eleven hours in the tin pan
God there's got to be another way
[chorus, long synthesizer segment, more chorus]
I know there's a place you walked
Where love falls from the trees
My heart is like a broken cup
I only feel right on my knees
I spill out like a sewer hole
Yet still receive your kiss
How can I measure up to anyone now
After such a love as this?
[extended chorus]

The lyrics are quintessential Townshend. They could involve a spiritual sentiment (especially the comments about "broken cups" and praying), a statement
about Townshend's marriage or children, or refer to the "audience's" undying
loyalty. In either case, the character merely "spills" out sewage and gains love
in return. The song's confessional tone extends the "Complaint's" thematic
qualities even though we are uncertain as to its narrative context(s).

"Love Is Coming Down" is a more direct statement in which the central
character appears to have had "four chances" with "love" and achieved varying
levels of failure. Consequently, the song begs the question: "I'm not a loser,
but did I really win/Can I afford to go through it all again/I hope I don't sound
as immature as I feel/But when I get wise I'll give you a call my friend."
"Love" (this could, after all, be anything) is not working for this individual;
thus, after the "fourth chance" the character proclaims: "I'm standing on the
ledge/Now I'm going down." "Love Is Coming Down" echoes *The Who By
Numbers* with its dark, defeatist imagery.

Between complaints about music and struggling relationships, we witness
the album's lone ray of hope. "Guitar and Pen" is an unequivocal statement
about the writing impulse and the value of perseverance. (Diperna [1994] observes that "Guitar and Pen" and "Music Must Change" also offer evidence of

Townshend's emerging "show tune" writing style—p. 54.) The song declares: "You can walk/You can talk/You can hide but inside you have something to write/In your hand you hold your only friend/Never spend your guitar or your pen." The songwriter's hymn proclaims:

> When you take up a pencil and sharpen it up
> When your kicking the fence and still nothing will budge
> When words are immobile until you sit down
> Never feel they're worth keeping, not easily found
> Then you know in some strange unexplainable way
> You must really have something, jumping, bumping
> Fighting, hiding away, important to say.

Townshend encourages perseverance. It may take years to get past bad rhymes, and you may play your guitar until your fingers bleed; nonetheless, you must push on. The song declares: "When you wanna complain/There's no one can stop you/But when your music proclaims there is no one can top you/You are wearing your heart on your dancing feet/Without a head start away from the street/But is that what you want/To be rich and be gone/Could be there's just one thing left in the end/Your guitar and your pen." The message is forthright: a "new song" may be risky, hurtful, and financially dangerous, but there is no alternative.

   Who Are You is a mixture of themes. It revisits the introspective images of *By Numbers* ("Love Is Coming Down" and "Who Are You"), reconsiders the deep-seated concerns over musical direction and the need for change that "Bobby" introduced in *LifeHouse* ("New Song," "Music Must Change," and perhaps, "Sister Disco"), and returns to the anthem format that extends from "My Generation" to "Won't Get Fooled Again," via "Guitar and Pen." "Pete Townshend's Complaint" focuses squarely on the music business, as he declares the need for innovation and the means through which that change may be achieved. That is, "never spend your guitar or your pen," because that is the only way the music will change—and the music *must* change. If one takes the "Who Are You" stanza regarding the capacity to "measure up" to such a "love as this" as addressing the audience, the songwriter's drive is nothing less than a moral responsibility.

   The critics' responses to *Who Are You* seem to vary in their degree of negativity. Robbins (1978) compares 1975's *The Who By Numbers* and *Who Are You*: "*Who By Numbers* was a total success as a musical and personal statement. It seemed that the Who had a second wind, that all the old venom was there, and was redirected to new targets. Three years later, the Who now seem to consider themselves tired and old. And *Who Are You* is a tired and old album, one that scarcely does them justice" (p. 69). In concurrence, the *San Francisco Chronicle* reports the album is "a jumbled, frantic and tortured album that would be pedestrian coming from any rock band, let alone the Who" and that Townshend "appears bogged down explaining his current inability to keep in step with swiftly changing musical times" (Selvin, 1978, p. 49). Two critics turned to sports analogies to convey their disappointment. *Creem* opens with the author's recollection of his childhood hero, baseball player Willie Mays, and the outfielder's poor performance in a World Series game: Mays "simply had gotten too old to play the game" (Altman, 1978, p. 56). The *Los Angeles Times* concurs: "Like an old quarterback whose knees just aren't the same, the Who can claim our respect merely for a game effort and for occasionally exceeding dimmed expectations" (Cromelin, 1978, p. 70). Yet Greil Marcus (1978) remains optimistic in his *Rolling Stone* review: "Pete Townshend recognizes the fact that, after a decade which seemed happy with its own dead end, bands like the Clash have broken through limits he had half-accepted. In this case, the child really is father to the man, and that means the chance to start all over again is at Townshend's finger tips" (p. 86).

All of these reviews share a common observation: The Who has grown weary, and it shows. The band's instrumental fire dissipated in direct relation to Moon's demise. Without Moon's chaotic (and original) drum work, the band lost its edge, settled into predictable patterns of instrumental and vocal performances (which Glyn Johns did his best to disrupt), and Townshend's pen chronicled the story. Instead of writing anthems that address generational, relational, or societal frustrations, Townshend now focused on *his* plight. The songwriter lost sight of his audience and, hence, his source of inspiration. Rock audiences no longer came to *experience* rock but to *observe*, and maybe celebrate, the art form. With the advent of punk rock, Townshend witnessed an audience revival; just the same, that reborn audience was not his. There may be hope for "rock" in the punk genre, but Pete Townshend still had to stand consistently before an audience that did not share his commitment and that obligation took its toll on the idealistic songwriter.

Townshend's remarks to Schulps (1978) in April 1978 capture his views regarding "the state of the Who" at that point in time: "We've been very lucky. Very, very lucky. And we're lucky to be together today, to be the same four blokes we always were. Because when you've known and worked with four people for 15 years, in the end you've got a power no one else can get unless they wait 15 years" (p. 35). That "luck" changed later that year. In early August of 1978 (sources disagree on the date), Pete Meaden committed suicide. On September 7, 1978 Keith Moon died. The previous evening Moon had attended a screening of *The Buddy Holly Story* hosted by Paul McCartney. Moon, accompanied by his fiancee Annette Walter-Lax, was reportedly in good shape. Yet upon returning home after the party he consumed a large amount of a prescribed anti-alcoholism medication and died in his sleep. Barnes (1982) and Marsh (1983) describe the situation in detail. The Who ended that morning, and "change" would, indeed, be at Townshend's "finger tips." But he would be slow in embracing that change. Townshend's "struggle" was far from over, The Who "changed," and for Pete Townshend that prescription would treat only the symptoms, not the disease. Several years later, Townshend described Moon's death in this manner: "It's amazing in a way how things have turned out. Keith died at a time when the Who really were finished.... We were at the end of an era about something else. We were about struggle and we stopped struggling" (Hilburn, 1982a). After a brief period of deliberation, The Who decided to continue, hired Kenney Jones to replace Moon (Jones worked on both the *Tommy* and *Quadrophenia* soundtracks), and added John Bundrick on keyboards.

All the while The Who contemplated its post-Moon future, the various film projects continued and, when joined with their soundtracks, assured The Who's commercial prosperity. The band re-formed and made its first public appearance on May 2, 1979, at London's Rainbow theater. On May 12 and 13, the New Who appeared at the 1979 Cannes Film Festival as part of the publicity associated with the two films' releases. The *New York Times* film critic, Janet Maslin, wrote mixed reviews of the two movies. Maslin (1979a) maintains director Jeff Stein missed the opportunity to tell The Who's story in *The Kids Are Alright* by focusing exclusively on the band's fans: "And even they may find this film chaotic, uneven and liable to raise questions rather than answer any.... [Stein] needed the structure of a novel to tell the Who's story; what he has come up with is barely an anthology" (p. 16). Stein had allegedly obtained treasured film clips of the band and failed to return them which once more created animosity within the group toward an associate. Maslin's (1979b) review of the *Quadrophenia* film is more generous: "This is a dramatic film, one that's gritty and ragged and sometimes quite beautiful. It happens to incorporate rock songs, and to be saddled with a silly title. Though it's by no means a movie for everyone, 'Quadrophenia' is something very special. It demands—and deserves—some special allowances" (p. 8). Apparently, Townshend made "special allowances" to Franc Roddam when the director elevated the story's violence. Townshend's original version featured Jimmy's mental images of intense violence while Roddam highlighted the "blood and guts and thunder" in order, as Townshend surmised, to "make good cinema" (Marcus, 1980, p. 412). Once more Townshend was willing to grant creative freedom in cinematic adaptations of his work.

Reactions to the two soundtracks are mixed as well. Swenson (1979) describes the changes in the *Quadrophenia* soundtrack: dropped from the original were "Sea and Sand" and "Drowned"; added were three Townshend compositions—"Get Out and Stay Out," "Four Faces," and "Joker James"—and a series of songs that Swenson terms "period tunes" (p. 70) by James Brown, the Kingsmen, and others. Greil Marcus (1979) considers the *Kids* soundtrack to be "a solid retrospective" that "lacks only excitement and surprise" (p. 57). The two films/soundtracks, a Mod revival in Britain, and curiosity about the new band certainly revived The Who's commercial operation. The question now was: how would the band respond? Just prior to the New Who's debut in America, Townshend elaborated on the post-Moon situation and his newfound attitude: "I can see more clearly now. I care more about the people on stage with me, and I don't have as many illusions about the fans. I used to think we couldn't let our fans down, that we were an important part of their lives. Now I know that about 10 percent really do care about us as people, that 25 percent are just street rats, and the rest are music lovers" (Rockwell, 1979a, p. 24). Such sentiments leave little doubt that Townshend had adjusted one of his most valued ideals. Now that the songwriter had modified his perspective about Who audiences, he was able to overcome his views regarding the pointless nature of a Who performance. Now, Townshend assured us, he cares more about his colleagues on stage, yet those "people on stage" had rarely been a source of inspiration for Townshend's pen, and his belief in them would not sustain his art.

The Who's U.S. debut involved a five-night stay at New York's Madison Square Garden. Prior to that opening, the band rehearsed in New Jersey in a 3,200-seat theater and unveiled the new band that featured Jones, Bundrick, and "three wind and brass backup instrumentalists" (Rockwell, 1979b, p. 22). Palmer (1979) writes the initial Garden show was "a splendid rock-and-roll concert that carefully balanced innovation and tradition" (p. 71). That balance of "innovation and tradition" would be the key to the new band's success. The Who's first U.S. tour without Keith Moon witnessed perhaps the greatest rock disaster to that point in time. Prior to a concert at Cincinnati's Riverfront Coliseum on December 3, 1979, eleven people were killed while attempting to enter the facility. Flippo's (1991) account of the incident is rich in detail; he outlines the poor security procedures that accompanied the concert's festival seating plan (first come, first served). The Coliseum had too few doors open, too few ticket takers, too few security officers, and too many warnings of potential trouble to make the tragedy comprehensible. (See Barnes [1982] for an insightful account from the band's perspective; he was traveling with The Who at the time.) Curbishley decided to go on with the show (fearing a riot if it were canceled) and withheld information from the band until after the encore. The Who was devastated. The band continued the tour (although several cities attempted to cancel shows), and the legal fallout from the disaster was considerable. The rest of the tour went reasonably well: Jones and the new members handled the pressure professionally, the band tried innovative promotions such as a simulcast to remote movie theaters in Chicago (with varying degrees of success), and The Who's financial enterprise no doubt profited greatly. Daltrey was optimistic in an interview with *People* magazine in which he suggested the band would tour for four more years and, "when the energy isn't there onstage, the records will go on" (Hauptfuhrer, 1980, p. 102). With such sentiments in mind, it was now time for the New Who to enter the studio.

FACE DANCES

The Who—with a new label, Warner Brothers, and a new producer, Bill Szymczyk—set about the task of recording a new album in its traditional fashion: Townshend prepared demos of songs for the band's consideration and adoption. This time Townshend received no feedback whatsoever: "I went and wrote four songs while everybody else was resting. When I played them nobody said anything, not a dicky bird. Eventually Rabbit said, 'I like such and such a song, that has some good bits in it.' He was trying to be positive because he was aware of this big pregnant silence. I just picked the tape up and walked out" (Barnes, 1982, p. 147). Without Kit Lambert "who acted like a buffer between [Townshend] and the band" (Barnes, p. 147), Townshend had to shoulder the bulk of the creative responsibilities without collaboration—much to his chagrin.

Face Dances contains nine tracks (running 38:59) with seven Townshend compositions and two Entwistle songs. The Entwistle numbers—"The Quiet One" and "You"—assume a serious autobiographical stance as the bassist writes about himself ("The Quiet One") and, one presumes, a failed romance (the very bitter "You"). Townshend's seven songs extend the "Pete Townshend's Complaint" plot in still another direction. Four of the tracks ("You Better You Bet," "Did You Steal My Money," "How Can You Do It Alone," and "Another Tricky Day") move from questions about self-worth (*By Numbers*) and the music industry (*Who Are You*) to interpersonal confrontations. The complaint remains, albeit in a more confrontational tone. The album's seventh track, "Daily Records," revisits the music business anxieties of the previous album and the numbers "Don't Let Go The Coat" and "Cache Cache" slip in stories of hope. The "search" that turned toward worldly matters with *By Numbers*' "Imagine A Man" returns from its brief respite and encourages us to, once more, persevere. I begin with Townshend's "interpersonal angst" and his confrontational response.

This edition of "Pete Townshend's Complaint" is an interesting mixture of direct complaint and nebulous story structure. The songs' grievances are straightforward and repeated in the chorus: did you steal from me, this is not some crisis but you having fun, and you respond to my expressions of love with "you better or else." After establishing the complaint, Townshend deploys a host of impressions that are difficult to fathom—he drives his complaint home through repetition, but leaves the details in doubt. For instance, "Did You Steal My Money" poses a direct question—"Did you steal it/Did you screw me/Did you peel it/Did you do me/Did you steal my money"—surrounded by a series of loose statements. Townshend writes: "Are you out there Mr. No-one/Is my investment growing/Sorry that I got so drunk/But I wrote you a poem/Did you search me/Did you turn me over/While I cold turkeyed/On the sofa/Did you steal my money." The song lightly reiterates the title throughout (voices whispering, "did you steal my money") and jumps in and out of vague scenes about a "veteran," a "trainer football," and a "female foot fall" as it advances the question: "Did you use me/Why did I trust you/Why'd you abuse me/I ain't going to bust you (no, no)." The grievance *is* the message, and the ambiguous scenes provide loose contexts for its expression. (No doubt this is personal stuff. When we consider Townshend's business dealings as well as the many Who-related financial debacles, there is no telling what he's working through.) "Another Tricky Day" also follows this impressionistic pattern:

You can't always get it
When you really want it

You can't always get it at all
Just because there's space
In your life it's a waste
To spend your time why don't you wait for the call
(Just gotta get used to it)
We all get it in the end
(Just gotta get used to it)
We go down and come up again
(Just gotta get used to it)
You irritate me my friend
(This is no social crisis)

The complaint—"You irritate me my friend/(This is no social crisis)/This is you having fun/(No crisis)/Getting burned by the sun/(This is true)/This is no social crisis/Just another tricky day for you"—is the song's focus with a series of phrases providing cloudy contexts. The song then turns to a specific point:

Another tricky day
Another gently nagging pain
What the papers say
Just seems to bring down heavier rain
The world seems in a spiral
Life seems such a worthless title
But break out and start a fire ya'll
It's all here on the vinyl.

From that rather pointed statement the song returns to the "this is you having fun/(No crisis)" cycle. I suspect Townshend is once again responding to the music press and its capacity to "have fun" at the artist's expense. "What the papers say" just induces depression; however, the truth exists "on the vinyl" for all to hear (shades of "However Much I Booze"). Townshend is complaining about deception and confronting the situation, albeit on his terms.

In "You Better You Bet" Townshend writes about what appears to be a demanding relationship. An opening chorus ("You better you better you bet") sets the pace:

I call you on the telephone my voice too rough from cigarettes
I sometimes feel I should just go home but I'm dealing with a memory that
    never forgets
I love to hear you say my name especially when you say yes
I got your body right now on my mind and I drunk myself blind to the sounds
    of old T-Rex
To the sound of old T-Rex—who's next?

The complaint is basically lighthearted and playful: "When I say I love you you say you better/You better you better you bet/When I say I need you you say you better/You better you better you bet/You better bet your life/Or love will cut you like a knife." The song admits "I don't really mind how much you love me/A little really is alright" and refers to the character's sartorial weaknesses ("I look pretty crappy sometimes") and physical prowess ("I still sing a razor line every time"). Again, it is difficult to discern if "you" represents the audience, Karen Townshend or something/someone else (characterological ambiguity, once again). Regardless, the point is never in doubt: the failure to meet "love's" obligations will "cut you like a knife."

While these songs advance the "Pete Townshend's Complaint" story line in a new direction; they do not reflect the dark, ominous tones of the two previous albums. Townshend is confrontational as he moves beyond wondering "how many friends do I really have" to the direct attack, "did you steal my money." The wistful resignation of "They Are All In Love" is replaced by the realization that "this is no social crisis, this is you having fun." Townshend's engagement extends to the music industry in "Daily Records," where he discusses his life in relation to his job:

This could be suffering
This could be pleasure
I'm unaware of any difference
My head is aging
My balls are aching
But I'm not looking for deliverance
This could be letting on
This could be highly cut
I'm unaware of any difference
One says it can't be done,
Then some one does it but
I am not looking for equivalents
I just don't quite know how to wear my hair no more
No sooner cut it than they cut it even more
Got to admit that I created private worlds
Cold sex and booze don't impress my little girls
Daily records
Just want to be making daily records
Try to avoid the bad news in the letters
Just wanna be making records
Play in—play out—fade in—fade out.

The song turns even more personal: "And they say it's just a stage in life/But I know by now the problem is a stage/And they say just take your time and it'll go away/But I know by now I know I'm never never gonna change." Here Townshend merges the drudgery of recording, his anxieties about "the stage," the negative response to his recent work (the "bad news in the letters"), his concern for his children ("cold sex and booze don't impress my little girls"), and his constant attention to fashion into one HUGE complaint. "Just wanna keep making daily records," he writes, "Can't exist no more in chains and fetters.... Just wanna be making daily records."

Face Dances features two songs of "hope" that appear early in the album. "Don't Let Go The Coat" (the album's second track) paraphrases Meher Baba's instruction "hang fast to the hem of my robe" (Marsh, 1983, p. 520), and "Cache Cache" (the third track) urges temperance in the face of uncertainty. This arrangement ("hope" before "confrontation") evokes a brief spiritual commitment theme as a preface to the interpersonal complaints. "Don't Let Go The Coat" speaks to the need for spiritual companionship; the character has "lost all contact with my only savior" and acknowledges "I can't bear to live forever like a loner." In typical Townshend style, the song's cryptic characterizations address a range of potential subjects (romance? the audience?) as the songwriter engages "you" about his anxieties: "It's easy to be sad when you lack a partner/But how would I react to a broken heart now/It ain't really true rock and roll unless I'm/Hanging onto you and when I hold it next time/I won't let go the coat." "Every lonely wife knows the way I feel," the character announces prior to a vow to persevere: "Your friends all pass for life is just a market/But you have to finish everything you started/So I live my life tearing down the runway/Sure to get the hang of hanging in there someday." The prescription "don't let go the coat" gains support through "Cache Cache" in which Townshend describes a series of dark, threatening scenes and concludes, "don't worry" because "there ain't no bears in there." The song asks "Did you ever lay on ice and grit," "Did you ever dream of a suicide pill," and "Did you ever pass the police at work/And hope they might take you in" as a preface to the realization:

> Don't jump in expectin' fun
> Don't swagger in there with an elephant gun
> Don't enter the cage wavin' chairs
> Cos I'll tell you something for nothing
> There ain't no bears in there (cache cache)
> Not a single bear in there (cache cache).

Although Charlesworth (1995) asserts "even with a lyric sheet" (p. 87) "Cache Cache" is "difficult to comprehend," these two tracks work in harmony to communicate the significance of spiritual attachment in an uncertain world. Things may be awful and threatening, these songs suggest, but there is nothing to fear. Still, Townshend warns against histrionics even if there "ain't no bears in there." "Don't Let Go The Coat" and "Cache Cache" are unique in this portion of the oeuvre that dismisses spiritual reflection in favor of worldly complaint.

Face Dances is an interesting mixture of introspection, anxiety, and hope. A new band with a new record label and a new producer rendered a new album that aggressively confronts old problems with an old attitude. That attitude— "don't give up and submit to your fears because everything's not as bad as it seems"—is the central point. Music critics share this observation as well. *Rolling Stone* opines: "As an album, *Face Dances* neither triumphs nor fails. Instead, it makes you wonder if the Who, without social—i.e., internal—crises, have any reason for being" (Nelson, 1981, p. 91). Selvin (1981) writes the album is "by no means...a piece done on the monumental scale of past works" but it is "rich, rewarding and powerful rock music by masters of the craft" (p. 19). That *San Francisco Chronicle* review concurs that *Face Dances* "hinges on" the four songs of complaint ("You Better You Bet," "Did You Steal My Money," "How Can You Do It Alone," and "Another Tricky Day") that, according to Selvin, "frame the entire album and seem to sum up Townshend's current concerns." Finally, the *Washington Post* maintains: "Pete Townshend has consistently set himself up as a mature spokesman, and it becomes rather tiresome. Perhaps this is a problem inherent in all long-term rock bands—running out of ideas, and thus, becoming too self referential" (Hull, 1981, p. B4). As these reviews suggest, the longer The Who continues as the mouthpiece for Townshend's pen, the more cynical and abusive the music press becomes.

Townshend's pen merely evoked his state of mind. The change that was once at his "finger tips" remained beyond his grasp. Shifting producers, musicians, and record labels were merely superficial adjustments that ignored the real problem. For insight into Townshend's state of mind at this crucial juncture, I turn to his Ealing roommate, Richard Barnes:

Pete got stranger and stranger, dropped his friends, had gone in for a succession of unflattering haircuts, taken to wearing makeup...and was "generally weird."... Talking about his degeneration became an almost full-time activity among Pete's associates and close friends. They were relieved when at one stage he was persuaded to take a couple of months rest. He stayed at his riverside country house alone, did some gardening and rowing, wrote some short stories, moderated his drinking, and completely cut out drugs. But after three weeks he was back, coked up to the eyeballs, twitching and shaking, and surrounded by the same old sycophants from the chic "living dead" of clubland. After one late night at a club his driver couldn't find him and assumed he'd returned in a cab. Pete was, in fact, fast asleep on top of a pile of old rubble and bricks in a builder's skip in the next street. Earlier that year he'd walked out of the Who tour in Austria and was discovered sleeping in the bear pit of the local zoo. (Barnes, 1982, p. 147)

(This last episode supposedly inspired "Cache Cache.") Barnes recalls that Townshend often flew to New York "only to spend most of his time sleeping in some hotel suite," and he cites a series of unsavory scenes (Townshend passing out in Mick Jagger's closet, vomiting in an ice bucket at an exclusive Paris hotel). Townshend's negative state of mind was enhanced by Kit Lambert's death in April 1981. Marsh (1983) relates that Chris Stamp attempted to have Lambert hospitalized for treatment of his various addictions, but to no avail. Lambert reportedly died from a fall down the stairs of his mother's home (with whom he was living at the time). And, according to Barnes, "Exactly two years and a day after Keith had died, Pete almost joined him." Townshend had been drinking at London's "Club for Heroes" when he drunkenly accepted heroin. Had it not been for his driver's decision to take him to a hospital, Townshend surely would have died that night. Barnes claims the incident "obviously shook" Townshend and that he attended a clinic for his alcoholism and, eventually, traveled to California for his treatment with Meg Patterson.

Meanwhile, The Who was once again in a state of internal turmoil. Daltrey was unhappy with Kenney Jones's drumming. Moreover, Daltrey and Townshend experienced performance lapses during a 1981 British tour. Manager Bill Curbishley called a meeting to decide the band's future. After several meetings the band agreed to record two more albums, conduct a tour of the United States in the summer of 1982, and then disband (Barnes, 1982). Townshend departed for California (and Meg Patterson) and afterward moved back in with his family as he resolved the intense financial problems mentioned in Chapter One (in 1997 Townshend reports that his various business ventures were sold for a profit). These were demanding times for the auteur; something had to give.

IT'S HARD

During his stay in California, the remaining band members worked on material for the new album since they felt Townshend's songs on *Face Dances* were too personal (Barnes, 1982). When the songwriter returned he asked what the group wanted to record, as he told Barnes: "I sat around with everybody and asked them, what do you want to fucking sing about? Tell me and I'll write the songs. It's a piece of piss! I've been writing songs for twenty years. D'you wanna sing about race riots? D'you wanna sing about the nuclear bomb? D'you wanna sing about Soya bean diets? Tell me!" (p. 148). After deciding they shared concerns about the planet, atomic weapons, and English politics, Townshend wrote the songs and Glyn Johns recorded them quite quickly (the whole process—including mixing—required approximately thirty days—very fast for contemporary Who sessions). The results were entitled *It's Hard*.

It's Hard contains twelve songs (running 47:29), nine by Townshend, three by Entwistle. The Entwistle numbers are dark, seemingly autobiographical songs about the complicated nature of life "up here on the ledge" (rock stardom) and passing the mantle to the next generation ("It's Your Turn"), how fear is a "dangerous" internal motivator ("Dangerous"), and diabolical romantic relationships ("One At A Time"). All of these songs stress negative views. The nine Townshend compositions extend the "Pete Townshend's Complaint" story line through an approach that I divide into a "societal complaint" component ("I've Known No War," "Why Did I Fall For That," "Cooks County," and "Eminence Front"), a general "life complaints" section ("It's Hard," "Cry If You Want," and "Athena"), and the resolution to the "worldly search" theme of this period ("A Man Is A Man"). The remaining song, "One Life's Enough For Me," is a tender love song (sung by Daltrey) that nostalgically reflects on teen love (its author reports in 1997 that he wrote this song for his wife). The song is brief, but poignant:

> There's a scene indelible, it hangs before my eyes
> In our teens, incredibly together with no ties.
> That was a life enough for me
> One life's enough for me

Throw back your head
Let your body curve
Into the long grass of the bed
Pull me down into your hair
And I'll push and swerve
As we both gasp in the evening air.

The song recycles these lyrics after a brief instrumental and, once again, demonstrates the flexible qualities of Townshend's pen. In an era of intense complaint, the writer's capacity to explore life's tender side suggests that his preoccupation with the negative may not be complete.

The final installment of "Pete Townshend's Complaint" is quite a contrast to "One Life." These songs offer evidence of the band's decision to address broader issues as opposed to Townshend's personal anxieties. Nevertheless, "I've Known No War" presents a theme that continues across the next several years—once again lending credibility to Townshend's claim that he tends to follow trains of thought for extended periods of time. Through the obvious antinuclear war statement, the songwriter embellishes patriotic frustrations that resurface in his solo projects:

I've known no war
And if I ever do I won't know for sure
Who'll be fighting whom
For the soldier's lonely tomb
Now opens as soon as the referee's gun starts to roar
I'll know no war, I'll never know war.
Galbraith took his pen
To break down the men
Of the German army defeated
On the nineteenth day
Of a spring in May
Albert Speer was deleted
And as soon as the battle was over
I was born in victorious clover
And I've never been shot at or gassed
Never tortured or stabbed
And I'm sure—I'll never know war.

(Notice the reference to Townshend's birthday.) The narrator will never know the honor of "front line battle cries" because if war ever arrives, the "glimpse will be short"—a "Fireball in the sky" that is launched by a "soul that's been bought." Afterward, the songwriter presents another glimpse of the "veteran's lament" first previewed in "Slip Kid":

In and out of reach loft
The medals are lost
They belong to a lone broken sailor

His provinces now
Are the bars of the town
His songs and his poems of failure
For his grandchildren can't see the glory
And his own kids are bored with the story
But for him they'd have burned behind netting
From the brink they were grabbed
And I'm sure
I'll never know war.

Townshend's interest in his conflict with his father's generation is intensifying as he introduces questions that he will eventually answer in his solo career. Furthermore, his ability to negotiate a personal theme within the context of a group decision offers a brief glimpse of the rhetorical style that had once guided The Who to commercial success.

The "societal complaint" theme continues via "Why Did I Fall For That." This track reiterates the message from "We're Not Gonna Take It" and "Won't Get Fooled Again" as it ponders, "why did we fall for that?"

The streets of the future littered with remains
Of both the fools and the so called brains
The whole prediction is enough to kill
But only God knows if it won't or it will
Nobody knows why we fell so flat
Some silly creature said we'd never crack
Most would just survive and then bounce back
But the rest are crying "Why'd I fall for that crap"
Why did I fall for that?
So many rash promises sincerely made
By people who believed that we were being saved
They made us all believe that we were acting while
But the truth is we've forgotten how we used to fight
Nobody knows why we fell so flat
We're impotent and neutered like whining cats
We've found the piper but we've lost the rats
But the kids are crying "Why'd I fall for that dad?"
Why did you fall?
It never rains under my umbrella.
Four minutes to midnight on a sunny day
Maybe if we smile the clock'll fade away
Maybe we can force the hands to just reverse
Maybe is a word. Maybe maybe is a curse
Nobody knows why we fell so flat
We've never been taught to fight or to face up to facts
We simply believe that we'd remain intact
But history is asking why did you fall for that?
Why did you fall?

Townshend may be addressing the music industry or domestic politics; as usual, the context is open to interpretation. The lament, however, is as forthright, as its similarity to "Won't Get Fooled" is striking. Both songs discuss "promises" that fell short of their aspirations. "Why Did I Fall For That" assumes a more reflective stance as the character's "child" asks the demanding question, "why did you fall?"

The two remaining "societal complaints" are powerful numbers as well. The hit single "Eminence Front" raises questions about trust and pretension (Townshend often states that the song is about egomaniacs and cocaine). The line "come and join the party, dress to kill" is evasive and merely provides a context for the pretenses people assume as they "forget" who they really are when they "put on" their roles. The song opens: "The sun shines/And people forget/The spray flies as the speedboat glides/And people forget/Forget they're hiding/The girls smile/And people forget/The snow packs as the skier tracks/And people forget/Forget they're hiding/Behind an eminence front/Eminence front—it's a put on." Townshend's impressionism is in firm control as he complains about social "put ons" through enigmatic symbolism. "Cooks County" does not share that ambiguity and mischief. To the contrary, the song directly states that people are "suffering," "hungry," "lonely," and "bleeding" as it prescribes: "So remember when you're looking for trouble/That trouble is already busy with weaker men" (Townshend notes in 1997 that this song was written for Cook County Hospital in Chicago). The character eventually complains, "This song is so long/It ends up where it begins," and it leaves us to contemplate the "lonely" and "bleeding" people. Both songs employ driving instrumentals that set up the short bursts of lyrics. By following this tactic, Townshend returns to the narrative strategy we observed in *Face Dances* in that the song's structure elevates the complaint through repetition, with the details remaining ambiguous.

These "general life complaints" assume varying levels of intensity and clarity. "Athena" is a light tune that portrays an internal struggle over whether or not to leave a lover. The song first notes how much the character needs "Athena" but quickly changes to "But I think I'll get along." The conflict is directly articulated in the chorus "She's just a girl—she's a bomb" (more metaphorical mischief?). Townshend writes:

Athena, my heart felt like a shattered glass in an acid bath
I felt like one of those flattened ants you find on a crazy path
I'd of topped myself to give her time she didn't need to ask
Was I a suicidal psychopath?
She's just a girl—she's a bomb [repeated] ...
Consumed, there was a beautiful white horse I saw on a dream stage
He had a snake the size of a sewer pipe living in his rib cage
I felt like a pickled priest who was being flambéed
You were requisitioned blonde
She's just a girl—she's a bomb
She's a bomb—I'm happy.

The track continues with more confused imagery and word games before it ends where it began, "She's just a girl—she's a bomb." Contrasting with "Athena's" metaphorical playfulness is "Cry If You Want"—a powerful, at times harsh song that reflects on the character's life and asks demanding questions about personal values. If the answers are hurtful, "you can cry if you want" ("Let your tears flow, Let your past go"). The final stanza's introspection seems fitting for the last Who song's conclusion:

> Don't you get embarrassed when you think about the way you were
> Yesterday the day before when you were young with much to learn
> Aren't you glad it's your last term
> No more acting lowly worm
> You can make the suckers squirm
> When you tell them how much you earn
> Don't you feel ashamed at all the bitterness you keep inside
> Does your ego save your face "I had to go—I really tried"
> Now you know your leaders lied
> Does it stop you acting snide
> Or are you still a boy that cried
> Tears now surely long since dried
> Cry if you want Cry if you want.

Townshend's power chords lead a furious instrumental pace that conveys the legendary Who anger. The other song of complaint, "It's Hard," falls somewhere in between the two previous tracks in terms of its intensity. The song draws attention to the difficulty of achieving excellence in contexts that range from sex ("Any stud can reproduce—few can please") to adolescent attributes: "Any brain can hide—few can stand/Any kid can fly—few can land/Any gang can scatter—few can form/Any kid can chatter—few can inform." Throughout the song Townshend seems to toss words about in a sportive fashion, either delving further into his impressionism or simply propagating gibberish. The song concludes without mystery:

> Anyone can do anything if they hold the right card
> So I'm thinking about my life now
> I'm thinking very hard
> Deal me another hand Lord, this one's very hard
> Deal me another hand Lord, this one's very hard.

These three songs seal the "Pete Townshend's Complaint" portion of the oeuvre through a narrative style that raises the negative and engages in various forms of word play. The writer's artistic philosophy tempers the "Complaint's" attacks by skirting around subjects through that cryptic symbolism.

I conclude this discussion of *It's Hard* with the final chapter of Townshend's search for worldly identity. After asking his audience to "Imagine A Man" at the outset, the songwriter now describes that "man" and his qualities:

You talk about your crazy affairs
You talk about your life as though it really mattered
You get your attention 'cos you block the stairs
Bragging about some bottles you have shattered
Well I met a man who really lives
He really does it all
But what really matters is the heart he gives
He makes your talk seem small
When a man is a man
He doesn't act to a plan
He don't have to perform like John Wayne in some
B feature flick
A man is a man
When he can offer his hand
Not afraid of appearing insane if he can't break a brick
I know a man who's a man.

The song continues: "I know a man who was once like you/But he opened his heart/No one is really bad right through/He's just another part." But Townshend's ideal "man" not only "opens his heart," he "drinks 'til he's canned" and "he's a looker...a dresser...a genius under pressure...a father...a brother...a rocker...a lover." The song closes with the prescription: "Be a man who's a man." "Imagine A Man" and "A Man Is A Man" are the brief bookends to a short search for worldly identity. Between these two songs are compositions about the value of "your guitar and pen" as well as the two songs of hope (*Face Dances'* "Don't Let Go The Coat" and "Cache Cache"). When considered together the songs appear to raise questions about what constitutes a "good man" and warn that if you understand these matters "you will see the end" (i.e., the "search" will be complete). Over time Townshend returns to *his* value structure (save your only friend, your guitar and pen, and the significance of spiritual companionship in an uncertain world), and he discovers the answer to his question when he describes his "ideal man" as a mirror of himself ("a genius under pressure...a father...a brother...a rocker...a lover"). That Pete Townshend appears to go nowhere in this "search" may suggest a great deal about his artistic vision during these troubled times. Or maybe it is another reiteration of "The Amazing Journey" narrative impulse: when you arrive at the top of the highest mountain, what do you find? Only yourself.

It's Hard dismisses the intensely personal subject matter that characterized Who albums since *Quadrophenia*. Perhaps Townshend's solo ventures provided an avenue for those subjects, or perhaps he took seriously the band's request to feature broader topics of interest to the general public. Or perhaps Townshend could, in fact, see the end coming, and that realization—in conjunction with his successful treatment in California, the resolution of his financial difficulties, and his return home to his family—inspired him to revisit the writing style that typified the "singles period" (i.e., the capacity to negotiate themes and satisfy diverse audiences).

Music reviews, once again, suggest such conclusions. Gilmore (1982) maintains the record is the "first Who album since *Who's Next* to assail the misrule of the world outside themselves and the misspent ideals of youth culture in particular" and concludes "this album was probably meant as the group's homeward-bound big statement." Joining the "homeward-bound" sentiment is the *Washington Post*'s review: "One thing...is clear: The Who couldn't have asked for more consistent, volatile and redeeming songs for their last hurrah than those found on its new album" (Joyce, 1982, p. B8). The *Kansas City Star* adds, "The Who will never be considered preachy, but we could all stand to listen" (Rassenfoss, 1982). The *Los Angeles Times* takes a different approach; it asserts, "This is not the sort of album upon which claims to greatness are staked" (Waller, 1982, p. 82), and it attacks Townshend: "Townshend has spent the better part of the past decade wrestling with the role of rock's venerated elder statesman. On this record, all he's succeeded in doing is emphasizing the *dull* in adulthood." Finally, we consider two reviews with contradicting conclusions. Both reviews appreciate *It's Hard*, but for conflicting reasons. The *Minneapolis Tribune* claims the new album is one of The Who's "strongest albums in years" and argues: "The album is lyrically potent with its mix of trenchant political and introspectively personal commentaries. Yet the music is less compelling" (*It's Hard*, 1982a). The *San Jose Mercury* describes the album as "the quintessential Who record, one that shouts its very Who-ness for all to hear," and yet it concludes the "lyrics would be embarrassing were they not backed by such gorgeous musical backgrounds" (Sumrall, 1982). With the number of music critics now under the employ of daily newspapers (recall the "singles period" and its dearth of commentary), such contradictions are no doubt common, and frustrating for artists.

The Who complemented its final album with a "farewell tour" of North America that resulted in a concert video and the double album set *Who's Last*. Loder (1982b) describes The Who's agreement with Schlitz beer (the tour's sponsor) and quotes a company spokesperson that the band will receive a "seven-figure amount" from "the biggest corporate-sponsored rock-music entertainment ever undertaken.... Meet the new boss" (p. 28). Palmer (1982a) reports that the tour anticipated "about $15 million from ticket sales alone" (p. 12) which—when combined with the tour's merchandising, the cable television pay-per-view broadcast, a taped show for Home Box Office, the concert video/disc, the live album, and the "new phenomenon, corporate sponsorship"— guaranteed The Who would exit with a major payday.

The 1982 tour most certainly reinforced the decision to end The Who. The *Los Angeles Herald-Examiner* chronicles an amazing story about a five-hour yacht cruise of the San Francisco Bay and the intense animosity the band members held toward one another. Fink (1982a) writes how the four musicians positioned themselves in separate areas on the boat and describes yet another "media conflict" between Daltrey and Townshend. Daltrey admitted that "this has been one of the most miserable tours I've ever done in my life" and announced: "Pete isn't the Who, nor is Roger Daltrey. No doubt about it. But when the Who gets it on, it's like magic. And it's just not worth analyzing. That's the problem. Pete is such a complete intellectual. He'll never understand." Apparently, during the cruise reporters would prod comments such as these from either Daltrey or Townshend and then scurry to the other side of the boat to get the other's reaction. The debate—such as it was—grew intense. Townshend proclaimed that Daltrey had a "secret reason" for ending The Who, to which Daltrey responded, "Pete says one thing one minute, and another thing the next. You don't ever know where you stand with the man." These two men had argued in this fashion for close to twenty years; the time to part was surely at hand.

Response to The Who's farewell tour ranged from Quinlan's (1982) view that the band performed "with the proficiency of the seasoned veterans that they are," to Mayer's (1982) conclusion that the tour "makes one hell of a retirement party," to Catlin's (1982) humorous observation, "One goes to Who concerts— and Stones concerts—the way you visit great-grandma at Christmastime, with the idea that this might be the last chance." Palmer (1982b) assumes a different stance and offers an insightful analysis of The Who's performance. The *New York Times* rock critic writes:

One goes to a Who concert knowing that Mr. Townshend will leap about and that Mr. Daltrey will twirl his microphone. But expectations that are this fixed don't leave much room for genuine spontaneity; they can become a kind of prison. Mr. Townshend and Mr. Daltrey must know that if they didn't jump and twirl and tried something different instead, most of their fans would be confused and disappointed. And that might have something to do with their decision to make this Who tour the last one. (p. 10)

While the tour received mixed reviews, the subsequent album, *Who's Last*, was thoroughly criticized. Loder's (1985) commentary is particularly negative: "I can't think of another band as committed and allegedly idealistic as the Who that has ended its career on so sour and sickening a note" (p. 60). The *Birmingham News* offers a mixed review of the Home Box Office production *The Who Tour 1982: The Final Show* (the Toronto show that was also distributed in video cassette/disc) in that it applauds the show as "one for the rock 'n' roll generation to savor" and yet regrets that the "*coup de grace* is missing...as we never see Townshend smash his guitar on the stage floor at the end of the night. It would have been the ideal exclamation point" (Carlton, 1983). To be sure, The Who was in an unique double bind: the performance style that pioneered the way for a new generation of performers was now tired and repetitive, and the rejection of "old tricks" such as auto-destruction met the disapproval of nostalgic critics. The Who just could not win.

Following the 1982 tour, The Who appeared at various events: Live Aid in 1985 and the 1988 British Phonograph Industry awards are two such instances (Harrington, 1989). Williams (1989) reports that Townshend's appearance during the 1989 Rock and Roll Hall of Fame dinner (where he performed with Mick Jagger, Tina Turner, and Bruce Springsteen) so "energized" and "inspired" him that when he was approached about a twenty-fifth-anniversary tour he agreed. The band re-formed in 1989 without Kenney Jones, added a large accompaniment of horns, singers, an additional guitarist, a percussionist, and Simon Phillips on drums. The Who again obtained corporate sponsorship and, from that starting point, planned two benefit performances of *Tommy* (one in New York, the other in Los Angeles) with proceeds going to the Nordoff-Robbins Music Therapy Foundation for Autistic Children and the Rock and Roll Hall of Fame (the Los Angeles show featured Phil Collins, Billy Idol, Patti La-Belle, and Steve Winwood in various roles). The Los Angeles show was released on video, and a concert "box set" entitled *Join Together* was issued as well. When joined with an intense merchandising plan, The Who's "The Kids Are Alright 25th Anniversary Tour" was a guaranteed financial windfall.

Responses to the tour varied in their tone. Grieve (1989) is quite negative: "A Very Large Band fronted by some Very Famous People played Oakland Coliseum Tuesday night. Sometimes the Very Large Band looked like the Who. Sometimes the Very Large Band even sounded like the Who. But it wasn't the Who...the Who...was nowhere in sight." In contrast, Pareles (1989b) observes: "Thursday's show [at Giants Stadium] was mammoth in every way—in attendance (54,000, for the first of four nights), in the size of the band (15 members) and in length (more than three hours of music).... The band revealed itself not just as earth-shaking stadium rockers...but as eccentric, even playful rock elder statesmen...the Who proved its place in the rock pantheon is secure" (p. 15). Most reviews, in fact, seem to reflect a combination of the "dinosaur-for-dollars" (King, 1989; St. John, 1989) assertion and praise (in King's case, about Townshend's performance: he "dominated the stage" with his guitar and vocals).

Efforts to reunite "The Who" in 1994 for a thirtieth anniversary failed (the band did release a box set, *Thirty Years of Maximum R&B*, that summer). While Daltrey's fiftieth birthday celebration in New York featured the remaining members (and many others) and his subsequent tour involved Entwistle and Simon Townshend, "The Who" did not reassemble until 1996, when the reissue of *Quadrophenia* inspired a dramatic rendering of Townshend's second opera.

As we have seen, the artistic *obligations* that surrounded The Who established a context for deterioration. Without entrepreneurial drive and creative inspiration (which was often a product of collaboration with Kit Lambert, Glyn Johns, or the band), stagnation set in, and Townshend's pen chronicled the entire episode through a writing style that emphasized direct complaint by way of cryptic characterizations ("Pete Townshend's Complaint"). This is, in many respects, a sad story: "sad" because Townshend's treasured rock ideals were overturned, his audience's eventual detachment and nostalgia threatened his performance instincts, and several of his close friends died. While Lambert's and Moon's contributions to Townshend's art had passed on long before they themselves died, their deaths sealed the songwriter's fate as a member of The Who. That *The Seeker*'s search departed from a self-actualized spiritual quest toward a worldly concern for physical survival, relational harmony, and musical

innovation is evidence of Townshend's shifting focus. The struggle to survive
The Who dominated the songwriter. But this "sad story" is only a portion of a
much larger tale. The auteur's narrative impulse may have taken a dark, introspective turn, but he would rebound from that state. Like the minstrel of old—
constrained and inhibited by his obligations to the Guild—Townshend would
now seek relief from a financially secure but uninspiring existence. Pete Townshend still had stories to tell.

PART III

The Minstrel's Resolution

5

The Solo Career: The Impulse's Opportunity

From tales of entrepreneurial aggression through stories of mindless commercial obligation, The Who's history is a revealing account of an artistic and commercial ebb and flow—all of which leads to a fascinating "irony of success" paradox: the potential for artistic freedom to stifle initiative, which in turn renders creative voids or fosters introspection. After years of financial success and artistic security, the incongruities that arise between freedom, obligation, and inspiration may overwhelm an artist. In response, creative teams break up (or reunite), members follow new (or revise old) agendas, and a process of rediscovery ensues. This may involve considerable *risk* in that the artist may place his/her career, *and the artistic impulse*, in harm's way. Still, there may be no other alternative: either take the chance insecurity's return will revive creativity, or fade away. I once more turn to the history of English minstrelsy to establish my point. The creative constraints imposed by either the guild system and its "charters" or the expectations that surrounded (and restricted) musicians inspired many minstrels to "hit the road" in search of creative rejuvenation. Although he might escape the drudgery of performing the same act repeatedly, the "wandering minstrel" faced a dangerous life. Rowbotham (1895) claims the wandering minstrel "laid down three distinct privileges" (pp. 174-75) upon this decision to roam: the protection and support provided by the patron, his "political rights," and his human rights. He could be killed, and remarkably, his murderer would not be charged. As Rowbotham explains, "The murder was not of a man, but of a minstrel."

While the contemporary musician who decides to leave an established career for new creative opportunities is rarely exposed to such physical danger, he or she is at considerable risk. Artistic standing, financial benefits, and industry support (among other things) are placed in jeopardy. Any relief the artist may hope for, therefore, may be short-lived. This chapter explores such a scenario as it unfolds in Pete Townshend's career. During a decade of declining devotion to The Who, Townshend quietly initiated a solo career. The relief he experienced through those projects played a central role in the ultimate decision to leave The Who and follow an independent agenda. The transition required years to complete; however, once Townshend dismissed The Who, his artistic impulse flourished.

THE SOLO CAREER: THE IMPULSE'S OPPORTUNITY

Pete Townshend's solo career is necessarily divided into two phases. The first involves a series of projects that emerged during his tenure with The Who, and the second pertains to his "post-Who" works. The first two albums, 1972's *Who Came First* and 1977's *Rough Mix*, were safe escapes from The Who, but they hardly qualify as "solo" projects; the former involved a number of Meher Baba followers, the latter Ronnie Lane and an all-star cast. Hence Townshend's third work, 1980's *Empty Glass*, was his first solo album. The fourth project, 1982's *All The Best Cowboys Have Chinese Eyes*, concludes the first phase of his solo career by way of a multimedia state-of-the-artist work. The last two entries were particularly risky, owing to their decidedly *personal* orientations— autobiographical stories that assume an increasingly impressionistic narrative form.

This chapter presents that first portion of Townshend's solo career. Since I have already discussed the various tensions surrounding his career at this time, I refrain from repeating those details except where warranted. Of principal interest here is Townshend's gradual move toward an individual career and the uncertainty associated with that professional shift. I begin with the first album following the *LifeHouse/Who's Next* project.

WHO CAME FIRST

The *Who Came First* album is not the result of an artistic longing for new venues or opportunities; rather, it is a product of Townshend's record company's (MCA) efforts to profit from a series of recordings honoring Meher Baba. Marsh (1983) reports that Townshend and other Baba lovers produced two albums—*Happy Birthday*, released in 1970 for Baba's seventy-seventh birthday, and *I Am* released the following year—that were to be distributed only within the group (only 2,500 copies of each album were pressed). The two albums caught the interest of Who fans, record collectors, bootleggers, and MCA. MCA persuaded Townshend to release the material "officially" (and disrupt the bootlegging) and promised to give the proceeds to the Baba organization. Believing that Baba's message would now reach an even larger audience, Townshend agreed.

The two original Baba projects featured poetry, comedy, and a variety of musical forms. Townshend's contributions included the demo for "The Seeker," several new compositions, and an extended version of "Baba O'Riley" (Marsh, 1983). Instead of merely transferring the materials from the original albums into a new format for MCA, Townshend recast everything. No doubt, that he was returning to the studio to do work in Baba's name soothed an artist still reeling from the *LifeHouse* debacle. Despite the *LifeHouse* failure, Townshend's dedication to The Who remained intact, and he articulated that position in the *Who Came First* publicity. The *Los Angeles Times* reports that Townshend did not feel "confined" by The Who; he viewed that responsibility "not as a problem, but as a healthy and stimulating limitation to work within" (Hilburn, 1972a, p. 58; a direct quote from the promotion featured below). Townshend (1973) articulates that point in an "advertisement" for *Who Came First* that appeared in *Crawdaddy* magazine:

The WHO, being famous for what they are famous for, don't turn out many ballads. They also don't turn out much that isn't heavy in some way or another. As a group we are self-consciously aware of our image—we were one of the English bands who grew up in that Beatle maniacal era when image was almost as important as sound, probably more important. We've never lost that feeling—it's somehow intrinsic in the mood of the band. When we stand together in a studio, or on a stage, we feel that image take over and become bigger than any single one of us. In the past, this has always precluded the possibility of ever being able to say anything other than what seemed right that the WHO should say. (p. 17)

Townshend explains Meher Baba's significance and how the album shares his feelings about his spiritual master:

Meher Baba is an amazing man. He's dead now, three years since, but one still gets the feeling of a NOW presence. No single thing that has ever happened to me has changed the way I see and do things in this world so much. This album is meant to reflect these changes. Allow them to breathe outside of the confines of the Who, and yet also feed back to the Who. Music is *really* communication.... Our bass player, John Entwistle, was well known to us to be a quietly accomplished musician—I've known him for nearly twelve years, played with him all that time—but I learnt more about him through the release of his solo album last year than in all that time.... On this album, in this context, [the album's music] is dedicated to Baba. Not for him to listen to, his ears aren't around, but so that he will be around whenever it's played.

In a *Rolling Stone* interview Townshend discussed the source of the material as well as his comment regarding Entwistle's solo album. He told Denselow (1972) the work is "in a way dedicated to Baba, but mainly dedicated to the people who want to know the way I feel about him...I find that when I try to talk about Meher Baba...I can't put it into words. So I thought maybe I should use my talent—with a small 't'—as a musician and try to put the feeling and the mood across that way." Townshend downplayed the album's significance: "If I were to do a proper solo album, I would probably show off more.... But then, I like the idea of people hearing what I do at home."

These remarks offer an insightful view from that point in time. Note that as of 1972-1973 Townshend remained committed to The Who. That commitment was based on his image of the band and its united front. When this ideal begins to disintegrate, Townshend's loyalties diminish. Next, notice how he defines the Baba project: there are "people who want to know" about *his* feelings for Baba, thus he is obliged to share them. For Townshend, *solo* albums are channels for self-expression (if not self-indulgence) in which artists "communicate" their views in a fashion that allows the audience to *learn about the author* and gain insight into that individual. His comments regarding the Entwistle project demonstrate that perspective. The Who's records had fed one image, and a "proper" Townshend solo album, one presumes, would feed another. Subsequently, as The Who's career entered its final stages and his image of a united front fragmented, the author offered a personal take on that demise ("Pete Townshend's Complaint") that displayed little regard for The Who's collective image. Townshend's capacity to write for others (industry operatives, Mods, commercials, adolescents, The Who) was evolving toward an expressive, multimedia style that would continue to reflect his artistic philosophy.

Turning to the album itself, the equivocal symbolism of *Who Came First*'s cover art—Townshend standing on dozens of eggs, dressed in his "boiler suit," a Meher Baba button pinned on his chest and a sour look on his drawn, bearded face—may say more about his state of mind than any of the album's songs (is he "walking on eggshells"? a "who came first the chicken or the egg joke"?). I work from the 1993 reissue that contains the original *Who Came First* material and the *Happy Birthday* project (fifteen tracks, running 59:37). The *Happy Birthday* portion consists of six Townshend compositions that pursue a single theme (two instrumentals, "His Hands" and "Lantern Cabin," the "The Seeker" demo, and three songs in praise of Baba: "Day of Silence," "Sleeping Dog," and "The Love Man") whereas the *Who Came First* tracks are more diversified: four Townshend songs ("Pure and Easy," "Let's See Action" [originally, "Nothing Is Everything"], "Time Is Passing," and "Sheraton Gibson"), a Ron Lane number ("Evolution"—a revision of his earlier "Stone"—Silver, 1972, p. 60), a Kate McInnerney/Billy Nicholls song ("Forever's No Time At All"), a cover of Jim Reeves's "There's A Heartache Following Me" (reportedly one of Baba's favorite songs), a musical version of Maud Kennedy's poem "Content," and a musical adaptation of a Baba prayer, "Parvardigar." The songs appear to fall into two categories, with one exception. The exception is "Sheraton Gibson," the stream-of-consciousness track discussed in Chapter One. In it Townshend merely strums his guitar and makes up the lyrics as he goes along: "I'm sitting in the Sheraton Gibson playing my Gibson/And boy do I want to go home/I'm sitting in the Sheraton Gibson playing my Gibson/And boy do I feel all alone." The other tracks may be divided in terms of songs written directly in praise of Baba or played in his memory, and songs from the *LifeHouse* project that employ spiritual themes.

The latter group involves three songs. The first two, "Pure and Easy" and "Let's See Action," are directly attributed to *LifeHouse* in the liner notes. The third track, "Time Is Passing," conveys *LifeHouse* themes in a prayerful manner. "Pure and Easy" is the pivotal song from the *LifeHouse* story, and the version featured here suggests the typical Townshend demo (a lighter, more serene style). Townshend writes: "There once was a note, pure and easy, playing so free like a breath rippling by/The note is eternal, I hear it, it sees me, forever we blend as forever we die/[chorus] I listened and I heard music in a word/And words when you played your guitar/The noise that I was hearing was a million people cheering/And a child flew past me riding in a star." Townshend's synthesis of Baba's teachings, his belief in a musical essence, and "Bobby's" metaphysics are evident in this *LifeHouse* remnant. "Let's See Action" also follows that approach. These two songs speak to two of the writer's signature topics: the belief in a musical essence ("Pure and Easy") and a fear of deception ("Let's See Action"). The second number opens with the simple lines, "Let's see action/Let's see people/Let's see freedom, Let's see who cares," as a preface to statements of distrust ("Rumor has it/Minds are open/Then rumors fill them up with lies") and uncertainty ("Future passing/Nothing lasting/I try to scream as nothing does/Nothing is, everything/Everything is, nothing is"). After repeating the "Let's see action" refrain several times, the song moves to the central point:

Get me a drink while I wash my feet
I'm so tired of running from my own heat
Take this package and here's what you do
I want to get this information through
I don't know where I'm going
I don't know what I need, but I get to where I'm gonna end up
And that's all right by me
I've been running from side to side
Now I know for sure that both sides lied
It's got so hard, but we gotta keep trying
I can't stand to see my people crying.

The song works on two planes. The first suggests a spiritual longing message in which the central character pleads for "spiritual action" as he/she floats through life. The character intuitively understands that everything will "end up" just fine, even though people have lied all around; perseverance will prevail. The second plane involves a statement of artistic frustration. This autobiographical reading reveals Townshend's frustrations over his inability to communicate through his work, the aimless qualities of that work, and his commitment to artistic progress. The "lies" that surround him make those efforts more difficult; however, he must push on: "Let's see freedom, Let's see who cares."

The third song, "Time Is Passing," also pursues this topic through its light, folksy instrumental style. The lyrics clearly evoke the musical essence and the distrust themes. To capture the song's rhythm, I present the lyrics in their entirety:

I'm playing my guitar
While my sister bangs a drum
The glass sets up a sound like people laughing
It's going to my brain and it's easing all my pain
I must hear this sound again
'Cause time is passing.
I'm walking by the sea and the seagull sings for me
The crabs are swimming down among the starfish
The rocks all scatter down, seagulls fly around
But the whole trip keeps it in that
Time is passing
Passing.
Find it, I've got to hear it all again
My heart has heard the sound of harmony
Blind to it, as my tears fall again
It's only by the music, I'll be free.
There's something in the whisper of the trees
Millions hear it still they can't believe
There are ripples of it crashing in the waves
As an empire of dead men leave their graves.
Don't listen to people talk
Don't listen to them selling souls
Don't listen to me or words from men above
Don't hear it in your needs
And don't hear it in your greeds
Just hear it in the sound of
Time a passing.

The message is straightforward and a direct reiteration of the *LifeHouse* story line: listen and learn from nature's symphony, don't trust anyone (especially yourself), and yield to the beauty of nature's harmony. Townshend is apparently tormented by the fact that he *has* heard that harmony and he will not be "free" until his "heart" hears it once more. Perhaps "Time Is Passing" represents Townshend's prayer for the *LifeHouse* project and conveys his dedication to its principles: "It's only by the music, I'll be free."

From these songs in praise of a "musical essence" we turn to *Who Came First*'s tribute to Baba. The Ron Lane and Nicholls/McInnerney songs, the Jim Reeves cover, and the Townshend compositions and adaptations all serve that end. Townshend's "Day of Silence" praises the healing power of silence and meditation, as we are encouraged to seek "oneness" with the Lord. "Sleeping Dog" is a Townshend prayer to Baba in which he acknowledges his efforts to "love" us all through song. While "dogs and children" sleep, the narrator is hard at work writing songs that communicate his love so that one day he may rest as well. "The Love Man" encourages us to "say hello to the love man, we can't afford to pass him by," and "Parvadigar" places a Baba prayer in a musical context: "The Parvadigar, the preserver, the protector of all/Without beginning, are you Lord, without end.... Imperishable beyond conception by our minds/

None can divide you, oh God you are eternal/None can see you but with eyes divine." The instrumentation complements the prayer format (slow, pleading). Finally, Townshend's adaptation of Maud Kennedy's poem, "Content," addresses the bliss that accompanies spiritual enlightenment: "I am ready, to learn and to grow/I am alone, with the truth/I am brave, what is there to fear/I am strong, God supports me/I am patient, each moment of eternity/I am able to help when necessary/I am happy swinging in the arms of love./I am balanced, keeping mind and heart equal/I am complete when I forget myself/I am receptive to each message of love/I am responsive to all that lives/I am happy swinging in the arms of love./Enough, I am content/I am content."

Who Came First is a transitional moment in Townshend's lifework. It looks back at the *LifeHouse* disappointment with a sincere belief in its principles, it examines Townshend's present through its spiritual themes, and it foreshadows his future in an instructive fashion. That is, solo albums are vehicles for self expression. That the auteur would one day package and release his home demos so that his audience may "hear what he does at home" and gain deeper insight into his work supports that point; *Who Came First* could easily be renamed *Scoop: A Preview*.

The critics' responses to *Who Came First* range from exorbitant praise to cynical condemnation. On the cynical side, Dave Marsh (1973) first swipes at Meher Baba ("Baba books and such have always seemed trite to me, without a whole lot to add to the body of cosmic aphorisms, but since he spent most of his life in silence, one doesn't expect much"—pp. 68-69) and follows with digs at Townshend: "It's inconsequential stuff.... *Who Came First* is there, if you want it, which I don't suppose I do, particularly. It's a curiosity, more than anything, or an idiosyncrasy" (p. 69). The *Los Angeles Times* describes the album as "more narrow than the Who's music" (Hilburn, 1972a, p. 58) and concludes: "There are portions of 'Who Came First' that suggest Townshend could well have made this a major musical philosophical work, but the bulk of the album indicates he stopped far short of that goal" (pp. 58, 60). Silver's (1972) review for *Rolling Stone* declares the project is "a brilliant and moving album...an amazing work" and contends, "As always with old panface Pete, the music manages to fuse high devotional feeling with commercial mastery resulting in powerful music" (p. 60). Silver pours praise on Townshend, calling the songwriter an "unarguable genius," designating him "the old Chuck Berrified cosmic chicken," and labeling the album "a godsend" (p. 61).

While Townshend may argue the work is not a "proper solo album," *Who Came First* and his media commentary offer evidence of his state of mind (artistically and spiritually), his perceived relationship with The Who, and his evolving narrative style. As such, this "snapshot" conveys compelling insight into the emerging solo artist and provides the foundation for his eventual move away from The Who. The band's image, its fans, and Townshend's desire to express *himself* (not articulate tales that feed The Who's image) would eventually lead to "proper solo albums" that build upon this starting point. *Who Came*

First may have been a throwaway for MCA, but it is a meaningful development within the oeuvre.

ROUGH MIX

The loyalty Townshend displayed for The Who just prior to *Who Came First*'s release was totally reversed by 1976. Hilburn's (1977) assessment of the state-of-The-Who in 1976-1977 conveys that situation: "the Who played with spirit and intensity on its '76 visit. Even so, the band lacked a compelling, purposeful edge. The evening had a sense of trying to recapture rather than extend the quartet's original vitality.... Pete Townshend warned it was a transitional time for the band" (p. 68). Townshend's anticipation of this "transition" was no doubt a product of his personal and professional anxieties—sentiments that constitute the crux of *The Who By Numbers*' lyrics, as Schulps (1977) explains: "It's been almost two years since we've heard anything at all from Pete Townshend. No interviews, no music, nothing. On *Who By Numbers*, perhaps the most intensely personal recording ever made by a major group, Townshend's bitterness toward his role in the rock world was unsettling, to say the least" (p. 76). Schulps argues that lines such as "'Goodbye all you punks, stay young and stay high, hand me my checkbook and I'll crawl off to die' haunted the listener" and—despite the songwriter's "complaint" that the lyrics were "over-analyzed"—motivated "listeners to anticipate the next offering like a housewife eagerly awaiting the next installment of *All My Children*." Schulps's sexism aside, the irony of success I described at the opening of this chapter had by now consumed The Who. In response, the band labored to "recapture" its "original vitality" in live performance, Townshend's pen moved from songs designed for The Who's image toward personal complaint, and, as Schulps observes, "listeners" eagerly awaited the next "installment." Unfortunately for these musical "housewives," Townshend was virtually incapable of delivering, as he told the *Los Angeles Times*:

Last year after the U.S. tour I was sick of working with the Who. I suppose it would have been just as easy for me to have rung up Roger Daltrey and arranged to have done an album with him. But I couldn't even conceive of the idea of writing songs. The last Who album, I barely wrote enough songs. 'The Who By Numbers' had no leftover songs at all, I'd stopped dead. But I was eager to do something in the studio with Glyn Johns, our producer, without the heavy pressure of a Who gig. (Mills, 1977, p. 68)

For relief, Townshend teamed with fellow Baba devotee and *Who Came First* participant Ronnie Lane. Lane—a member of the successful act the Small Faces, and later the Faces—had grown tired of the rock world and retired to a low-profile solo career. After several relatively unsuccessful ventures, Lane was in financial trouble. Marsh (1983) says that Lane approached Townshend in late 1976 to discuss his situation and they resolved to help each other with their respective problems: Lane would benefit financially, and Townshend would gain relief simply by working outside of The Who. With a cast of all-star musicians (Eric Clapton, Entwistle, Charlie Watts, and others) and with Glyn Johns at the helm, Lane and Townshend rendered *Rough Mix.*

Rough Mix contains eleven tracks (running 41:28) and features five Townshend compositions ("My Baby Gives It Away," "Keep Me Turning," "Misunderstood," "Street in the City," and "Heart To Hang Onto"), two Lane songs ("Nowhere To Run" and "April Fool"), one Townshend/Lane collaboration (the instrumental "Rough Mix"), two Lane collaborations (Lane/Lambert/Clapton's "Annie" and Lane/Lambert's "Catmelody"), and one cover (Holyfield/Williams's "Till All The Rivers All Run Dry"). There is no dominant theme or technical style guiding Townshend's contributions to *Rough Mix*; instead, we receive a sample of the songwriter's various narrative signatures (what I term "The Pete Townshend Sampler"). His songs range from a humorous satire ("My Baby Gives It Away"), to a spiritual message delivered somewhat tongue-in-cheek ("Keep Me Turning"), to a dark statement of interpersonal angst ("Misunderstood"), to a plea for relational sincerity ("Heart To Hang Onto"), to a strong piece of foreshadowing ("Street in the City"). True to the venture's transitional qualities, Townshend's contributions revisit the past, embrace the present, and unveil the future. Still, this was a low-risk project: there were many "stars" involved, and Townshend would in no way have to shoulder the responsibility for the project's success (or failure).

"My Baby Gives It Away" and "Misunderstood" take us back to *The Who By Numbers*, the playfulness of "Squeeze Box," and the darkness of "However Much I Booze." In the former, the narrator describes his girlfriend's penchant for free love and invites participation:

> My baby wakes in the deep of the night
> She doesn't need it but she says it's alright
> My baby digs into some rolling away
> My baby gives it up everyday
> My baby gives it, she gives it away
> My baby gives it up everyday
> My baby
> She just gives it away.
> When you're alone in some city hotel
> You can get company by ringing a bell
> You might go pick up a girl on the street
> But my baby gives it up totally free
> My baby's counting won't cause you alarm
> My baby's brother never breaks your arm
> My baby
> I-I-I love her.
> She's cheap.

Just as "Squeeze Box" was a marked departure from the remaining *By Numbers* songs, "Misunderstood" is a stark contrast to "My Baby." Here the central character longs to be "misunderstood," since according to the character's reasoning, "misunderstanding" fosters power: "I want to be feared in my neighborhood/Just want to be a moody man/Say things nobody can understand." This character aspires to be "obscure and oblique/Inscrutable and vague," which in turn makes him/her "hard to pin down" and, more importantly, superior: "I want to leave open mouths when I speak/Want people to cry when I put them down." And yet, this person has a problem:

> I want to be either old or young
> Don't like where I've ended or where I begun
> I always feel I must get things in the can
> I just can't handle it the way I am.
> Why am I so straight and simple
> People see through me like I'm made of glass
> Why can't I deepen with graying temples
> Am I growing outta my class.
> I always feel I should be somewhere else
> I feel impatient like a girl on the shelf
> They say that I should live sera sera
> But I am such an ordinary star.

These lines revisit the introspective themes of *By Numbers* while they preface the "entertainer-artist" anxieties that engulf *Who Are You*. Townshend's character longs to be a "cool walking, smooth talking, straight smoking, fast talking" star whose mysterious qualities elevate his/her celebrity status. While that character may aspire to be mysterious and vague, the complaint about the music business and its obligations is direct: "I always feel I must get things in the can/I just can't handle it the way I am."

"Keep Me Turning" and "Heart To Hang Onto" are statements of longing presented through an impressionistic narrative style. "Keep Me Turning" uses word games and theatrical metaphors to communicate what appears to be a Townshend spiritual statement. "Keep Me Turning" begins:

> Rivers getting higher
> No wood for the fire
> They saw the messiah
> But I guess I missed him again
> That brings my score to one hundred and ten.
> The water's getting closer
> Better ring up the grocer
> Stack up the potatoes
> Poor Jack are you ever coming back
> Will your operatic soul turn black.
> Keep me turning
> Oh keep me on
> Keep me burning for your son
> Keep me turning

Don't leave me till very last
Keep me turning
I'm hanging on
Stop me yearning
I've had enough
Keep me turning
Want to hand in my backstage pass.

Townshend next describes children "smiling" and parents "whining" before he turns to a concert metaphor for one's ascent to heaven: "I got a ticket/Just gotta get past the picket/They say the trick is to walk in backwards, like you're walking out/I guess the Lord's wearing glasses now." The light instrumentals and the urgency of Townshend's voice suggest the heartfelt qualities of these rather cloudy lyrics. Just what Townshend's metaphors mean to him is a matter of speculation; nevertheless, the vague, obscure, and potentially mischievous nature of the song's contents represent major stylistic signatures from this time frame. Dave Marsh (1977) agrees:

"Keep Me Turning" is a spiritual parable that is undoubtedly much clearer to its author than to any other listener. The organ, guitar and drum interplay makes the song exciting, but what draws me back time and again is the yearning and vulnerable quality of Townshend's vocal. This is spiritual rock & roll in the very best sense: it doesn't make sense except in the heart, which won't ignore it. Its wit and charm strike beyond the confusion of its verses to the heart of the chorus, where the devotional imagery is the most complete. (p. 82)

The author stated that "Keep Me Turning" pertains to his "midlife crisis" (White, 1990, p. 223) and to the idea of "keep me young, don't tell me this is all there is, don't tell me I've got to stop now, don't tell me I can't ever be infatuated with somebody; just allow me to go on doing what I'm doing 'cause I like it." In that interview Townshend explained the line regarding his "backstage pass" meant that he "wanted the ritual to end but the real thing to continue." Such are the flexible qualities of Pete Townshend's lyrics.

"Heart To Hang Onto" is a more accessible tale in which Lane and Townshend articulate the interpersonal needs of three characters. Lane's vocals describe the characters: "Johnny" is a bar fly who "sees his life crystallized through his jar," "Sally" has her "finger on the pulse of every guy," and "Danny" wants "to save for a new guitar." And yet, "deep in [Johnny's] heart there's a cry of fear," Sally cries "deep in the night," and Danny's musical aspirations are destined to fail. The chorus explains why. Each character needs "a heart to hang onto" in general, while Johnny needs "a soul that's tailored new," Sally "a life that's tailored new," and Danny "a suit that's tailored true." In every case, the story returns to the need for somebody or something "to hang onto" for stability.

Finally, "Street in the City" is a complicated track that uses complex musical orchestrations (conducted by Townshend's father-in-law, Edwin Astley) to revisit themes that permeate the oeuvre. Townshend's concerns about "lies" and observations about "street life" are presented through an instrumental style that Altman (1977) describes as "more of a show tune than a regular pop song" (p. 64). Townshend's character leans against his/her "wall," observes the daily routines on the street, and hopes for bad things to happen. For instance, the character watches a man "up on that ledge...cleaning windows" ("What a shame/Who's to blame for the pain/We live in") and, for some unknown reason, resolves to "lean back on my wall/And pray for him to fall." The song depicts street happenings such a man entering a bank with a "bag full of very important paper," a street musician and his "new flute," the newspaper headlines concerning the "Cambridge raper," and the activities of "girls" who pass by everyday and play games "till they can claim their personal man," while Townshend's character decides to "lean back on my wall/And pray for her knickers to fall." In the closing scene, the narrator denounces the press, describing a man who "was charged with telling lies again." Townshend writes:

> I see the world go by as I lean against my wall
> I watch as Fleet Street makes new heroes rise and fall
> The news is written in the eyes of us all
> One is a sinner the next is a saint
> Most of us worry about showing up late
> I'm going to lean back on my wall and pray for him to fall.

This song introduces what will become a major trend in Townshend's post-Who writings. Not only will his writing style evolve toward a "show tune" format (this song has truly beautiful transitions, and Astley's orchestrations heighten the piece's dramatic value—Townshend is in his element here), but his penchant for psycho/sociological observation will expand via stories about individuals, relationships, neighborhoods, society, and the press. In this case, I suspect, Townshend's character is a "reporter" with an eye for sensational news copy, but one never knows.

The critics' responses to *Rough Mix* are somewhat unusual for this point in Townshend's career in that the reviews are generally positive. Marsh (1977) contends that the "juxtaposition" of the album's spiritual messages and its rock format "might be one meaning of *Rough Mix*" (p. 81) but the album "is worth the turbulence, for it touches closer to the heart of the rock & roll experience than almost anything I know" (p. 82). Schulps (1977) writes: "Townshend-watchers will be delighted that *Rough Mix* shows him in a slightly more healthy frame of mind than *Who By Numbers*...while the songs here aren't bubbling with bright-eyed optimism, neither do they sound suicidal. The rampant pessimism seems to have made way for a jokingly ironic cynicism" (p. 76). Hilburn (1977) argues that these songs offer "evidence that the doubts about the Who's future need not also apply to Townshend," since the album's "gently soothing, subtly spiritual tone comes across both honest and eloquent" (p. 68). And Altman (1977) says the work "is a rather startling album because, as a writer who most of the time hides himself behind narratives, allegories and personaes [*sic*], one is totally unprepared for the nakedness which Townshend shows here" (p. 64).

That *Rough Mix* was a positive step in Townshend's "transition" away from The Who is evident in virtually every facet of the project. *Rough Mix* offers yet another valuable glimpse of the auteur's evolution—this time, by way of "The Pete Townshend Sampler." On another level, the project provided Townshend an opportunity to work with others and this songwriter truly needs collaborators. But *Rough Mix* would prove to be but a brief respite; he quickly returned to his monolithic control over The Who. Even though he claimed *Rough Mix* rejuvenated him ("Now I've got 40 songs ready for the next Who thing"—Mills, 1977, p. 68), that feeling would be short-lived. To be sure, a number of those "40 songs" found their way onto *Empty Glass*, my next topic.

EMPTY GLASS

Townshend's career takes a decisive turn with his 1980 release *Empty Glass*. This record represents the first time that the songwriter placed *his* work above The Who. By 1979-1980, Townshend was more than prepared to disband The Who in order pursue his own creative agenda. Part of that decision, he told *Rolling Stone*, involved the ascendance of the punk rock movement: "It freed me. It allowed me to be myself. It dignified me, in a way, to be cast to one side" (*Empty Glass*, 1989, p. 11). He explained what *Empty Glass* meant to his career: "[It] was the most important thing I've ever done for me—to allow me to have a new beginning, to actually grow." Townshend hired Chris Thomas (who produced punk acts, such as The Pretenders and Sex Pistols) and a cast of musicians who would appear on most of his future projects (e.g., "Rabbit" Bundrick on keyboards, Simon Phillips on drums, Peter Hope-Evans on harmonica). When asked about the album's thematic content, Townshend told the *Trouser Press* he "just decided to *write*—to write straight from the hip and offer everything to the project that's going at the time" (Murray, 1980, p. 17).

Empty Glass contains ten original compositions (running 40:01) that reflect Townshend's "write from the hip" orientation. As a result, the album offers a compelling state-of-the-auteur snapshot. The project's dominant theme is spiritual in nature ("I Am An Animal," "Let My Love Open The Door," "A Little Is Enough," and "Empty Glass"), with brief commentaries about music journalism ("Jools and Jim") and assorted topics, several of which reflect Townshend's emerging penchant for word games and free association: the epitome of "writing from the hip." One point is certain: Townshend's impressionistic writing style is expanding.

I begin with *Empty Glass*'s spiritual songs. The liner notes establish this album's spiritual tone through a quote attributed to Avatar Meher Baba: "Desire for nothing except desirelessness, hope for nothing except to rise above all hopes, want nothing and you will have everything." These spiritual songs are, indeed, arranged haphazardly. Those messages seem to unfold in a three-stage fashion: first, Townshend introduces the "spiritual need," by way of the album's title cut and ninth track, "Empty Glass"; second, he articulates a "spiritual dilemma," through "I Am An Animal"; and third, he offers a "spiritual answer," through two equivocal tunes, "Let My Love Open The Door" and "A Little Is Enough." "Empty Glass" appears to open with autobiography:

> Why was I born today
> Life is useless like Ecclesiastes say
> I never had a chance
> But opportunity's now in my hands.
> I stand with my guitar
> All I need's a mirror
> And I'm a star
> I'm so sick of dud TV
> Next time you switch on
> You might see me...oh what a thrill for you.
> I've been there and gone there
> I've lived there and bummed there
> I've spinned there, I gave there
> I drank there and I slaved there.
> I've had enough of the way things have been done
> Every man on a razor's edge
> Someone has used us to kill with the same gun
> Killing each other by driving a wedge.
> My life's a mess I wait for you to pass
> I stand here at the bar, I hold an empty glass.

After an instrumental interlude, the song repeats these verses (with a few minor changes) and pauses for a brief, but important, resolution: "Don't worry smile and dance/You just can't work life out/Don't let down moods entrance you/Take the wine and shout."

The extent to which Townshend uses "Empty Glass" as a vehicle for auto-biographical complaint is, as always, uncertain. At first he seems to address The Who ("opportunity's now in my hands"), next he sarcastically comments on his celebrity status, then he presents his character's experience, and closes with a generational complaint. The chorus ("My life's a mess.... I hold an empty glass") is ripe for all sorts of interpretations—typically, that Townshend is embellishing his alcoholism. The author used media interviews to clarify his point:

The spark-off for the song was when I read Ecclesiastes again, and it was so powerful it just reminded me of the way Britain is today.... Bringing it closer to home, to my age group, after winning the war you end up with fuck all. You got King Solomon talking about how after he's fucked everybody and had everything and gone through everything, the only piece of advice he's got is that life is useless. But it also contains some great inspirational poetry: "There is a time" and all that. It really reminded me of a lot of Persian Sufi poetry, that it's only in desperation that you become spiritually open.... This thing that I was talking about before about the empty glass: it's this whole thing about the innocence and purity of the heart; whatever you do the heart will remain pure. But you have to go out and suffer life; you can't just sit there going, "I am pure. Peace will come to me." The song's about this guy sitting at the bar and waiting for life to come to him and say, "you have won a star prize!" (Murray, 1980, pp. 20-21)

Townshend's comments are rich, and the elaborate spiritual message *requires* that commentary to gain coherence. The song, in and of itself, is so chaotically impressionistic that *Townshend's* message is buried. Still, it introduces two major themes: his views about British society and its impact on men of Town-shend's generation (shades of "Slip Kid"), and his belief that regardless of what we do in *this* life we all end up in heaven eventually (a partial restatement of "Let's See Action"). Entire projects will be based on these two themes over the next fourteen years. Moreover, notice Townshend's reiteration of the *Quadro-phenia*-Jimmy dilemma in which he claims purity is the product of desperation (one must destroy one's self in order to come to grips with that self). Later, Townshend sharpened his "Empty Glass" analogy: "Hafiz...used to talk about God's love being wine, and that we learn to be intoxicated and that the heart is like an empty cup. You hold up the heart and hope that God's grace will fill your cup with his wine. You stand in the tavern, a useless soul waiting for the barman to give you a drink—the barman being God" (Marcus, 1981, p. 407). There he offered a Baba version of the "Empty Glass" analogy that recalls his Mod heritage: "It's also Meher Baba talking about the fact that the heart is like a glass, and that God can't fill it up with his love—if it's already filled with love for yourself."

After establishing the need to hold out your "cup" to receive God's "wine," Townshend's spiritual message turns to the worldly dilemma that fosters that spiritual need. "I Am An Animal" addresses life's spiritual journey and the sig-nificance of a spiritual foundation (I think!). Again, the author's impressionism invites a host of readings:

I was always here in the silence
I was never under your eye
Gather up your love in some wiseness
Every memory shall always survive
And you will see me.
I am an animal
My teeth are sharp and my mouth is full
And the passion is so strong
When I'm alone, loneliness will change me.
I am a vegetable
I get my body badly pulled
And I'm rooted to the spot
Nothing will rearrange me.
I'm looking back and I can't see the past
Anymore, so hazy
I'm on a track and I travelling so fast
Oh for sure I'm crazy.

The narrator declares, "I am a human being" ("I don't believe all the things I'm seeing/I've nowhere to hide anymore/I'm losing my way") and, "I am an angel" ("I booked in here I came straight from hell/And I don't know how to lie anymore/I'm boozing to pray"). All indications are that this character is either "lost" or fears that he/she is "lost" and is no longer able to cover it up ("And I don't know how to lie anymore"). Consequently, he/she turns to a worldly answer, "boozing to pray." The song seems to continue with more role confusion, as the character acknowledges the dilemma that has rendered the introspective confusion: "And I don't know where you are anymore/I've got no clue." Using imagery suggestive of "The Amazing Journey" poem, Townshend's character is off the path, has lost his/her master, and is unable to look back down that path and its spiritual lessons. The author appears to be saying that we are complicated entities—part animal, vegetable, human being, and angel (these references could also be personal metaphors)—but we are nothing in the absence of spiritual drive, an imperative that requires we hold out our "glass" and remain focused on our personal "Amazing Journey."

"Empty Glass" and "I Am An Animal" are two introspective songs that convey Townshend's spiritual confusion during a very demanding portion of his life. The album's two-part spiritual resolution does not share that intensity. In "Let My Love Open The Door" and "A Little Is Enough," he returns to a song-writing style that employs cryptic characterizations to mask his point (is the song about a romantic relationship? a spiritual message? or some combination?). "Let My Love Open The Door" urges the listener to keep the faith in the face of life's difficulties. The narrator offers comfort; just when you think "love" is impossible or "when everybody seems unkind," a remedy is available ("Let my love open the door/To your heart"). The song declares:

> I have the only key to your heart
> I can stop you falling apart
> Try today, you'll find this way
> Come on and give me a chance to say
> Let my love open the door
> It's all I'm living for
> Release yourself from misery
> There's only one thing gonna set you free
> That's my love.

The story's ambiguity is its strength. When considered in light of the previously discussed songs, the track's spiritual message is focused and clear; however, in the absence of that framework, the song is open to a romantic reading as well. This strategy also appears in "A Little Is Enough." Here Townshend's lyrics gain in complexity, as he tosses about images that, once more, suggest autobiography:

> They say that love often passes in a second
> And you can never catch it up

> So I'm hanging on to you as though eternity beckoned
> But it's clear that the match is rough
> Common sense 'd tell me not to try 'n continue
> But I'm after a piece of that diamond in you
> So keep an eye open
> My spirit ain't broken
> Your love's so incredible
> Your body's so edible
> You give me an overdose of love
> Just a little is enough.

The song continues with sexual/drug related imagery: "I eat an oyster and I feel the contact/But more than one would be a waste," "Some people want an endless line that's true," and "Your love is like heroin/This addict is mellowing." These images converge, again, on a reiteration of "The Amazing Journey" poem and Townshend's commitment to stay on the path:

> Just like a sailor heading into the seas
> There's a gale blowing in my face
> The high winds scare me but I need the breeze
> And I can't head for any other place
> Life would seem so easy on the other track
> But even a hurricane won't turn me back
> You might be an island
> On the distant horizon
> But the little I see
> Looks like heaven to me
> And I don't care if the ocean gets rough
> Just a little is enough.

Dave Marsh (1980) concurs that these two tracks evoke romantic imagery when he writes the songs "might sound purely romantic on the radio, yet their imagery is shaped by religion (Whose body is so 'edible,' after all, as the Lord's?)" (p. 72). Townshend moves away from the direct complaint that characterized Who songs from this era and returns to a narrative signature from the singles period: open stories that communicate value-laden messages through ambiguous characterizations. That Townshend strategically employs such characterizations is evident in his comments about "A Little Is Enough":

It was *purely* personal: instant, and purely transparent. It's very emotional, but it's also very straightforward and clear. Just the fact that you can't fucking have the world.... I suppose I wrote the song about a mixture of things: I wrote it a little bit about God's love. But mainly about the feeling that I had for *my wife*—and the fact that I don't see enough of her, and that when we are together there's lots of times when things aren't good.... Because love, by its very nature, is an infinite quality, an infinite emotion—just to experience it *once* in a lifetime is enough. Because a lot of people don't—don't *ever* experience it. (Marcus, 1981, p. 407)

Pete Townshend's songs are "purely personal" to the point that characterological ambiguity, metaphorical games, and lyrical tomfoolery occasionally emerge
as a given song's principal feature. The extent to which Townshend uses these
narrative devices to camouflage personal views varies from song to song; nevertheless, the consistent use of such storytelling techniques offers evidence of
artistic style and, when joined with the story's content, creative vision. Hence,
an idea may be "straightforward and clear" to the auteur while its public articulation produces a rather cloudy story.

Townshend's narratives, as we know, assume other structures as well. In the
album's fifth track, "Jools and Jim," he turns to a direct narrative style
to complain about music journalism and, in particular, reporters Julie Birchill
and Tony Parsons. Here we note the writer's capacity to hit his audience
straight on with an explicit message:

> Anyone can have an opinion
> Anyone can join in and jump
> Anyone can pay or just stay away
> Anyone can crash and thump.
> But did you read the stuff that Julie said?
> Or little Jimmy with his hair dyed red?
> They don't give a shit Keith Moon is dead
> Is that exactly what I thought I read?
> Typewriter tappers
> You're all just crappers
> You listen to love with your intellect
> A4 pushers
> You're all just cushions
> Morality ain't measured in a room
> He wrecked.
> Anyone can buy some leather
> Ain't no better than wearing sheep
> Anyone can sell lucky heather
> You can see that words are cheap!

The song continues by assailing "Jools and Jim" for having "a standard of perfection there/That you and me can never share" before shifting moods and
turning pensive:

> But I know for sure that if we met up eye to eye
> A little wine could bring us closer, you and I
> 'Cos your right, hypocrisy will be the death of me
> And there's an i before e when you're spelling ecstasy.
> Did you hear the stuff that Krishna said?
> Or know for you that Jesus' blood was shed?
> Is it in your heart or in your head?
> Or does the truth lay in the centre spread?

The song concludes with the "Anyone can have an opinion" stanza prior to the closing lines: "Oklahoma/Oklahoma/Oklahoma...OK." Although Townshend said he changed the song's title from "Jools & Tone" to "Jools & Jim" because the song is "not directly about" Birchill and Parsons ("it's about taking a stance and believing what you read. It's just another 'don't believe what you read' song"—Murray, 1980, p. 20), the song's direct complaint on Keith Moon's behalf as well as the remarks about listening "to love with your intellect" and displaying a unique "standard of perfection" are quite pointed. That observation aside, "Jools and Jim" initiates several themes and stylistic features that reappear for some time to come. Thematically, the introspective nature of a line such as "'Cos you're right, hypocrisy will be the death of me" foreshadows the *All The Best Cowboys Have Chinese Eyes* project, and the "don't believe what you read" angle—specifically, the "Or does the truth lay in the centre spread?" line—is a central element of the *PsychoDerelict* project. In terms of narrative signatures, the song's use of purposeful gibberish ("And there's an i before e when you're spelling ecstasy"), word games ("Anyone can join in and jump...Anyone can crash and thump"), and idiosyncratic metaphors (assuming the "Oklahoma" lines are metaphoric, they could represent more games) preview forthcoming trends. And finally, notice how the song turns from an attack toward reconciliation ("A little wine could bring us closer, you and I") in the same fashion as "La La La Lies."

Further evidence of Townshend's impressionistic writing style may be found in three of the album's less coherent tracks: "Keep On Working," "Cat's in the Cupboard," and "Gonna Get Ya." These songs use pleasant—and at times, powerful—musical structures to articulate loosely framed messages. "Keep On Working" appears to discuss Townshend's financial problems and the respite his children provide as his creditors demand that he "keep on working" (Townshend told Garbarini [1982b] that the song is a failed attempt to copy the Kinks). "Cat's in the Cupboard" is a fast-paced, powerful track that conveys the character's frustrations over his/her inability to "get an answer" ("No one's answering me/Can't get an answer"). Just what this person is unable to get a response to is unclear in the song. Townshend is either using a "rat" and a "cat" metaphor in some obscure fashion or merely playing word games. Consider this excerpt from the song's opening: "Cat's in the cupboard/You've got to set him free/Cat's in the cupboard you've got to set him free/Cat's in the cupboard/You've got to set him free./Rats on the high street/You've got to let 'em be/Rats on the high street/You've got to let 'em be/Rats on the high street/Can't you let them be./While your racing/People wasting/Life's enthralling/People calling/While you're weeping/Blood is seeping/While you're dancing/No one's answering me/Can't get an answer."

When we consider that Townshend admits the tenth song, "Gonna Get Ya," is a word game (as he told Murray [1980], the song is "nonsense...just a word game. I don't think it means anything" [p. 21]), "Cat's in the Cupboard" may follow a similar strategy as well—although the "rats" and "cats" relationship may hold the key to unlocking this track. In 1997, Townshend reports the song is "not really a word game" at all; in fact, it was written for the "Rock Against Racism" concert. Hence, the "cat-rat" segregationist metaphor is a helpful reading.

The two remaining tracks—"Rough Boys" and "And I Moved"—represent two of the oeuvre's more complicated, and in several respects controversial, entries. The liner notes dedicate "Rough Boys" to Townshend's children and the Sex Pistols, while "And I Moved" was originally written for Bette Midler. The album's first track, "Rough Boys," opens with powerful, sustained guitar chords as Townshend sings:

Tough boys
Running the streets
Come a little closer
Rough toys
Under the sheets
Nobody knows her
Rough boys
Don't walk away
I very nearly missed you
Tough boys
Come over here
I wanna bite and kiss you.
I wanna see what I can find
Tough kids
Take a bottle of wine
When your deal is broken
Ten quid
She's so easy to blind
Not a word is spoken
Rough boys
Don't walk away
I'm still pretty blissed here
Tough boy
I'm gonna carry you home
You got pretty pissed dear

From there the narrator promises, "Gonna get inside you/Gonna get inside your bitter mind." The song rotates between portrayals of strength (above) and weakness ("What can I do?/I'm so pale and weedy/Rough fits/In my Hush Puppy shoes/But I'm still pleadin'") and uses vague sexual references to create a "rough love" message that is wide open for interpretation. Carr (1980) describes "Rough Boys" as Townshend "railing and pleading and boasting and confessing all at once" (p. 67) through a "very complex" song that "shifts perspective from line to line." Cromelin (1980) contends the song is "'My Generation' from the other side" and asserts: "The song drives and slashes, running on a friction between the fascination and alienation the subject inspires. Townshend acknowledges the generation gap, and his determination to bridge it comes across with an erotic intensity." The author's comments about "Rough Boys" vary between sources. In *Rolling Stone*, Townshend discussed the gay community's response:

A lot of gays and a lot of bisexuals wrote to me congratulating me on this so-called coming out. I think in both cases ["Rough Boys" and "And I Moved"] the images are very angry, aren't they? In "Rough Boys," the line "Come over here, I want to bite and kiss you" is about "I can scare you! I can frighten you! I can hurt all you macho individuals simply by coming up and pretending to be gay!" And that's what I really meant in that song, I *think.* (*Empty Glass*, 1989, p. 11)

In an interview with Timothy White (1990) Townshend was more direct about the song's homosexual orientation. When asked if the song was written for The Who, he responded: "No, no. How could 'Rough Boys' be written for the Who? It's about homosexuality" (p. 224). He explained:

What, in a sense, "Rough Boys" was about was almost a coming-out, an acknowledgment of the fact that I'd had a gay life, and that I understood what gay sex was about: it was not about faggery at all. It was about violence in a lot of senses. It leans very heavily into the kind of violence that men carry in them. If men have a violence which cannot be shared with women, then it can't be shared with them sexually. And so there's only one place for that violence and that's with other men. (p. 225)

In contrast to this "rough love" message is "And I Moved," with its smooth, flowing piano instrumental that establishes a musical context for an ambiguous lyrical statement. The song contains but two stanzas: "And I moved/As I saw him looking in though my window/His eyes were silent lies/And I moved/And I saw him standing in the doorway/His figure merely filled the space/And I moved/But I moved toward him./ [extended instrumental] /And I moved/And his hands felt like ice exciting/As he laid me back just like an empty dress/And I moved/But a minute later he was weeping/His tears his only truth/And I moved/But I moved toward him/I moved toward him." In classic Townshend style, we have no idea who "he" is or why the character is attracted to "him." However, the description of "his hands" and the line "As he laid me back just like an empty dress" are suggestive of a sexual encounter. Interestingly, "his" response to the event is intense and, perhaps, deceptive. To that end, Townshend told White (1990) that he wrote the song for Bette Midler, hence, his use of pronouns. He continued:

One of the things that stunned me when *Empty Glass* came out was that I realized I'd found a female audience, just by being honest. Not necessarily by saying, "I am gay, I am gay, I am gay." But just by being honest about the fact that I understand how gay people feel, and I identify. And I know how it feels to be a woman. I know how it feels to be a woman because I *am* a woman. And I won't be classified as just a man. (p. 225)

Townshend's comments were highly publicized and reprinted in a variety of media. His response to that publicity is somewhat humorous: "Scandal is fabulous. No artist ever suffers from it. The people who suffer are the artist's family and friends. When Reuters put out on the wire that I was a transsexual, cross-dressing sheep-fucker, I was laughing until I saw my cleaning lady's face. It was a weird day. Those things are difficult. It's not that all publicity is good publicity" (Gill, 1993a, p. 104). In 1994, Townshend's reflections about this incident were intense:

["Rough Boys"] is ironic because the song is actually taunting both the homosexuals in America—who were, at the time, dressing themselves up as Nazi generals—and the punks in Britain dressing the same way. I thought it was great that these tough punks were dressing as homosexuals without realizing it. I did an interview about it, saying *Rough Boys* was about being gay, and in the interview I also talked about my "gay life," which—I meant—was actually about the friends I've had who are gay. So the interviewer kind of dotted the t's and crossed the i's and assumed that this was a coming out, which it wasn't at all. But I became an object of ridicule when it was picked up in England. It was a big scandal, which is silly. If I were bisexual, it would be no big deal in the music industry.... But I was bitter and angry at the way the truth had been distorted and decided never to do any interviews again. Not because I had been manipulated but because I didn't trust myself to be precise about what I was saying. (Sheff, 1994, p. 148)

Regardless of the various interpretations and commentaries, these two songs offer strong evidence of Townshend's narrative style in that the songs' ambiguity invites a variety of possible readings. That tendency is wholly consistent with the auteur's artistic philosophy: the message is there, if you want it, but its intensity has been tempered. Pete Townshend is not going to "hit you over the head" with his "idea of the month," even though that style may facilitate controversy.

The critics' responses to *Empty Glass* appear to share the view that the work is intensely personal. In its review of the 1980s, *Rolling Stone* reports "Pete Townshend chronicled the personal tumult he was experiencing and initiated an adult style of songwriting that helped reenergize the singer-songwriter tradition of the Eighties" (*Empty Glass*, 1989, p. 11). The *Village Voice* uses its review for a state-of-the-artist commentary: "Poor Pete...still spare and sparky and hardly even dazed by his early middle age, he just has his great intelligence, his rampaging doubts, his extreme intensity and his Remy Martin Cognac" (Carr, 1980, p. 67). From there, Carr assesses the album: "Devoid of fun-pop whimsy or allegorical bombast or anthems for his or anyone else's generation it is...strictly personal. Poor Pete: alcoholic, quadrophenic, and honest...the Remy bills must have been staggering" (p. 67). (That last line is a liner note reference, which I discuss in a moment.) The *Los Angeles Times* comments on the songwriter's writing style and uses lyrics from "Jools and Jim" to communicate its point: "Throughout the album Townshend unleashes fusillades of words, like a man compelled to articulate positions whose essence is uncertainty and dislocation.... That won't hurt the album's commercial potential, true, but it bothers us typewriter tappers, who find his rare blend of spiritual and temporal concerns worthy of more inspired framing" (Cromelin, 1980). Marsh (1980) describes how "Townshend the preacher" (p. 72) uses *Empty Glass* to "step down from his pulpit to wander once more through his peculiar parish." The writer notes that Townshend "fashions his music from sermons and confessions" and concludes: "*Empty Glass* isn't just an album with vaguely religious connotations. It's as consciously spiritual as any rock & roll record ever made."

Empty Glass is a watershed in Pete Townshend's career. With this project the auteur turns the corner, moves away from The Who, and initiates a solo career based on personal expression. In so doing, Townshend relies on a narrative style that incorporates old and new traits. First, he employs ambiguous story structures that avoid "hitting his audience over the head" with his spiritual themes. Equally traditional is his capacity for direct complaint, as he goes straight after music journalists in "Jools and Jim"—a tight narrative structure that leaves little doubt about the song's message. Townshend also introduces an equivocal style that deliberately misleads or confuses the message; unlike the "ambiguous" signature that allows a choice, this signature is deceptive. This stylistic tendency leads to "word games" in which Townshend employs powerful instrumental patterns to establish a context for purposeful gibberish; the track sounds super but says little (at least at a surface reading). The author may view solo albums as vehicles for conveying how *he* feels about *his* life; however, he expresses those sentiments through a stylistic lens that adheres to an avowed artistic philosophy.

With regard to this "snapshot" of the artist at this point in time, perhaps *Empty Glass*'s liner notes sum up the situation best: "Thanks to Remy Martin Cognac for saving my life by making the bloody stuff so expensive" (he also dedicated the album to Karen Townshend). Assuredly, 1979-1980 were troubling times for Pete Townshend; losing Keith Moon, the decaying Who situation, domestic and lifestyle complications, and other things made this a difficult period. And yet, Townshend *believed* in his art: "I hold rock above most forms of art because it is one of the few forms of communication where there are people who are idealistic in the medium. And there is a very high percentage of people who *listen* who are looking for idealism and are disappointed when they get empty crap. I aspire to music that has brains, balls and heart" (Arrington, 1980, p. 31). That aspiration would provide the strength for Townshend to move beyond The Who and follow his artistic agenda, but the artist would "destroy himself still further" before he would "face himself" and his situation.

ALL THE BEST COWBOYS HAVE CHINESE EYES

The extent to which *Empty Glass* represents a pivotal point in Pete Townshend's career is evident in the *All The Best Cowboys Have Chinese Eyes* project. *Chinese Eyes* revisits one of Townshend's long-standing principles: in order to move forward, you must first step back. Like *Quadrophenia*'s "Jimmy," when this writer faces a crossroads his first response is to step back and take stock of the situation (perhaps "The Amazing Journey" lessons). When Townshend faced the crossroads between writing singles and accepting the pretentious challenge of the "rock opera," he revisited the single's best friend, radio, as a transition. When he entertained the choice between artistic innovation and industry prescriptions, Townshend returned to his first opera and the *Tommy* film. Now, as he prepares to exit The Who and enter the risky world of an independent career, he pauses for a look back and evaluates his personal and professional life to that point in time. Townshend realizes these transitions are not simple matters, and his art conveys that understanding.

Subsequently, *Chinese Eyes* offers another state-of-the-auteur snapshot (our last) as we consider Townshend's reflections on his life. These ruminations address a range of topics on a variety of levels, with varying clarity. Townshend assesses his spiritual state, his views on stardom, and celebrity's impact on his life through a narrative style that employs multiple media. To capture fully the scope of *Chinese Eyes*'s message one must consult the album, the short essay printed in the liner notes, the "video EP" of the same title, and, of course, Townshend's extensive media commentary.

I begin with the album's liner notes. Townshend's essay is without a title and simply appears on the liner notes' final page. It begins:

There have always been times like these. The multi-coloured spheres crash and collide, the triangle expands and explodes: eventually there is nothing.

They were being attacked from all sides, everything seemed hopeless. There seemed to be no language in which they could communicate to their adversaries, to beseech them for mercy. At a crucial moment a natural leader emerged. His horse was dry and cool when all others were frothing and bleeding, his leather clothes dusty and worn. His face was keen and firm, lightly lined and weather beaten. The most remarkable thing about him was his eyes; half shut against the wind blown dust and the noise of guns. The pupils seemed hidden and colourless, dilated so much by the brilliance of the sand-reflected sun they appeared like needle points.

Townshend's hero "saved them all by skilful organising and rallying rhetoric," making the tough decisions that led to victory. When "they" returned home, everything fell apart: "Once home it didn't take long for them to lose their way again. They lost husbands and wives, the closeness and changes of their children and families, the regular contact with old friends and lovers, their hold on normality (particularly vis a vis money), and finally somehow, somewhere, they lost God."

The essay shifts context to "Hollywood" where "fools learned how to behave like stars under a Caligulan sky" and briefly establishes Hollywood's connection with the end of World War I: "When the twenties arrived men who are now British grandfathers became free again—no more uniforms" (a rather displaced statement with thematic implications for this and future projects). He next describes the "star's" lifestyle ("At night they drank freely, smoked, tasted cocaine and made love. The boredom was fundamental.") and contrasts that luxury with the Depression's poverty. The work moves to what appears to be a description of film audiences, their efforts to recapture the memory of "the man who had redeemed them years before," their frustrations over their inability to do so (because "they had confused real heroism with power"), how "they" became "atavistic," and their susceptibility to an "ironic justice" ("had they actually become like one of those pathetic pedestal souls they wanted to emulate—insular and alone—they might have drowned in a very confused sea"). Next, we pause for a twenty-five-line poem about the sea in which Townshend offers descriptions of the water's functions ("For some the sea runs with oil and gas.... To some the sea holds fish.... For some the sea evokes an idea of God.... For others the sea is a dumping ground") prior to the narrator's account of the sea's significance:

> For me once the sea was a promise,
> A memory of what seemed an endless love.
> It proved not to be endless but enough perhaps.
> Now the sea is a vast accessible wasteland;
> An infinitude in which to hide our cupfuls of tears.
> Tomorrow the sea will be the place to dive and swim,
> To flow and timelessly drown in Pacific patience.
> Then again, the sea will be the sea.
> And me? I will still be merely me.

The prose resumes with "stardom" and the writer's view: "The movie made the star and the star made movies, but somewhere men with calculating screwed up eyes—a little like our hero's—made the real killings. Years later rock and roll, a half grown teacher, tried to create stars. The men with the snake-like slits for eyes reaped again, but is the pusher really worse than the junkie?"

The essay shifts context with a new paragraph. This time Townshend writes: "Everyone needed someone to blame. Some accused politicians, some whole races of people different to themselves, some pointed fingers at established religions." He describes people who "ended their lives because they felt too ordinary...too uniform"; all the while "they were placing blame" as well. The next paragraph continues the accusatory theme, describing the "evil" everyone observed in everyone else, noting that "the potential for evil is within—not without," and observing that a "smile" is "the greatest force to hurl against suffering." That paragraph concludes: "But look at the smiling cowboy, the natural leader and champion of the downtrodden soul. He smiled as he urged them all to war, 'Just once more.'"

The piece closes with a brief paragraph about how "they arrived alive" and "found the broken bottle trail without help." "All stars, great and small, shine under God," Townshend observes: "It was only impudence and frivolity that conspired to make any one of them try to get higher. A smile is still merely a smile. Anyone for snooker?" With those lines the essay ends and a seventeen line poem follows:

> I walked between identical houses,

In towns so similar the memory of each blends.
I walked through forests;
God paid attention to detail
But on the surface one forest is much like another.
I walked between identical soldiers.
They belonged to opposing armies.
Armies so similar they fought one another for history.
Those who survived resumed living together.
I walked with children,
Their faces painted and streaked, their clothes preened,
I watched their delight in being alike.
I heard music drift down,
Cello struck vamps of twitching lethargy.
I looked at the heroes
And the junkies in the billiard hall —
All the best cowboys have Chinese eyes.

Townshend's impressionism—complete with its characterological ambiguity, nebulous plot progression, and cryptic metaphors—make this essay rough going. The work seems to address the inherent hypocrisy of celebrity by tracing its evolution from the "frontier" to "Hollywood" to "rock and roll," and by noting the dysfunctional qualities of the "star-audience" relationship. Hypocrisy and manipulation run rampant in this somewhat uneven tale. Townshend explained his "hero" theme to Kurt Loder (1982a):

Basically, it's about the fact that you can't hide what you're really like. I just had this image of the average American hero—somebody like a Clint Eastwood or a John Wayne. Somebody with eyes like slits, who was basically capable of anything—you know, any kind of murderous act or whatever to get what was required—to get, let's say, his people to safety. And yet, to those people he's saving, he's a great hero, a knight in shining armor—forget the fact that he cut off fifty people's heads to get them home safely.... And I've taken this a little bit further—because I spent so much of my time in society, high society, last year—to comment on stardom and power and drug use and decadence, and how there's a strange parallel, in a way, between the misuse of power and responsibility by inept politicians and the misuse of power and responsibility by people who are heroes. If you're a really good person, you can't hide it by acting bad; and if you're a bad person, you can't hide it by acting good. Also—more to the point, really—that there's no outward, identifiable evil, you know? People spend most of their time looking for evil and identifying evil outside themselves. But the potential for evil is inside you. (p. 18)

The *Chinese Eyes* video (directed by Chalkie Davis and Carol Starr; produced by Genevieve Davey) is a thirty-minute production that stresses themes that both complement and contrast the liner note essay. The "video EP" is a mixture of music video tomfoolery and Townshend commentary with an overriding emphasis on his recovery from his substance abuse problems. The video contains ten scenes of varying length, complexity, and clarity. It opens with the song "Prelude" and video of a grassy, open garden area. As the song moves through a piano instrumental (a soft, pensive sound), Townshend walks out from behind a group of trees, dressed in a robe, head down, left arm extended across his body holding his right arm. The scene relates Townshend's "recovery" as the song begins: "Sometimes, walking through the streets of this city/I see all the faces of the winners and the losers/Oh why, can't I see a change/Just one sign/Before I say goodbye/Before I say goodbye." The one-minute, thirty-two-second scene establishes Townshend's physical state and his longing for a "change" in his life.

That scene shifts abruptly to the song "Face Dances Part Two" and a silly video featuring Townshend's morning rituals. The opening shot shows him lying in bed (arms and legs spread apart), waking up, and moving to the bathroom to shave. As he shaves, small "talking head" machines "sing" the song, while the video cuts in and out of his high-speed shaving, the talking head machines, and scenes of Townshend singing behind a double-neck guitar and various instruments. The song's conclusion takes us to a kitchen scene in which a Townshend voice-over discusses his situation while he makes breakfast (much silliness here: attempting to use a chain saw to cut his bread). The voice-over relates:

There are no great revelations about the songs [on the album] except one. And that's that this is the first record I've ever made during which I felt that there was no hope whatsoever to try to repair my lost love for my wife and family or to repair the damage I felt I'd unwittingly laid on my friends and my relationship with the other guys in the band, The Who. And the songs, as a result, each a reflection of an aspect of what it's like to feel alone, I think, and yet still be yearning for lost emotions and power. "Prelude" the opening song you heard is a simple prayer for change in a world that from my viewpoint had gone crazily wrong. "Face Dances," the second song you heard, is the anthem of the soul in solitary confinement.... It's like feeling in jail. And the face that I sing about is my own, I wrote the words while I was looking in a mirror. [Pause to start the chain saw, to no avail.] The cause of the loneliness is partly obvious, I've become incredibly confused over the years with The Who. I think anybody that's read interviews I've done over the years and seen the work of the band knows the kind of confusion and perhaps its a kind of self-inflicted torment. I know a lot of people reckon I couldn't live without it. A lot of the values I'd held to be important in the early part of the band's career and in the early seventies—spiritually and morally and creatively—got let down somehow, compromised. I think because I wanted an easier, happier life, I've always found it difficult to say no and I think that applies also to "no" when somebody asks you for a favor and also "no" when somebody is trying to [enter] into your life in some way. And I'd spread myself really thin in this pursuit of the good life and my wife and I lost touch, even living in the same house and the drinking habits became downright selfish. And the business pursuits I'd got involved in outside of music distracted me from my creative work. And almost two-thirds of the way through this record I came to my senses, thank God, and with a lot of help from friends I got back to my work and my family and my wife and I began again. And lonely breakfasts aren't part of my routine anymore and neither is brandy in the coffee or chain saw hangovers, thank God. It's incredible to think that music began so simply for me when I was a kid in Acton and I had no idea how much it would challenge me when I got older. And how much the simple thing I call rock and roll could give and how much it could take—try to take.

Townshend concludes as a telephone rings and the video cuts to the song "Communication." The music video rotates between scenes of a recording studio, Townshend singing into a telephone, and an interpreter for the deaf (a middle-aged white male) signing portions of the song (basically signing "communication" over and over). The video is full of communications-related imagery, with jumps between scenes (one scene featuring Townshend in the grassy area shown in the opening, playing his guitar, and getting entangled in his guitar cord as he spins around and around).

The video shifts to the song "Stardom In Acton" with scenes of a highway leading into Acton (England). With shots foreshadowing the *White City* movie, the video offers various views of the town and its people. The crux of the video involves cuts between Townshend walking around town (missing a bus because he stopped to give his autograph to a young girl, holding open the telephone booth door for an older lady, simply walking the streets with his hands in his pockets) and a group of four young men (clearly a band—carrying guitar cases, drummer with drum sticks in hand). The imagery is unequivocal: Townshend and the youngsters co-exist in the same "neighborhood," walk the same streets, and yet they remain separate.

From there, another music video unfolds; this time, featuring the song "Exquisitely Bored." Here Townshend picnics in an area much like the grassy spot of the opening scene (he rows down a river, goes ashore, empties his picnic basket, hits golf balls, enjoys his meal and tea). The various scenes suggest Townshend was "exquisitely bored" during his stay in California and the audience is afforded a glimpse of that recuperation. Afterward, the video moves to a another voice-over segment that features Townshend walking along the Thames River, talking about his fascination with rivers and the songwriting process. The remarks about "the river" are revealing:

It always reminds me of a soul irrevocably plodding on towards God. It's full of food for fish and it provides London with most of its water and yet its also treated like a rubbish dump...people chunk their cars in and their beer cans, their used contraceptives and everything else. And many rivers still get used as sewers and yet they all get to the sea in the end. And so the analogy with the human soul always appeals to me [the song "The Sea Refuses No River" emerges in the audio background], the fact that it doesn't matter how clean or dirty you are, you get there in the end. It reminds me constantly, the river, of my immortality and of my goal and in a strange way—however I feel—it reminds me of my permanence.

Townshend notes that his life has "come round full circle" by the summer of 1982 and that songs such as "Slit Skirts" are now "new anthems" in his life. The commentary ends with this observation: "Love always wins out in the end, but when you're down it's hard to believe that." With that, a studio performance of "Slit Skirts" precedes another music video. The song "Uniforms" provides a context for a strange and goofy portrayal of Townshend working as a waiter in what appears to be a country club setting. He "serves" customers (mostly mannequins) while he "sings" the song. The EP ends with a solemn

Townshend (dressed in black in a dimly lit set) playing the piano instrumental from "Prelude" as the credits roll.

The *Chinese Eyes* video employs a collage presentational style that takes the viewer from one scene to the next for no apparent reason. And yet when Townshend's personal situation is taken into consideration, a more coherent message emerges, and that message is distinct from—and yet complements—the liner note essay. While Townshend's commentary and the "Stardom In Acton" video speak to the heroism/stardom theme, the bulk of the video delves into his recovery, his frustrations over the difficulties of communicating with his audience, and a "state-of-the-auteur" message (his relationship with punk rock, his spiritual standing, and the vicissitudes of middle age).

The *Chinese Eyes* album was released only a few months prior to The Who's final studio album, *It's Hard*. The album contains eleven tracks (running 41:25), with nine original Townshend compositions, one Townshend/Andy Newman collaboration ("Prelude"), and one "traditional" ("North Country Girl"). The album was produced by Chris Thomas and features Townshend's now-standard cast of musicians. When the work is examined in its entirety, I contend, its message may be broken into two parts: a statement of spiritual realization and an extended commentary on the author's life with an emphasis on "stardom's" impact. The latter portion speaks to four areas: his wife Karen, his work, his lifestyle, and personal frustrations over his current situation.

I begin with Townshend's spiritual statement. As the video EP indicates, "The Sea Refuses No River" represents the author's understanding that "it doesn't matter how clean or dirty you are, you get [to heaven] in the end"—a direct extension of "Let's See Action" and "Empty Glass." Townshend opens with a music business complaint and quickly turns to the moral of the story:

> I remember being richer than a king
> The minutes of the day were golden
> I recall that when the joint passed round
> My body felt a little colder
> But now I'm like a sewer channel—running lime and scag
> Let me get at the master panel—let me at my stack.
> The sea refuses no river
> And right now this river's banks are blown
> The sea refuses no river
> Whether stinking and rank
> Or red from the tank
> Whether pure as a spring
> There's no damn thing stops this poem
> The sea refuses no river
> And this river is homeward flowing.

Townshend is anxious over his financial troubles and his art's direction, but his belief that all will turn out well comforts him in those anxieties. He seems to acknowledge the end of The Who ("We tried not to age/But time had its rage"), his personal problems ("There once was a fool in a dressing robe/Riding out the twilight hour/Lonely and cold in an empty home/Trying to assess his power/But now he's like a stream in flood/Swollen by the storm/He doesn't care if he sheds his blood/Let him be reborn"), and the realization that "the river is where I am."

"The Sea Refuses No River" lyrics are generally consistent with Townshend's remarks in the video EP. Moreover, he told Resnicoff (1989a) that the track is "about the idea that no matter how *awful* you are, you will, in some way, prevail" (p. 82), and in the premiere edition of *Rolling Stone's One on One* (1993) he stated that the song is "about destitution." Elsewhere Townshend explained that the song "has not got anything to do with my preoccupation with oceans"; it is "the Townshend family motto" (Loder, 1982a, p. 54). There he recounted a story about his daughters meeting "a London socialite" and their fascination with the man's family heritage (his family portraits and family crest). When his daughters inquired as to the Townshend family artifacts, he referred them to the photographs in the "desk cupboard" for the portraits and to the "Book of Proverbs" for the family motto. With her mother's help, Emma Townshend discovered the proverb "the sea refuses no river." Her father observed: "It's just what this family's all about. And I got very involved in the idea, the true expression of the proverb and turned it into a song." That song is the oeuvre's capstone spiritual statement. Townshend's subsequent work may suggest spiritual themes, but *White City*, *Iron Man*, and *PsychoDerelict* all move in other directions. The auteur has achieved a resolution to his spiritual quest and that resolution echoes Meher Baba: "Don't worry, be happy, and leave the rest to God," for God will accept us all in the end; the heavenly sea refuses no earthly river.

From this spiritual resolution, I turn to Townshend's views on his personal and professional situations. I begin with his assessment of his marital life and his relationship with Karen Townshend. The writer is direct on this matter. "Stop Hurting People" is a prayer to be reunited with his wife: "I suddenly broke down and scribbled it out on a piece of paper, and didn't realize until later quite to what extent it was a prayer" (Salewicz, 1982, p. 31). "Stop Hurting People" opens with these lines:

A love born once must soon be born again.
A spark that burned, then died, leaving cinders to be fanned
By the wind and thrown to flame;
Flames like tongues impassioned in a moments burst.
Tell me friend—why do you stand aloof from your own heart?
The truth confronts you—the truth confronts you as the sea
Crushing without detail,
Impassioned and detached,
Killing with love and power in God's name.
People, stop hurting people
People, stop hurting people.
Love conquers poses. Love smashes stances. Love crushes angles
Into black. So you, without question, know your first love

Is your last. And you will never—you'll never-never-you'll never love again.
I always wished to walk with her into restaurants. (It's a clammy tale).
To be seen beside her at the public bar foot rail.
I always wanted to be matched with her —
Yet her beauty was so different to mine.
My "beauty" needs an understanding, and a knowledge of what I am.
Hers is enough. Earned through eons; for that is what true beauty is —
Time's gift to perfect humility.
May I be matched with you again
I know the match is bad
But God help me —
May I be matched with you again.

The track concludes "without your match there is no flame" and repeats the "people, stop hurting people" chorus. The lyrics—which Triplett (1982) feels "would be a beautiful poem on its own"—speak to a recurring question in Townshend's work, the search for beauty. In this case, "true beauty" resides in "time's gift to perfect humility" and the peace that comes from their relationship. Although Townshend told White (1990) that he has never written a "proper love song" (p. 224), he identified "Stop Hurting People" as such in 1993: "['Stop Hurting People'] is a love song.... I actually wrote that for Karen, my wife, when we were separated briefly...well, it wasn't that brief" (*Rolling Stone's One*, 1993). Townshend's "prayers" are assuming more complicated, lyrically dense, structures.

Complementing "Stop Hurting People" is the track Townshend designated as a "personal anthem" in the video EP, "Slit Skirts." The extent to which the song discusses its author's marital life, marriage in general ("A Legal Matter" fifteen years later), or middle-aged angst (or a host of combinations) is uncertain and characteristically left to the auditor. In all cases, however, the song is a complaint:

I was just thirty-four years old and I was still wandering in a haze
I was wondering why everyone I met seemed like they were lost in a maze
I don't know why I thought I should have some kind of divine right to the blues
It's sympathy not tears people need when they're the front page sad news
The incense burned away and the stench began to rise
And lovers now estranged avoided catching each other's eyes
And girls who lost their children cursed the men who fit the coil
And men not fit for marriage took their refuge in the oil
No one respects the flame quite like the fool who's badly burned
From all this you'd imagine that there must be something learned.
Slit skirts—Jeannie never wears those slit skirts
And I don't ever wear no ripped shirts
Can't pretend that growing older never hurts
Knee pants—Jeannie never wears no knee pants
Have to be so drunk to try a new dance
So afraid of every new romance.

Several of Townshend's most poignant lyrics appear here. Notice how he blends autobiography with generational complaint to address a relational boredom that is apparently stifling. The generational angst of "My Generation" has entered middle age, and Townshend is charting its maturation. The track continues:

> Let me tell you some more about myself, you know I'm sitting at home just now
> The big events of the day are passed and the late TV shows have come around
> I'm number one on the home team but I still feel unfulfilled
> A silent voice in her broken heart complains that I'm unskilled
> And I know that when she thinks of me she thinks of me as "Him"
> But unlike me she don't work off her frustrations in the gym
> Recriminations fester and the past can never change
> A woman's expectations run from both ends of the range
> Once she woke with untamed lover's face between her legs
> Now he's cooled and stifled and it's she who has to beg.

The lyrics take a decisive turn as the narrator complains about his relationship. He laments his partner's inability to cope with the past and, as Triplett (1982) observes, displays the logic of "a man facing middle age when he's still a kid at heart." The songwriter has paused to assess a situation of consequence to his generation through an idiosyncratic style that features an uncertain blend of fact and fiction.

Townshend's reflections on his work appear in two songs, "Prelude" and "Stardom In Acton." "Prelude" is the brief track that opened the video EP with its plea for a "change." I suspect Townshend is revisiting "Bobby" and the *LifeHouse* project, as the author wonders if the much-desired—indeed required—"change" will ever emerge. Yet, the *Chinese Eyes* video uses "Prelude" in a very different fashion. There the song assumes a more personal stance in that the visuals directly associate the message with Townshend's recovery and a personal "change." Typical Townshend, the song easily serves both ends.

The "Stardom In Acton" project is an autobiographical statement about Townshend's youthful ambitions in Acton when stardom offered such romantic promise. Quite unlike the video portrayal, the song's lyrics emphasize a bitter stance when considered alone:

> Stardom in Acton that's all they got [repeat three times]
> Just like the grub that wriggles to the top of the mass
> I'm the first to get hooked
> Just like the stub of that long cigarette full of hash
> I'm the last to get booked
> But I'm capable
> My love's inescapable
> Conquering lethargy
> I've got energy.
> Stardom—I want a hit
> Want my tan, want my cash, want my innocence

Stardom—I want a script
Want my band, want my stash, want omnipotence.
I'll go where the senescent soldier retires
And shiver in south California
Watching the storms and the tangling wires
And rivers that meet on the corner
Like some prostitute
Handling round the loot,
I am not ashamed
I will stake a claim.

Townshend's chorus proclaims: "Stardom—born in a trunk/Got my home, got my car, got stability/Stardom—Hollywood's son/All alone don't admire anonymity." At this point the song turns to a confrontation with an unidentified entity:

I'm so angry that you turned me on,
I didn't remain your friend too long
I'm so angry that you turned me on,
I didn't stay your friend for too long,
I'm so angry that you let me see
My totally futile destiny.
I'm so angry—you interrupted my dream
Now I know that the power rest in me.

The song closes by combining the two "Stardom" choruses and Townshend's observation, "All alone don't admire anonymity." An interesting aspect of this particular song involves the stanza in which Townshend expresses his anger. Is he angry at "stardom" for interrupting his artistic vision? Is he talking about Keith Moon or Kit Lambert? Is he talking about "rock" itself? Once again, Townshend's cryptic characterizations camouflage a central part of the story and leave us to contemplate a superficial complaint. Considered in isolation, these lyrics place a very different spin on the message delivered by the video version. Apparently, the song also confused music critics who misread the track's title. Pareles (1982) and Browning (1982) both read the title as "Stardom In Action"—which was, of course, misleading. The "Stardom In Acton" message is complicated and requires a consideration of the song lyrics as well as the video presentation and liner note essay.

From Townshend's views on marital life, middle age, and stardom we move to his comments about his lifestyle. Three songs address this subject with varying degrees of clarity: "Somebody Saved Me," "Face Dances Part Two," and "Uniforms (Corp d'esprit)." "Somebody Saved Me" portrays anxieties over an encounter with a woman, live performance, and a lost friend with a slight spiritual reference. In all cases, "somebody" saves the character from various plights, or at least he/she learns to face a situation honestly. The song opens with the narrator's attempt to seduce a woman ("I was such a bore and I lied to her/I said I didn't really want her ass"), only to be "saved" from a "fate worse than heaven/'Cos if I'd had her for just an hour/I'd have wanted her forever/Somebody saved me." (We must exercise care with regard to Townshend's use of pronouns—recall "Rough Boys".) The song continues with that scene for several lines and suddenly turns to a comment about the music business:

> I don't know about guardian angels
> All I know about staying alive
> I can't shout about spiritual labels
> When little ones die and big ones thrive
> All I know is that I've been making it
> There have been times when I didn't deserve to
> Every show there's been more faking it
> But right at the point of no return.

The narrator next describes how he/she left his/her "folks" to pursue the "Truth" prior to the loss of a close friend (Kit Lambert?):

> I lived hippy jokes getting stoned insane
> Till the rain looked just like snow
> But there was a soul in whom I could depend
> He worked himself crazy while I laid in bed
> I never leaned on a person like I leaned right then
> And when I finally woke up clean
> My friend was dead—stone dead.

The song ends with the "somebody save me" chorus and these lines: "Somebody saved me—I ain't ready for heaven/If I'd seen you for a second I'd have wanted to see you forever/Somebody saved me." The autobiographical aspects of this song are, predictably, uncertain.

"Face Dances Part Two" and "Uniforms" appear to address the presentation of self in public situations and through one's clothing. Both songs are rich in their metaphorical and characterological playfulness. For instance, Townshend's description of "Face Dances" in the video EP adds an interpretation that makes much sense as one considers the lyrics; however, in the absence of that explanation, a very different impression emerges. The song opens:

> I watch you sit and twitching
> With a match between your teeth
> You seem to have a knack of moving it
> It's in time to the beat.
> [chorus] Face dances tonight
>   Fate chances moonlight
>   Face dances tonight
>   Fate chances moonlight
> I can't be distracted
> By the stuttering of the kids

I just sit enraptured
By your fluttering eyelids
[chorus]
I can only stare
You make me feel like
I don't care
I can only stare
You make me feel like
I don't care.
Your eyes explain a story
That never had a start
Your brow reveals the glory
That's hidden in your heart.
[chorus]
Your skin is fine china
White as winter snows
Your lips are always shining
Turning up your nose.

Townshend's references to "fluttering eyelids," "skin" as "fine china," and shining "lips" camouflage his video EP claim that the song speaks to a "soul in solitary confinement."

"Uniforms" does not share that impressionism. Townshend is straightforward with his point, presented in the song's opening lines: "I don't matter you don't matter/Neither does this mindless clatter/It don't matter where you're from/What matters is your uniform." After describing how "you" wear your "Doctor Martens on your feet.... For credibility on the street" and declaring "We are marching as to war/We won't be obscure no more/In uniform—In uniform," Townshend briefly mentions the insecurity that accompanies such sartorial awareness ("I am frightened, you are frightened/Should we get our trousers tightened?"). The author's perspective is insightful:

People think we dress alike to segregate identities
Pills or drink or puffing pipes in integrated entities
Then they wink and snort their line and say how great their Bentley is
They feel so warm when they conform.
They say that nakedness is what our Lord intended
When we stand naked then we all appear the same
But it's just faking it if we all try pretending
Are we just making all our prayers in the rain
Heaven knows I need new clothes.

"Uniforms" evokes one of the oeuvre's more dominant themes: personal identity through clothing. In this case, the liner note essay, video EP, and song lyrics all work in harmony to create a single image. Marsh (1983) argues that "'Uniforms' comes close to summing up in a single lyric what *Quadrophenia* had evaded for an hour" (p. 519). Townshend supported Marsh's conclusion in an interview with Greil Marcus (1981):

There is that deeply ingrained sense of class, and it shatters down now into separatism—but it goes a little bit deeper. There's a need for uniforms; and to some extent it doesn't matter which uniform you choose, just so long as you choose a uniform.... What's important about the uniforms is that they're so extreme.... I think it *invites* a them-and-us situation, wherever it occurs.... Quite why there is the need for uniforms, I don't know. I'm still trying to work that out. (p. 413)

On another occasion, Townshend seems to have resolved his curiosity regarding the "need for uniforms," as he related to Vic Garbarini (1982b): "To me, fashion is always an indication of a need for some kind of identification and unity with other people, and of changing moods in society. That's why I've always felt it's one of the first places to look for change and volatility" (p. 52). The track demonstrates the sincerity of that last remark when it proclaims "I need new clothes!" (a reference to a personal or professional transition?).

I conclude with Townshend's commentary regarding several personal frustrations from this point in time. In his arrangement of the traditional "North Country Girl," we hear him sing of nostalgic recollections about a beautiful young lady with red hair who dwells "up there near the Roman wall." The song requests that we "drink her a toast" as our narrator is "exiled in a lonely place." Townshend's anxiety over his "exile" is apparent in "Exquisitely Bored" as well. Here the song and video work in harmony once more as he articulates his frustrations over his condition ("And I'm still hardly here") and offers his views on life in southern California:

The peasants here are starving,
They look like barrels out in space.
Pray TV looks like pay TV to me,
It's just a curse on the human race.
I take a drive up to L.A.,
In my gas guzzling limousine.
There's a whole lot of crazy people up there,
Living out a life in sweet ennui.

Consistent with the *Chinese Eyes* essay, Townshend merges his view about the boredom of recovery and his assessment of life in Hollywood into a highly personal complaint.

"Communication" may very well be the oeuvre's most ironic song. The song is complete gibberish. Townshend makes up words and strings along phrases ("Selbstdarstellung/Gay Talese/Ronald Rocking/Euthenasia") that readily fit the song's powerful instrumentals, for instance: "Use the words like flowing river touches/Embraces parting hard steel surfaces revealing pages/Beneath the water skin broken like ice flows/Smashed by iron bows and the back of the whale." Portions of the song focus on the word "communicate"

("Comma comma comma comma/Commi commi commi commi/Commu commu commu commu/Communi commu communicate") as Townshend urges us to "Never never hesitate" to "communicate." Again, the video works with the song's lyrics to "communicate" the author's point, as he explained to Garbarini (1982a):

I deliberately take the word communication and break it up into bits. I mean I literally hurl the letters of the word at the listener. And then I show a literal example of how not to communicate, which is with flowery, meaningless prose. You know "briolette tears drip from frozen masks, the back of the whale cracks through the ice floe," blahblah blahblahblah—who needs it? (p. 52)

Pareles (1982) criticizes Townshend for the tactic: "But what does he think he's saying...the (throwaway) lyrics dissolve into gibberish—a cute joke only if Townshend realizes he's done more or less the same thing throughout the album" (p. 48). Browning (1982) also takes a dark view of this strategy: "[The song] is unmusical, unexpressive and singularly ugly in its screed against the abuses of language—exactly as Townshend meant it, no doubt; but hardly a tune that any but the most attentive of his disciples will probe for insight" (p. D4). Townshend takes issue with these views in 1997. First, he notes that the remarks to Garbarini were inspired by the journalist's lack of attention. Second, he expresses pride in his "liquid" and "ocean" metaphors even though he realizes they "don't communicate the essence of the message.... They are there to evoke something in me as the performer" (Townshend, 1997). He says the song was intended to communicate: "I'm in this spiritual place of impressionist images...this is where I am, where are you?"—hence "the urgency of the music, the insistence of it, the demandingness of it contrasted with the pseudo-classical, rippling kind of sound." Townshend does concede, however, that the lyrics contain a form of "personal language" that he denotes as a "kind of cod [i.e., idiosyncratic] poetic stuff"—further proof of the narrative depth associated with a song that, on the surface, appears to be a lyrical throwaway.

Assuredly, the *Chinese Eyes* project is an impressionistic review of the Pete Townshend's life. From the spiritual reckoning of "The Sea Refuses No River" to the deeply personal assessments of his private and professional life, *Chinese Eyes* represents a long, hard look back at a life that "started so simply as a kid in Acton" only to become "exquisitely bored" in a California "clinic." And remember, according to the author, this is a "solo" album's function. Music critics may vary with regard to their judgments as to *Chinese Eyes* aesthetic value, but there is widespread agreement over that work's function. To that end, *Rolling Stone* comments that Townshend "acts like someone in therapy, coming across as sincerely and forthrightly as he can, using the apparatus of rock stardom—airplay, interviews—as one big couch" (Pareles, 1982, p. 48). Browning (1982) praises Townshend for his "courageously open" (p. D4) approach and observes, "Introspective often to the pain threshold.... Highly confessional in tone and structure, the record seeks to spell out the hard lessons of a career that spans two decades, the better that we should neither emulate nor envy Townshend.... Townshend doesn't flinch from the pain of this introspective tour de force." Pareles (1982) asserts: "As far as I'm concerned, every bit of Townshend's malaise about stardom may be true, and earned, but it's just not my problem" (p. 48). Garbarini (1982a) ponders the record's relationship to *Empty Glass*: "The [latter], a near perfect blend of power, passion and grace, utilizes references to the alchemical transformation of water and wine to depict an inner ascension, a glimpse of the goal; while the [former], with it's tangled imagery of mud, streams and rivers documents the painful but necessary struggle to separate the fine from the coarse—and forms a therapeutic chronicle of Townshend's recent dark night" (p. 51).

Townshend (1997) essentially agrees with these observations, as he notes that the project was the "process" through which he separated his "fantasy" from his "reality." Yes, the risks of self-disclosure are certainly high. The *Chinese Eyes* project joins *Sell Out*, the *Tommy* film, and later, *PsychoDerelict* as one of the four major transitional statements in Pete Townshend's oeuvre. All of these projects venture a considerable look "backward" as a preface to a "forward" surge in the lifework. That the *Chinese Eyes* album was dedicated to "Meg" (California therapist , Meg Patterson) signals Townshend's appreciation for this particular transition's facilitator.

Here the author's narrative signatures take a turn toward the storytelling style that will henceforth control the oeuvre. First and foremost, from this point on all Townshend musical projects involve multimedia packages. Just as he once demanded that his live audiences *work* toward his treasured "rock ideals" (the aggressive reciprocity of the performer-audience encounter), Townshend now requires that his audience *work* in order to grasp his messages. A Townshend solo project is a complex mix of music, prose, film, and stage action, with each project employing its own unique blend of media. No single facet of a project yields his message. For thorough commentary, we must consult all aspects of a given project, his often-protracted interviews, and supplemental materials. Other signatures evidenced in *Chinese Eyes* include his use of autobiography, word games, impressionism, and plots of varying clarity (ranging from obscure, value-laden statements—as in "Communication"—to direct expressions of complaint—as in "Slit Skirts"). With *Chinese Eyes*, Townshend settles into a narrative groove that will guide his pen for the next decade.

This introspective look back signals Townshend's good-bye to The Who and all its trappings. How interesting it is that the capstone statement regarding this period of his life would appear not on a Who or Townshend project, but by way of a song he authored for David Gilmour's 1984 album *About Face*. Townshend penned two songs for Gilmour's project, "All Lovers Are Deranged" and "Love On The Air." I think the latter song accurately captures Townshend's views about his career to this juncture. He writes:

Love on the air
I keep transmitting but reception is hazy

I don't get an answer
Keep sending it faster
Always knew it was crazy
To put my love on the air.
No one will hurt me again
No one will cause me to lie
No one control me by pain
No one will cause me to cry
I was looking for love
In wandering eyes
Like a ship trying to fix on a beacon
I learned how to sigh
On the ribbon and wires
It's a habit that's so hard to weaken.
No one will every manipulate
Make me promise to do or die
No one can make me hesitate
What can I lose if they try
I was looking for love
Like the very first time
Didn't realise love never left me
Contradicted—conspired
I connived and designed
Nothing on earth could arrest me.
Reception is hazy
When you put your love on the air
Always knew it was crazy
To put my love on the air
But I only communicate
When I put my love on the air
You don't have to consummate
Love on the air.

Just as the successful but bored minstrel's search for inspiration required him to
risk everything in order to satisfy his artistic urges, Townshend's need to
"communicate" moved him to accept the risk of "wandering" away from The
Who. This chapter demonstrates that Townshend's evolution was slow. Each
of the projects cited here appeared during his tenure with The Who; thus his
disillusionment and subsequent introspection are evident.   He nevertheless
achieved resolutions to problems that dominated his career to that point. Like
the narrator in "Love On The Air," Townshend searched for lost emotions that
were, in fact, embedded deep inside himself—shades of the "Amazing Journey"
poem; one travels to the highest peak and finds only him/herself. With his departure from The Who and the resolution to *The Seeker*'s spiritual quest, the
auteur would once again assume the risks associated with placing his "love on
the air."

6

The Solo Career: The Impulse's Victory

To this point we have observed how commercial success in the popular music industry may be a double-edged sword. The presence—as well as the absence—of professional conflicts, expectations, and obligations have both positive and negative implications for artists. Such conditions may be further complicated by an additional consideration: an artistic imperative may drive an artist to an alternative or complementary means of expression. A photographer may turn to video, a poet to prose, or a singer to acting in order to achieve some artistic or commercial end. The possibilities are endless. The motivating force—the creative impulse—may know no boundaries, and the work may be pushed in a variety of directions simultaneously. English minstrelsy, once again, provides a strong case in point by way of the English and French "trouvères." Rowbotham (1895) writes that the "separation between the music and the poetry" grew in "a most pronounced form," such that "a race of trouvères" eventually "branched off from the troubadours" (p. 125). He explains: "Their [the trouvères] distinguishing characteristic was to carry to excess the love for long elaborate poems, to prefer the historical style to the amorous, and finally most naturally to discard the employment of music in the recitation of their compositions" (p. 125). That is, the troubadours' evolving stylistic inclinations required a shift in expressive forms. Although this change may be considered a victory for the creative impulse, different tensions are invited into that artist's world. New structures must be acknowledged, new audiences embraced, and new critics encountered. While not as risky as the wandering minstrel's decision to "hit the road," shifting art forms takes a musician into an uncertain professional world.

I have already cited Pete Townshend's involvement in various film, stage, and publishing projects throughout his protracted career. Now I focus on four major *Townshend* projects that demonstrate his narrative impulse's evolution toward other means of expression. As the stylistic variations expand, new venues are entertained and new risks encountered. Just as the trouvères adjusted their music for their poetry; Townshend takes rock 'n' roll to music theater.

THE SOLO CAREER: THE IMPULSE'S VICTORY

We now move to the second portion of Townshend's solo career. Here we observe an extension of the multimedia format initiated with the *Chinese Eyes* venture. These projects offer a compelling view of the writer's creative vision through their synthesis of Townshend's state of mind, artistic philosophy, and storytelling style. Such is the stuff of the "narrative renaissance" that results from The Who's passing. We open with the two projects that initiated this creative resurgence: the book of short stories, *Horse's Neck*, and 1985's dual film-album project, *White City: A Novel*. Afterward, I move to his 1989 adaptation of Ted Hughes's work, *The Iron Man: The Musical*. I close with the songwriting oeuvre's capstone statement, 1993's *PsychoDerelict*. We begin this final segment with yet another transitional statement, *Horse's Neck*.

HORSE'S NECK

Published by Harper and Row, *Horse's Neck* contains thirteen chapters that, according to Townshend's preface, represent a "collection of prose and verse...written between 1979 and 1984." There the author states the book's purpose: "I have never wanted simply to tell my own story. But I have tried here to attend to a wide range of feelings." To that end, Townshend introduces two themes that run throughout the book. The first is essentially implicit: "My mother features in this book, but her character changes constantly because this 'mother' is many mothers, many teachers." The second theme is more explicit: "Each story deals with one aspect of my struggle to discover what beauty really is." That search for "beauty" is full of dark images and scenes of despair. *Horse's Neck* is a probing, searching work.

Townshend claimed he moved from song lyrics to prose because his "notebooks" contained "notions that resisted conversion into song" (McKenna, 1986, p. 50). Moreover, since he "didn't feel the need to entertain" (p. 65) his audience, a more expressive style emerged: "Most of the book was written with the feeling that I was just laying it out there, and if you didn't like it, tough, because the things I was trying to share were very painfully observed by me and there was no way to sugarcoat them." As he shared these "painful observations" he envisioned his traditional audience: "I'm sure there were a few new readers, but I wasn't looking for a new audience. If I wanted a new audience, I'd use a nom de plume—and then I'm sure I'd sell zero copies." In his most poetic (i.e., expressive) project to date, rhetorical (i.e., commercial) factors remain evident in Townshend's intentions.

There was another reason why Townshend wanted to speak to his traditional audience. Several years prior to publication, he told Kurt Loder (1982a) that *Horse's Neck* offered an opportunity to comment about his generation and its problems: "I feel that I've woken up from a bit of a dream, with all my faculties operatin' and my sixth sense operatin', and I do know that there's something very *wrong* going on. And it has to be talked about and dealt with, and I think, as always, writers are the first people to start to express that" (p. 54). In response, he brought his artistic impulse to a new venue through which he could "commentate" on contemporary society and, in turn, present *his* views to his readers (again, a "solo" project's function). In doing so, he relied on the narrative signatures that typified his songwriting to this point: an uncertain blend of autobiography and fiction, a penchant for metaphorical mischief, and occasionally, cryptic or equivocal characterizations.

Horse's Neck opens with "Thirteen"—a combination of verse and prose that introduces a parental anxieties theme. "Horses" follows, with its three-level "horse" metaphor and a powerful statement about the value of "dreaming." The third entry, "The Pact," embellishes a maternal angst theme by way of a "letter" from a "mother" to her "son." "Champagne on the Terraces" delves into a recovering alcoholic's propensity for dreaming and his daily struggle with sobriety. In contrast, "Ropes" (the book's fifth story) presents a "life on the road" tale of decadence and depravity that culminates in a startling "Christ" dream. "Ropes" is followed by "Tonight's the Night"—a straightforward yarn about a young lady's sexual history and its impact on her life—and "Fish Shop" (a story of violence, distrust, and disillusionment). The book's eighth entry, "Pancho and the Baron," is a mix of verse and prose that seems to probe Townshend's feelings regarding Keith Moon's and Kit Lambert's deaths. "Winston" follows, with its intense diatribe on "stardom." "A Day in the Death of" (the tenth chapter) is a dark tale that uses a confessional tone to convey both the narrator's state of mind and how journalists shape realities to suit their agendas. *Horse's Neck*'s longest story, "The Plate," is a richly detailed account of a "detective" and his obsession with a case. The book closes with "An Impossible Song" and "Laguna. Valentine's Day, 1982." In the former, the narrator reflects on his mother, her love of horses, and his acceptance of his life; in the latter, the book resolves the dilemma introduced in "Thirteen."

Horse's Neck unfolds in a linear fashion, as Townshend explores specific themes that weave in and out of the work (maternal angst, guilt, celebrity anxieties, the value of dreaming). Only "Fish Shop" seems out of place in that the book establishes its thematic foundation in its first three chapters ("Thirteen," "Horses," and "The Pact"), embellishes various fear and loathing in life scenarios across the next seven entries, breaks for a tale of obsession ("The Plate"), and closes with a two chapter resolution. "Horses" uses three levels of a "horse" metaphor to articulate what appear to be personal frustrations: a pantomime horse, a horse trapped in a church, and a "pure" white horse that contains a "bloated snake" in its rib cage (imagery that also appears in the song "Athena" on *It's Hard*). From there, the work explores these anxieties as they manifest in various contexts by way of a series of narrative vignettes.

For a few moments let me attempt an overview of the various structural and thematic tendencies evidenced in these writings. I begin with *Horse's Neck*'s three poems which appear to feature Townshend's responses to three relationships of considerable importance: his mother, Moon, and Lambert. "Thirteen" opens with a twenty-four-line poem *from* the narrator's mother:

> What did I do for him?
> I gave him life
> I foresaw the danger
> I prepared him
> I hardened him
> I nurtured his femininity
> I praised his maleness
> I deliberately failed him
> I scorned his teammates
> I judged his fellows
> I was his conscience
> I was his inquisitor
> Gave him his freedom
> Encouraged his fantasies
> Sneered at his inadequacies
> I lost him to another
> But I produced him
> I conceived him
> I breast-fed him first
> I screamed with him first
> I adored him first
> I rejected him first
> What did I do for him?
> Only what any mother would have done.

Afterward, the narrator describes a beach scene—"I remember the noise of the wind moving through the coarse grass, the sanctity of our protected spot never threatened even by the sea before us, blue-gray and green"—and his recollections of "a dreamy afternoon, languorous and drawn out, without detail or punctuation." Suddenly, his parents appear, racing toward him on horseback (*the mother winning*): "As though riding out of the sea and up to the dunes where I played, they were breaking the spell of my loneliness. Now I knew what I waited for, what I missed, but they stayed only for a minute and were gone, galloping off again laughing and waving. This is my earliest memory." The narrator claims he was but two years old at the time ("only one month into my second year") and concludes: "But I do remember, and to this day I have never felt inclined to ride a horse." The brief tale establishes parental anxieties that seem to relate Townshend's frustrations with his mother and her impact on his life.

The writer employs the same style in "Pancho and the Baron" and the two twenty-four-line poems that appear there (one *from* Pancho/Moon, the other *from* the Baron/Lambert). For "Pancho," Townshend writes, "And what did I do?/What a boring question!" He continues: "At first I did little/Except thunderous drumming/I hated his cynicism/Was afraid of his keenness/His sharp perspicacity/His need to be leader.... And then I submitted/Admitted I loved him/And dared to display this/What did I do?/Only what any brother would have done." The work shifts to prose and the narrator's account of Moon's death: "When I first heard that Pancho had died all I could think of was that I had survived. I had outlasted him. In a sense, I had won." The story moves to "The Baron's" death and recollections regarding the day our narrator first heard of his manager's passing. After scenes involving the seduction of two women ("When we got back to the hotel I was accompanied by a girl who looked very much like the girl I slept with on the previous night"), Townshend presents the third poem: "And I?/I challenged him/Seduced him from the bosom/Drew him from the sycophants/Fought off the leeches/Recognized his greatness/Flattered youth's ego/Overrated his vitality/Ignored his flatulence/Resisted his attraction/Listened to his babbling/Acknowledged his genius/Lived with his impudence.... I was his mentor/I was his manager/What did I do for him?/Only what any father would have done." There are autobiographical elements in these writings; however, to attribute any aspect of any story to any person or group is risky business. Townshend consistently splits up characters in curious blends of fact and fiction that, no doubt, camouflages specific portions of the story, and stimulates reader mischief.

"The Pact" also employs vague characterizations that invite attribution. There a "mother" writes a detailed account of her frustrations over her physical attractiveness ("My beauty is often a burden.... It's always me who suffers") and follows with a contradictory statement about how she manipulates her looks to her advantage ("Most wonderful is the freedom of choice beauty ensures"). "She" writes:

I know you dream of me. You further idealize me in your reverie.... Sometimes you write to me possessively: *I could make you happy*, or *I can't live without you*. At other times you write in an offhand way.... Sometimes you attack me....

I am special. To be beautiful is to be lucky; to be lucky is to have received grace; to receive grace means you have been chosen. Too late now to turn back. I am beautiful and must suffer the consequences.

I am never entirely sure what a man wants from me. That is why I have always preferred horses. I can't entirely trust a man who tells me he appreciates my looks, because there are so many others with good looks.

The "letter" ends with the woman's aspirations for a "young partner" who is "as lucky as I am so that we might suffer equally as our luck runs slowly out until our death." That chapter closes with the opening scene (the "son" sitting along the river, reading the letter, and giving it to the narrator to read) and the "son's" observation that his "mother" is a "bit unhinged."

While "Thirteen," "The Pact," and "Pancho" establish maternal or relational anxiety themes, "Horses" is a two-pronged story that visits a series of frustrations and follows with a prayer for the lone avenue of escape. At first, the narrator recalls a pantomime horse ("How the back end bloody well followed the front end in darkness and humiliation") and how he "longed, for a second, to be that man trapped inside the colored horse." Next, we move to two dream sequences. The first involves a horse trapped in a "ruined church set on the edge of a hill" and the beast's futile efforts to escape. For the narrator, the "circling horse was an oblique warning that I would repeat the same mistake eternally" (echoing *LifeHouse*'s Bobby: "Can anything continue without change? Nothing else in nature behaves so consistently and rigidly as a human being in pursuit of hell"). The second dream features a long description of a "Cotswald village" and its cottages before the narrator comes upon the white horse with the snake in its ribs: the narrator's "perfect horse, my symbol of purity." The story shifts quickly and closes with this revelation:

With infinite dream potential I can believe in everything. This is a gift from God, a presentation of his grace. If it arrives with the package torn I can't argue. I'm ready to be humiliated, to suffer, to go through whatever I need to go through. I won't betray God or his world.

Another cigarette, then to bed, please God to dream again, to be refreshed. There is no blood like the blood that flows within one's own body. No dreams like those that spark from one's own mind. Nothing is necessary except a dream. A dream can set off reality; the smoke ring rises vertically, perfectly round and in equipoise, then wavers and collapses.

Nothing has anything to do with you or me.

An elementary reading of the "horse" metaphor suggests that each application addresses a different anxiety: the pantomime horse and drugs, blindly following where the drugs lead; the trapped horse and Townshend's career, ensnared in an endless cycle; and the corrupted pure horse, his disillusioned spirituality. And yet, one never knows.

Townshend's faith in the power of dreaming is considerable; "dreams" directly appear in nine of the thirteen chapters. In "Champagne on the Terraces" the recovering alcoholic's wife observes, "Since you've been on the wagon all you do is sit and dream" (and she's right; the story is a mix of dream scenarios and their implications for the alcoholic's dry reality). Throughout this piece Townshend employs images and phrases that appear in songs such as "Slit Skirts," "Somebody Saved Me," "North Country Girl," and "Athena." That writing also assumes a dreamy stance, as this description of the "wife" illustrates:

Looking at her, he knew that his extremes had been his way to keep her love and interest in him alive and fresh. He adored her, but he dreaded her in his heart; this was so different from the way he had buffeted her in his arms. He whip-panned between true recognition of her perfect soul and his steam-kettle lust for her down-pillow bosom. Her eyes tolerated him, praised him, rebuked him. He hid from them, wearing his body like a space suit. Then the shy smile would be sweetly won, the firm persuasive lips would seek out their nipple-sweet opposites and lovers would blend smoothly like butter and flour cooking in a roux.

The wistful introspection of "Champagne" is a marked departure from the "life on the road" scenarios featured in "Ropes." Through various scenes of life with Ray, Rastus, The Baron, and assorted women (all of whom the narrator deems his "rodent family") Townshend embellishes the "exquisite boredom" of the celebrity's life that he mentions briefly in the *Chinese Eyes* essay. "Ropes"—a variation of "Eminence Front" and its "layers upon layers of cheap nightclub hypocrisy"—concludes with an alarming dream sequence. The narrator describes returning to his room after a typical evening of decadence: "I had developed a slight temperature during the day. It suddenly threatened nightmares and I became irrationally scared." Eventually, he drifts into a dream. In it a "sexually alert" woman in a "black cowl" approaches him and leads him into an adjoining room with a "large pillar" located in the center:

She led me gently around the pillar, leading me by my cock. On the other side of the pillar was a gigantic cross, nailed to it suffered the Christ, his beautiful, racked face gazing down on me, tortured and forgiving.

"You caused this." The woman squeezed my hardened phallus, her voice and manner totally evil now.

"No! No. God forgive me—please forgive me."

I woke up wet and writhing…. The final image of the dream was still burned into my retina—I had denied my Savior and, after a brief reprieve, left him in the torture chamber in which he faced his doom.

It was getting harder and harder to live with the truth; impossible to be honest because the truth was too awful. I was therefore ever a hypocrite, the punishment eternal and unbearable. It all seemed that serious to me at the time; Christ and the girls and sleeping alone.

Such dreams/fantasies cut in and out of "A Day in the Death of," "The Plate," and "An Impossible Song" in unpredictable ways. Townshend's interest in "beauty" weaves its way into the various chapters as well (directly featured in every chapter). The writer's descriptive powers focus on minute details. Consider this description of "Miss Lazenby," in "The Plate":

She was a fairly plump girl of about twenty-three with blond hair. Her face was weary, and small dark crescents capped her green eyes, which were hypnotizing and slightly reptilian. Her look was spellbinding and gave her heart away: she was sad, and she was sick. Behind those dilated pupils there was a mystery flashing that intrigued me. There was a call from her body that had me opening and closing my hands involuntarily. She did not appear beautiful at first—her chin was too petulant, her lips too thin and her hard eyes too widely spaced—but if you had a soul with a nose, you were sunk.

Townshend's observations are not restricted to women; he describes landscapes, horses, sexual acts, and male features such as "Jaco's" strong qualities in "Fish Shop"—the complement to the song "A Man Is A Man." As in his songwriting, when the auteur *complains*, he relies on a direct storytelling style that leaves little doubt about his thesis. "Winston" is a compelling case in point. Here our narrator recounts the first anniversary of John Lennon's death and a party at "the home of a big music entrepreneur" in New York City. During the party participants discuss the late Beatle's final days and his apparent state of mind, to which the narrator quips: "Oh, the tight friendships, the shared secrets, the unique and privileged intimacies between a star and his so-called friends." The affair was interrupted by the appearance of a drunken "Van Smith-Hartley" (a friend of the narrator's who "had lost his band only a year or two before") who promptly treated the party to his views on stardom. "Smith-Hartley" begins with this declaration:

We've brought our children up to sit with glued-on headphones while they scribble away at their homework, music throbbing in their mental genitals. They confuse sex with aspiration, violence with fortitude.... They analyze the words of songs that might just as well be written in a foreign language, the interpretations are so high-flown and pragmatic. It belies the fact that all rock and its so-called stars ever did was stand up and complain.

"Smith-Hartley" turns to a bitter discussion of "The Star" as "Messiah" and his intense frustrations over his own situation: "And the poor Star who finds himself hounded from restaurant to doorstep...what of him? While I stand waiting for the blind to see, for the seekers of truth to scream for me, these dilettante pretenders are worshipped, an audience of millions hanging on their every word." The diatribe continues: "Stars are attributed with intelligence they don't have, beauty they haven't worked for, loyalty and love they are incapable of reciprocating, and strength they do not possess.... They are treated like a beautiful vase of cut flowers. When wilted, simply replaced with new blooms." Townshend's character rails on for several more lines (with slight references to Lennon) before the chapter simply stops: "The anniversary dinner party was apparently over. Van got up and left without another word." Pete Townshend's views on "stardom" reach new levels of complaint through Van Smith-Hartley's monologue.

Horse's Neck's resolution is startling. After multiple scenes of personal anxiety in "A Day in the Death of "—a cloudy story in which the narrator seems to describe his sad state for a journalist whose editor insists that account be transformed into a story more to *his* liking—and "The Plate's" tale of obsession, we reach the end. That closure begins with "An Impossible Song" and a young narrator's conversation with his mother (yes, about "horses"), his response to an overheard telephone conversation in which one woman tells another, "I rode him—just like a horse," and his attempt to overcome his fear of horses by riding a "hobby horse" (posing with the horse, like posing with a guitar, is preparatory). At this point the narrator pleads: "Why am I ashamed to let anyone know

I am afraid? What's wrong with fear?" The story suddenly shifts to an adult narrator and this account of his situation:

So you see, my story is much like yours. I have a mother whom I loved more than I ever knew; sometimes I thought that love had turned to hate, but it hadn't. I have a father whom I respected and idealized above all others; now I see he is just a man, I respect him among others. I have had friends whom I abused and who abused me; all that has become neutralized. I now have a wife and I have children; I hope that saying they are part of my life doesn't deny them freedom.

I am very ordinary. I have made mistakes and found it hard to forgive myself, just like you.

The narrator admits his belief in God as a preface to the "I am special" scenario the beautiful "mother" espoused in "The Pact": "I sound conceited but I think I'm special. Why should I pretend otherwise? If I'm not special, then I must be unusually lucky, and if I'm that lucky with no talent and no guardian angel, then that makes me special." Next a naked narrator attempts to ride a foal, to no avail. Here he specifically denies the "horse" imagery has anything to do with drugs ("The horse I feared to ride was a real giant, not a circus clown's prop"), admits his own weakness ("Given the truth just once, I would hardly know what to do with it"), and concludes:

What a terrible fate it is to be young. To be faced with life's razor-edged pathway, a withheld freedom in any case, only safe for the strong or ugly.

So beauty is rarely seen; youth is rarely at liberty; fear becomes a discipline, once again, for the frail and the beautiful.

And what of the misfits? We are able to roam free. We observe and become commentators and artists. Our freedom is absolute.

It's a bitter irony, then, that the beautiful have come to be envious of the ugly just as the frail covet the freedom of the strong.

Townshend's resolution is nearly complete. With "Laguna. Valentine's Day, 1982," the writer ends what began in "Thirteen." There he describes an escape to the ocean side and its silence: "All of us believed we were trapped inside that tormenting place of change and strain. Yet the doors are open. I didn't need a key. I just walked through." Sitting near the beach, he sees two people approaching on horseback. He rises and moves toward the riders. As they venture closer, he notices both that they are leading a white horse and his own physical response to the beast: "As the riders get nearer I realize, without any shame, that I am naked and my phallus is erect and enormous, like Dionysus.'" The riders stop "a good hundred yards off"; the narrator is unable to see them clearly (they are wearing the same clothes the parents wore in "Thirteen"). The "man" releases the white horse, and the couple rides away ("they appear to ride straight into the sea"). The white horse arrives, the narrator caresses the animal, and *Horse's Neck* ends with this statement:

Then I walk behind the beautiful creature and, brushing aside the tail, slide deeply into it. When my orgasm comes it is without sensation. I am no longer an animal. My phallus diminishes and my horse flicks its tail and stands on its back legs, magnificent.... I grab its mane and pull myself up. We are suddenly and rapidly off at a canter. At last I can ride. I am in perfect control. I urge the horse into a gallop and the wind cools my face. I am riding towards the water's edge.

With that, Pete Townshend ends this long look back at a series of serious frustrations. All of the distrust, disillusionment, decadence, and detachment ends in a physical denouement. Like a river flowing into the sea, our narrator rides his symbol of purity toward an all-accepting ocean.

Townshend's prose employs the narrative style that typifies this phase of his lifework. His mysterious blend of autobiography and fiction (shades of *Empty Glass* and *Chinese Eyes*), the value-laden impressionism, the project's linear qualities (although individual segments may employ uneven flashbacks for strategic reasons), and his thematic emphasis on beauty and dreaming all reflect signatures from this portion of the oeuvre. The book—like Townshend's songwriting—rotates between an impressionistic diary style with its "heartfelt" presentations of "painful observations" and a tightly structured format; the latter is used principally as a tool for complaint. The various entries also display multiple levels of meaning that may or may not be used to camouflage a personal message: the metaphorical mischief of a "musical practical joker." As Townshend told to the *Chicago Tribune*: "If anybody asks, I say it's all fiction. Because I really don't know if I can tell the difference, looking back. I know I can tell the difference now. But certainly there was a whole period of my life...[about] 1979-80, where I really just didn't know the difference. I really didn't" (Kolson, 1985b). Years later, he suggested that "Fish Shop" was autobiographical:

That was the most real story that I had in that book. Most of the stuff was complete fiction. I was trying to write a [Charles] Bukowski kind of thing, actually taking people through a really quite nightmarish thing and then out the other side, and little bits of autobiographical things slipped in. You know, you only have one life and only one set of influences. And, if something slips in which anybody can recognize as being real, they immediately think the rest of it must be real. (Resnicoff, 1989a, p. 74)

Townshend's (1997) contemporary views stress that "Fish Shop" represents a *blend* of biography and fiction (with an emphasis on the fiction). Whether "real" or fictional, *Horse's Neck* is a valuable portion of the oeuvre in that it demonstrates the flexibility of the auteur's narrative impulse. Here he embraces a new medium by way of a narrative style that is a direct manifestation of the structural and thematic songwriting signatures evidenced thus far. *Horse's Neck* achieves a form of thematic closure for Townshend as well. *Empty Glass*, *Chinese Eyes*, and *Horse's Neck* work, in harmony, to embellish and resolve a decade of introspection that began with *The Who By Numbers*. Townshend now moves away from personal introspection toward multimedia complaints that articulate a generational angst predicated on his "observations" about contemporary English society.

WHITE CITY: A NOVEL

For years Pete Townshend said that he was more interested in making a movie than doing another Who album. With The Who's demise, Townshend was free to turn to this long-standing ambition. Here his subject matter shifts from introspective commentaries about his spiritual life, the music business, and his lifestyle as the writer who penned "My Generation" explores that generation's situation in considerable detail. The *White City* movie offers a detailed account of Townshend's artistic rationale in a monologue that appears after the film. There he describes the White City area:

White City is an estate built before the last war and I think its intention was to create a kind of small garden city, we call them in Britain. I was driving through the area quite a lot—I found a short way home—and I became...struck by the fact that all the street names were connected with the British Empire. And I'd been working on an idea which was based on my roots as a post-war child and the way it related to the decline of the British Empire. It wasn't so much because it was where I was brought up—I was brought up very near there—White City was a kind of a legendary place to me as a kid [He describes the area as "a very electric and alive place" with a large "immigrant community" that is "mixed in with the obviously indigenous community"].... It's bordered on one side by what used to be the White City stadium, on another side by a great big highway, and its defined by four walls—it's very much like a fortress.

The monologue continues with the project's evolution, Townshend's discussion of the director's role, and the story's place in the lifework:

I started thinking about this particular film last May, in May 1984, and the original idea was simply going to be twenty-four hours in the life of somebody who spends a day literally wandering through that area. By the end of the summer, around August-September, I'd completed a draft script of my own and about six songs. And in November, I started recording. What was interesting for me—and something that I was determined to do—was to make sure that whatever happened to the story, whatever happened to the script, that the music would be allowed to evolve with that. And, in fact, it's worked out very well. When I first met our director last year, we stripped away quite a lot, we stripped away a lot of the music which we felt was superfluous and the whole thing did evolve...in small steps, I'd do a bit of recording and then we'd together do a bit of writing for the screenplay. We were inching forward step by step.... The music in *White City* is an extension of everything that I've done before.... The story is a follow on from *Quadrophenia*.... Jim might be Jimmy from *Quadrophenia* twenty years on. It's set in the present day amid flashbacks to about fifteen years ago, ten-fifteen years ago. The film is not meant to be a period piece in any sense, the story is what's important. The story of the relationships and the way in which these two people work out their relationship.

Note Townshend's reference to the film's director, Richard Lowenstein, and the collaboration that emerged during the project: "I've learned working with Richard...that he has a role very similar to a record producer for me. I need...a record producer because I need somebody to bounce performances off.... We have to attempt to move forward together." As they "moved forward," commercial factors emerged via the rationale for a two-dimensional project: "I'm really interested in video.... But realistically, a video won't sell more than 150,000 units, at best, so it was necessary to have the album, and I wound up putting key elements in both" (Hinckley, 1985).

Here again, Townshend makes the audience *work* to grasp his message. The songs—in and of themselves—focus on the impressions and emotions associated with the story. As a result, the individual tracks may be taken out of that context and auditors may do as they wish with them. To appreciate *Townshend*'s message, we are obliged to consult all aspects of the project (the album, film *and* interviews). The story operates on two planes. The first involves the "life in the White City" yarn and Townshend's "English Boy Syndrome." For generations, as Townshend told *Spin*, English men "have somehow been brainwashed into sacrificing themselves for causes which are said to be greater than themselves and which they don't understand" (McKenna, 1986, p. 49-50). The absence of these national crises renders a "tragedy of emasculation" for Britons, who are unable to secure employment and assume traditional domestic roles which, in turn, leads to societal instability—and often, domestic violence, as Townshend related: "I work with a refuge for battered women in England, and working there has led me to conclude that domestic violence is often the last resort of men who are lost and emasculated."

The story's second plane features Townshend's status as a "heroic veteran" who has traveled the world, made good for England, and returned home to help the old neighborhood. In the post-film monologue he describes that facet of the narrative as he elaborates on the story's three characters and unveils the intersection where the film's two planes meet:

In the film I play very much myself really; somebody based on somebody of my age with my accomplishments.... The two main characters, Jim and Alice, are younger than me, a little bit. My generation—I was born practically the day the war ended—I think I was brainwashed, like so many people my age, into believing that success was tied up with the pursuit of heroism and that seems to be very much what the first wave of sixties rock and roll musicians perpetuated. And when I went to look at the kind of story that I wanted to tell I wanted to talk about people that were breaking those traditions.... Jim for example hasn't done what I've done, he hasn't felt the need to escape, he hasn't felt the need to run off and travel the world. He hasn't felt the need to make lots of money, he's not been driven in that same way, he's quite happy to live on the estate and his life completely established in the microcosm that it represents. And she is one of the new breed of women: she thinks for herself, she acts for herself, she doesn't accept the old role.... And I feel that when I look at people maybe five or ten years younger than me—I wouldn't say I'm jealous of them, but I do admire the way that they've started to break with the old traditions which I do feel very embedded in me. You know, I still feel the best thing that could have happened to me was that I'd been called up, put in the army, and sent out to some battlefield. I mean people might think that that's sick, but I think I was brought up to do that, trained to do that and I respected people that did that. My father did it, my grandfather did it, and I had to do it in rock and roll.

Townshend's heroic status is evident in the album's cover art: a profile photo of him standing in front of two apartment buildings, wearing a black jacket with a medal pinned over his heart.

The *White City* film features three main characters—"Alice" (Frances Barber), "Jim" (Andrew Wilde), and "Pete" (Pete Townshend)—and traces their activities as they unfold over a single day. Originally, Jim's character was "brutally disabled" (Townshend, 1997) by an accident, "beaten up" after that incident, and was widely known for "beating his wife." Noting that the story was based on his experiences at the "battered women shelter," Townshend hoped to extend this tale of "disablement" and how one may be "stopped in your life by an accident." Negotiation ensued, and Lowenstein cut this facet of the story. The resulting film (running 44:45) contains eight scenes or segments of varying depth (this designation is technically difficult because of the heavy use of inter-cutting flashbacks).

The opening segment—the film's longest (9:03)—initiates the "day in the White City" theme with shots of the estate at dawn. With "Give Blood" providing the musical context (slowly emerging in a heartbeat rhythm), the visuals move from a large highway, past a "White City Pool" sign, to various views of the neighborhood as the night gives way to the morning (apartment buildings, shops, lots of barbed wire and fences communicating the estate's four "walls"). Suddenly, a fast-paced visual collage appears featuring Jim "struggling" underwater (lots of slow-motion shots—one offering a glimpse of Alice in the pool as well), Pete in a recording studio, and the activities of the estate (on the street, in apartments, etc.). The scene contains but one piece of dialogue. As Jim walks down the street (back to camera), Pete says: "Jim was a few years younger than me. But we both grew up on the same estate. The White City." The music resumes full volume as we witness more shots of White City people. Obviously, the estate is "alive."

The brief second scene (1:07) relates Jim's and Alice's unemployment (both are waiting in line to receive their unemployment checks). With "Brilliant Blues" playing softly in the background, these characters convey the embarrassment of state assistance as well as the tension that exists between them. Alice takes her check and dashes out; Jim follows, arrives too late to speak to her, and stands on the sidewalk, clearly confused.

In the third segment (running 6:51), Pete meets with Jim and later Alice, and a series of flashbacks unfold that established Jim's troubled youth. The scene begins with Jim sitting quietly listening to a "street preacher" (foretelling the apocalypse) as Pete walks up. The two men walk away and reminisce as a group of skinheads kick and throw cans about in front of an old fish shop. Throughout Pete and Jim's conversation the video cuts back and forth to black-

and-white film of "young" Jim and Alice talking to a camera (the "kids'" and Pete/Jim's dialogues track simultaneously). Next we travel to the White City pool, where Alice and Pete talk about their past (they used to spend the afternoons "in bed" while she was "seeing" Jim). That scene cuts in and out with black-and-white images of young Jim (maybe ten years old) misbehaving in an all-girl dance class. Here the film establishes that Alice coaches a synchronized swimming team that will be performing at a benefit "disco" that night featuring Pete's band. As the girls practice their swimming routine to "White City Fighting," the video rotates back to "young Jim" and his attention seeking (pushing the girls around, not doing what he's told, being admonished constantly). Young Jim is horrible, and his teacher decides to spank him as the girls watch and giggle. While Jim receives his punishment, Townshend sings the "street preacher's" warning of impending doom and the need for a "cleansing fire" that removes societal injustice.

The movie's fourth segment (running 6:17) establishes Jim's problem. It opens with kids playing around the pool while Pete prepares for a sound check. Jim enters for a swim. With Jim swimming toward the camera, the band begins a spirited version of "Secondhand Love" while the film cuts back and forth between a flashback of Jim and Alice having fun, the band performing, and black-and-white shots of young Jim: this time walking up a flight of stairs until he enters a room where his mother is lying on a couch with a man. His mother screams at him; Jim simply stands there, stunned and confused. Throughout, the adult Jim contorts (literally struggling) underwater in slow motion.

From here, we move to the fifth scene (running 4:00), featuring Pete and Jim in Jim's mother's bar with Alice and several girlfriends interacting across the room (laughing and talking). Jim recounts a childhood story about a bar patron tickling him in bed late one night, how his mother intervened and punished *Jim* (she locked him in a room and left him in the dark). All the while, Pete sits quietly and listens (this character says very little). As Alice and her friends get up and dance (to "Hiding Out"), Jim's mother enters and offers him work, but Jim despises his mother and looks away. She pleads her case to a silent Pete. While the girls dance, another flashback of Jim and Alice appears. First, they dance slowly together (basically ignoring one another) at the same bar; afterward, they enjoy a wonderful time washing dishes at home. During the fun, Alice expresses her concern over Jim's unemployment. Jim dismisses her inquiry, claiming that he will get a job "in the morning"; however, Alice is not satisfied and asks if she should look for one as well. Jim is stunned. He stops, stares down, and communicates a sense of failure.

The story's sixth scene (running 8:30) presents the benefit disco. Pete stops by Jim's apartment (walking by and noticing a hole punched in a wall), the two men arrive at the pool. There Pete resolves a dispute between a female box office employee and a young female patron ("Let her in," he urges). He goes off to find "the lads," as Jim moves about the pool and Alice readies her swim team for the show. Pete emerges dressed in a gold sequin jacket, baton in hand, and leads the band through an energetic version of "Face The Face" (the bulk of the scene: the band performing, with shots of Jim, Alice, and the swim team).

With the song's conclusion we are taken to the pivotal seventh scene (running 2:26). After the disco Jim and Alice sit by the pool, and Jim relates: "I want to tell you a story. It's about a boy who lived in a pub, he was brought up in a pub. His father was an alcoholic and his mother ran the bar. And he was always being sent away to his granny's for months on end, just so his mother could get rid of him. And the mother was always having affairs...and the boy looked on in confusion until he grew up and he met a girl." All the while he talks, the video shifts back and forth to an intense fight between Jim and Alice. At first, they stand toe to toe cursing each other, but the fight quickly escalates. Jim destroys the apartment (he does not, however, strike Alice). He continues: "And he never knew how good it could be to be wanted by somebody...and they eventually got married...but something seemed to go wrong." Again, the film depicts Jim's rage (throwing clothes, tossing furniture, and punching through a wall—the hole Pete noticed earlier). The song "Come to Mama" begins softly in the background as Alice responds, "I just couldn't stand being cooped up in that place one more day, I had to get out." Jim concludes, "I guess we both should've got out of there a long time ago," pauses, and smiles at Alice. The video fades into a water montage.

The film's eighth and final scene presents the next morning, when Jim awakens by the pool. He coughs, undresses, and slips in the pool ("Come To Mama" getting louder and louder) just before Alice enters with a group of kids. The kids play loudly as Jim and Alice sit in the pool staring intently at one another, then laughing: all is well between them. Pete suddenly appears walking around the corner of a busy street (a facial shot growing tight, Tighter, TIGHTER). He says: "Me? I went back on the road with the boys. We're still playing soldiers. We'll never learn." The camera pans past a "Commonwealth Avenue" sign toward an apartment building, and the credits roll to "Crashing By Design."

While the movie has an ambiguous ending, Townshend (1997) reports this was not the original plan: Lowenstein ran out of film, and the project was curtailed. The original plan featured a reunion between Pete and Alice, not Jim and Alice. Townshend recalls, "we wrapped it up as best we could," and that he shot the final scene without Lowenstein (the "Pete walking down the street" tag). Once again, such are the negotiations that constitute the commercial art industry.

That aside, the film communicates a complicated situation in an impressionistic style that requires multiple viewings to comprehend. Townshend's heroic role is the most direct: he listens to Jim and Alice empathetically (never judging), he does the benefit concert for the community, and breaks up the fight between the ticket taker and the young woman. Jim's frustrations over his unemployment and Alice are apparent, yet the film seems to stress Jim's difficulties with his mother more than those matters. In fact, the film *dwells* on Jim's maternal anxieties: he gets no attention at home so he disrupts the dance class, his mother sides with a pub patron over the tickling incident (and leaves him alone), and Jim has a considerable problem with women.

The *White City* album echoes the film's impressionism; moreover, it initiates a storytelling trend that will henceforth dominate the musical portion of Townshend's oeuvre. While the narrative may employ flashbacks from time to time, the *White City*, *Iron Man*, and *PsychoDerelict* albums join *Tommy* and *Quadrophenia* in their linear expositions: each track builds on the previous songs in a manner that allows the story—or facets of the story—to unfold. Unlike *Empty Glass* or *Chinese Eyes*, or Who-related works (*Who By Numbers*) that feature coherent messages articulated in a chaotic order, these multimedia projects render albums that unfold systematically, albeit in Townshend's writing tradition: the song order may be linear, but the various tracks may be quite cloudy as they communicate value-laden *impressions* that embellish the narrative's structure. Thus, as we examine the various tracks on the *White City* album, that interpretation is informed and guided by the film. For example, nowhere in any lyric does the name of any character appear (only pronouns are used). A brief essay in the liner notes provides insight as to the story's plot (or at least part of it). There Jim relates:

When I get up in the morning I look out onto the estate. What a view! Two dustbins and a Ford Cortina. Some people have flats right at the top of the highest buildings. Their view must be amazing. I sometimes imagine them all in their secure little cells. They stand naked like prisoners, I can see only their backs. They are all semi-silhouetted against their windows: a little boy watching the traffic stream past as it builds up under the sunrise; an old woman like my mother, her skin quite loose, watching the black kids down in the street as they head off for school; a pretty girl holding up her hair. I wonder what they all feel when they first get up. On another new morning, they are waiting for it to sink in that they still belong to the White City. Like me.

The album contains nine original Townshend songs (running 38:40) which pursue a variety of narrative functions. The songs introduce the characters ("Give Blood" and "Brilliant Blues"), the situation and its needs ("Face The Face"), Jim's plight ("Hiding Out"), why Jim is hiding out ("Secondhand Love"), Jim's destination ("Crashing By Design"), Jim's response to his situation ("I Am Secure"), Pete's return home ("White City Fighting"—written with Dave Gilmour), and the crux of Jim and Alice's problem ("Come To Mama").

The album and film begin with Townshend's "veteran's lament," "Give Blood." Here the writer articulates the "war veteran-rock veteran" analogy through a song that stresses how "veterans" give everything only to return home to additional demands. The song opens:

Give Blood
But you may find that blood is not enough
Give Blood
And there are some who'll say it's not enough
Give Blood

But don't expect to ever see reward
Give Blood
You can give it all but still you're asked for more
Give Blood
But it could cost more than your dignity
Give Blood
Parade your pallor in iniquity
Give Blood
They will cry and say they're in your debt
Give Blood
But then they'll sigh and they will soon forget
So give love and keep blood between brothers
Give love and keep blood between brothers.

The song is vague. It suggests "give it all" and hope for the best, while it conveys the wisdom: "Give love, not blood." The song seems to elaborate on the "war veteran's lament" that first appeared in "Slip Kid" and emerged in later songs (such as "I've Known No War" and "Empty Glass").

"Brilliant Blues" is equally ambiguous, as it relates "say goodbye to the brilliant blues" because "it's time" to do things (to live, give, teach, preach, trust, and thrust). The song relates that the good times are gone ("The brilliant blues/Have faded into sadness and pain/And now it's time to say...it's time") and that "it's time" to deal with the problem: "You and me are going to finally sail away/We'll get far away from the blues and the mist and the rain/You and me are going to fight until we reach the day/For now is the time that we must say goodbye/To the brilliant blues." The track suggests the extent of Alice and Jim's conflict and their need to face each other and deal with the situation. Townshend (1997) explains that the "Brilliant Blues" was a Satchi and Satchi advertising ploy designed to introduce the "New Tories" in the British elections of that period: hence, the film's presentation of Jim and Alice's initial encounter regarding their unemployment benefits. That message advances with the album's next track, "Face The Face." "Face The Face" evokes one of Townshend's long-standing rock principles: face your problems and "dance all over them." The number employs a big band sound that starts slowly and builds into an intense musical statement. With backing vocals singing "Face the face...got to...Face the face," the song declares: "You must have heard the cautionary tales/The dangers hidden on the cul-de-sac trails/From wiser men who have been through it all/And the ghosts of failures spray-canned up on the wall." Townshend urges us to "judge the judge," "scheme the schemes," "stake the stakes," and finally, "Try to place the place/Where we can face the face." The message is straightforward: we must "keep looking" until we find the "place" where we can "face the face" (confront our problems and deal with them or submit to "the dangers hidden on the cul-de-sac trails").

Jim, however, is content "Hiding Out" on the estate. The album's fourth track, "Hiding Out," communicates Jim's strategy by restating the liner notes essay. He sees the world from his "window"—"From my window I see roads/

They lead to darkness, leading home/And in the midnight of a soul's unsleeping/I hear the waterfall of women weeping/I hear the distant noise of traffic stalling/I hear the prostituted children calling/Calling out"—and resolves "I am safe hidden here/Hiding out." Jim is "hiding out" because he has a problem, and Townshend addresses that difficulty in the album's fifth track, "Secondhand Love." "Secondhand Love" relates Jim's personal "war" with his mother (this is abundantly clear in the film). The song is misleading at times; for instance, the character complains: "Don't bring me secondhand love/He's been leaving his scent on you/I can sense it from a mile/All my money is spent on you/But you're still selling your smile." (The lyric here seems to depart from the story.) The "give your love, and keep blood between brothers" line emerges midway through the song, as the final stanza communicates Jim's anxieties: "I want first call on your kiss/Answer me one question; can you promise me this/I want my defenses laying in your hands/I don't want to rest in the palm of another man/I don't want your secondhand love."

These songs build into Jim's plight, "Crashing By Design." The sixth track opens with the chorus—"Nothing must pass this line/Unless it is well defined/You must have to be resigned/You're crashing by design"—and moves into a direct expression of Jim's dilemma:

> You once believed that crazy accidents were happening to you
> You were chasing a capricious wind
> Whenever bad luck and trouble happened to pursue you
> The dice would surely save your skin
> But when you look back you must realize
> That nothing in your life's divine
> Everything that's ever befallen you
> Happened simply 'cause it crossed your mind
> You're crashing by design
> [chorus]
> In your single-room flat in a courtyard building
> You sit alone just like a broken toy
> Where's your mother, where's your lover
> And where are the children
> Are you a man or are you still a boy?
> Who left you behind, or did you run
> From the crush of so many options?
> Now you know the special despair of the man
> Discussed, debated and offered for adoption
> [chorus]
> Another man without a woman
> Dropped like a tool that's no longer required
> A man who longs for the stifling
> Milk flowing bosom, a fool who's
> No longer desired.
> Another man without a woman
> Too many rages have cost you this time

Another man among a hundred children
You're just a child who is lost in time.

Jim is crashing by his own hand, and unless he faces his problems and acts, he stands to lose even more. Still, the next track indicates his unwillingness to respond. "I Am Secure" opens with a long instrumental that sets the mood for Jim's response. First, we revisit "Hiding Out," with a description of the view from his room ("My room looks out to the wide open spaces/My heart is touched by awakening faces.... I see the city laid out like a patchwork"); afterward, we hear the response:

Alone I am free from hatred and blindness
I hope this life is frozen and timeless
My man is here we're growing by inches
Tomorrow I'll walk among heroes and princes
I feed the boys, I hear secrets whispered
I know the hearts that are battered and blistered
I am secure in this world of apartheid
This is my cell, but it's connected to the starlight.

(This last stanza is completely different from the one printed in the album's liner notes. That version stresses "I see a boy with his mother's ambition/Performing for love, trained in submission." Those lyrics are not sung in the recording, but they are insightful.)

The next track returns to Pete and the "Give Blood" thesis, by way of "White City Fighting." The song opens: "The White City/That's a joke of a name/It's a black violent place/If I remember the game/I couldn't wait to get out/But I love to go home/To remember the White City fighting." Pete-the-veteran drives through the estate in his "German car" and proclaims: "Prone to violence, and prone to shame/I glide in silence, my pride in vain/For no one remembers not that I can see/That we were defenders—we were the free." The White City is a violent place where "blood was an addiction," but Pete-the-veteran has to return: "I guess I'm violence prone/To remember the White City fighting." The story ends with "Come To Mama"—a fascinating title that actually speaks to the crux of Jim's problem. Yet the lyrics seem to pursue another angle, with indirect references to Jim's maternal anxieties:

Pride is like a bandage
He is wrapped in a warm cocoon
His pride is just like heroin
He is back inside the womb
His pride is like an ocean
Encircled by a reef
His pride's an hypnotic potion
His memory is a leaf.
[instrumental]
Her pride is like an armour

Flaming ring of fire
Her pride is like a blindness
An ever tightening wire
Her pride is like a razor
A surgeon's purging knife
Her pride is like a censor
She's slashed out half her life.

"Come To Mama" suggests that Jim's and Alice's "pride" has interfered with their relationship and that once they overcome their pride all will be well. And yet, we do not know what happens. The story just ends with that realization—if they do realize that point.

The complexity of the *White City* project—and the corresponding need to consult multiple sources to grasp the story—is evident in the critics' response to the work. Williams (1985) declares the album "jumps out of the speakers" instrumentally, but the songs are "joined by the thinnest of threads." *Rolling Stone* describes the work as "a clear, organic parable of hope triumphing over despair" (Tannenbaum, 1986, p. 48), one communicating that Townshend "seems to have finally found comfort in maturity, and that feeling warms and informs" the project. In sharp contrast, Altman's (1985) review for *Spin* is extremely negative:

To explain this a lot more simply than Pete "Call Me Egghead" Townshend ever would, *White City (A Novel)* isn't a novel at all, but an album that's the basis *of*—but not exclusively the soundtrack *for*—a film.... Having not *seen* the thing, I can't tell you much more about any "plot" except to report that, from what I've been able to glean from the uncredited liner notes, it appears that Petey (or, as they say at the publishing house where he's now an editor, his *persona*) once upon a time lived in a housing complex called White City Estates...what we have here...is a, for the most part, serious-minded contemplation of the sociopolitical ramifications of life inside a racially mixed housing project. Or something like that. Like I said, I haven't seen it, so I can't be sure. There's really only one thing I *can* be sure about: *White City* is one of the most pretentiously boring records I've heard in quite some time.... Oh well—no one ever said growing old and in the way was going to be easy. (p. 28)

The intensely personal—and unnecessary—qualities of this commentary complement the writer's ignorance of the film to discredit the review (one has to wonder about personal agendas here). Nevertheless, Townshend's insistence on complex—and at times fragmented—projects increases the potential for this type of response (an inherent risk). With time, the author responds to these critics through the very tactics they so deeply abhor.

Evidence that Townshend's narrative impulse follows a specific train of thought over extended periods of time may be found in the *Chinese Eyes* and *White City* projects. Interestingly, he chose to introduce the heroism theme in *Chinese Eyes*, when in fact *Chinese Eyes* says little about it. That theme joins the maternal angst story line to form *White City*'s centerpiece. While popular critics may consider the continuity of this particular story line as re-treading old material (a short cut, not an inspiration), that consistency indicates Townshend is probing deeper and deeper into his subject matter. As such, *White City* revises and extends several narrative signatures through its use of word games, multimedia, and the open-ended narrative structure (the story just stops, as per *Tommy* and *Quadrophenia*—albeit for a different reason). Furthermore, whereas *Empty Glass* and *Chinese Eyes* afforded snapshots of the state of the auteur in a manner that informed an interpretation of those projects, Townshend now moves away from the "personal snapshot" narrative strategy toward "statements" about various life conditions. Thus, the second portion of Townshend's narrative "renaissance" yields a storytelling style that takes positions on subjects of significance to the writer through an impressionistic style that relies on multimedia formats. That trend continues with 1989's *The Iron Man*, our next topic.

THE IRON MAN: THE MUSICAL

The *Iron Man* project is as big an artistic turning point as any within Pete Townshend's lifework. Fittingly, this important step toward music theater—the production of a full fledged musical—was accompanied by a rather profitable look back: *Iron Man* was released just prior to The Who's 1989 25th Anniversary Tour. A wave of media interviews appeared in conjunction with the tour, and they offer insightful glimpses of the state of the auteur. Those interviews focused on a variety of topics ranging from nostalgic recollections about The Who, Keith Moon, and other historical matters to Townshend's assessments of the music industry, to the nature and extent of his hearing disorder, and to his thoughts regarding his most recent album. Townshend used a *Washington Post* interview to explain his adaptation of British poet laureate Ted Hughes's story:

What is at the center of "Iron Man" is a little boy who is isolated and afraid. It's the "Tommy" story, it's the "Quadrophenia" story, it's my story, which is why I was attracted to it in the first place. What I found when I got deep into it, it's also about that little boy taking power, taking control of his own life and doing it with such a vengeance that he actually overcomes fear by taking control of the very things that are threatening him. And in a sense, I think that's what I've done in my life and what I intend to continue doing. (Harrington, 1989)

Elsewhere, Townshend elaborated on his revision of Hughes's work and its relevance to contemporary society. He acknowledged that he added a chorus of animal friends for the boy as well as a love story; otherwise, he remained true to Hughes's concept. There he argued the story "is very pertinent to modern life" (Boren, 1989) as it portrays "fear and deprivation of children and the ignorance we display towards both history and nature." Townshend reinforced those views in a *Musician* interview, "it's about the moment when a child balances those symbols of fear and smashes them against one another and grows up" (Young, 1989, p. 69). After a brief reference to domestic violence and children,

Townshend launched into a statement that would, no doubt, please the fictional
Van Smith-Hartley:

But the thing about brutality is that it's valuable when we're united against a common
enemy. We can drain ourselves of all emotion and kill. We should be mobilizing all this
brutality we have to clean up all this shit we've created.... People of conscience on this
planet *have got to be prepared to be brutal.* It does no good being nice about it: "Please
don't do that crack. Please don't beat your kids. Please don't shoot one another."
We're dealing with dogs—*rabid, fighting dogs.* I'm not suggesting brutal policing. The
people who care have got to be prepared to die for the cause. We've had wars and expected young people to go off and die in some far-off country. I'm surprised people
aren't prepared to expect some of their young men and young women to die for the cause
right here and now.... If you vote, vote with a big cross. Make a nick in your hand and
vote with your blood. I feel that passionate about the way the world is going at this moment.

Such commentary suggests that Townshend's metaphorical adaptation of
Hughes's work may run rather deep via this continuation of the English Boy
Syndrome. While he admits his construction of the *Iron Man* story contains a
blend of *Tommy, Quadrophenia,* and autobiography, Townshend chose not to
focus on *his* condition (as per the previous artistic "snapshots") but instead uses
Hughes's work to make a socio-political statement about social responsibility
and individual heroism (shades of the *Chinese Eyes* liner essay).

The *Iron Man* album is but a portion of a much larger project that was compromised by economic concerns. Townshend claimed he had prepared "20
songs and a score" (Young, C.M., 1989, p. 72) but had to restrict the work "for
financial reasons." The author's explanation sheds considerable light on both
the negotiations that surrounded the venture and his artistic future:

I got a nice deal from Atlantic in the States and Virgin worldwide, but I had to contract
all the different singers on the record and I spent two years in the studio. It cost me a lot
of money. I couldn't afford a double album because neither company was willing to pay
me a double album rate. They would have put it out, but I wasn't willing to risk my own
money. It would have taken another six months and another $200,000. John Lee
Hooker would have sung five or six songs as opposed to two.... My aim is to change the
music we hear in musical theater, not to take musicals to stadiums. I'd like to produce
music for people who don't want to go to stadiums anymore. I enjoyed *Les Miserables,*
and I enjoyed *The Phantom of the Opera.* Everything was great about them except the
music was very old-fashioned. More than old-fashioned. Half of it was crap. The
problem with Broadway is that no one in rock has paid any attention to it.

The Iron Man: The Musical is a product of serious negotiations, conditions that
are leading the auteur to new artistic venues.

Iron Man is the tightest, most direct entry in the oeuvre. Although the
project extends beyond the materials reviewed for this study (a forthcoming
feature- length animated film), the combination of the album's music and liner
notes offers a clear, coherent story. Townshend's songs continue to employ an

impressionistic style that expound on moments or aspects of the story; however, when joined with the script a linear narrative emerges. To be sure, there are some adult takes on human affairs articulated within the context of Hughes's story (providing an endless number of metaphorical possibilities); yet Townshend sustains the innocence that one associates with a children's tale.

The album contains twelve tracks (running 47:25), featuring a variety of characters: Townshend as Hogarth (according to the liner notes: "a ten year old boy; the story is told from his point of view"), Deborah Conway as "The Vixen" (Hogarth's "conscience, always urging him to be brave, upright and quick thinking"), John Lee Hooker as "The Iron Man" ("a large self-maintaining robot programmed to destroy any machinery or system that ultimately threatens man"), Nina Simone as "The Space Dragon" ("an enormous anarchic spirit from space in the guise of a dragon"), Roger Daltrey as "Hogarth's Father" ("a farmer who leads a futile people's revolt against the Iron Man"), and a chorus of "Woodland Creatures" (Chyna as "The Crow," Nicola Emmanuel as "The Jay," Billy Nicholls as "The Frog," Simon Townshend as "The Owl," and Cleveland Watkiss as "The Badger"). Also featured are Townshend's usual cast of musicians (Simon Phillips, John Bundrick), a chorus (including "The Children of St. Stevens and Orleans Schools"), as well as a "vocal music director" (Billy Nicholls) and an "orchestral director" (Chucho Merchan). "The Who" is listed as "special guest" (performing "Dig" and "Fire"). All of the songs are Townshend originals with one exception, "Fire" (by Brown, Crane, Ker, and Finesilver). The album was produced by Pete Townshend.

The liner notes begin with "The Coming of The Iron Man" (credited as the "opening chapter of the original book") and its splendid description of the Iron Man's mishap and recovery. The Iron Man falls off a cliff by the sea and he slowly reassembles himself: "But as soon as the eye and the hand got together the eye looked at the hand. Its light glowed blue. The hand stood up on three fingers and its thumb, and craned its forefinger like a long nose. It felt around. It touched the eye. Gleefully it picked up the eye, and tucked it under its middle finger. The eye peered out, between the forefinger and thumb. Now the hand could see." Afterward, Townshend's adaptation takes over:

At dawn, somewhere in the English countryside near a rockface by the sea, Hogarth is fishing in a peaceful but fast moving river. The sky is a strange mixture of colours and there is an air of tension. Distant bells ring out an eiry sound and he can hear some beautiful singing. He becomes afraid, but is quite exhausted from a night without sleep, and begins to doze. Suddenly he is surrounded by a group of inquisitive woodland creatures led by a Vixen. He starts with a scream. The animals urge Hogarth not to be afraid and he is cheered by their friendship. —I WON'T RUN ANY MORE—As they sing, a strange new star appears in the sky.

These lines preface the album's first song, "I Won't Run Anymore." The woodland creatures sing, "Don't be afraid of the night/Only you hear the scream that you scream/Don't turn away from the light/Only you see the dream that you dream" and Hogarth responds: "I'm not gonna run anymore/I'm not gonna run/Away from this honeymoon/I'm not gonna run anymore/I'm not gonna run/Like a rat to a piper's tune." Hogarth is joined by the Vixen, and they harmonize: "We're not gonna lie anymore/We're not gonna lie/In ignorant ecstasy/We're not gonna cry anymore/We're not gonna cry/At a figment of fantasy/For you and I/Will grow together now/You and I/Will go together now." The project's rhythm is established at the outset. To follow the story, one must read Townshend's prose in the liner jacket which complements the songs. The prose carries the story. Furthermore, notice the appearance of several of Townshend's thematic signatures in the opening number: the appreciation of "dreaming," his defiance of societal expectations ("I'm not gonna run/Like a rat to a piper's tune"), his rejection of "lying," and his refutation of "fear." The writer's personal manipulation of the story line is skillful.

The story continues with the Iron Man's accident. Hogarth witnesses the happening and hurries to inform his father. John Lee Hooker performs "Over The Top" and chronicles the Iron Man's rebuilding project. As "old soldiers" sing "Over the top we go/Yey yuh yair yuh ye-uh," Hooker describes his character's plight ("I lost my arm/I lost my eyes/I broke my feet/I bruised my thighs") and communicates his resolve ("I've no idea where my maker ran/But I am a fearless Iron Man"). Townshend's prose resumes:

Hogarth's father hears his son's story and finds it hard to believe. But across the countryside, some awful machine has eaten up every bit of metal in his path: barbed wire, farm machinery and electrical pylons. The Owl who has followed Hogarth observes wryly that this machine was obviously built by men to protect them from their own awful inventions.

The prose leads into "Man Machines" and the Owl's brief description of the situation ("Man makes machines.... To break the machines/That make the machines"). The story moves to the father's efforts to assemble "a group of old farmers" to dig a trap for the Iron Man. The old farmers sing, "We old ones, have seen two wars" to which the father (Daltrey) replies: "When you're sick and afraid/And there's danger around/Take a pick and a spade/And cut into the ground/Away from the light/Away from the sound/Make a trap for the beast/Dig his burial ground." Once the trap is set, the farmers await the Iron Man. The Iron Man moves near the trap, and "Hogarth lures him into the abyss by tapping a nail on a knife edge." The farmers quickly bury him; however, Hogarth "feels remorse" because the Iron Man trusted him. The woodland creatures assemble, and Hogarth contemplates the value of friendship in the album's fifth track, "A Friend Is A Friend." Hogarth and the animals sing of the value of a "life long alliance" that "won't be betrayed" and conclude: "A friend is a friend/Nothing can change that/Arguments, squabbles/Can't break the contract/That each of you makes/To the death, to the end/Deliver your future/Into the hands of your friend."

After "some carefree but messy picknickers" disturb the Iron Man with the "sound of their metal knives, forks and kettle," he manages to pull himself out of the ground (with Hogarth's assistance) and goes on an eating rampage (consuming "military equipment wherever he finds it deployed against him"). While the "government plans an all-out nuclear attack," the Iron Man (Hooker) sings "I Eat Heavy Metal": "I eat heavy metal/Gargle premium gas/I drink heavy water/Nitro-demi-tasse/I eat heavy metal/I chew up limousines/I munch barbed wire/In my submarines." Hogarth saves the day by leading the Iron Man to a junk yard where he may munch forever. A threat remains, as Hogarth, the Vixen, and "her posse of woodland creatures" all agree that the "star" Hogarth observed earlier "represents a strange new force entering [Hogarth's] life and great suffering will have to be endured before everything comes right." Hogarth, the Vixen, and her posse join to sing "All Shall Be Well"—a smooth, flowing song that follows the story all the while it interjects several traditional Townshend themes. The song begins with Hogarth's observation: "You can wake deep in the night/And know that out of sight/A dangerous passion grows/A force you can't oppose." Townshend's characters sing about love's demands (Hogarth: "You can demand that your love's defined/Before you jump in blind/Keep everything to plan/So you can remain a man") in a powerful track that offers several seasoned realizations about love; especially for a ten year old: "You have imprisoned half your soul/You have denied the love that you hold/Your angry heart never seems to break/You've learned to give, but not to take." Throughout the song, the creatures reiterate "all shall be well" and Hogarth concludes, "But right under your nose/A revolution grows."

The story moves to the falling star and Hogarth's image of a "beautiful girl" trapped inside. In "Was There Life" Hogarth explores "love" still further ("Was there life before this love/Was there love before this girl I can see"), contemplates his feelings, and wonders if he's in a dream: "If this scene is in a dream/Then I'm perfect for the part I play/You can count on me to stand and say/'Was there ever life before this wonderful day?'" The story quickly shifts back to the star. It crashes on the earth and contains not a beautiful girl but a Space Dragon the size of Australia. Townshend writes: "All the nations of the world join together to bombard the monster with their weapons. But they cannot hurt her. She gives a final ultimatum: she wants living flesh to eat or she will destroy the entire planet." This situation leads to the album's ninth track, "Fast Food," and the Space Dragon's (Simone) culinary demands ("I want food—fast/I want fast food/Frisky little children/Served up in the nude").

Since the star yielded a hungry monster instead of his lifelong love, Hogarth feels foolish and states his case in "A Fool Says." A mature Hogarth opines: "A fool/Says love is like a melody/Or something like a symphony/But this love is cacophony/Never changing key/We/We can't fool our audience/We put up such a poor pretense/Don't hide a shred of evidence/We have no defense." (The remarks about "our audience" are intriguing.) The woodland creatures harmonize "A fool says/Love is foolproof," while Hogarth embellishes his plight. Here the story takes a decisive turn:

But Hogarth wants to defeat the Dragon and free his beloved, and runs to the Iron Man for help. The Iron Man agrees to be his champion. The Iron Man challenges the Space Dragon to an ordeal by fire on one of Australia's enormous white-hot beaches. The Space Dragon accepts believing that she can easily beat the relatively tiny Iron Man. The Iron Man must endure being heated to melting point on a massive grid that has to be fired up by Hogarth's father. The Space Dragon is so big that she has to fly into the heat of the sun, the only fire large enough to encompass her.

"The Who" performs the album's eleventh track, a cover of Arthur Brown's "Fire." Next, we witness the Space Dragon's demise: "She lands back on earth for the last time, so badly burned that her skin has hardened into precious gems which scatter all over the earth." Not only is Hogarth's "beloved" freed, but "the souls of millions of children all crying for liberation" are also released. The album's final track, "New Life," ensues in which the woodland creatures and Hogarth celebrate the Iron Man's victory. The Badger and Crow sing, "What we want is a brand new year/Open your heart and set us free/What we need is a brand new life/We'll decide on our own destiny," to which the woodland creatures harmonize: "What we want is a brand new life/For every brother and sister—husband and wife/For the single and lonely, living in fear/What we want is a brand new year."

The story concludes with the Space Dragon's explanation for her attack ("she used to fly around [space] singing the beautiful music of the spheres, but the awful things that men were doing on earth distracted her, and she wanted to join in"), the Iron Man's response ("The Iron Man tells her she must go to the dark side of the moon so that she can make her music without frightening people"), and these final lines: "As the joyful people sing ['All shall be well/And all shall be well/And all manner of things'], the Iron Man sits once again in his yard, chewing up scrap. The Space Dragon takes off to the moon filling the air with music." What becomes of Hogarth and his newfound love is left to the audience's imagination.

That Townshend used *The Iron Man* to articulate a political stance is beyond question. However, his stylistic approach was consistent with his artistic philosophy in that he refrained from "hitting his audience over the head" with a straightforward polemic. Instead, he used a children's story that employed traditional Townshend themes to weave a tale of hope: "all shall be well" if the world is willing to do what must be done ("give blood") to save the planet.

The Iron Man received a variety of responses basically free of the mean-spirited commentary we have observed previously. While Townshend had combined two elements—a children's story and a musical—that rock snobs and purists could easily condemn, the reviews consulted here seem to treat the work on its own terms as opposed to measuring it against some idealistic Rock Standard. Fricke (1989) describes the project's "Broadway elegance" (p. 91) and refers to *Iron Man* as a "highbrow *Cats*." Fricke places the work in the context of Who history: like the Who "morality plays" (*Tommy*, *Quadrophenia*) the story stresses "youth's enormous capacity for courage and love, the power of faith and the drive for a greater common good." Brown (1989) writes the "often dazzling but inconsistent record" (p. 20) represents Townshend's attempt to claim "Andrew Lloyd Webber's turf" and observes that several major musicals began as albums "long before they were staged" (the author cites "Jesus Christ Superstar" and "Evita" as examples). Boren (1989) considers *The Iron Man* "an infectious success," and the *Atlanta Journal* reports: "What might seem a silly subject for an album turns out to be just the right creative vehicle for Mr. Townshend.... Despite one or two rusty spots, 'The Iron Man' is a soulfully spirited work of art" (Thomas, 1989). The *Oakland Tribune* considers the album to be "Townshend's tightest and most accessible work in years" (Kelp, 1989) in that—despite the diversity of the cast—the author "managed to keep a single focus, make it all sound like a unified whole, and deliver some rousing music along the way." *Spin* magazine (often a source of heavy anti-Townshend sentiments) opens with this observation: "Yep, that's Pete Townshend's face next to the dictionary entry for 'ambitious'" (Young, J., 1989). Young asserts that the "large cast of voices suggest something as uncool as a Broadway show" but concludes the album "benefits from this diverse lineup." Finally, the *Los Angeles Times* describes Townshend as "rock's most eloquent man/child" (Hochman, 1989, p. 58), as a preface to this observation: "After all, the story deals in Townshend's own essential themes: wonder vs. temptation, and submission to confusion vs. submission to comfort."

The Iron Man represents a major turning point in Pete Townshend's career. Townshend now embraces *his* creative urges through an established narrative style that benefits from collaboration (here, with Hughes's original work and the "actors"). Absent are overbearing autobiographical statements and word games. While Townshend continues this evolution toward music theater, he once again takes a look back. This time those reflections extend beyond a summer Who tour as the auteur pauses to bring closure to some unfinished business.

PSYCHODERELICT

PsychoDerelict—the album—is a "musical play" (WFBQ, 1993) featuring a mix of dialogue, sound effects, and music. *PsychoDerelict*—the stage production—is a blend of stage action, sound effects, screen projections, and music (using extended instrumentals not found on the original album). This multimedia venture is as complicated as any Pete Townshend project. *PsychoDerelict's* principal yield, therefore, may be in its demonstration of Townshend's willingness to assume a significant *risk* in a transitional project. As he risks commercial and artistic condemnation via yet another technologically innovative work, Townshend turns to a mix of recurring themes for his subject matter. *The Seeker* now focuses on specific social situations through which Townshend advances his take on contemporary English life. Weaving its way through those scenes are statements regarding the value of *dreaming*. *PsychoDerelict* represents the quintessential Townshend project: a technologically innovative format is used to articulate the importance of individual initiative.

Townshend defined the term "PsychoDerelict" in a *Good Morning America* interview: "I think it fits the idea...of a destitute generation that's been pilloried for having created everything that's wrong with the world through having had a dream...this idea that we were crazy and now we're washed up." In *Rolling Stone's One on One*, he elaborated: "That's about the dream, you know, the lost dream of the hippy years, about how its all got kinda chewed up by the mechanism of information technology and the exactness of the press. That in our effort to define everything that we dreamed of we reduced it to nothing." *PsychoDerelict* functions as more than an account of the "lost dream of the hippy years" in that it represents a thematic closure for the songwriting oeuvre. Townshend acknowledged the project's transitional qualities:

I think it's a question of me always having been very transitional as a writer, I'm trying to find an end to the job that I started in the '60s. Maybe there's no end to it, but I think I'm more and more finding forms that suit me, and they are in music theatre and drama, with story and music both carrying the ideas. As I'm approaching 50 I know I've found some answers. I can't pretend I'm 19 years old anymore and be just unbelievably angry that people older than me have fucked up the world. I have some answers now and I have to give myself the space to project them into artistic forms that can carry them. (Tingen, 1993, p. 24)

That *PsychoDerelict* represents Townshend's attempt to bring about closure to his "old job" is also evident in the extensive publicity associated with the project. The writer's propensity to explain his work through media interviews reached new heights in 1993. One gains an impression he desired understanding—and, correspondingly, closure. The compact disc *Pete Townshend: Interview with a PsychoDerelict* (produced by Andy Denemark and Dia Stein for Eel Pie Productions) is a case in point. That promotional disc presents an interview (running 29:18), song excerpts, and edited commentary that lend themselves to alternative means of presentations (simulating interviews, etc). There Townshend maintains that the *PsychoDerelict* "story was written after the music" since he had already "delivered" the album of songs. A subsequent bicycle accident damaged his right wrist, and he believed his guitar-playing days were over. He told Tingen (1993) he had "126 stiches" (p. 26) in his hand and that the injury prohibited guitar playing for "18 months." He decided "to drop the whole thing" (*Interview with*, 1993) but changed his mind. In his efforts "to give it a last stab" Townshend realized he "was kind of coming at it as though it was the last thing that [he] was ever gonna do." Consequently, he enlisted ex-roommate and longtime colleague Richard Barnes for editorial assistance.

PsychoDerelict is "an adaptation of a 1989 Townshend short story entitled *Ray Highsmith and the Glass Household*" (Tingen, 1993, p. 26). The author explained the project's evolution for *Guitar Player*:

Through a series of unfortunate accidents and predicaments, I ended up doing things in a better order than I had planned. I wanted to write songs about the nature of truth, how it's changing in the modern world, how computers—data banks and computer preservation of newsprint in particular—are elevating fact to a level of truth. Facts, as I say on the record, don't always lead to truth. They should, but they don't always.... When I first put the songs together for *PsychoDerelict*, I was unhappy with them. I felt that I failed in my original mission. I thought some of this stuff is good and some of it isn't, but it doesn't do what I want it to do. Then I fell off a bike and smashed my wrist.... I abandoned the record completely, went off to La Jolla to gun up *Tommy*, sat in Shakespeare classes, learned what dramaturgy meant, and met dramaturgists.... I was embraced in theater. I came back to this album and thought, "Fuck it. What I'll actually do is *say* what this thing is about. I'll use a play or drama to describe what I'm trying to get across. The music can act as highlights." Had I not had the accident, had I not worked on *Tommy*, I probably would have gone back and done another bunch of tracks. (Gill, 1993a, p. 102)

The music-dialogue innovation—which Townshend referred to as a "black art" (Tingen, 1993, p. 28)—proved satisfying. He explained why he had not tried this approach earlier: "I was obeying the old set of rules, which is that you don't fuck with people when they're listening to music. You don't play them a piece of music and slip them a subversive idea that happens to be your idea of the month" (Gill, 1993a, p. 102). All the while he used the radio play format to deviate from the "old rules," he paused to revisit his past through synthesizer work from the *LifeHouse* project, as he explained: "I'm taking stock.... I'm trying to work out what there is...we need to go back and look at the building blocks and the great things that we've all contributed to.... That's what I'm doing now" (Gill, p. 106). On another occasion, he declared: "I can be like Shakespeare. I can come back and re-write everything I've done and nobody can fucking stop me. I've done that with *Tommy* and I might revisit *Quadrophenia* too" (Tingen, p. 24).

In preparing *PsychoDerelict* Townshend endeavored to "write grown-up songs" (Tingen, 1993, pp. 26, 28) that embrace his life's lessons. This "adult" songwriting remained ambiguous: "For example, if there's a love song on the record its not just a song about love its also about...attraction or the way that love happens, but also about the way that its distorted and changed and the way that we play games with it as well" (*Pete Townshend's*, 1993). He discusses the work's autobiographical qualities and his songwriting:

Well, obviously every writer, every individual that creates, has to draw on their own experiences and when I set out to write songs I shoot from the hip—I don't actually write for any particular voice—except that I'm always writing for the first commission I ever had, you know, the Shepherd's Bush Who fan who was so delighted when I wrote "Can't Explain" and "My Generation" and "Anyway, Anyhow, Anywhere" who came up and said "Listen, that's what we need, that's what we wanna say, that's what we wanna say to the establishment and to the world." And I've been fairly faithful to that all the way along, so I tend to write songs for where those people are at today.... But the play here is actually addressing things which I've learned, which I bring my experience to. So I thought—you know, listening through to the songs—I thought that maybe what I should do is I should give my personal take on it. So to that extent, it's autobiographical. But to the extent that I always write for that Shepherd's Bush kid—if this is sort of chapter twenty-six in his continuing story—then this is the usual kind of eighty-twenty break-down. It's eighty percent my take on other people's lives. (*Interview with*, 1993)

The project involved intense collaboration, as Townshend worked with Barnes, the various actors, and his now-traditional cast of musicians ("I like them there for spiritual reasons"—*Interview with*, 1993). Negotiations also extended to radio programmers, who posed a unique problem, since dialogue often appears in the middle of songs and, on occasion, uses strong profanity. In response, Townshend released a "music only" version for radio and, later, for the general public.

The various activities weaving throughout *PsychoDerelict* result in a busy production. The original version (containing twenty-one tracks running 63:04) features over fifty transitions in and out of songs or scenes. The "music only" version (containing fifteen tracks and running 59:09) is much less complicated. To rely on either version is to omit several valuable aspects of the production; as a result, I turn to the stage performance as my story guide. Townshend conducted his first solo tour in 1993, and *PsychoDerelict* was the show's centerpiece. An August performance in New York City was distributed live on pay-per-view television. An edited version of that performance was aired in December 1993 on the Public Broadcasting System's *Great Performances*. Another edited version of that show was released as the videotape/disc *Pete Townshend Live* (an abridged version was released in CDi form as well). The *Pete Townshend Live* video provides our guide through *PsychoDerelict*. The show's playbill (Townshend, 1993a) introduces our characters:

I hope that you have heard and enjoyed my new CD *PsychoDerelict*. This show will give you a different slant on the concept of setting pop-music and spoken drama together in the same package.... Meet RAY HIGH—ageing rock star with a dream; RUTH STREETING—sharply critical journalist; RASTUS KNIGHT—Ray's worried manager; SPINNER—the young hero and ATHENA—the female villain of Ray's dream-story. On the CD and in this show I am the seventh "character," not so much a narrator as an observer. I play myself and speak my own thoughts. The songs are very personal to me, but the drama—which is I think full of both smart and stupid theories—is not, even though there are some autobiographical aspects to the story.

(With regard to Townshend's role as an "observer," he enacted that role in various ways. In a Chicago show, for example, he moved about offering reactions to the story; in New York, he was more detached in his response to the actors.) Townshend's interviews shed much light on his characters and—since characterization drives this story—I spend a moment with those descriptions. Townshend discussed "Ray High" with New York's WNEW (1993) and established that character's connection with *White City*'s Jim:

I suppose what actually made him turn to rock & roll in the first place. Those post-war years in the late 50s and the early 60s in England where they stopped conscripting people into the army. They said: "Listen there's gonna be no more war. We've solved that problem. We don't need you anymore." And I think there are a lot of kids running around England trying to find something to do and I think some of us came up with rock & roll—English style. And the song is really about that. Its about the old English idea and also the fact that those boys, those men, those people are kind of made redundant, in a sense, by peace...by peace time and now being held up, in some way, responsible for many of the things that are wrong with modern society.

High's English Boy Anxieties are exacerbated by his commitment to the "Gridlife"—read, *LifeHouse*—vision: "The problem that Ray High has is he has a creative vision.... You know, a dream that was maybe rooted in the sixties, a GOOD dream, a good idea, a good take, a good feeling about what rock and roll was gonna do, what music was gonna do, what young people were gonna do in that first flush of sixties rock which was then somehow forgotten in the seventies" (*Interview with*, 1993). A complex web of independent themes—the English Boy Syndrome, the value of individual aspiration (dreaming), the role of journalists in the truth-fact dichotomy, music business angst, and artistic insecurity (there are more)—converge into a single characterization, "Ray High."

The show's account of Ruth Streeting's character is intriguing: "What's interesting about her is she's not meant to be just a bitch; she's actually meant to be, in a sense, a maternal function. She knows this man.... She knows his weak points. She knows what's gonna get him going and she knows that what he's really hooked into deeply, most deeply...is what he feels is his sacred relationship with his fans" (*Interview with*, 1993). The remaining characters, quite frankly, are either underdeveloped (Spinner and Athena) or blatantly stereotypical (the superficial Rastus). Ray High and Ruth Streeting drive this story.

The show's set design positioned Townshend on a riser in the middle of his band (also on risers): guitarist Phil Palmer, bassist Pino Palladino, and drummer Simon Phillips appeared on Townshend's right; pianist John "Rabbit" Bundrick, guitarist/singer Andy Fairweather Low, singers Katie Kissoon and Billy Nicholls, and Peter Hope-Evans on "mouth organ" stood to Townshend's left. Three large projection screens were placed behind the band with television monitors of various sizes located around the stage. And to the left and right of Townshend, directly in front of the musicians, were two open areas for the stage action. "Ray High" was played by John Labanowski, "Ruth Streeting" by Jan Ravens, "Rastus Knight" by Linal Haft; Donny Kerr and Sage Carter were the voices of "Spinner" and "Athena," respectively.

PsychoDerelict opens with "English Boy" (the projection screens spell out "P-S-Y-C-H-O-D-E-R-E-L-I-C-T") and fades to Ruth's radio program (she sits at a desk with two telephones [one red] and an "ON THE AIR" sign over her shoulder): "Hello Ruth Streeting here.... This is the show that dishes the dirt on the dirt. Strictly no rock star bullshit on my show. I talk about anything I like, or anything I hate. Speaking of which, remember that clapped-out sixties hell raiser Ray High? (Camera cuts to opposite side of stage and Ray lighting a cigarette) Rumor has it the sad old lush can't do it anymore, I mean make records." With Union Jacks blazing on the projection screens, "English Boy" resumes:

> I'm an English boy, I was brought up right.
> Hold me down and I will bite.
> I show no fear, I serve with joy.
> I'm proud to be here, an English Boy.
> I feel like a stray dog, blurred like a movie.
> You say you've come to arrest me but you're just trying to test me.
> I'm fucking bored with your prejudice spreading like a fever.
> Your promises to train me are just attempts to restrain me.
> I'm an English boy, precisely made.
> You can pin me down, I am not afraid.
> I show no fear, I will serve with joy.
> I'm proud to be here, an English boy.

After citing how English Boys are used "like a headline, cut pieces to pieces," and warning, "if you raise your dress, I will bite," Townshend presents the English Boy Syndrome: "And I don't know where I'm gonna go, I don't know where I been/I just keep going round and round on the Circle Line like some demented kid in the mirror, I'm trying to avoid paying for my ticket/I'm a lost soul/I read about myself in the newspapers/I'm a pig, I'm a thug/I've got nowhere to go but down." The song is interrupted once again by Streeting's assault on High ("The only thing Ray's writing these days are large checks to his booze merchants"), as the video shifts to Rastus (shaking his head) and Ray (pouring a glass of wine). The reporter closes: "Poor little sausage. Life's a bitch, and so am I." Townshend returns: "Feel like I'm kicking at a dead man, kicking in the chorus/I'm broken by hatred while politicians just ignore us/You never give me any value, you didn't give me any reason/There's no tools and no toys for any English boys." As "English Boy" fades, Ray and Rastus appear. Ray declares, "Look, I need something more than playing empty halls for you and your fucking Free Mason cronies," to which Rastus replies: "What you need Ray is a kick up the bloody ass. Look, I'm running out of your money. If you must be introspective, at least do it in public. Millions wanna share in your loneliness and misery." Ray hangs his head: "But the press slaughtered me Rastus. I need to be back in control of my own existence, other then, leave off." Rastus asserts: "How can you stand this solitude after all that fucking fun. I mean, look at you. What are you now? You're mature." Ray erupts: "Mature! I'm not mature! I'm just derelict! Look, inside I'm the same as I ever was!"

Next the first *LifeHouse* instrumental bridge emerges—the synthesizer-based tracks entitled "Meher Baba M3," "Meher Baba M4 (signal box)," and "Meher Baba M5 (Vivaldi)." The Baba instrumentals signal a shift to the "Gridlife" portion of the story and its rapid projection-screen activity. First photographs of Ray appear, followed by pictures of "young Ray" and scenes of the flower-power era (1960s fashions, concert photographs, hairstyles, etc). While the music intensifies, chants of "We demand the Universal Grid" emerge, projections of crowds carrying banners ("We demand the Universal Grid") flash, and Athena appears in an advertisement for the Universal Grid. The music fades to Ray, logging onto a "Gridlife Chronicles" computer program. There he reports that he was listening to some of his work "from 1970." "It's got something," he enters, "I could really dream then, it ain't such a bad dream either."

The story moves to a night on the town with Ray and Rastus. Dawn approaches, and Ray is tired of chasing publicity. Rastus urges him to continue ("You got to play the game!"); they argue and stop in front of a "club" frequented by Ruth Streeting. Ray protests, "That bloody cunt wrote that I'm ugly." Oddly, the solicitous Rastus responds, "Well you are actually"; they squabble, and a reluctant Ray enters the club. The song "Let's Get Pretentious" ensues: "Let's get pretentious, put on an act/Let's be portentous, embroider fact/Exaggerate it, dress up the bland/Let's over-rate it/Let the critics be damned." Townshend's 1990s version of "Eminence Front" pauses for Ray's observation: "This club is full of journalists and I hate the fucking lot of 'em!" Ray drinks while Rastus works the crowd, always reminding Ray to "play the game." Ray grows introspective: "You know what I think? You got beauty or talent and you're gonna end up in prostitution. I mean that's all my life was on the road. Prostitution. It's inevitable. We're all cunts after all. Get us another drink, will ya?" A patronizing Rastus declares, "As you know Ray, I find all this fascinating. It's a pity Ruth Streeting's missing it." Ray assures Rastus, "She'll get it alright, but my way. Don't you worry, my story'll get told." "Let's Get Pretentious" resumes: "Let's find a market for sparkling wit/Let's make a target of anyone with a hit/Let's keep some secrets, let's make them up/Put them together, then break them up."

A synthesizer interlude introduces another "Gridlife" segment: this time, the heavy projection screen activity yields to Spinner's image and his complaints about Athena, an "experience program" programmer who is not "doing her job." Spinner explains how the "grid life suits" are substitutes for life: "The programmes replace life" (a concept straight from *LifeHouse*). Spinner's image fades, and the rhythmic projections/music slide into a nightclub scene. Ruth dances out of the shadows and happens upon Rastus on the "dance floor" (Rastus complimenting Ruth's leather outfit, Ruth replying, "It's not leather you jerk, it's rubber"). The exchange turns to Ray and Rastus's frustrations, "all he seems to do is read his fan mail.... I don't know what would fire him up." Sassy Ruth responds, "I bet I could fire him up." An eager Rastus answers Ruth's inquiries about Ray's fan mail and promises to "cut her in" if she is successful. Ruth appears confident but warns her idea "would be dangerous, especially for Ray."

The busy production cuts to a photo of Athena ("You are safe from harm on the Grid") and rapid projections of famous people: John Kennedy, Elvis Presley, Marilyn Monroe, and various glamorous people and scenes—including the Mona Lisa. As the track "Early Morning Dreams" unfolds, a song/advertisement for the Universal Grid appears: "This is the dream that I wake up dreaming/Lovin' my lover under dawn-pink skies/Perfect design that

I wake up scheming/What I recall when I first open my eyes." There Athena sells the Grid's virtues via projections of luxury and fantasy ("I wanted it to go on forever," one perfect male voice sighs). The plot takes a complicated turn when Ray—sitting in his robe, writing and then reading a letter to a fan, Rosalind ("Your dream sounds wonderful")—offers help with her career. Ray stands, disrobes, and "dives" into a "pool" via swimming sound effects. While swimming, he describes the letter to Rastus (sitting poolside, telephone in hand) and its photograph of Rosalind lying naked on her mother's grave. Ray points to Rosalind's unique physical features and her erotic appeal: she has "witches teats" (two extra nipples on her breasts). After Ray explains Rosalind dances at a topless bar in "San Francisco"; his manager jokes "With four nipples I could get her a double fee." The pool scene cuts to a brief segment from Ruth's radio program. Ruth notes that Ray has "been seen out" since her last broadcast, expresses her sympathy for Rastus ("I've always had a soft spot for Rastus and I've often seen him looking at it"), and condemns Ray's "peace and love" philosophy. From that scene, the show turns to its first uninterrupted song, "I Want That Thing." While Townshend sings, he points to the projection screens and their Gridlife imagery. The narrator longs for the Universal Grid:

[chorus] Free ride to the house of life,
       Free ride to the house of life. (repeated several times)
I work hard at my job.
I save and I save.
I know what I deserve after all that I gave.
You know I want that thing, you know I want that thing.
Put aside a little money almost every day.
When I think that I'm close it just gets further away.
You know I want that thing, I want that thing.
[chorus]
Don't know if it's truth, don't know if it's lies.
I just can't be aloof to what you advertise.
I have to have that thing, I want that thing
I want that dream [repeated] ...
I can't wait any longer to choose.
If I can't get my own, I'm gonna fucking take yours from you.
I want that thing, I really want that thing.

The song segues directly into the next track, "Outlive The Dinosaur." The music fades to Ray reading another letter to Rosalind in which he responds to her longings for "security" ("insecurity is the principal driving force we performers share"). Ray confides that he too endured childhood problems but that he learned from his misfortunes: "The only power available to you lies in your submission. Isn't that what the photo was all about? Remember, you don't have to bury the pain. You can use it." "Outlive The Dinosaur" resumes with lyrics that are not easily placed in the story's context: "I breathe, my throat clinches, clutching to exclude a dozen different stenches/In Falmouth Bay a blue whale rolls/Gonna drown in the swill from sewer holes/Summers longer, deltas gashed, ancient trees uprooted, smashed/Time is generous—more, take more [repeated]/I must out run the dinosaur." The music fades to Ray and additional advice for Rosalind. He sends her a song ("Flame"), urges her to sing, and closes with this lesson: "Remember, the great artist is just like a child and needs to submit to the audience. Do you begin to see the secret?" Townshend's impressionism resumes with images of "battle scarred temples" and general, *negative,* confusion: "The strong survive to wean more brutes who grow and seed, extend their roots.... Like monkeys trapped in monkey suits."

A synthesizer interlude takes us back to Gridlife and Spinner's reservations about the system. Colorful, rhythmic projections accompany Townshend's guitar and *LifeHouse*-era tape while Spinner raises the central question: "The Grid always provides facts, but facts don't always reveal the truth." Spinner argues, "You need truth to develop morality and decency." The brief segment closes with that complaint (the projections feature a computer menu with choices of beautiful people, Nazis, and others). The music fades into "Flame"— the song Ray wrote for Rosalind—and Ray's final letter in which he praises her singing, warns her that she "must serve the press as well as the audience," and confesses his love for Ruth. There High describes how Ruth's disgust motivates his art, that somehow his contempt evolved into love. Townshend walks up behind Ray and places a consoling hand on his shoulder. The music softly shifts to "Now And Then," which is performed uninterrupted:

> [chorus] Now and then you see a soul and you fall in love.
> You can't do a thing about it [repeated].
> In you I saw someone that I recognized.
> I had no idea what was in your mind.
> I met your eyes and I was hypnotized.
> I let our lives become entwined.
> [chorus]
> I feel so badly darlin' all the time.
> I have tortured you so long
> But I am helpless in this pantomime.
> I am aware that I was wrong.

The song's flowing instrumentals continue with the narrator's remorse and regret: "But it was me who had the most to gain/Despite the fact that I now have lost/The only love that ever caused me pain/I feel like a double head was tossed."

Upon the song's conclusion a telephone rings; it is Ruth phoning Rastus. She leaves a message regarding her impending success (it's "gonna be so big") and mentions her "commission." The action cuts immediately to the song "I Am Afraid" and Townshend: "I stand beside you, I face the future/I'll admit to you I am afraid/I am afraid/As I stand beside you I have denied you/I am afraid/ I am not drunk now/I am not pilled down/My window's wound down/I am not brain-washed/My bet's still riding/I am not hiding/I am not running/I am afraid." The song breaks for Ruth's radio show announcing the "Porno Pen Pal" story featuring Ray and Rosalind. As newspaper headlines flash on the projection screens (e.g., "Exposed. Star's Sexy Sordid Secret," "Has-been Star's *Promise to Sexy Teen,*" "Extra: Ray High Hits New Low"), Townshend offers impressions of despair and fear: "I hear you crying/Your brother's dying/Be no more lying/I am afraid.... By my religion I stand here naked/I cannot fake it, with God as witness/My little children who wait for feedin', I watch you bleedin'/I am afraid." Ruth returns: "High, one time psychedelic flower child now turned alcoholic vegetable, encouraged a steamy correspondence which climaxed in the innocent fourteen year old's now infamous photo with its suggestion of nakedness...and incest." Ruth acknowledges that High's albums have been reissued, but contends that "decent, normal" people will want to hear *Rosalind*'s new single ("Flame") produced with the reporter's assistance: "She's a brilliant singer and with my help has just released a brilliant new record."

Heavy projection screen activity and a synthesizer interlude follow. Eventually, Spinner announces plans to "secretly commandeer" a Gridlife studio in order to stage a live rock concert (shades of *LifeHouse*). The story shifts back to Ruth's studio and a confrontation with Ray. He goes straight after her: "What the fuck do you think you're playing at!" She remains calm, "Just doing my job." Ray asserts, "With this line of crap?" Again, Ruth comforts, "Just wait, you'll see." Ray demands to know what's going on between Ruth and Rastus ("So that's how you got the photo"); again she dismisses him, "Do me a favor." The projection screens go dark, and Townshend performs "Don't Try To Make Me Real" (uninterrupted):

> [chorus] Stop trying to make me real.
>> I haven't got the kind of heart a lover can steal.
>> Stop crying, I just can't feel any sympathy for someone trying to make me
>> real.
> Make me of shit in a two-tenner deal.
> Make me of pornography in a pedophile wheel.
> Whatever I do, whatever I feel, by your double standards I will never be real.
> [chorus]
> Why can't you settle for a fantasy?
> You're so convinced that I'm the man to see.
> I can't live up to what you give up to.
> I fail to see the perfect man in me.

The protracted number concludes, and the story turns to a sex scene, a silhouette of Rastus whipping Ruth. Ruth screams "Why so bloody hard" and warns that "Ray would be so jealous." Rastus inquires why, she responds that Ray admitted his love in a letter to Rosalind. Rastus grunts, "Don't talk crap" and strikes her even harder before asking her to "turn over." As she faces Rastus, the manager inquires about her physique (she too has "witches teats"), and the scene closes with Ruth's masochistic pleasure ("Harder! Harder!").

Townshend dances (literally) his way through the next song, "Predictable," and its tale of romantic bliss: "Your love is so predictable/I can rely on you to blow my brain/You always know which trick to pull/I can predict you'll drive me wild-insane.... Your body's so delectable/I know for sure I'm gonna be amazed/You get me so erectable/I know for sure you're gonna leave me raised." The uninterrupted song concludes with the sound of a radio tuning in Rosalind's "Flame." (The only song not written by Townshend; Simon Townshend, Josh Phillips-Gorse, Gavin Lewis, Mark Brzezicki, and Jaz Lochrie share authorship.) Ruth—"riding in a car" with Rastus (who pretends to "steer" the "vehicle")—laughingly says she can't wait to see Ray's face, to which Rastus replies, "I can't wait to see Rosalind's fucking face, but of course I won't will I...that photo was of you, you dirty cow." Rastus concedes the "witches teats" gave Ruth away. Both characters embellish the plan's success, yet Ruth refuses to admit that Ray wrote "Flame," saying, "That would be telling." With that, the characters walk across the stage and meet Ray. Ruth confronts Ray about Rosalind ("You manipulated her!") and warns him to watch what he says ("Careful what you say, I might print it"). Ray reacts, and Rastus urges him not to get "introspective" since "we're back in calculator country." Ray insists he "helped" Rosalind with "her problem" and that if she were present, she would agree. Sassy Ruth responds, "You didn't help her, you just made her a fucking star."

Once more, the story cuts to rapid projections, a Baba synthesizer segment, and Spinner's voice. Echoing *LifeHouse*'s Bobby, Spinner proclaims: "You will each hear your own song.... It's your own note. Your own vibration in the cosmos. All of you will know one another through the other's song. You'll blend and get in harmony. As you blend, your song will change. And in the end your music will turn into a sound so complete...it will show us that we all are one. Free. We're all in tune." The busy story cuts back to Ruth, Rastus, and Ray. Ray reports that he knows the truth. Ruth fails to grasp his point and replies that she knows what he has done as well: "I've seen all the letters. What a fool you are Ray Highsmith." Ray responds that he "knew all the time" (a potentially equivocal line). Ruth's surprise yields to "Fake It": "You can fake it/Hold my hand/If you fake it I will understand/I don't care if you fake it/I don't give a damn/I don't care if you fake it/Don't you understand/You might laugh at me later but please just smile at me now/Don't ever feel like a traitor/You're not letting me down/Fake it, fake it, I can take it/Love's just an end, it's the means we feel." Afterward, Rastus pays Ruth "five percent, that's sixty grand." She complains that she's getting very little for such a successful plan; Rastus cracks: "It's not bad, fifteen grand a nipple." Rastus promises "loads more" since Ray is "back where he belongs, on top and no more bloody letters." The video pans across stage to Ray, writing a letter to "Lily," expressing his gratitude for the increase in fan mail and photographs ("And for that, I'm very thankful"). Ray and Townshend exchange smiles.

PsychoDerelict concludes with a brief "Now And Then" reprise before returning to Ray (with guitar), Rastus, and Ruth in a recording studio (images of a studio are projected). Rastus bubbles "What a team," as Ruth encourages Ray: "OK Ray love. Now I know this is difficult for you sweetheart but you do have such a wonderful dream to share. You must bring it to the world." Ray hangs his head (with a shy smile) while Rastus screams "yeah, Yeah, YEAH," Ruth yells "shut up Rastus" and tells Ray, "OK Ray, when you're ready, in your own time sweetheart." A long, pleasant reprise of "Now And Then" follows. A synthesizer segment introduces Spinner's last appearance and a statement originally featured in the 1971 "letter" from "Bobby" printed in *Melody Maker*: "Music and vibrations are the basis of everything. They pervade everything...atoms are vibrations between positive and negative forces...some very subtle, some complex, but it's all music." As the music rises, Ray stands with his guitar and launches into *LifeHouse*'s climax (Ray: "The crowd rushes in, three circles closing fast"). Ruth abruptly cuts him off: "I've cut all this crap! Go straight to the single." Nothing has changed after all.

And that is exactly what happens. "English Boy" returns via a compelling performance in which Peter Hope-Evans and Townshend exchange solos and antics: Townshend admonishing Hope-Evans as the "English Boy" who steals from people, while Hope-Evans runs around the stage teasing Ruth and Ray. Interestingly, Townshend sings "English Boy" in the *past tense*: "I was an English boy, I was brought up right/You could hold me down and I would bite/I served with joy, I knew no fear/I was an English boy, proud to be here." He also adds lyrics that provide a sharper edge than the initial version: "You spray like a tom-cat, piss like a stray dog/Swear like a sailor, speaking in gang-tongues/Kicking in the chorus, stabbing to order/Slashing like a blind man, lost like a soldier." Townshend demands, "Stand up when I'm talking to you boy/Stand up/Stand up" (Hope-Evans is running around, doing his thing at this point), and the powerful rendition closes, "I was an English Boy." The music fades to Ray's final lines:

Gridlife was a vision. A real vision. Not a fiction. Not a fairy tale. A glimpse of the future. Today, twenty years later, the apocalypse it foresaw is nearer. But whatever you read in the newspapers, we still don't have any alternative reality. It's all games now. It's all lies and deceit. What happened to the truth? What happened to the dream? What happened to all that lovely hippy shit?

With those words a rooster crows (a new dawn?), and the show concludes (at 67:49). Townshend thanks the actors, the band, and the show's technicians, and closes the performance with a set of old material.

At this point, we would be wise to pause and consider the author's comments about his work. Again, that commentary was, to say the least, extensive. Townshend makes us *work* once more; however, when those materials are assembled, a clear, coherent message emerges. Much of his commentary focuses on the English Boy Syndrome. Although he claimed the song could easily be entitled "American Boy" (Gill, 1993a, p. 110) since it is a follow-up on the 1982 Who song "I've Known No War," his explanations reflect an autobiographical slant. Townshend described the song as "a cross between 'My Generation' and 'Face The Face'" (Wild, 1993, p. 21) and reiterated the *White City* story of male frustration: "These boys are the product of first generation fighters, winners of wars, men who were expected to stick bayonets into a German at any given moment," and yet they "never get a job, are never given any prospect of getting a job and are always told that they're wankers" (Martin, 1993, p. 41). Through Ray High, Townshend takes Jimmy, Jim, and their English Boy Anxieties into the 1990s.

Compounding the English Boy Syndrome is the story's other major theme, the value of dreaming. Townshend explains: "There is...a need for the dream...we've lost sight of the dream...there was a dream that we had in the 60s and it went up in a big puff in the 70s, bang the bubble burst and now we've got millions of bubbles all around us and they're all very interesting. But we need the big bubble back" (WNEW, 1993). For the author, that "big bubble" involves the *means*, not the ends: "And I say this as somebody who's lucky enough to be creative and realize some of my dreams. The great dream is the pursuit of the dream itself" (Duffy, 1993b, p. 43). In order to give life to this aspect of the story, Townshend revisited the failed *LifeHouse* for two reasons. The first is primarily a social statement. That is, the media's capacity to usurp the individual's power over his/her destiny: "the moral issue is that more and more of what's affecting us in our lives is brought to us by messengers. We're not in contact with our own village anymore, with our own direct experience" (Tingen, 1993, p. 26). The second involves Ray's characterization. Townshend believed High needed a "history...a dream and a vision" (WNEW, 1993), and since Townshend enjoys revisiting his original demos, he turned to the *Life-House* material.

Townshend's "truth-fact" theme runs throughout the work, although he camouflages many of those statements. Whereas the Gridlife portrayal of the "truth-fact" dichotomy is direct, other applications are cloudy. Townshend's remarks about the song "Now And Then" are instructive:

This is a hard song to talk about. It's just a song that I wrote for somebody that I care about and addressed the original idea of the whole album which is really whether or not when you actually feel, or say, that you're in love with somebody that you actually know what you mean. It was the first principle for trying to find out whether what we say...when we think we're speaking the truth whether it's possible for us to ever know that we're speaking the truth. And then, if that's true in relationships, then is it possible that when we accuse the totalitarian media of sometimes bending the truth—which obviously, in this particular story I do to some extent—are we actually being hypocrites? Are we actually saying listen...you have to be exact, you have to be precise, you have to tell us the truth always. Don't censor, don't shield us. We can handle it. When we don't really know how to say what we really feel ourselves because we don't really know how to get in touch with it. That was the first song that set up this idea for the record that, in a way...when you see somebody, when you experience...when you look in their eyes there's something goes between you and you both recognize that and you both might feel very very different things. But if one of you decides that it's—let's say love—what that actually can set up is a very kind of fatal circle. (WNEW, 1993)

Townshend's complaint is without mystery: how can we blame the media for misleading their audiences when, in fact, people follow the same strategy in life's most significant interpersonal context, loving relationships? The author's career-long struggle with hypocrisy reaches new heights in *PsychoDerelict*.

Other traditional Townshend themes appear as well: the performer's relationship to the audience and its submissive nature, the power of the critic to impact an artist's work, the commercialization of artistic dreams (via Athena, Townshend's "female Rupert Murdoch of the future"—WNEW, 1993), and the fear of aging. Throughout all of these scenes and themes, Townshend speaks to various levels of a "truth-fact" dichotomy by way of a purposefully ambiguous narrative strategy. In *Interview with a PsychoDerelict* he describes the situation between Rosalind and Ray and how the audience cannot be sure of Ray's story, "He might be making out, she might never sent him a photograph." When asked if Ray triumphs in the end, Townshend responds:

You decide, I don't know. I don't know whether Ruth and Rastus have pulled off the coup, whether Ray knew that Ruth was Rosalind or Rosalind was Ruth, whether in fact there really is a Rosalind, we don't know that. We don't know whether Ruth has actually used the song that Ray sent or not, we don't know whether that "Flame"—the song that we hear Ruth sing—is actually sung by Rosalind and she's taken Rosalind's song and paid her off in San Francisco or shot her. We don't know whether Ray wrote it. None of these things are stated and that's deliberate, I want to leave that open, that's for you to decide.

The *Pete Townshend Live* version does not appear to be as vague as he suggests; however, his intentions are apparent. In a 1997 conversation Townshend specifically cites how Richard Barnes made every effort to keep the story as open-ended as possible.

PsychoDerelict blends autobiography, professional complaint, and psycho/sociological observation to render commentary regarding English society, interpersonal relations, and professional life. The project also seeks thematic closure for its principal author. Just as "English Boy" wraps around *Psycho-Derelict*, the song serves as the songwriting oeuvre's capstone statement. The track is a generational complaint, a direct manifestation of the "Can't Explain"/"My Generation" anthems. The communication problems associated with a generation unable to articulate its inner emotions either to one another or outsiders have expanded to the point of being a social dilemma. These conditions pose a threat to two areas of concern for the auteur: they threaten and stifle individual initiative ("the dream" theme)—hence, the English Boy Syndrome-Dream tensions—and they promote and extend dysfunctional communication patterns in both personal and professional contexts. The Shepherd's Bush youth who could not explain himself and found himself in a dishonest world now endures an extremely complicated life. That inarticulate kid now over-thinks everything as an adult as his life has evolved into a diabolically complex web of perspectives in which people anticipate behavior patterns predicated on various role expectations. The dialogue also conveys anxieties over celebrity status, journalistic practices, and the performer-audience relationship in a direct manner. Rastus's blatant superficiality, the Gridlife's commercialism, Ray's views on celebrity "prostitution" (where Townshend briefly revisits *Horse's Neck* and the "burdens" of beauty/talent theme), and the intensely negative portrayal of the "publicity game" all communicate Townshend's traditional stance on these subjects.

Critical responses to *PsychoDerelict* are as varied as the project's content. Comments range from insightful analyses of the project's strengths and weaknesses to mean-spirited attacks on the artist. Several "typewriter tappers" focus on Townshend's use of dialogue during and between songs and how that innovation is a potential distraction. For instance, Gill (1993a) writes the "record breaks rules and challenges listeners" (p. 100), but since the dialogue "often interrupts the music, it may annoy listeners who simply want to boogie to the tunes." *Time* magazine contends the dialogue "wears out its welcome" (Simpson, 1993, p. 55) even though "the dramatic format appeals" to Townshend's "love for the theater." After describing Townshend as Andrew Lloyd Webber's successor (the new "king of New York musical theater"), Morison (1993, p. 170) maintains the project's "hooky choruses and rock drive" will bring the audience "back to *PsychoDerelict* even after the dialogue has worn thin" (p. 172). Martin (1993) notes that "people yawn at the idea of another Townshend concept" (p. 17), Tingen (1993) argues the work is another "disturbing psychological drama" (p. 23), but—unlike *Tommy* and *Quadrophenia*—this "comic book radio play...is in places genuinely funny and the ending a happy free ride for all." Calling the project an "aural movie," Evans (1993, p. 76) describes its author as a "compulsive seeker whose questing sometimes recalls John Lennon's embarrassing honesty." *Spin* advances its traditional anti-Townshend position by stating, "Townshend's brutal cynicism...sure tests the devotion of his erstwhile fans" (Foege, 1993, p. 78). The mix of critical responses is revealing and, perhaps, suggestive of journalistic agendas.

The extent to which Townshend actually uses the *PsychoDerelict* project as a capstone statement for his songwriting career is uncertain at this writing. To be sure, the mixture of unresolved themes from days gone by, the unprecedented solo tour, and the success of Broadway *Tommy* seem to establish a context for such a decision. As we observed with Townshend's spiritual themes, the auteur is capable of resolutions. Just as "The Sea Refuses No River" concludes the spiritual dimension of *The Seeker*'s quest, Townshend achieves a measure of closure with *PsychoDerelict*: interpersonal distrust and uncertainty are ubiquitous, the music industy is duplicitous, and dreams/visions are the last refuge of hope. After *PsychoDerelict*'s long, serious look *backward*, Townshend has opened the way to music theater.

THE *SCOOP* PROJECTS

Before closing, I must pause for a brief discussion of the *Scoop* series of home "demo" compilations. Townshend explains the project's rationale in the initial entry's liner notes:

For many years it has only been the people close to me who have heard the music I made for myself or by myself. I have always called these recordings "demos." Demos they have been whether made for my amusement, for film soundtracks, for experimentation purposes or to submit material to The Who. (I have rarely written for anyone else).... Making demos is where I find peace and sometimes even a feeling of prayer. Right now words are still something I am newly grappling with on a day to day basis, trying hard not to let too much of myself get in the way. I am trying to isolate my music and lyric writing and once again recording becomes both a hobby and a creative outlet.... Away from sophisticated studio techniques and repeated soul destroying takes the real joy I get from playing and writing comes through, and that joy is something I want to share. I have hundreds of such demos, this isn't meant to be a definitive collection, just a scoop.

Most of the songs featured on these compilations appear elsewhere in the study; however, the two albums also contain unreleased compositions from several unrealized projects and songs omitted from existing albums. In short, the *Scoop* ventures are invaluable artifacts, even though they take the various songs out of context and restrict the critic's ability to assess their significance within the oeuvre's development. The first edition contains twenty-five tracks (running 74:53), with sixteen previously unreleased songs (by my count, anyway). The album features leftovers from *Face Dances* ("Zelda," "Dirty Water," "Popular"), *Empty Glass* ("You're So Clever"), and *Chinese Eyes* ("Body Language"), to name but a few. David Fricke's (1983) review in *Rolling Stone* captures the project's significance:

No one in rock & roll has spent more time revealing the motivations for making music, the private energies and obsessions that drive one to it or the intimate details of the process than Pete Townshend. For that reason alone, *Scoop*...is essential Townshend, the ultimate unburdening of a chronic confessor. A logical extension of the passionate searching and naked, rock-star, menopausal fear...this album is an open invitation into the root experience of songwriting, a rare glimpse of those secret explosions when words first collide with music. (p. 66)

To Fricke, the album presents "a pure, expressive Pete Townshend free of the responsibilities of being *the* Pete Townshend" (p. 67) and, in turn, provides an "art in progress" experience. The *Los Angeles Times* adds: "Rather than intensely search his soul before our eyes, Townshend here takes us on a tour through his attic.... Townshend has some uncommonly interesting throwaways, and his insights and obsessions always have been the most intriguing in rock" (Pond, 1983).

Townshend's second demo collection, 1987's *Another Scoop*, builds upon the first edition. That volume contains twenty-seven tracks (running 87:38), with fourteen previously unreleased numbers. This compilation moves away from Who/Townshend album leftovers in favor of unrealized projects and musical experiments. For example, two songs from an aborted Who project, *Siege* ("Cat Snatch" and "Ask Yourself") are featured along with the "experimental" song, "Prelude, The Right To Write." At times, Townshend's liner note comments are insightful, such as this remark about the early Who song "Call Me Lightning": "The song is a very clear example of how difficult it was for me to reconcile what I took to be Roger's need for macho, chauvinist lyrics and Keith Moon's appetite for surf music and fantasy sports car love affairs." Such comments suggest the negotiations Townshend endured with the early Who. In his review of this second release, Fricke (1987a) writes that the artist who "dedicated his life to the proposition that rock & roll is a communal experience...shows that he wrote some of his best songs and made some of his most affecting music playing to an audience of one—himself" (p. 146). Fricke suggests this view of Townshend in "his private song lab, testing and editing his creative impulses before broadcasting them to the world" (p. 148) reveals an artist free of the tensions that engulf the world of commercial music. When those ideas, songs, and stories emerge from that "song lab" they join their author in the negotiations that constitute the musical world. Some survive, some do not. But without the *Scoop* compilations, we could never fully comprehend the scope of Townshend's writing—if, in fact, that is possible at all.

As we have seen, the second portion of Pete Townshend's solo career presents an artistic evolution. Just as "The Sea Refuses No River" closed *The Seeker*'s spiritual quest, *Horse's Neck* achieved closure for Townshend's personal search for worldly understanding. *The auteur* reached an *individual* denouement to his tale about the interpersonal, marital, parental (mostly maternal), professional, and sexual anxieties that dominated the oeuvre to that point. "Laguna. Valentine's Day, 1982" represents that resolution. From that point on, Townshend complained not about his *personal* condition but about the generational angst introduced in "I Can't Explain" and "My Generation." This complaint—the English Boy Syndrome—supports the *White City* and *Psycho-Derelict* projects and appears metaphorically in *The Iron Man*. Townshend's proclamation "I was an English boy" signals that aspect of *The Seeker*'s search may have also achieved resolution. The moral of the story is consistent with the auteur's previous resolutions: no matter the difficulties of contemporary life (abandonment, deception, and creative commercialization), cling to your dreams, your relationships, and your neighborhood and they will sustain you. Townshend's penchant for long, elaborate expressions (making his audience *work*), his preference for the "historical" over the "amorous," and his decision that the "words are the most important thing" recalls the trouvères and their shift in artistic forms. Pete Townshend combines those structural and thematic signatures to chronicle the resolution to *The Seeker*'s quest, end his "old job," and embrace a "new job" in music theater. After a long, dark, and lonely struggle, the impulse is victorious.

7

The Minstrel's Dilemma: The Case of Pete Townshend

That the artist is not as a rule consciously concerned with communication, but with getting the work, the poem or play or statue or painting or whatever it is, "right," apparently regardless of its communicative efficacy, is easily explained.... He cannot stop to consider how the public or even how especially well qualified sections of the public may like it or respond to it. He is wise, therefore, to keep all such considerations out of mind altogether. Those artists and poets who can be suspected of close separate attention to the communicative aspect tend (there are exceptions to this, of which Shakespeare might be one) to fall into a subordinate rank. (Richards, 1924, pp. 26-27)

I. A. Richards's idealism certainly contrasts the pragmatism Henry Raynor conveys in this book's introduction. Richards's writings regarding the artistic impulse may provide the conceptual foundation for this examination of Pete Townshend's lifework, but his comments on the creative process are apparently void of the tensions and negotiations that characterized the songwriter's commercial career. In fact, Richards's position reminds us of Raynor's observations about "nineteenth-century conceptions of art as pure activity" and its naive stance on commercial art. Townshend's narrative impulse may have aspired to "get the work right"; however, that inclination often yielded to other—at times equally important—factors. While this book demonstrates that Pete Townshend is most certainly an *auteur*, it also uncovers the complex negotiations that rendered that art.

Throughout this volume I have characterized those negotiations in terms of "the minstrel's dilemma" analogy. I began with a fledgling stage act and its *aggressive* approach, moved to the *expectations* that accompany commercial success and creative potential, proceeded with the *obligations* that follow stardom and its mindless commitment to a domineering industry and nostalgic audiences, and I closed with the *risks* connected with the decision to abdicate security in favor of independence or innovation. In every case, this "minstrel" endured tensions that both facilitated *and* debilitated the articulation of his artistic vision. In every case, negotiations ensued.

I conclude with an overview of those negotiations, Townshend's artistic signatures, and the resolution of this "minstrel's dilemma." My discussion of those creative/commercial tensions—and the auteur's stylistic response to such conditions—speaks to the study's theoretical yield (what I term the "negotiation thesis"). Flowing from that starting point is my treatment of Townshend's narrative signatures and *The Seeker* composite text. Townshend's artistic philosophy employs specific stylistic tendencies that evolve as the oeuvre unfolds. These stylistic features intersect the negotiation thesis at the critical juncture that is the art's *function*—an attribute that changes in response to the particulars of the moment. Unlike I. A. Richards's example, as Pete Townshend labored to "get the work right" he paid very close attention to its "communicative efficacy" and its various creative and commercial implications.

THE MINSTREL'S DILEMMA: THE NEGOTIATION THESIS

The complex web of activities that constitute the contemporary musical world clearly moves the modern music critic away from "nineteenth-century conceptions of art as pure activity." If this study of Pete Townshend's work reveals anything at all, it exposes the degree to which he was *required* to compromise between ideals and practicalities (among other things). *Quads* rendered one song, "I'm A Boy." *Tommy*'s spiritual journey accommodated pinball. *LifeHouse* never happened. The *White City* video required an album. The *Iron Man* project was curtailed. From all this, I argue that Townshend actively participated in five levels of negotiations throughout his career. The intensity of the respective tensions varied in relation to the artistic context: an aspiring band and its songwriter were more responsive and flexible than an established group of seasoned—financially independent—professionals.

The five areas of negotiation I discuss are: within the artist, within the band, between the artist and producer, between the artist and the industry, and between the artist and the audience. Townshend's internal tensions are described in terms of three phases of perceived responsibility that involved negotiations between musical aspirations and commercial factors. The tensions within The Who are presented through three historical phases that are defined by their level of intensity. Townshend's relationship with producers is characterized via three professional orientations (the argument is chronological but not necessarily developmental). The artist-industry negotiations are presented by way of three phases of development, and the artist-audience relationship is described in terms of three historical phases. The negotiations associated with Townshend's art may be more extensive than those cited here; nevertheless, these five levels of activity influenced the oeuvre to such an extent that their recognition is essential to an understanding of a given project's communicative function.

Townshend's comments regarding his perceived professional responsibilities, our first level of negotiation, are plentiful. His attitude toward his audience, his band, the direction of his music, and his understanding of the music industry affected his writing in various ways. These internal tensions fall into three phases that directly correspond with The Who's history: the tensions between musical aspiration (here, "quality") and commercial image (the singles period), tensions between musical aspiration (here, "artistic progress") and commercial expectations (the opera period), and tensions between musical aspiration (here, leaving the band) and commercial obligation (the end of The Who). Once The Who disband and Townshend's solo career advances (the "renaissance"), these internal tensions gradually subside, and the writer's creative/commercial dilemma dissipates.

Townshend's slavish devotion to The Who's commercial image was the driving force in his early songwriting. The musical sensationalism of The Who's early years was a gimmick-ridden approach that subordinated substance to style, and Townshend's pen supported that strategy. After all, the auto-destruction, guitar feedback, athletics, and staging satisfied Townshend's artistic inclinations (the performance *was* the art), hence his songwriting readily reinforced that orientation. The group's emphasis on "singles" oriented to specific audiences—the Mods, the pop art fad, and later the "rock" movement—demonstrated Townshend's capacity to tailor his creative instincts for the band's commercial aspirations. A song such as "Anyway, Anyhow, Anywhere" may emerge from Townshend's appreciation of Charlie Parker's music and his desire to achieve a similar artistic effect (see Barnes, 1982), but he quickly abandoned that ideal in service of The Who's commercial agenda. Thus, Townshend and Daltrey adjusted the original idea in a fashion that fed the band's rowdy image. Townshend's ability to copy The Kinks' music in order to persuade Shel Talmy (on "I Can't Explain") and his willingness to shift "My Generation's" tempo and add the Mod "stutter" are two more examples of his early artistic-commercial flexibility.

That orientation changed with such musical experiments as *Quads*, the mini-opera, and "Rael." The artistic satisfaction gleaned from the stage gradually faded in favor of more complex storytelling; as a result, Townshend eagerly pursued extensive writing projects that would have to be tempered in order to fulfill the commercial demands upon the band. *Tommy* is the prime example of Townshend's negotiations between musical aspiration and commercial demands. The writer's consistent references to the commercial "desperation" that inspired *Tommy*, his willingness to include the pinball element, and his frustrations that *Tommy* diluted Meher Baba's message all exemplify the compromises associated with that project.

The third phase of internal negotiations featured a tired, disillusioned songwriter, no longer willing to subordinate his ideals to The Who's commercial needs but who continued to do so, at his own expense. To suggest Townshend *hated* the commercial obligations The Who faced is a supportable claim. Remember Roger Daltrey's comment regarding the various pressures evident during the crucial post-*Tommy* era and how the audience's expectations proved stifling ("you stop doing what you want to do and you're startin' to do what everybody wants you to do and that's fatal as an artist"). *Quadrophenia* provided no relief, the *Tommy* film contributed to the band's concentration on its past, and the last round of Who albums chronicled Townshend's dilemma. Townshend's cynicism was evident in these remarks to Vic Garbarini (1982a): "What's the point of trying to make a really great record, when we know that just a well-constructed, well-produced piece of crap is gonna sell six million copies.... And to be brutal for a second, I think one of the dangers of middle age in rock 'n' roll is that it's very easy to take the easy way out. You have to be very angry, in a sense, to stay honest" (p. 54). Perhaps Townshend's "anger" sustained him to the point where, upon the conclusion of The Who's career, his renaissance was possible. His post-Who work indicates the extent of his anger over his generation's plight (the English Boy Syndrome), the rock industry's acceptance of the Hollywood star system, rock journalism, and various social causes. More often than not Pete Townshend's work is a conscious compromise between artistic ideals, commercial factors, and his perceived audience's situations; negotiations that emerge from the auteur's philosophy that artists must *inform*, or "*commentate*," through *entertainment*.

The tensions that existed within The Who—our second level of negotiations—are the stuff of legend. Band members not only physically fought with one another but experienced innumerable artistic and commercial conflicts as well. I present these events in terms of three historical phases: the era of combative confrontation, an acceptance of roles phase, and the dissolution of the band. Townshend characterized the combative confrontation of the band's early years as a "democracy of total negativity" (Garbarini, 1982a, p. 52), in which personal and professional agendas constantly clashed. Popular writers may claim that The Who represented the quintessential "rock gestalt" musically, but beneath the united stage front was genuine, intense turmoil. These dynamics changed with *Tommy* and The Who's acceptance of Townshend's creative leadership. Since *Tommy* provided a meaningful role for Daltrey and financial security for everyone, tensions relaxed temporarily. Although Townshend's efforts to use the *LifeHouse* project to transcend *Tommy* ultimately failed, the band supported his idea initially. The author's—and the band's—frustrations over his unrealized ambitions were no doubt placated by the commercial success of *Who's Next*; thus, *LifeHouse* did not immediately disrupt the band's chemistry. *Quadrophenia* did. Townshend's total domination of The Who's second opera destroyed the band's internal harmony and established a context for renewed conflict. The Who willingly granted Townshend creative control over the project, yet Daltrey, and even Entwistle, were quick to condemn the control they so readily ceded the songwriter. From that point on, the period of internal harmony ebbed and an era of personal and professional deterioration advanced.

What is particularly interesting here is that even while the deterioration intensified, the band still accepted Townshend's creative leadership. That Daltrey
would publicly denounce his band mate and then enter the studio to record
Townshend's idiosyncratic, impressionistic writings is a genuine curiosity. Recall how these two men fought via the media as they debated ending the band.
Much grandstanding was taking place, as The Who attempted to orchestrate one
image for public relations purposes while the dissolution advanced. Townshend's comments after the *Face Dances* release indicated the band's situation:
"I don't think we were really quite working together. Roger says that you could
feel on *Face Dances* that the band wasn't a *band*. And what I'd like to see happen on the next album is for the Who to *feel* like a band, and *work* as a band"
(Loder, 1982a, p. 19). That never happened. The conflict that typified the early
Who was a source of creative inspiration for everyone involved. The acceptance of roles within the financially secure band initiated, ironically, the group's
demise. The band evolved from an united group with a shared purpose—Swenson's "rock gestalt"—into a gathering of individual acts. Townshend desperately wanted to push his work *forward*, but in the absence of incentive—
motivations that often emerged from competition within the band—his
aspirations faded into "Pete Townshend's Complaint" and the group's
termination. Such is the "irony of success" cited in Chapter Five's introduction.
    The tensions associated with the artist-producer relationship assume a fun-
damentally different tone. I describe these happenings in terms of three types of
professional relationships: dictatorial, emotional, and rational. In terms of the
dictatorial style, Shel Talmy's dominating approach to The Who's early recording was certainly stifling in the studio; nevertheless, that style was standard
operating procedure for the times. Townshend described Talmy's perspective:
"Shel's attitude was 'You're just a load of punks and I made you; you should be
happy you've got where you have because if it wasn't for me you'd be nowhere,' and the other thing was that he had a specific sound which he would
impose on the group and it became very inflexible" (Swenson, 1979, p. 33).
Talmy's dictatorial production techniques joined his lackadaisical approach to
the American market and the pitiful quality of The Who's financial contract to
ensure that this relationship would be short-lived. Still, several positive developments emerged from this era in that the band met engineer Glyn Johns
through Talmy, learned the error of its financial ways through its mistakes, and
it provided a context for Kit Lambert's emerging role.
    Kit Lambert was special. He truly understood his band and that under-
standing was not *technical* in nature but *emotional*. Townshend's recollections
indicate Lambert's value to The Who and its songwriter:

The main thing that made me confident was Kit Lambert...his conviction that I could
"through compose"—as he used to call it—a piece.... What actually happened first is
that in the singles band period of The Who I was already, almost on my third song,
starting to think about conceptual pieces. This actually happened because of a joke. I
had an apartment in London and I let this friend of Keith's stay there—it was a big studio

in Soho.... He said I've got this libretto for an opera and I'd like you to write the music of it. So we spent an evening doing this joke opera...called "Gratis Amatis." It was all written in Cod Latin. It was a bit like Gilbert and Sullivan. [It contained] about five or six songs and it ran for about ten minutes or something. And I played it to Kit and Kit laughed.... But when Ray had gone, he said to me "You know this is very interesting that you can do this. I know it's a joke but you know you can do this Gilbert and Sullivan stuff. You can do it as though you were born to do it." He said you should continue to try to do that kind of thing. (*Rolling Stone's One*, 1993)

Perhaps no statement addresses Lambert's nurturing relationship with Townshend better than the poem "The Baron" featured in *Horse's Neck* (I must, however, exercise caution with that attribution). Lambert supported Townshend's intuitions, contributed to his musical education, disciplined his intellect, and coped with his personality. Lambert's emotional support extended to the studio as well. Recall Chapter Three's description of the *Tommy* sessions in which Lambert would readily stop the proceedings on the basis of his intuitions about the group's mood (regardless of the financial costs). No one ever understood this group as well as Kit Lambert.

Whereas his technical expertise was limited, his emotional support may very well be the most significant factor in The Who's development. That Townshend endeavored to do for others what Lambert had done for him is evidence of his appreciation for Lambert's role. Townshend told Schulps (1978) that he was building a studio in which bands could rehearse and receive assistance without charge, as he explained: "What I'm getting at is that when the moment comes— this is the important part of any band's career—then what they need is guidance, the kind of guidance we had from Kit Lambert.... Behind every band is some sort of mentor figure, some Svengali. This is the thing. That can't be provided without love, care and full-time attention" (p. 18). After *Tommy*, The Who no longer needed that "guidance," and besides, Lambert was losing his ability to provide it. As an experienced, financially stable band, The Who now required *technical* expertise. Thus, the band entered the Glyn Johns era, in which Johns's technical knowledge joined his commitment to musical innovation to introduce a new producer-artist orientation.

Entwistle's remarks about simply "needing someone in the booth" to handle the technical aspects of recording and Townshend's comments about Richard Lowenstein's role in the *White City* film indicate an approach distinct from earlier periods. Both statements reveal the need for rational, technical expertise as opposed to the emotional support that mentors provide. Throughout The Who's final years, the band turned to technicians to bring a rational understanding of the recording process into the studio. Such a trend continued in Townshend's solo work as well. Townshend's need for emotional support returned with time, and his reliance on the same cast of musicians for virtually all of his solo projects indicates from whence he gained that understanding.

The fourth level of negotiations, the artist-industry domain, is presented in terms of three historical phases that reflect The Who's professional relationship with the music industry: the age of aggression, a period of bargaining, and the acquiescence stage. Each phase displays meaningful implications for the auteur's songwriting, as Townshend aggressively tailored his words for specific purposes, compromised his projects in response to industry demands, and endured the lack of motivation that occasionally accompanies commercial success. Of course these tensions extended beyond the songwriter to include the band's managers and their respective approaches to industry level-happenings (publicity, touring, and recording).

The aggressive qualities of the band's early commercial strategies are as much the stuff of legend as The Who's internal fighting. Not only did Townshend write songs for specific audiences, but the band's appearance, performance style, and demeanor all followed Pete Meaden's, Lambert's, and Stamp's relentless drive for commercial success. Lambert and Stamp's stage innovations, promotional stunts, publicity seeking, and creative accounting were recklessly aggressive. Stamp's efforts in the United States (the Murray the K show) and the management team's legal maneuvers represent compelling examples of The Who's assertive approach. The pinnacle of the aggression phase, the *Tommy* project, was an all-or-nothing endeavor in which the band risked everything for the money to record the project, adjusted the story for commercial reasons, orchestrated the album's premier before an infant rock press, and pursued unprecedented venues for the opera's performance. The sheer aggression of the *Tommy* project is its most dominant feature. As I have said repeatedly, it is hard to imagine a more aggressive commercial operation than the Lambert/Stamp/Who coalition.

This aggression subsides slightly in the latter portion of the singles period. Just after "Happy Jack's" release, Lambert expressed fears of overexposure. A band that readily changed its lyrics to suit American radio (as per "Substitute") later angered the industry with the *Sell Out* album cover (Marsh [1983] writes that the cover was the first "in pop history" to omit song titles—p. 286). *Tommy* provided a much-needed boost, and the band's aggressive assault on the industry resumed briefly (*Tommy*'s controversial qualities facilitated that surge). The group soon tired of this relentless commercial push (and of *Tommy* as well). The band that once recorded "Coke" commercials and recruiting spots for the American armed services now asserted that it would perform its first opera one more time at New York's Metropolitan Opera House and resisted participation in the original Woodstock festival. The Who's aggressive managerial tactics now faded into a *bargaining* period in which the band exercised the freedom of choice that success offers. Several significant developments accompanied The Who's commercial momentum and independence: the industry was increasingly willing to take and sell anything the band offered, Lambert lost interest, the audience grew nostalgic, the group began to lose its "united stage presence," and Townshend grew more detached.

All of this leads to the acquiescence phase. Townshend's remarks to David Fricke (1987b) leave little doubt about the auteur's assessment of the industry. There he laments that rock has "adopted the Hollywood star system"

(p. 180) and offers his perspective on an industry that had consistently disappointed him for over fifteen years:

There is a quick condemnation you can make. You can just say it's all crap. The important thing is that every now and then a unique musical event happens. But most of it is utter garbage. The machinery behind it is financially, spiritually and morally corrupt. And I don't think there is any point in standing on a soapbox trying to get the music industry to honor the music itself. In the end, it becomes futile. The importance of people like Kit Lambert is what he said to me from day one. He went even further. He said all great art was crap.... We read that Mozart was doing commissions on motifs, numbered motifs, and selling his copyrights. "Oh, the bloody prince of Denmark wants another piece of music, and I'm so busy. Give him fifteen of number twenty-two, six of number four, nine of number fifty-eight...." It was very much like computer music. And, of course, Bach was a mathematician. And these have all been elevated to some kind of artistic gods. (p. 182)

Through a statement reminiscent of the fictional Van Smith-Hartley, Townshend articulated his deep-seated disaffection for an industry unwilling to push its craft in new directions. The "anger" that Townshend felt a middle-aged rock star must sustain to remain "honest" slowly but surely consumed him. The artist-industry tensions that inspired an aggressive artistic style yielded to a state of give-and-take that eventually resulted in a collapse of inspiration. Townshend's artistic impulse requires *tension*; without it, his creative instincts fail to achieve their potential.

Townshend's creative requirements provide the segue to our final area of negotiation, the artist-audience level. I divide Townshend's relationship with his audience into three historical phases: discovery, dedication, and detachment. Here we witness an evolution in which a local artist's ability to draw motivation from his audience—an intense artist-audience reciprocity—grows into a dedicated following that places serious demands on that artist and eventually yields to a nostalgic relationship predicated on a celebration of the band's history. The ebb and flow of Townshend's relationship with his audience has had a crucial impact on his temperament and correspondingly his art. Therefore, this level of negotiation may very well join Kit Lambert's influence as the two most important factors in Pete Townshend's professional maturation.

That Dave Marsh (1983) opens his book on The Who with "Irish Jack" and the band's early Shepherd's Bush following suggests the audience's significance within Who history. Townshend's Ealing education stressed the audience's importance, and that lesson was reinforced through the band's relationship with the Mods, as Townshend explained to Perry and Bailey (1974):

What the Mods taught us in the band was how to lead by following.... I mean, you'd look in the dance floor and see some bloke stop dancing the dance of the week and for some reason feel like doing some silly sort of step. And you'd notice some of the blokes around him looking out the corners of their eyes and thinking, "Is this the latest?" And on their own, without acknowledging the first fellow, a few of 'em would start dancing that way. And we'd be watching. By the time they looked up on the stage again, *we'd* be doing that dance, and they'd think the original one had been imitating *us*. And next week they'd come back and look to us for dances. That kind of feedback and interchange goes on in all the popular arts, I think, but particularly in rock & roll. (p. 16)

This aggressive reciprocity was the driving force in The Who's formative years. Townshend's 1994 assessment of the band's relationship with its initial audience is also insightful: "The Who were supposed to be a reflection of what the audience was feeling. If it worked, if The Who were successful, it was against all fucking odds. We were horrible, ugly, noisy, scruffy, arrogant, intimidating, inconsiderate bunch of assholes. We became successful, I think we became successful because that's what the audience were like, too" (*Thirty Years*, 1994). Few stage acts have attained the level of audience-artist reciprocity The Who and the Mods achieved during the band's formative years.

A period of total dedication followed. The generational complaint that flows throughout Townshend's work is a direct manifestation of that "Shepherd's Bush voice" he mentioned in the *PsychoDerelict* interviews. In a 1993 interview with *Musician* magazine Townshend noted that the "kids from the Goldhawk Club in Shepherd's Bush" (Duffy, 1993b, p. 36) claimed "I Can't Explain" as their anthem and pleaded with him to "write some more straight away." After penning "Anyway, Anyhow, Anywhere" and "My Generation," Townshend realized that he was writing for a specific "voice," as he acknowledged: "I think I'm still writing for that voice, that same group of people, who weren't all boys by any means. And I think I wrote *Tommy* for the same voice. It's only in the last six months that I've realized that." Roger Daltrey offers this assessment of Townshend's early work:

He had an incredible perspective on what was happening around him. He writes with incredible courage and incredible honesty and it's not always easy to write like that; especially in those early years of your life where you're all mixed up and you're not sure about this and not sure about that. And he obviously...he just had his finger on the pulse of what so many people were thinking, but not...maybe not saying and managed to say it for them in music. (*Who Rarities*, 1994)

Writing for that "voice" at times constrained Townshend. He told Garbarini (1982a), "We have a responsibility to the fans who've grown up with us, and don't want us to change too fast, because they're worried about literally losing their grasp on what's going on; the responsibility to not change suddenly in mid-stream, to evolve slowly" (p. 53). With time, "those fans who've grown up with" The Who faded into a relatively small portion of the audience, and Townshend's attitude about his "responsibilities" shifted. In Chapter Three I mentioned Edwards's (1974) views regarding the changing nature of Who audiences and its three tiers: early club fans, *Tommy*-era fans, and "contemporary" fans that saw the band as a "classic" act (and that was *1974*!). The Who's movement toward stadium venues and complex shows (*Quadrophenia*'s use of taped segments) increased Townshend's detachment from his audience. The 1974

Madison Square Garden shows sealed the matter. Townshend's reflections in 1982 demonstrated his attitude in a fashion that was, no doubt, beyond his understanding in 1974: "Occasionally, I do have contempt for the audience.... I think the audience's current reaction is to what the band represents, or to what the band has been. People are coming to see us and applaud our history.... I would much prefer to feel that people were responding on another level" (Fink, 1982a). In that same interview, Daltrey countered Townshend's reasoning by asserting that the Who-audience relationship is simply "magic... just not worth analyzing." Daltrey concluded: "Pete is just such a complete intellectual. He'll never understand."

While there is merit in Daltrey's point, *he* failed to understand the secret to Townshend's artistic motivations: a drive for excellence that is firmly rooted in his perceptions of and responsibilities to his audience. One is not surprised, therefore, that Townshend's capstone statement, *PsychoDerelict*, speaks directly to his construction of the artist-audience relationship and its "submissive" nature. Townshend's submission to his band, his producers, the industry, and his audience (including rock journalism) created the internal conflicts I discussed earlier. When his commitment to his perceived audience was no longer reciprocated, he retaliated through detachment. Complicating that situation was the growing complexity of rock journalism and Townshend's inclusion of journalists as part of his immediate audience. Unlike Roger Daltrey, Townshend never surrendered to the mindless obligations of audience nostalgia—unless, that is, it served his purposes. *PsychoDerelict*, Broadway *Tommy*, 1994's "Townshend Tribute" (staged by Daltrey), The Who's *Thirty Years of Maximum R&B* set, and the 1996-1997 *Quadrophenia* tours work in harmony to achieve closure for the auteur *on his terms*. Townshend may effectively appeal to his audience's nostalgia for personal, commercial, or artistic reasons, but he does so via his stylistic twist on the event: *PsychoDerelict*'s dialogue with its use of *LifeHouse* themes and music industry complaint join Broadway *Tommy*'s revised ending, Townshend's limited participation in the Daltrey "tribute," his commentary about the boxed set, and *Quadrophenia*'s commitment to music theater (topics I turn to shortly) as compelling evidence of his resolution of the artist-audience conflict Simon Frith described in this book's introduction. The tensions that emerge from the "permanent contradiction between being an artist—responsible only to one's own creative impulses—and being a star—responsible to one's audience's perceived values and needs" require constant, and considerable, negotiation. Beginning in 1993, Townshend slowly resolved those conflicts on his terms and Roger Daltrey may "never understand" that resolution.

In the *Chinese Eyes* video cited in Chapter Five, Townshend laments how a craft that "started so simply" when he was a boy in Acton rapidly became a complicated and demanding profession. This discussion demonstrates the relevance of Townshend's statement for critics of artistic communication. Perhaps the writer captured this notion best in an early song, "Substitute," when he wrote, "the simple things you see are all complicated." Critics who assume the rhetorical (persuasive) or poetic (expressive) qualities of commercial art without a close scrutiny of a given artifact's history may very well miss crucial elements in their analyses and as a result dilute their respective contributions to our understanding of artistic communication. Pete Townshend's career offers conclusive evidence of the negotiation thesis's centrality to an understanding of commercial art. To omit or disregard this fundamental component of the creative process may result in serious errors in judgment—if, that is, music criticism is taken seriously.

THE MINSTREL'S DILEMMA: THE SIGNATURES

When the various narrative strategies evidenced in Townshend's lifework are construed in light of the negotiations that rendered his art, compelling support for the writer's status as an "auteur" emerges. An at times raw impulse may inspire the author to pursue some creative end, but a steady staple of storytelling strategies shaped that idea's articulation. Here I present these signatures as they evolve throughout Townshend's career; afterward, I discuss the "master signatures" that appear across the oeuvre.

In order to evaluate the storytelling tendencies within Townshend's lifework, I turn to narrative synthesis. Narrative synthesis contains three steps: a determination of the story's function, the reduction of the work into its essential parts (characters, values, and plots—the structural signatures), and the creation of a composite text that exposes the work's theoretical or aesthetic qualities. The first two steps organize the subject matter prior to the creative act that is the composite text's construction. Throughout, Townshend's characters, values, and plots are examined individually (by song, album) and collectively. When those constituent elements are construed as a whole, they produce *The Seeker* composite text (and its thematic signatures). As we have seen, the five phases of Townshend's writings reflect gradual shifts in narrative function that offer insights into both the writer's lifework and the necessity to determine function in studies of commercial artistic communication. One just cannot say if a given song serves a rhetorical/persuasive function or a poetic/expressive function without inquiry into that work's history (hence, the "negotiation thesis"). In response, I have charted Townshend's movement across the artistic communication rhetoric-poetic continuum. In this case, creative context and narrative function are related: early songs written for instrumental purposes stress one spin of *The Seeker*'s quest; later songs written for more expressive reasons emphasize another. Such an analysis reveals not only the continuity of Townshend's writings but a consistent adherence to a guiding artistic philosophy as well.

Townshend's "singles period" contains four signatures that establish the narrative foundation for his career. Three minor signatures also emerge that reappear in varying degrees throughout subsequent periods. The singles period signatures are: the presence of tight narratives written for specific audiences, an emerging theatrical style that aspires to extended storytelling venues, a penchant for characterological ambiguity, and the advent of "the search" theme. The three minor signatures are: Townshend's use of humor, the "deception" theme, and the "Face Dances" theme (a concern for the presentation of self in social contexts).

The singles period is dominated by tight narrative vignettes written for particular audiences. Townshend penned songs to hook Shel Talmy ("I Can't Explain"), for the Mods ("Anyway, Anyhow, Anywhere," and "My Generation"), and for the band's image ("Out in the Street," and all of the above). His capacity to write commercials—both real ("Little Billy") and fictional (for *Sell Out*)—demonstrates his ability to shape his words to suit strategic ends. Of these various subject areas, Townshend's tales of adolescence represent *the* dominant thematic signature of the singles period. He explored teen frustrations about self-expression ("I Can't Explain"), doubts over identity ("I'm A Boy" and "Tattoo"), sexual frustrations ("Pictures of Lily"), youth's mean-spirited nature ("Happy Jack" and "Little Billy"), and the teens' desire for segregation ("My Generation" and "The Kids Are Alright"). The young songwriter's capacity to construct tight stories for specific audiences is impressive.

While he told tales of adolescent life for the singles market, Townshend's narrative impulse longed for more extensive venues. The "opera" prepared for Keith Moon's friend cited earlier in this chapter, the aborted *Quads* project, and the commercially inspired mini-opera all foreshadow the writer's future. Central to this trend was Kit Lambert's cooperation and his synthesis of Townshend's talent and the band's commercial needs. Thus, when the band issued its first concept album, *The Who Sell Out*, an important compromise was achieved: Townshend pursued an extended work, while The Who responded to the marketplace. "A Quick One" and *Sell Out* display an internal continuity that demonstrates Townshend's emerging theatrical style—a talent that eventually saved the band from financial ruin.

The third dominant signature from this period involves Townshend's use of ambiguous characterizations. The writer may produce a tight little ditty for a particular audience, but he could also camouflage his messages. Songs such as "It's Not True," "I Can't Reach You," and "Sunrise" employ pronouns (typically "you") that facilitate flexible interpretations. The song may be construed as a spiritual statement or a romantic ballad—the decision is the listener's. Such an approach is wholly consistent with Townshend's philosophy which refuses to "hit his audience over the head" with an idiosyncratic message; moreover, it is our first glimpse of his emerging impressionism.

The final major signature from this period involves the advent of "the search" and *The Seeker*'s quest for identity. At this point the search is present but unfocused. Characters such as the young man in "The Kids Are Alright" realize that something is "out there," although he does not know what it is (expressed as the need to "get out in the light"—whatever that means). The search for identity is more of an *urge* than anything else; however, Townshend introduces that urge by way of adolescent anxieties over personal appearance ("Substitute"), masculine identity ("I'm A Boy" and "Tattoo"), and group solidarity ("My Generation" and "The Kids Are Alright"). With time, these essentially superficial searches begin to assume a spiritual tone (in *Sell Out*) that is also un-focused and evasive.

The minor signatures that emerge in the singles period represent specific tendencies that creep in and out of the oeuvre from time to time. Townshend's use of humor is a stylistic variation that often suggests his state of mind. No-where else may we find the level of humor that appears in the singles period. The lighthearted appeal of "A Legal Matter," the insightful comedy of "Pictures of Lily," the playful moralizing of "Little Billy," the silliness of "Tattoo," and the craziness of "I'm A Boy" all demonstrate Townshend's sense of humor in ways that are unavailable elsewhere. The remaining minor signatures are the-matic and serve *The Seeker* text in varying degrees throughout the lifework. Townshend's concern for "deception" is initiated via songs such as "La La La Lies," "It's Not True," "Substitute," and "I Can See For Miles." Furthermore, tracks such as "Happy Jack" offer indirect or brief references to lying and mis-representation. Equally present is the "Face Dances" notion in which anxieties over the presentation of self appear in such social contexts as the generational anthems and interpersonal situations. The teenage posturing evident in "Any-way, Anyhow, Anywhere," "Substitute," "Out in the Street," and "Disguises" (to name but a few) conveys the psychological insecurity often associated with adolescence.

The Who's singles period may have emphasized the band's commercial im-age and performance style, but it also introduced a writer with a vision. That vision may be unfocused and raw, yet the budding auteur's ability to balance the band's commercial agenda and his creative inclinations established a context for stylistic distinction. Townshend eventually dismissed the adolescent themes, however, his emerging theatrical style, his use of ambiguous—and at times strategic—characterizations, and the unfolding nature of the search for identity join the deception and "Face Dances" themes as a stylistic baseline for a thirty-year career.

The opera period reveals four signatures that both build upon and deviate from those of the singles period. The minor signatures are evident as well, al-though Townshend's use of humor dissipates rather quickly. The four major signatures are: the use of nebulous plots that emphasize characterization, a the-atrical style that requires collaboration, an emerging autobiographical trend, and a focused "search" that stresses a sociological orientation. The three projects from this period—*Tommy*, *LifeHouse*, and *Quadrophenia*—presented a fasci-nating double bind for the writer in that they simultaneously afforded an oppor-tunity for expansion *and* placed Townshend in a creative cul de sac. *Tommy* freed Townshend's pen but dominated his band to the extent that it stifled that creative freedom.

The most significant shift from the singles period involves Townshend's move away from tight narrative vignettes with ambiguous characters toward vague plots that stress characterization (the longer a Townshend project goes, the weaker its plot becomes). For instance, the two operas and the *LifeHouse* story are virtually without endings: Tommy is left alone, Bobby disappears, and

Jimmy sits on a rock in the rain. Just as Ken Russell observed, *Tommy* seems to begin in the middle of the story as it focuses on the various characters and their respective traits: Tommy and his preposterous pinball machine, Cousin Kevin's bullying abuse, Uncle Ernie's sexual desperation, the Acid Queen's psychedelic perversion, Sally Simpson's celebrity confusion, and the parents' guilt frustrations. These value-laden characterizations *are* the story. *LifeHouse* might have deviated from this trend, yet the remnants that make up *Who's Next* are incoherent in terms of the original plan. *Quadrophenia* offers a tighter story through its emphasis on Jimmy's plight; however, the promised four parts of Jimmy's personality (which never materialize) would have represented the epitome of characterization. Instead, the story focuses upon Jimmy's Mod angst as he floats in and out of various contexts. The cryptic characterizations of the singles period evolve into the nebulous plots of the opera period and, once more, suggest an impressionistic style that is on the verge of dominating Townshend's pen.

Correspondingly, Townshend's theatrical style of composition prospers in the opera period. An essential element of this trend is the writer's need for collaboration. No Who project enjoyed *Tommy*'s level of collaboration: Lambert prepared the script, Entwistle wrote songs, Moon invented scenes, Daltrey gave life to the story's central character, and Nick Cohn inspired a twist in the project's plot. Townshend consulted musicologists, psychologists, and computer experts in preparation for the *LifeHouse* project; still, once he returned to the band with his ideas, he worked in complete isolation. Townshend's colleagues—in Kit Lambert's absence—could not even understand the *LifeHouse* plan, much less implement it. The trend intensified with the *Quadrophenia* project in that The Who granted Townshend complete control over the venture. Townshend's attempts to bring unfinished demos to the band for the type of assistance he had received with *Tommy* were fruitless. He was left to his own devices, and without the collaboration he needed, he drifted further into himself. Townshend's theatrical-collaborative signature is a prominent aspect of his art; therefore, the presence or absence of such conditions plays a significant role in his artistic direction.

The third signature from this period, Townshend's emerging autobiographical style, is a direct consequence of these first two points. Whenever the respective projects expanded and the amount of collaboration decreased, he turned to personal experience for his subject matter. Consistent with his artistic philosophy, Townshend employed various blends of fact and fiction that camouflaged personal messages within an entertainment package. The writer's awareness—or lack thereof—of these autobiographical tendencies is intriguing. The 1993 Broadway *Tommy* interviews indicate that several of the original *Tommy* characters represent subconscious manifestations of personalities from Townshend's youth: the Acid Queen evokes his family's gypsy heritage, the love triangle at the opera's opening recalls his parents' marital problems, and Uncle Ernie (although written by Entwistle) conjures memories of an incident with a friend of Cliff Townshend's (an incident very similar to the tickling scene Jim describes in the *White City* film). These autobiographical traits operate on a more conscious level with Bobby in *LifeHouse* (essentially, Bobby *is* Townshend) and Jimmy in *Quadrophenia*. I dare not suggest that Jimmy and Townshend are one and the same, yet the auteur had direct experience with Jimmy's plight—Mod angst—and he closely identified with Jimmy's social and spiritual dilemma. In all cases, the evidence suggests that as The Who slowly disintegrate, Townshend's autobiographical impressionism begins to compensate for his creative loneliness.

The fourth signature, the thematic qualities of *The Seeker*'s quest, evolves from an unfocused urge into a sociological phenomenon in which characters turn to groups or institutions for personal insights. Tommy becomes a pinball messiah, whose "disciples" pursue a blind ambition toward an uncertain destination. Here the pinball element conveys Townshend's anxieties over celebrity status and hero worship—whether that worship is spiritual or secular. Bobby develops a "rock church" that provides relief from a domineering government. Although Bobby avoids Tommy's messianic features, he does discover his own "burning bush," which supports a social revival. And Jimmy displays a confused, albeit complete, dedication to a peer group that ignores him. Jimmy's character is a turning point in *The Seeker*'s search in that his failure to gain relief from the Mods prompts him to look inside himself, which initiates the search's next phase. Interestingly, *The Seeker*'s sociological phase emphasizes failure: Tommy's disciples reject him, Bobby and his followers just disappear, and Jimmy sits on a rock. When these three stories are considered together it is as if Townshend is saying that there is no relief to be gained from institutions or groups—hence, "meet the new boss, same as the old boss"—and the story returns to an emphasis on the *individual* (a "How fantastic am I" reprise).

The opera period's minor signatures vary in their intensity. The humor evidenced in the singles period assumes a dark tone in *Tommy* (if one finds child molestation and physical abuse funny) and then simply disappears. There is no humor in *LifeHouse* and *Quadrophenia*. The deception and "Face Dances" themes are present in each project. Tommy's parents' attempt to cover up the lover's murder, the vacuous qualities of celebrity, and the cheap indoctrination of the holiday camp offer evidence of *Tommy*'s use of the deception theme. Moreover, the government's use of experience suits to control the polity in *LifeHouse*, and Jimmy's frustrations with his parents, his girlfriend, his doctor, his job (and the workers' attitudes), and the Mods all suggest deception, or at least Jimmy's fear of dishonesty. In many respects, Jimmy longs for honesty—a trait absent as a result of the third minor signature, the "Face Dances" theme. Everywhere there is posturing in this segment of the oeuvre. Tommy's followers pretend to aspire to "salvation," Bobby encounters a programmed society, and the Mod angst that haunts Jimmy is the quintessential example of the "Face Dances" notion (the *required* fashion, scooters, music, rebellion, group segregation). Once more, nothing is resolved in the opera period, but the sociological aspects of these minor themes directly serve *The Seeker* composite text.

That Townshend raised many questions during the opera period and answered none of them is indicative of both his state of mind and artistic philosophy. Consistent with the latter, Townshend avoided preachy messages that imposed his worldview on his audience, even though he bludgeoned that same audience with questions that haunt him. One cannot read too much into *Tommy*, since it is a hodgepodge of ideas and loose themes. But *LifeHouse* and *Quadrophenia* are different matters: Townshend's belief in a musical essence and its capacity to transcend societal evils *is* (not *was*) genuine. The auteur may have sought closure for his adolescent themes in *Quadrophenia*, yet his effort with the four-personality characterization raises complex questions regarding the *individual* outside the group context. Instead of forcing a message upon his audience, he simply placed Jimmy on a rock and left him (and everybody else) to contemplate that situation. And that was exactly where Pete Townshend was at that time. His inability to answer those questions would now lead to the next phase of the oeuvre.

The lifework's third phase—which I characterize as the end of The Who and "Pete Townshend's Complaint"—revisits the storytelling style of the singles period through its use of tight narrative structures. The phase differs, however, in its thematic emphasis on Townshend's dissatisfaction with his perceived situation. This is clearly the oeuvre's darkest moment. Four signatures control this portion of the lifework: the use of tight story structures that focus on individual complaint, the absence of theatricality, an extension of the autobiographical trend, and a pause in *The Seeker*'s spiritual quest in favor of worldly matters. In terms of the three minor signatures, these four albums (*By Numbers*, *Who Are You*, *Face Dances*, and *It's Hard*) feature very little humor, although the deception and "Face Dances" themes abound and directly serve the "Pete Townshend's Complaint" story line. All of the signatures evident in this phase emphasize straightforward, autobiographical complaint.

One of the more fascinating aspects of this study involves the extent to which The Who readily recorded Townshend's introspective compositions. The level of self-analysis is staggering. Songs skirt around direct attacks on certain individuals through cryptic characterizations, yet Townshend's first-person narrations leave little doubt about his subject matter. He complains about his lifestyle ("However Much I Booze"), his friends ("How Many Friends"), his profession ("New Song"), and his generation ("Why Did I Fall For That") in a relentless fashion. Whereas the absence of Townshend's theatrical style—and its corresponding need for collaboration—occasionally leads the auteur toward introspective impressionism, this is not the case here. Townshend *complains* through a coherent, direct style that is reminiscent of the singles period's narrative vignettes.

These trends lead to the third signature from this period, Townshend's autobiographical orientation. The auteur's confessional angst (*By Numbers*), his anxieties over the music business (*Who Are You*), and his confrontational songs (*Face Dances*) are deeply personal. His ability to weave in *personal* complaint with *the band's* desire for societal statements on *It's Hard* recalls the songwriter's capacity to write for others while simultaneously satisfying a personal agenda. Where this phase differs from the singles period is in the auditor's attribution of the song's contents. The adolescent themes from early songs featured autobiographical elements that were either camouflaged by ambiguous characterizations or evoked widely shared identifications. "Pictures of Lily," for instance, may involve a Townshend incident with his parents (supposedly they caught him masturbating), yet the song transcends that personal experience—everybody has a "pin-up" period. That trend continues in "Pete Townshend's Complaint," if the auditor is lucky enough to have a serious drinking problem, untrustworthy friends, domineering lovers, devious business partners, pretentious social relationships, anxieties about his/her place in society, or a complete disregard for his/her profession. We are, most assuredly, talking about "introspection to the pain threshold," and I find it remarkable that Roger Daltrey was willing to sing these very, very personal songs.

This introspection establishes the context for *The Seeker*'s thematic evolution—our fourth signature from this period. As I noted in Chapter Four, the search for identity virtually disappears, as Townshend emphasizes his various complaints. A thin narrative thread weaves its way through these four albums as Townshend seems to pause briefly to question his role in society. Songs such as "Imagine A Man," "Guitar and Pen," "Don't Let Go The Coat," "Cache Cache," and "A Man Is A Man" articulate the need for personal strength, artistic commitment, spiritual perseverance, and individual integrity. In particular, "Imagine A Man" and "A Man Is A Man" appear to speak to Townshend's search for "manhood," the male's role in society, and the acceptance of one's worldly state. Beyond question, these songs preface the solo career's English Boy Syndrome.

This emphasis on complaint is evident in the minor signatures as well. The comical "Squeeze Box" is the lone source of humor in this truly dark songwriting phase. The deception and "Face Dances" themes are integral parts of the various complaints. The deception in "How Many Friends" and "Did You Steal My Money" complement the social angst of "Sister Disco" and "Eminence Front" to reinforce the complaint's value orientation. This phase contains little mystery; the auteur uses straightforward narrative structures to weave value-laden elegies, as Townshend deviates from his artistic philosophy and relentlessly pounds home his point of view.

The oeuvre's fourth phase—featuring the solo projects *Who Came First, Rough Mix, Empty Glass*, and *All The Best Cowboys Have Chinese Eyes*—reflects a mixture of the narrative styles observed thus far since all of these projects overlap Townshend's tenure with The Who. The stylistic signatures from this period are: the presence of value-laden stories of varying clarity, an absence of theatricality, an increase in the auteur's impressionism, an extension of the autobiographical trend, and a decidedly spiritual turn in *The Seeker* text. The deception and "Face Dances" themes recur as well and directly support this phase's emphasis on spirituality, societal roles, and relationships.

The most dominant characteristic of this phase is its emphasis on *The Seeker*'s spiritual quest. Little doubt, the *Who Came First* and *Rough Mix* diversions were just that: opportunities to pray about (*Who Came First*) and celebrate (*Rough Mix*) Meher Baba's presence. In *Who Came First* Townshend's spiritual messages assume a prayerful stance through a light impressionism that urges the auditor to seek spiritual satisfaction on his/her own terms. *Rough Mix*'s lighthearted style provides a transition to the intensity of the *Empty Glass* and *Chinese Eyes* projects. Townshend may beg questions about spirituality and sexuality through equivocal characterizations that sound like love songs and street machismo "on the radio" ("Let My Love Open The Door" and "Rough Boys," respectively), but that quest for understanding is passionate. The intense spiritual search featured in *Empty Glass* is actually resolved in *Chinese Eyes* (via "The Sea Refuses No River") and, in turn, represents the first of *The Seeker*'s thematic resolutions. That resolution—that all worldly matters are eventually resolved in heaven; we all get there in the end—signals an acceptance of the individual's spiritual destiny and, correspondingly, echoes Meher Baba's philosophy, "Don't worry, be happy, and leave the rest to God." The *individual*'s complaints that "I Can't Explain" how "I" feel about *my* God, *my* loves, *my* parents, *my* friends, and more are now displaced by Townshend's concerns for *mutual understanding* in loving relationships, friendship, and society. With the individual's spiritual quest resolved, that person now turns to his/her responsibilities in various social situations of consequence.

Townshend articulates these thematic matters through four structural signatures that revise and extend previous trends. This phase's variation in plot strength is attributable to the stories' emphasis on values. Characterizations and narrative progression are subservient to prayer, introspection, and impressionism. Remember, Townshend acknowledged that he uses solo projects to explore and share his *personal* views; as a result, the public prayers that constitute *Who Came First* evolve into *Empty Glass*'s introspection and *Chinese Eyes*' resolution. That narrative trend is supported by another signature, the absence of theatricality, in that Townshend's creative isolation facilitates his propensity for self analysis. Whereas evidence of Townshend's theatrical style appears in the flowing prayers of *Who Came First* and the show tune format of *Rough Mix*'s "Street in the City," the absence of creative collaboration renders a pause in this facet of the auteur's writing.

The remaining structural signatures (increased impressionism and autobiography) are a natural consequence of this narrative trend. The intensely personal aspects of the spiritual quest join Townshend's extension of the "My Generation" complaint (the English Boy Syndrome) to elevate the autobiographical dimensions of his writing. Here Townshend's impressionism assumes a mischievous posture. His proclivity for word games ("Gonna Get Ya," "Cat's in the Cupboard," and "Communication") and metaphorical folly ("Uniforms" and "Empty Glass") extend his impressionism in a rather predictable fashion; as he endeavors to camouflage his autobiographical elements or avoid prescriptive messages, he drifts toward idiosyncratic expressions prone to equivocation. Even in one of the most volatile periods of his career, however, there is evidence of Pete Townshend's artistic philosophy. The auteur may probe his life and its anxieties, but he does not prescribe remedies. Instead, he searches himself—again, "introspection to the pain threshold"—and offers impression-istic commentary about that experience.

The "Face Dances" theme is the most prominent of the three minor signa-tures. Whereas the lighthearted humor of "My Baby" is fleeting, the deception theme recurs, as characters continue to lie to one another. The search for self is complicated by such issues as role confusion, celebrity anxiety, spiritual angst, and societal injustice which impact how characters present themselves to others (the "deception"-"Face Dances" connection). The resolution of the spiritual search achieved in "The Sea Refuses No River" displays meaningful implica-tions for the presentation of self in everyday life: the inherent deceit of the "Face Dances" theme begins to subside in favor of internal bliss, and later, social responsibility.

Townshend's book of short stories, *Horse's Neck*, also employs this narra-tive style in which introspection produces ambiguous characters, nebulous plots, and idiosyncratic metaphors. His penchant for complaint recurs via the opposite narrative path, tight tales that clearly articulate personal or professional stances. *Horse's Neck*'s principal similarity to the initial solo phase is found in its reso-lution. Just as *Empty Glass* engages an impressionistic self-analysis that is re-solved in *Chinese Eyes*, *Horse's Neck*'s final chapters answer the questions posed in its initial entries. These projects work in concert to reveal Town-shend's willingness to embrace artistic and commercial risks in order to satisfy personal impulses. That inclination provides a foundation for the oeuvre's final songwriting phase in which Townshend uses a multimedia format to frame lin-ear narratives that take stands on interpersonal and societal matters.

The final phase of Townshend's lifework opens with the resolutions achieved in *Horse's Neck* and moves on to three multimedia projects that dis-play five features: linear narrative frameworks that provide a context for im-pressionistic songs, multimedia formats, the return of theatricality (and collaboration), an extension of the autobiographical trend, and a shift in *The Seeker*'s quest toward worldly matters, such as social justice, relational under-standing, and the value of individual initiative or "dreaming." *White City*, *Iron Man*, and *PsychoDerelict* also feature humorous scenes as well as the deception and "Face Dances" themes, in varying degrees. This phase of the oeuvre repre-sents a capstone statement; recurrent structural signatures are used to achieve closure for a thirty-year-old thematic trend.

I begin with *The Seeker*'s search for social justice and relational under-standing. Throughout this quest the value of dreaming floats in and out of the story: Jim dreams of a domestic stability that has forever eluded him, Hogarth dreams of a childlike utopia filled with interpersonal and societal bliss, and Ray revisits Bobby's *LifeHouse* dream of individual aspiration and musical salva-tion. Townshend's recognition that the value of dreaming is more important than any single dream invokes his artistic philosophy and spiritual resolve (there are "many keys," or many "rivers," in life). That perspective provides the nar-rative starting point for *The Seeker*'s final phase.

Townshend's English Boy Syndrome is the principal manifestation of this phase's search for social justice. Directly introduced in "Pete Townshend's Complaint" and embellished in the *Chinese Eyes* project, the English Boy Syndrome probes the social angst of a generation that, according to the story, has been abandoned by British society. (In fact, the English Boy Syndrome's roots extend from the "My Generation" single all the way through *It's Hard* in one way or another.) Townshend's explanations about this trend are thorough, and he carefully used media interviews and commentaries to establish a context for his impressions on the subject. *White City*'s Jim accepts "the estate" as his home and suffers the emasculation that unemployment and failure to achieve traditional roles brings. The *Iron Man* project depicts social situations that foster the condition: thoughtless elders, reckless military innovations, governmental ineptitude. And *PsychoDerelict*'s Ray High is the very embodiment of the English Boy Syndrome. High directly represents the young Briton who pursues heroism through rock and roll—the autobiographical notion Townshend describes in the *White City* film's commentary. The heroic qualities of *White City*'s "Pete" evolve into *PsychoDerelict*'s "Ray," as the older Ray is forced to cope with the societal rejection Pete avoids by remaining "on the road with the boys." Once off the road, severe introspection ensues, and Ray, in search of comfort, revisits his dreams. The power of those dreams sustains the embattled Ray as he confronts a morally corrupt music industry. *Dreams* are the only hope, the story says, to escape the English Boy Syndrome and the dysfunctional relationships it fosters.

This leads to the second facet of *The Seeker*'s quest in which characters search for relational understanding. *White City*'s Jim and Alice face their pride. Jim copes with maternal anxieties in order to overcome the powerful combination of the English Boy Syndrome and maternal abuse. Hogarth transcends his elders' naivete and saves the Iron Man through the relational bonding that is friendship. And relational problems abound in *PsychoDerelict*: the distrust between Ray and Rastus, Ruth's abuse of Ray, the superficial escape provided by the Gridlife, and the mean-spirited interplay between artists and the press (there are more!). The auteur resolved that condition in a fashion similar to his spiritual resolution in that he encouraged acceptance, patience, and a continued belief in one's dreams.

The structural signatures through which Townshend expressed these thematic trends are suggestive of the writer's future. These projects used various combinations of film, prose, and stage action to articulate coherent packages for the audience. As I noted previously, just as Townshend demanded that his audience *work* to obtain the maximum benefit from Who shows, he now insists that we work to comprehend the totality of his messages. For instance, to understand fully the *White City* project one must consult the liner note essay, Townshend's commentary after the film, the film, his media interviews about the project, and—last but not least—the album. When taken as a *package*, a linear narrative emerges. If the album is construed in isolation, Townshend's impressionism dominates in a fashion that facilitates the auditor's identification with the work on the auditor's terms, not the auteur's. Hence, one may enjoy "Face The Face" for a personal reason, but to understand *Townshend*'s use of that song one must move beyond the record. This trend is particularly evident in *Iron Man*. *Iron Man* is the most accessible of these multimedia projects in that the listener needs only the liner notes and the album to enjoy Townshend's version of Ted Hughes's story. Yet if the album is considered without that prose, Townshend's commentaries on love, social responsibility, and friendship emphasize mature impressions about these complicated subjects which in turn muddles Hogarth's story.

What anchors Townshend's impressionism and his tendency to use word games, oblique metaphors, and cryptic characterizations to mask his autobiographical elements is the level of collaboration he experienced with each of these ventures. In *White City* Townshend worked with Richard Lowenstein (on song development and use, dialogue, and filming), the actors, and the set itself (the White City estate and its occupants). In *Iron Man* he worked from Hughes's original work and with the various singers and musicians. And in *PsychoDerelict*, Townshend consulted Richard Barnes and worked with the stage actors, the musicians, the projection-screen technicians, and more. Consequently, Townshend presents his autobiographical impressions about maternal abandonment, the value of friendship and loving relations, the significance of dreaming and individual aspiration, the potential evils of technology, and the depravity of social irresponsibility in a more coherent fashion than in "Pete Townshend's Complaint" or the first portion of the solo career. Without such collaboration Townshend drifts either into straightforward complaint or a cloudy, evasive impressionism.

Supporting these major signatures are the three minor trends we have observed in varying degrees thus far. Townshend's humor returns via the lighthearted moments in the *White City* film, Hogarth's playfulness and the Iron Man's boyish qualities, and Rastus Knight's caustic tongue and Ruth Streeting's bossy style in *PsychoDerelict*. Townshend's sense of humor appears to rebound in collaborative situations, once more a result of the tamed introspection creative assistance brings. The deception and "Face Dances" themes support all three projects. English society deceives its male youth, Hogarth tricks the Iron Man into the farmers' trap, and Rastus and Ruth will do whatever it takes to achieve their goal. *PsychoDerelict*'s treatment of the truth-fact distinction, and technology's capacity to diffuse it, represents the ultimate in deception. All the time this deception abounds, its colleague—"Face Dancing"—assumes increased importance. The clever masquerades at the White City pool's disco, Rastus's search for publicity (and the complaint in "Pretentious"), the beautiful people in the Gridlife ads, and Ruth's never-ending posturing all indicate the centrality of the "Face Dances" theme in these projects. These occasionally humorous portrayals of interpersonal and societal deceptions foster artificial responses ("Face Dancing") that serve the dominant thematic signatures of this period.

The extent to which Townshend endured the artistic and commercial risks of these innovative multimedia projects also sheds light on his ability to negotiate with the industry. Townshend may assume the artistic liability of imposing dialogue over music in *PsychoDerelict*, yet the subsequent tour, music-only version, pay-per-view telecast, PBS broadcast, and video-cassette release all temper the commercial risks associated with the venture. The auteur may aspire to a film; however, he compensates for potential commercial losses by issuing an album to accompany that video (*White City*). Also his ambitions for a lengthy musical are tempered by the industry's limited support (remember, Townshend was unwilling to finance *Iron Man*). Townshend's poetic aspirations are constantly constrained by the realities of the commercial industry; thus, he turns to a long-standing skill: the capacity to negotiate a "product" that both fulfills his artistic ambitions and satisfies a given external audience.

Having established the various traits associated with the respective phases of Townshend's career, we close with the four dominant stylistic tendencies that recur throughout his lifework. These four "master signatures" are: his narrative impressionism, his capacity for direct complaint, his need for collaboration, and his need for explanation. The four master signatures weave their way in and out of the oeuvre in highly predictable ways; for instance, in the absence of collaboration, autobiographical impressionism flows; when introspection inspires complaint, direct stories follow. Let us begin with the auteur's impressionism.

Townshend's impressionism is a direct manifestation of an artistic philosophy that requires the artist to inform or—in his words "commentate"—through entertainment. While this orientation seeks to convey knowledge of life's situations, it purposefully avoids dogmatic personal prescriptions. Therefore, Townshend's impressionism camouflages his personal explorations in a manner that elevates the moral of the story; that is, the "moral" transcends the author's experience. That impressionism employs three tactics: characterological ambiguity, nebulous plot structures, and metaphorical mischief. The writer's ambiguous characterizations begin in the singles period and his tight narrative vignettes about adolescence. The story's values and plot progression are straightforward, but his characters assume a vagueness that facilitates an interpretative flexibility. This trait is particularly relevant to Townshend's early spiritual/love songs. The songwriter's characterizations allow the auditor to do with the song what s/he wishes, while Townshend articulates his stance on his terms. Even during the dark moments of "Pete Townshend's Complaint," in which concrete complaint dominates the oeuvre, we do not know who Townshend accuses of stealing his money, personal and professional trickery, and deceptive posturing.

The auteur reverses that style in the larger projects in which nebulous plots are dominated by strong characterizations. Much time is allocated to developing Tommy's dilemma, Jimmy's angst, Jim's insecurity, Hogarth's honesty, and Ray's dedication; however, how these characters end up is a complete mystery (what does happen to Jim and Alice, Hogarth and his new love, and Ray, Ruth, and Rastus?). Townshend uses these characters to discuss an individual, interpersonal, or societal condition; invites his audience to share in his impressions about that situation; and leaves the audience to form its own conclusion. Unlike

Tommy and *Quadrophenia*, the post-Who multimedia projects are suggestive of positive endings, although closure is not explicitly achieved.

These impressionistic tendencies are extended further through Townshend's use of idiosyncratic word games, purposeful gibberish, and evolving meanings that are the direct consequence of his penchant for metaphorical mischief—our final impressionistic signature. The fact that Townshend's "meanings" evolve with his perspective on his work is one of the lifework's oldest traits. The writer recognized very early that his lyrical meanings changed within *him*, and his media interviews chronicled those shifts in perspective. Such a trend expanded into the word games and purposeful gibberish of later songwriting periods. Townshend's interviews either specifically state alternative readings, suggest that such readings are possible (or impossible), or admit to his internal confusion regarding his impressions. Nowhere is this more evident than in the "Rough Boys" commentary and Townshend's vacillating statements about the Sex Pistols, punk rockers, his daughters, alternative lifestyles, and his personal feelings about gender roles. Interestingly, Townshend often encourages his audience to refrain from over-analyzing his texts, yet the understanding that he camouflages personal statements within his impressionism invites dedicated fans to pursue those messages. In all cases, the auteur's impressionism is nothing less than a direct implementation of an avowed artistic philosophy—a creative worldview that remained remarkably constant across a thirty-year career.

Complementing our initial master signature is the writer's capacity for direct complaint. Townshend's ability to weave elegies is a striking manifestation of his early proclivity for narrative vignettes. That Townshend maintains a capacity to write a tight story about a specific situation or for a particular audience is evident throughout the lifework. For example, the generational angst of the Mods evolves into the English Boy Syndrome. Anxieties over the music business that emerge in the singles period (concerns for journalistic misrepresentation) mature into serious complaints about the industry's creative stagnation, the artist-star conflict, and music press abuse. Insecurities over the presentation of self in interpersonal and societal situations move from adolescent anxieties over self-expression, through superficial attempts to create personal identities, to sophisticated social posturing and deception, to the ultimate relational dilemma: the truth-fact dichotomy of *PsychoDerelict*'s "Now And Then." And Townshend's aspiration for spiritual bliss is introduced early in the oeuvre, discussed in a "half-baked" manner in *Tommy*, omitted in "Pete Townshend's Complaint," and resolved in the *Chinese Eyes* project. There Townshend seems to say that if you accept that "we all get to heaven in the end," the anxieties over your individual social dilemmas, professional situations, and relational predicaments will dissipate proportionately.

Townshend's need for collaboration—the third master signature—likewise emerges rather early in his songwriting career and also gains momentum during the opera period. This particular master signature assumes both direct and indirect forms of collaboration. That Resnicoff (1989a) and Garbarini (1982a) cite Townshend's propensity to borrow ideas from diverse sources supports this point. The songwriter's close relationship with his initial audiences virtually elevated that audience into the role of co-author. Townshend would gaze into his audience, work the crowd between sets, read his fan mail, and afterward, write songs specifically for that group. Hence, the auteur's use of borrowed ideas and his capacity to embrace his audience create a context for an unique form of collaboration in which Townshend responds to his environment and shapes his work accordingly.

Kit Lambert's influence is a crucial element in this third master signature. Not only did Lambert expand Townshend's musical education through his knowledge of classical music (e.g., Townshend "borrowed" Purcell's use of suspensions and transformed them into his trademark "power chords") but Lambert and Townshend's work on *Tommy* refined the young songwriter's compositional skills. Through Lambert's early nurturing, Townshend's theatrical inclinations matured to the point that *Tommy* became possible. During the creative portion of the *Tommy* project, Townshend received unprecedented levels of cooperation from Lambert and the band. Subsequently, Townshend developed a growing dependency on collaboration. Without that creative assistance the auteur's pen drifts toward an unrestrained impressionism—both in technological and thematic matters—that may, or may not, serve Townshend's artistic intentions (e.g., the technological *and* thematic aspects of the *LifeHouse* and *Quadrophenia* projects). In short, the Ealing College "ideas man" prospers best in a supportive creative environment—an attribute that is quite apparent in his multimedia solo projects.

The final master signature is an interesting characteristic. The number of popular writers noting the irony that the author of a song entitled "I Can't Explain" spends so much time trying to explain his actions is too great to list here. Pete Townshend's *need* to analyze and explain his work is as old as his professional career. Of particular interest here is his use of journalistic encounters to do more than explain a song's or project's meaning. The *Tommy* and *LifeHouse* projects prove that Townshend thinks out loud in interviews and media statements in a fashion that occasionally places him in a creative bind. Chapter Three noted that Townshend talked so much about the *Tommy* project that he had to do it. Moreover, the "Pete Townshend Page" accounts of Bobby and the *LifeHouse* experiment floated the idea before the public as Townshend worked through the project's logistics. Townshend's tendency to wander through projects during media encounters is a genuine oddity for a writer so prone to personal statements.

Yet it is precisely the personal qualities of these impressionistic accounts that seem to motivate the explanation. The promotional campaign that accompanies a new project requires Townshend to submit to countless interviews. In the contemporary musical world, such promotional plans extend to devices such as Eel Pie's *Interview with a PsychoDerelict* compact disc mentioned in Chapter Six. What separates Townshend from his peers is what he *says* in these sessions. His self-revelations occasionally surprise even him (and his family), but still he continues to use these encounters to explain his work, his life, and his perspective on that day's topic. Few artists have carried on the level of public dialogue that Pete Townshend has sustained throughout his professional career.

We have, then, the auteur: the unique blend of biography, artistic philosophy, thematic orientation, and stylistic tendency. Townshend's impressionism joins his capacity for complaint, his need for collaboration, and his media commentaries to form a creative core through which a consistent story is told. Perhaps the most impressive aspect of Townshend-the-auteur is the growth we have observed across a thirty-year period. *The Seeker* story—the search for spiritual, relational, and societal identity—unfolds through a narrative style that is responsive to its commercial environment. Through negotiation, the vision accommodates the moment: youthful searches for personal identity appear as generational anthems, spiritual quests make way for pinball machines, science yields to commerce, aspiration succumbs to suicide notes, movies require records, expensive projects are compromised, and bicycle accidents result in Tony Awards. Such was the ebb and flow of a commercial career that spanned four decades. Such was the nature of the Pete Townshend's version of the minstrel's dilemma.

THE MINSTREL'S DILEMMA: THE RESOLUTION

I now move to Townshend's most recent—and perhaps final—career transition. The combination of Broadway *Tommy*'s success, Roger Daltrey's tribute, and the *Thirty Years of Maximum R&B* project prefaces yet another career turning point. Here I discuss Broadway *Tommy*'s evolution and how the show's revisions join the Daltrey escapade and the *Thirty Years* boxed set and video to achieve closure for the lifework. When these happenings are paired with the thematic resolutions realized in the *PsychoDerelict* project, the final elements of *The Seeker*'s quest are resolved. I begin with the perennial turning point, *Tommy*.

For years, a variety of production companies expressed an interest in bringing *Tommy* to the theater, yet Townshend resisted all inquiries. The author explained his "wait and see" attitude to the Cable News Network ("I've been sitting on *Tommy* like a mother hen for about fifteen years"—*Show Biz*, 1993a) and Fox TV: "I've always kept that publisher's hat on, so looking at *Tommy* I've always thought, 'I published this. I'm responsible for making sure that its done right by.'... This is not my inheritance. This is my children's and grandchildren's inheritance" (*Backstage on Broadway*, 1993). Townshend bided his time, protected his family's inheritance, and waited for the right director, technology, and audience temperament. He actually *wanted* to stage *Tommy* for personal reasons, as he told Duffy (1993b):

I think what I really wanted was an ending. I know that sounds very trite, but that's what I wanted. I still want an ending for *Quadrophenia*. I want an ending for all of the work that I've been involved in.... I think stories need indications of endings even if you don't wrap up, if you want to leave people to draw their own conclusions, at least give them some way to go. I was reading *The Painted Veil* by Somerset Maugham the other day. At the end of that, a girl who's been quite errant in her life, and has given her husband and her family a hard time, goes back home and decides to commit the rest of her life to her father. That's where you're left in the story. It's both an end and a beginning. That's the kind of ending I've always striven for. (p. 36)

Since Townshend, Kit Lambert, and their lawyers had wisely "registered a grand right" (*In the Studio*, 1993) for *Tommy*—thereby prohibiting any public performance without the author's permission—the auteur was in a legal position to wait for the proper moment to stage, and *end, Tommy*.

That moment arrived via a bicycle, a pothole, and Des McAnuff. The pothole left Townshend with a smashed right wrist; McAnuff left him with a Tony Award-winning director (for Roger Miller's *Big River*), a high-tech production plan, and a theater—McAnuff is the artistic director of the La Jolla Playhouse in California. McAnuff aspired to direct an "official version" (*The Who's Tommy*, 1993) of *Tommy*; thus, he "wanted to get Pete's approval and, if possible, Pete's involvement." A meeting was arranged, and Townshend was persuaded by McAnuff's preparation, his willingness to return to the original record for insight, and his understanding of "what bringing *Tommy* to the stage was about...adapting something that was already a stage piece" to music theater (Townshend's words—*The Who's Tommy*, 1993).

A 1993 *Los Angeles Times* article traces *Tommy*'s evolution from La Jolla to Broadway and cites the initial plans of the Pace Theatrical Group (PTG) for the production. According to Scott Zeiger (PTG's president), the original plan involved a tour of "arenas and amphitheaters" (Pacheco, 1993) across North America, with high-profile stars playing key roles (Michael Hutchence of INXS as Tommy, David Bowie as Captain Walker, Tracey Ullman as Mrs. Walker). PTG changed that approach with Dodger Productions and Des McAnuff's involvement. McAnuff and Townshend shifted the emphasis from casting to the music; as McAnuff stated, "I think we realized early on that the music was the star." With that strategy as a guiding principle, *Tommy* made its official theatrical debut.

The initial responses to the new *Tommy* were mixed. Hilburn (1992) observes that Daltrey, Entwistle, and Townshend sat through opening night "twisting anxiously like parents at a child's first recital," as a preface to this review: "It's an undeniably dashing, dazzling, frequently witty, extravagant, grand-standing work.... What was once a probing, cutting-edge musical experience has become a mostly conventional 'feel good' showcase." The *Orange County Register* concurs: "The production by the La Jolla Playhouse is a visually astounding and flawlessly performed spectacle that downplays the rebellious spirit and critique of celebrity status in the original. Call it a 'Tommy' for the '90s" (Niesel, 1992). The *San Jose Mecury News* proclaims "it looks as though the next big British rock musical to hit Broadway may come from a California theater" (Green, 1992), describes the production (it "takes your breath away"), and advances the view that the show "is profoundly conservative...this is a parable that preaches the virtue of family." Townshend, of course, used media interviews to respond to charges that the new *Tommy* had lost the original's perspective. He told the *Los Angeles Times*:

So Tommy is about the way an individual is made into a star, and the way he deals with that. And hopefully [about] the fact that he deals with it in a very wise way. What I'm trying to say is that it's fools who become stars; it's wise folk who don't. It's people who stick to the tried-and-tested roads; it's people who stay with their group, who value their family and friends and things they've actually done, more highly than dreams and visions and fantasies. And what happens at the end of "Tommy" is that, being given this mantle of people saying, "Listen, you're the boss," what he then says is, "Thanks. Thanks for that, but it's not right for me. I've had weird things happen to me, but, you know, it's what I am. That's what I am, not what you're trying to make me." He's just saying, "I'm gonna live my life, you're gonna live your life." (Walker, 1992)

Irony, once again, has its way with Pete Townshend. In his attempt to bring closure to the *Tommy* story, he ran straight into his old nemesis: nostalgic audiences. The auteur just could not win: "I know some people are going to come in with their interpretations of the ending and be pissed because we haven't honored that.... I'm not pretending here that what 'Tommy' can do is what I dreamed both rock and 'Tommy' could do in the 60s, which was to raise people up. I actually believed that. I think that was a mistake, and I learned that lesson quite quickly" (Walker, 1992).

Still, Townshend and McAnuff had more revisions in mind. While they were satisfied with La Jolla's first act, the second act required further attention, as Townshend observed: "For one thing, it didn't have an end. And we didn't really deal a lot with the nuances and subtleties of character and relationship which aren't necessary in the rock 'n' roll condition but which you do have to resolve in the theater" (Pacheco, 1993). In an effort to appeal to both the theater and rock audiences, the story's time frame was moved to a post-World War II setting (according to McAnuff, "It's very much about Pete's life and times and it seemed very natural to set the story kind of post World War II"—*The Who's Tommy*, 1993), a song was added to sharpen the story ("I Believe My Own Eyes"), and another "starless" cast was selected (many, from the La Jolla cast). The new song was designed to shed light on the parents' frustrations over their experiences with Tommy "when he's grown up" (*Today*, 1993). Townshend did not shy away from the new song's "Broadway value" (*The Who's Tommy*, 1993) and admitted that "I Believe My Own Eyes" was a challenge to write for that reason. Armed with the wisdom obtained through La Jolla, *Tommy* moved to Broadway.

The show opened on April 22, 1993, at the St. James Theater and was an immediate success. Thigpen (1993) reports that by "midnight on the day after Tommy's opening on April 22nd, ticket receipts totaled $494,897, beating by $98,000 the record set by *Guys and Dolls* one year before" (p. 22—Stearns, 1993b, and Larkin, 1993 confirm Thigpen's numbers). Broadway *Tommy* "crossed the $3 million mark" (Thigpen, p. 22) by its fifth day and the show's producers "were scrambling to extend box office hours." Townshend's (1993b) book *The Who's Tommy: The Musical* offers a thorough treatment of the show's history, photographs of the Broadway production, interviews with the cast and production team, and the story's script. A cast recording was also issued, and Townshend recruited George Martin to produce the venture. When asked how Martin's version compares to the original, Townshend responded: "I think it is really for people who have seen the show" (Gillen, 1993, p. 104). In *USA Today*, Townshend's attitude toward the recording—and Martin's role— was more enthusiastic: "I love not having the responsibility!" (Stearns, 1993c, p. 4D). With a cast recording, a book, a CD-ROM (*Pete Townshend Presents Tommy: The Interactive Adventure*—Strauss, 1996), and countless souvenirs available (hats, T-shirts, pins, posters), the Broadway *Tommy* team left no commercial stone unturned.

The most frequent response to Broadway *Tommy* involved the story's new ending and Tommy's return to his family. The so-called "Nancy Reagan ending" became a point of consternation for parts of the audience, as this *New York Times* commentary indicates:

> Though it springs from the era that's despised in conservative politics, this musical might even pass muster in the heart of Republican Central, even with that narrowest of minds, Jesse Helms, who was culture cop under Presidents Reagan and Bush. That's a suspicious development.... The Broadway "Tommy" is tame, almost Reaganesque in its domestic tranquillity.... Listen to the original recording. Rent the movie. Bring both to bear on the Broadway musical. Don't let Pete shed the past so easily. (Staples, 1993)

McAnuff's response featured an interesting political argument: "That's the typical self-destructive side of the intellectual left...we've allowed the right wing to abscond with basic notions like family or patriotism. We just sit back and allow them to do it, accepting that it must be correct. I've never met anybody who didn't consider families important" (Maslin, 1993, p. 27). Townshend's response was mixed. In a *Guitar* interview, he declared that he was "not suggesting a return to family values" but that "the family is the fucking battle field in which we grow up, and I think that rock 'n' roll is about the moment when we leave it and become alone" (Tingen, 1993, p. 24). Though Tommy returns to his family, Townshend explained, "he goes back alone" and does not "pretend that the family is going to provide an answer" (p. 24). In *Time*, the author called on his critics to "grow up" (Simpson, 1993, p. 55). Elsewhere he acknowledged Broadway *Tommy*'s ending is the result of a visit with Betty Townshend and a conversation about his youth and his "clinically insane" grandmother:

> What I discovered in returning to *Tommy* was that in all its vagueness, it's a story about a *real* person and a *real* family. I discovered that Tommy's awful neglect and traumas, the terrible abuses, the lovers, the murders—emotional murders—all of those things actually happened. They happened to me. I saw them as a young child. I saw the adult world at its worst. And I saw it at its best, because my parents finally got back together again.

But I saw an *ending*. And so I do have an ending to *Tommy*. Which is that one forgives one's awful parents for everything they've done. Because if you don't, you'll spend the rest of your life going fucking crazy. (Heilpern, 1993, p. 138)

Hence, Townshend's artistic intentions—and their autobiographical connotations—are once again conveyed via media interviews that attempt to explain perceived misunderstandings or controversies. The more things change, the more they remain the same.

The media's responses to Broadway *Tommy* were more positive than the California reviews of the La Jolla production. The *New York Post* issued two opinions: Barnes (1993) declares the show to be a "blazing triumph" (p. 27) and concludes that Broadway "will never be the same again.... Brilliant, bloody brilliant!" while Aquilante (1993) had "expected a yuppie trap" (p. 27) that was "designed to tap the bulging billfolds of people too old to really rock 'n' roll and too young to die," but he discovered he was wrong: "This Broadway rock opera made sense of the original work and brought it to life." The New York *Daily News* offered contrasting opinions in which Farber (1993) praises the "first fully linear Tommy" (p. 53) as a fleeting "distraction, not unlike an amusement park ride matched to a deathless score," while Kissel (1993) argues: "As theater, 'Tommy' is dumb. As packaging, it's great. And since our theater has less and less to do with theater and more and more to do with packaging, maybe 'Tommy' is a breakthrough.... The contents may be *vodka ordinaire*; the bottle is Absolut" (p. 53). Winer (1993) writes that Townshend and McAnuff "have flattened the evocatively ambiguous song cycle into a doggedly literal, very straight, square and joyless psychodrama" (p. 108) that "drained the mystery from this heretofore edgy, mythic tale of childhood angst and messianic disillusionment." Stearns (1993a) says the show "stimulates senses you didn't know you had" (p. D1), Kuchwara (1993a) writes the production is "a musical made in MTV heaven," and Ridley (1993) describes the show as "a stunner, an explosion of kinetic energy and high-tech stagecraft that grabs you by the throat and never lets go." Just as the original *Tommy*, people may like or dislike the work, but everybody has something to say, and their remarks are usually intense.

The most anticipated review was that of the *New York Times*'s Frank Rich. Rich's (1993) comments were no doubt a godsend to the Broadway *Tommy* team; the review begins:

The Broadway musical has never been the same since rock-and-roll stole its audiences and threw it into an identity crisis. For three decades, from the moment "Meet the Beatles" usurped the supremacy of such Broadway pop as "Hello, Dolly!," the commercial theater has desperately tried to win back the Young (without alienating their elders) by watering down rock music, simulating rock music and ripping off rock music. A result has been a few scattered hits over the years, typified by "Hair" and "Jesus Christ, Superstar," most of which have tamed the rock-and-roll revolution rather than spread it throughout Times Square.
Until now. (p. C1)

Rich deems Broadway *Tommy* to be "the authentic rock musical that has eluded Broadway for two generations" and argues "the show at the St. James is so theatrically fresh and emotionally raw that newcomers to 'Tommy' will think it was born yesterday." After praising the cast and the production, Rich closes by returning to that one song lyric that will never die:

"Hope I die before I get old," sang the Who in "My Generation," its early hit single. A quarter-century or so later, Mr. Townshend hasn't got old so much as grown up, into a deeper view of humanity unthinkable in the late 1960's. Far from being another of Broadway's excursions into nostalgia, "Tommy" is the first musical in years to feel completely alive in its own moment. No wonder that for two hours it makes the world seem young.

Broadway *Tommy* was nominated for eleven Tony Awards and won five: musical score (Pete Townshend), director, musical (Des McAnuff), scenic design (John Arnone), lighting design (Chris Parry), and choreography (Wayne Cilento). A "special Tony Award for continued excellence by a regional theater" was awarded to the La Jolla Playhouse as well (Kuchwara, 1993b). In the fall of 1993 versions of Broadway *Tommy* toured major U.S. cities, the show opened in Germany in 1994, and *Tommy* returned home to London in 1996 (and eight Olivier nominations).

The author was pleased by the Broadway *Tommy* experience, telling the *Today* show: "I think what's been the most gratifying thing...has been the fact that most of the big critics loved the show" (*Today*, 1993). When Jay Leno asked for Townshend's response to the Tony Awards, he said: "Maybe I should've got an award like that twenty years ago for the music work that I did, I mean it's strange for me to get it from a completely new and different industry like theater but it was a kind of a 'kind embrace' for me to get that because it felt as though the work that I was doing on Broadway was being acknowledged...a touch of the establishment theater saying welcome, you know, we embrace you" (*Tonight with*, 1993). Townshend's comments to Anthony De-Curtis (1993) are more revealing: "You know, the Tony is the first artistic award I've ever had.... At this time in my life, it's like getting a knighthood" (p. 107).

Awards aside, Townshend seemed genuinely surprised by his "new job" as a "composer"—reporting that the "most moving" aspect of the Broadway experience "is people call me the author, the composer, they don't say, 'Oh he's the bloke who wrote the songs'" (*The Who's Tommy*, 1993). He also enjoyed an aspect of the experience that revitalized him in a highly predictable manner: "And it's a great thing for me to actually be in a collaborative team which is what being in a rock and roll band is supposed to be about, it isn't always like that" (WFBQ, 1993). Townshend elaborated on this fundamental, master signature in a *CD Review* article: "I thoroughly enjoyed working as a team... there's only so much that can be done by an individual.... I find it's a far richer experience as a writer than anything else I've ever done. There are so many people that feed me with ideas, issues, responses, feedback" (Korte, 1993, p. 53). The Ealing College "ideas man" found a creative home in an artistic environment that nurtured his talent as a storyteller: "I do see myself as a dramatist now, as pretentious as it sounds. I think that anything I do as a songwriter or a composer is going to be linked in some way to live storytelling" (DeCurtis, 1993, p. 108). Townshend—the rock auteur who perceived an artistic "responsibility" to inform through entertainment—now embraces a new obligation: "I have long felt that I have a place in musical theater; I feel I have a function there, a duty" (Sheff, 1994, p. 55). That "duty" involves giving "Andrew Lloyd Webber some competition." He continued: "Rock and roll needed to be brought to Broadway, and in doing that I always felt that Tim Rice and Andrew Lloyd Webber, with *Jesus Christ Superstar*, rode off with part of my inheritance. I wanted to claim it back. Now I've done so. And *Tommy* is my way in. I plan to become more involved in musical theater."

What a fascinating twist of fate: from a bicycle accident to New York's Great White Way, an opportunity that rendered a serious revision of the *PsychoDerelict* project, the songwriting oeuvre's thematic closure, and Broadway *Tommy*. As we have seen throughout his protracted career, Pete Townshend's first move in a career transition is to step back and assess the situation. This time, he stepped back to his family's inheritance and, subsequently, achieved another personal and professional resolution. On a personal level, Townshend's revelations regarding his "dark period" with his grandmother and its impact on his art effectuated closure for that part of his life. On a professional level, Townshend—the flexible storyteller who needs collaboration and public explanation in order to ply his trade—now embellishes the "teamwork" and public forum that music theater offers. Little wonder he returned to the scene of the bicycle accident; as he told Jay Leno, "So whereas at first I used to be very angry about this biking accident and this spot where I fell off, last time I went back...I kissed the spot and said 'thank you hole in the ground'...it was such a lucky break" (*Tonight with*, 1993). The auteur's sense of humor, once again, suggests his state of mind.

The resolutions achieved via the Broadway *Tommy* project were complemented by two events from 1994: Roger Daltrey's tribute and The Who anthology, *Thirty Years of Maximum R&B*. The evidence indicates that Townshend's relationship with these happenings sealed his career with The Who in a capstone manner that sharpened his focus on music theater. The Daltrey show, entitled "Daltrey Sings Townshend," was held on February 23 and 24 at New York's Carnegie Hall. It featured The Chieftains, Alice Cooper, Daltrey, John Entwistle, Sinead O'Connor, Linda Perry, Lou Reed, David Sanborn, The Spin Doctors, Townshend, Eddie Vedder, and a sixty-five piece orchestra from the Julliard School of Music, directed by Michael Kamen. The three-and-one-half-hour show was taped over two nights, and the video was edited into a pay-per-view broadcast and later a compact disc package. During "Daltrey Sings Townshend" the various participants added their unique musical spins to Townshend's lyrics, often recasting the material in innovative ways. Townshend appeared for but two songs ("And I Moved" and "Who Are You"), accompanied by the musicians from the *PsychoDerelict* tour and the Julliard orchestra.

Daltrey announced his desire to sing Townshend's compositions as a celebration of both the work and his fiftieth birthday. He explained his plans to *Rolling Stone*: "I know this is going to sound cliched...but I was the guy who sang, 'I hope I die before I get old.' And I've survived, much to my surprise.... I wanted to celebrate my 50th birthday in a grand way with music, because without rock & roll, I would have been a factory worker" (Strauss, 1994, p. 20). Townshend's comments during the show suggest his thoughts about his music and its relationship to his host, Roger Daltrey:

> The interesting thing about most of these songs...most of the songs that I've written that Roger...has done the best job on, is they were written about fear. I think it's interesting that it takes a big strong man like Roger to sing about fear and not look afraid. I think he was probably afraid inside tonight.... I wish him a happy birthday, a happy fiftieth birthday. And I wish, I wish I knew what fear was.

The music press, in general, condemned the show. Farber (1994) writes: "Too many arrangements felt haphazard, little rapport arose among the musicians, the hall often sucked the center out of the songs, and the pace limped badly" (p. 45). Robbins (1994) took exception to Daltrey's motives, asserting that "the vocalist was there strictly for his own benefit" (p. 79), and arguing: "With 28 Townshend tunes providing the evening's music, it was impossible to discern the line between celebration and exploitation." Stearns (1994) praises Townshend's performance but ridicules Daltrey's "strutting showmanship" (p. 1D) as "an odd ritual from times past." Aquilante (1994) turns to tradition and uses the "hope I die before I get old" line as the lead into this view: "the former Who lead singer died a little death paying tribute to ex-bandmate Pete Townshend with a strange lineup that didn't make you think Who. It made you think why. Daltrey wasn't the problem, although since he said, 'This was all my idea,' he is to blame" (p. 69). Jon Pareles (1994) contends that Daltrey's vocal "limitations" (p. C3) actually "allowed the songs themselves to shine through, revealing Mr. Townshend's brilliance and scope."

The extent to which Roger Daltrey resolved any anxieties over The Who's retirement is uncertain (the three remaining band members appeared together only in the finale, "Join Together," with everybody else). He did, however, attempt to stage the show across the United States later in the year, but with marginal success. A more successful endeavor appeared in the summer of 1994 with the release of the *Thirty Years* anthology with its four CDs, a two-hour video, a thorough booklet (with discography), and—if one purchased the proper package—a commemorative T-shirt. Much publicity accompanied the anthology's release, and the various interviews shed considerable light on Townshend's attitude. For instance, he told WXRT-Radio Chicago that he is "very proud" of the boxed set and that it conveys how the band was "obsessed with ideas, not just with the essence of musical entertainment, there was always a drive to try to do something new." More importantly, he acknowledged that the project "somehow helped me to emotionally let go of the band" and that his "future is going to be somewhere else.... I can tell you now, you won't see me on the road with The Who." He explained:

I will be concentrating on writing, on developing some kind of...better dramatic skill...also finding a way to continue to enjoy life because I've had a much better life in the last four or five years than I've ever had before, I'm much happier, I'm more settled.... I nearly said more in control, I think in a way, I'm less in control than I ever was before. Maybe that's what I'm enjoying: I'm letting life come to me rather than the other way 'round.

John Swenson prepared *Rolling Stone*'s review of *Thirty Years* and awarded the boxed set a perfect five star rating. Swenson (1994) argues the work "changes the perception of the Who as the band that recorded *Tommy* to one of the Who as rock's greatest live rock group" (p. 76). Swenson describes Townshend's songwriting as one that "elevates the rite of rock & roll passage into a spiritual quest for freedom, self-knowledge and eventually salvation" that "kept trying to find new ways for technology to take his songwriting to another level." With an anthology containing over five hours of music and well over two hours of live shows and interviews, a two-song performance at a "tribute" to his work, and the successful staging of his most enduring project, Pete Townshend advanced toward a new creative outlet.

Townshend's move to music theater continues to feature a blend of his past, present, and future. The reissues of Who albums and *The Best of Pete Townshend* (released in 1996) revisit works from yesteryear, while new projects incubate. To promote the greatest-hits record, Townshend conducted a brief "supper club" tour, in which he and Jon Carin (on keyboards) performed mostly acoustic renditions of Townshend/Who classics. Townshend's 1995 New York appearance on behalf of the Children's Health Fund (with Paul Simon, Annie Lennox, and others—Pareles, 1995) featured his first public performance on the piano and, no doubt, set the scene for the brief 1996 "supper club" promotional tour. Newquist (1996) describes Townshend's ability "to play the crowd" (p. 65) during a New York show through a "gregarious" stage presence. Of that show, Farber (1996a) proclaims "What a privilege to behold!" while Watrous (1996) and Williams (1996a) concur with Newquist regarding the artist's demeanor. Townshend closed that particular show by announcing that The Who would regroup to perform *Quadrophenia* later that summer: "It won't be a Who reunion...but it will be a Who *thing*" (Newquist, 1996, p. 65).

Actually, Townshend predicted a *Quadrophenia* revision during the *PsychoDerelict* tour and publicity ("I can be like Shakespeare. I can come back and re-write everything I've done.... I've done that with *Tommy* and I might revisit *Quadrophenia* too") and mentioned his desire to achieve closure for his second opera in a fashion similar to Broadway *Tommy*. In 1997, he reveals the rationale for revisiting Jimmy's Mod angst: his displeasure over the audience's inability to grasp the original *Quadrophenia*'s ending (the widely held perception that Jimmy commits suicide). To deal with that perceived problem, Townshend used the *Quadrophenia* reissue, his desire to work with Roger Daltrey, and MasterCard's financial support for a charity show in London's Hyde Park— for the Concert for the Prince's Trust, also featuring Alanis Morissette, Bob Dylan, and Eric Clapton (Gundersen, 1996; DiPerna, 1996). He explained his aspirations for a Daltrey creative reunion: "This is the beginning, hopefully, of a creative, collaborative partnership, which is something very different from anything we've ever had before" (DiPerna, 1996, p.91). Consequently, Townshend/Daltrey turned to a combination of the celebrity *Tommy* shows (from 1989) and the *PsychoDerelict* production format to elevate *Quadrophenia*'s ending.

After the June 29, 1996 London performance, *Quadrophenia* moved to a six-night appearance in New York's Madison Square Garden (July 16-22, 1996). The show featured Townshend (on acoustic guitar), Daltrey, Entwistle, Zak Starkey (drums), Jody Linscott (percussion), Simon Townshend (guitar, vocals), Geoff Whitehorn (lead guitar), John Bundrick and Jon Carin (keyboards), actor Phil Daniels as "Jimmy" (Daniels played that role in Franc Roddam's film adaptation), singer Gary Glitter as the "Godfather," singer Billy Idol as the "Bell Boy/Ace Face," a five-piece horn section (Neil Sidwell, Simon Gardner, Paul Spong, Steve Sidwell, and Andy Fawbert), and four backup singers (Billy Nicholls, Suzy Webb, Sonia Jones, and Peter Howarth). The performance opened with *Quadrophenia*—using multiple projection screens, dialogue segues by Daniels (often working from Townshend's original liner notes essay), sound effects, video interludes, and stage action (featuring Daltrey, Glitter, and Idol)— and closed with three or four Who classics (acoustic versions of "Behind Blue Eyes," "Won't Get Fooled Again," "Naked Eye," or "Magic Bus"). An interesting aspect of the London and New York shows involved Phil Daniel's contemporary take on the Mod-Rocker battles of thirty years ago. Daniel's recollections combined with video footage to present a historic look back on Jimmy's struggle for identity. Daniel's performance added much to the show's dramatic value.

The New York media's responses to *Quadrophenia* were loud. The *Daily News* proclaims "Rock Like It Oughtta Be" (Farber, 1996b, p. 45) in its headline and describes the show as "one of the most electrifying performances this critic has experienced, a spectacular take on one of rock's most virile works." The *Post*'s Dan Aquilante (1996) writes: "For anyone looking for a major negative about this show, there isn't one in this review. The band, carried by enthusiasm for rock and a score that's as good live as it is on disc, performed what will be remembered as one of the great triumphs and possibly the top rock and roll performance of the year" (p. 36). *Newsday* observes the show "was pumped with passion, videos that enriched rather than sabotaged the show, and was notable for generating rock's circle of life as invented by The Who three decades ago: that giant, invisible spinning hoop that transfers energy between band and audience" (Williams, 1996b, p. B3).

Later that summer, with the New York success as inspiration, The Who toured the United States—and later England—with a stripped-down version of the original production (fewer backup singers, Simon Townshend assuming lead guitar duties, Phil Daniels replaced by a video Jimmy). The show extended into 1997 with a tour of Europe and America. Townshend's frustrations over the audience's inability to grasp the story's ending are now gone: "With the confidence of having delivered the piece dramatically—without changing any of the text—just simply by nailing it down and presenting it in the proper chronological order dramatically on the stage. Everybody understands...that Jimmy experiences a spiritual" renewal (Townshend, 1997). Once again, the auteur achieves thematic closure for a project that—in his view—has been widely misunderstood for twenty five years.

With Townshend's move to music theater firmly in place, the generational angst that demanded the *individual*'s search for spiritual, relational, and social identity is resolved via a three-pronged conclusion: we all get to heaven in the end—that "sea refuses no river" (the spiritual resolution); we must forgive our parents, relatives, and friends for their various indiscretions (the relational resolution); and we must fight the potential travesties associated with a technologically driven society (the English Boy Syndrome/societal resolution). *The Seeker*'s quest is resolved and Townshend—free of his old "job" with "The Who"—turns toward another, more "specific way" to work via a medium that anchors his impressionism through collaboration. Townshend may return to work with Who band members, yet those endeavors reflect a commitment to music theater, not a celebration of "The Who's" history. The elusive "ending" that evaded Townshend for so long is achieved, the auteur's creative impulse is victorious and free to explore new opportunities.

THE MINSTREL'S DILEMMA: THE CASE OF PETE TOWNSHEND

This study's findings support this claim: no other artist in the history of popular music has achieved the artistic scope of Pete Townshend's career. No other popular musician's lifework displays the creative diversity of an *oeuvre* featuring songwriting, poetry, prose, screenplays, operas, musicals, radio plays, music videos, films, as well as an innovative performance history (the auto-destruction and athletic guitar antics). Throughout that career Townshend negotiated a contemporary version of "the minstrel's dilemma" by way of a consistent artistic style that now offers new creative possibilities. All the while certain aspects have remained constant. He has always been a philosophical artist who is more than willing to share his perspective on life, art, or that day's topic. With that in mind, I searched for that one Townshend statement that captures his outlook best and I believe I found it in a remark to Kristine McKenna:

To a great extent, life is a lottery. The only thing you can do is throw the dice and hope it comes up the right way, and if it doesn't you've got to keep throwing. It seems that

the essence of all wisdom is an acceptance of the nature of your own power over yourself
and the circumstances that surround you. The most important thing for a human being to
understand is that there are certain things they can, and therefore must, do, and there are
certain things they can't change and must accept. People who are consumed by bitterness are trying to avoid the acceptance of their own frailty by blaming others and the circumstances around them.... No aspect of nature seems to have the resilience of the
human soul. (McKenna, 1986, p. 65)

Like so many of Townshend's philosophical ruminations, his lifework provides
concrete evidence of that orientation's implementation. Pete Townshend kept
"throwing the dice," as he learned what he *could* do and—many times—what he
could not do. The "bitterness" of "Pete Townshend's Complaint" conveys his
experience with that emotional state, just as his survival—and eventual prosperity—demonstrate his "resilience." Townshend's view that "no aspect of nature
seems to have the resilience of the human soul" is a product of direct experience, and that experience consistently informed his art.

I close with Townshend's reflections on his past, his assessment of his present, and his outlook on his future. Broadway *Tommy*'s success in 1993-1994
provided many opportunities to expound on his career, and the commentary
aired via the television program *Rolling Stone's 1993 Year in Review* was rich in
this regard. First, let us consider Townshend's perspective on his past:

You know I grew up in a show business family. It's all in the blood, it's DNA. That's
what performing is about to me. I'm not comfortable with it, I don't like it. It's almost
like being a boy born to a tailor who has to cut cloth all his life and he can do it, but
really wants to do better than his father, wants to do some other job. I've always wanted
to do some other job than the one that I'm best at. The one that I'm best at *used* to be
playing the guitar in The Who. I don't feel that playing guitar with John Entwistle
playing the bass as a support guitar player to Roger Daltrey is my destiny. I also don't
think it's the most important thing I can do anymore.

He continued with reflections on Keith Moon and The Who's early years:

Now I spent my life with Keith Moon. We share this truth: if you stand on the edge of
the building and you dance about on one leg, you fall off. He died. People die. So,
having experienced that reality, then say, OK we smashed our guitars, OK we were crazy
kids. One of us died and then we...grew up. We stopped. Don't hold us down to the
things that we did when we were stupid kids. Let us grow up and let us be men.

Townshend closed with these words: "I'm trying to keep myself engaged in the
place that I've landed, which is, I think, somewhere between music theater and
rock and roll. And trying to be honest with what I've found and honest with
what I've had, but also honest with the fact that I'm 48 years old and I want my
dignity."

An assessment of Pete Townshend's present, then, starts with these observations and his efforts to maintain his "dignity." He continues to argue that rock
stars—especially "aging rock stars" (*Show Biz*, 1993b)—have a responsibility to

pursue artistic progress: "We rock artists who are aging need to start to refine our craft rather than let it blunder on like a lumbering machine until it crumbles to dust" (Campbell, 1993, p. 17). For Townshend, music theater is a place where "aging rock stars" may "refine their craft" and preserve their "dignity," as these comments to *Billboard* indicate:

I feel that [music theater] has opened a door for me and other artists like me.... I am urging people like Lou Reed, people like Billy Joel and Bruce Springsteen to try something like this, to tell us where they are *now*, at this point in their lives, and not on Thunder Road. There are a lot of people Des and I hope will be encouraged to write for the stage without feeling they are being pretentious—something the Who have always been saddled with. (Gillen, 1993, p. 104)

Elsewhere he reinforces that perspective: "Everything I do should have a musico-dramatic reason for being.... I don't think anybody is as positioned as I am at the moment in show business to do the kind of work which I can do" (Townshend, 1997). To stage his work Townshend plans to "use the craft" that he "developed" when he "was writing songs like 'Little Billy'...[and] the more specific songs for *Tommy* and *Quadrophenia*." He explains:

I should use that craft combined with the ability that I have to touch a certain kind of heart, to write for dramatic pieces. And, also, I should continue to collaborate.... I think that that is something that I'm now much more confident about, much more skilled at, and I'm of an age now when I should really be working with other people because I will benefit more and they will benefit more.... And I do think that what's important now is to accept that some of the Greek theater traditions from which—not just music theater grew—but of which theater itself grew...and lots of storytelling grew...are very much the appropriate vehicles for popular song to evolve.

As he turns to music theater as a "vehicle" for popular song, Townshend's thematic orientation is evolving:

I'm now trying to write about the subtleties and intensities of the daily domestic grind and the simple pleasures and difficulties of domestic life. Things we all understand. Not the extreme and excessive. We all understand passion. We all understand danger and risk. We all understand futility. We all understand desolation, desperation. Everybody writes about "I can't live without you." It would be interesting to write about "Honey, we can't go to the party yet because I have to change a wheel on the car." Or, "Help me, I've forgotten how to tie a fucking bow tie." Or, "Yes, I would love to make love to you, darling, but it's my period and you know you hate blood." The stuff of real life. (Sheff, 1994, p. 60)

Townshend has "landed," and his interest in telling stories about domestic life through music theater projects appears to be the channel through which he now pushes his art, transcends the stagnation associated with aging rock performers, and—hopefully—maintains his dignity. The program distributed during the 1993 *PsychoDerelict* tour captures these ambitions:

In the '90s I am still primarily a song-writer. I usually write songs for the adult male voice and like to record my own compositions. But in the future I see myself writing biographical material for other voices. Notice I say "biographical" and not "autobiographical." I have always felt a part of, and written for a Group. Not just a rock group but also a social group; a bunch of people from a small neighbourhood in a big city. I am always trying to tell their continuing stories. (Townshend, 1993a)

Whether or not Townshend stays on the artistic course he appears to have plotted is uncertain; however, the thematic turn toward "domestic issues" or biography represents a direct extension of *The Seeker*'s resolution. To that end, Townshend's artistic plate is full. Warner Brothers is currently producing an animated version of *Iron Man* (renamed "Iron Giant," because of the comic book character "Iron Man") that, in Townshend's (1997) view, is in "the Disney tradition of musicals...in animation the Hollywood musical lives." There he reports that a *LifeHouse* project (with John Fletcher) is still in the works (*LifeHouse* is the epitome of Townshend's view that you must "keep rolling" those dice), a film script of the "Fish Shop" story exists, and a series of three one-act plays that run consecutively is in development. The three one acts would portray what Townshend terms "avuncular" women (that is, "preposterous, beneficent, non-maternal women") and "the role that avuncular women play with young men in their lives." He acknowledges that this is a conscious effort to write for a "female voice." The three plays are: "Stella" (based on a character from Arthur Miller's *Timebends*), "Chloe" (a story of a woman heroin addict, her violent husband, the husband's murder by her adolescent son, her son's stay in jail, and her subsequent recovery from addiction), and "Trilby's Piano" (an semi-autobiographical account of Townshend's relationship with an aunt and her piano). Each act features but two characters, the woman and young man. Townshend is also working on a "grand musical" of *Daniel Deronda* with Siri Hustvedt, a "dramatization" of *PsychoDerelict* with Roger Daltrey for the Ordway Theater in Minneapolis, and he "writes a song every now and again." However, Townshend has no intentions of producing an album since he views that type of project as a major "distraction." Such a project poses a simple problem: "How do I market this? I don't want to go on the road with it, I don't want to go on TV, I don't want to talk about it." Indeed, negotiations remain.

Rock composer Pete Townshend now describes himself as a "minstrel" (Duffy, 1993b, p. 39) committed to "advancing rock 'n' roll." This minstrel is quite clear about his ultimate destination:

But what I still aspire to is to continue, as far as it goes, and to close the circle...to try to get to the point where—I felt that this was happening with punk, it didn't happen—when somebody walks into the door and does to me what I did to my dad. So I can retire. Because until that happens I can't retire...until that happens I don't think I will be able to look at my son Joseph and say "now you do it...now you pay the rent, so I can go and play golf." (Townshend, 1997)

(Townshend's reference to his father involves his view that the electric guitar ended his father's musical career and introduced his own; simply, he suggests, "why play forty musicians when you can pay four for the same job?" Townshend's autobiography will shed considerable light on this topic.)

How this minstrel uses that motivation to advance rock and roll through music theater and, in turn, "close the circle" is the subject of future projects. This book has charted the auteur's maturation from a young, defiant, aggressive commercial artist into a mature, cooperative, savvy commercial artist. Just as in the Somerset Maugham example Townshend cited earlier, this study does not "wrap up" that career as much as it gives it "some way to go."

References

Abraham, G. (1979). *The concise Oxford history of music*. London: Oxford University Press.

Aledort, A. (1994, June). Maximum rock 'n' roll. *Guitar World*, pp. 57-66.

Allan, M. (1993, July 20). Fire doesn't burn as hot for older Pete Townshend. *Indianapolis Star*, pp. C1-2.

Allman, E. (1982, July 2). This may be Pete's best. *Baton Rouge Morning Advocate* (NEWSBANK).

Altman, B. (1977, December). Townshend/Lane sing the almost middle-aged blues. *Creem*, p. 64.

Altman, B. (1978, November). Adios El Kabong. *Creem*, p. 56.

Altman, B. (1985, November). Review of *White City*. *Spin*, p. 28

Anderson, D. (1989, June 18). The Who: Bassist John Entwistle reflects on the legend—and the tour. *Buffalo News* (NEWSBANK).

Apel, W. (1969). *Harvard dictionary of music*. Cambridge: Belknap Press of Harvard University Press.

Aquilante, D. (1993, April 23). Score's a score for pinball wizard. *New York Post*, p. 27.

Aquilante, D. (1994, February 25). Who cares about TV. *New York Post*, p. 69.

Aquilante, D. (1996, July 17). Who makes sure "Quadrophenia" is well worth the wait. *New York Post*, p. 36.

Arrington, C. (1980, November). Pete Townshend: Who's he? *Creem*, pp. 28-35.

Atkins, J. (1995). Who's Next and the Lifehouse project. *Who's Next* (liner notes).

Attali, J. (1985). *Noise: The political economy of music*. Minneapolis: University of Minnesota Press.

Backstage on Broadway: The Who's Tommy. (1993). Produced by Fox TV.

Bangs, L. (1975, December). Pete Townshend's last detail. *Creem*, p. 62.

Barnes, C. (1993, April 23). "Tommy" terrific. *New York Post*, p. 27.

Barnes, H. (1985, December 19). Blue suede studies. *London Review of Books*, pp. 19-20.

Barnes, R. (1982). *The Who: Maximum R&B*. New York: St. Martin's Press.

Barnes, R. (1996). Deaf, dumb and blind boy. *Tommy* (liner notes).

Barnes, R., and P. Townshend. (1977). *The story of Tommy*. London: Eel Pie.

Bishop, P. (1982, September 29). The Who make their finale a grand musical goodbye. *Pittsburgh Press* (NEWSBANK).

Bloodworth, J. D. (1975). Communication in the youth counter culture: Music as expression. *Central States Speech Journal* 26: 304-309.

Booth, M. W. (1976). The art of words in songs. *Quarterly Journal of Speech* 62: 242-249.

Bordwell, D. (1989). *Making meaning: Inference and rhetoric in the interpretation of cinema.* Cambridge: Harvard University Press.

Boren, R. (1989, August 11). Pete serves up treat for lovers of music and stories. *Deseret News* (Salt Lake City, Utah) (NEWSBANK).

Brooks, M. (1972, May/June). Peter Townshend. *Guitar Player*, pp. 26-28, 30, 32, 36, 40.

Brown, J. (1989, July 7). Who's Townshend: Proscenium rock. *Washington Post*, p. 20.

Browning, B. (1982, August 5). Confessions of Pete Townshend. *Washington Post*, p. D4.

Campbell, M. (1993, April 18). Rediscovering the magic at the Wizard's core. *New York Daily News*, p. 17.

Cannon, B. (1993, October 29). See him, hear him, read him. *Entertainment Weekly*, p. 56.

Carlton, B. (1983, July 15). The Who invades living rooms, courtesy of HBO. *Birmingham News* (NEWSBANK).

Carr, P. (1980, May 26). Daddy who? Daddy punk! *Village Voice*, p. 67.

Carr, R. (1975a, September). Pete Townshend: The punk as godfather. *Creem*, pp. 36-41, 76-77.

Carr, R. (1975b, October). Pete Townshend: The punk as godfather II. *Creem*, pp. 52-54, 76.

Catlin, R. (1982, October 31). Fans flocking to see Who, "just in case." *Omaha World Herald* (NEWSBANK).

Catlin, R. (1989, April 25). The Who to reunite, play Hartford July 4. *Hartford Courant* (NEWSBANK).

Charlesworth, C. (1982). *The Who.* London: Omnibus Press.

Charlesworth, C. (1995). *The complete guide to the music of The Who.* London: Omnibus Press.

Childs, E. (1975, February). Review of *Odds and Sods. Crawdaddy*, p. 82.

Christgau, R. (1969, June 12). Rock & roll: Whooopee! *Village Voice*, pp. 36, 42.

Cocks, J. (1979, December 17). Rock's outer limits: Through turmoil and triumph, The Who makes music that will last. *Time*, pp. 86-94.

Cohn, N. (1970, March 8). Finally, the full force of The Who. *New York Times*, p. 2.

Collins, M. (1974, June). Pete Townshend: Busy days. *Rolling Stone*, p. 20.

Considine, J. (1982, September 22). The Who say farewell—maybe. *The* [Baltimore] *Sun* (NEWSBANK).

Cott, J. (1970, May). A talk with Pete Townshend. *Rolling Stone*, pp. 32-35.

Cromelin, R. (1978, August 20). New Who LP: Game, but limited effort. *Los Angeles Times*, p. 70.

Cromelin, R. (1980, May 25). Townshend sings to new generation. *Los Angeles Times*, p. 64.

Crowe, C. (1974, December). Peter Townshend. *Penthouse*, pp. 95-99, 127-128, 130.

Daltrey, R. (1966, September 24). Pop think in: Roger Daltrey. *Melody Maker*, p. 12.

DeCurtis, A. (1993, December). Opera man. *Rolling Stone*, pp. 105-109, 182.

Denselow, R. (1972, October). Townshend prays, writes new opera. *Rolling Stone*, p. 52.

Denselow, R. (1989). *When the music's over: The story of political pop.* London: Faber and Faber.

DiMartino, D. (1993, July). Review of *PsychoDerelict. Musician*, p. 86.

DiPerna, A. (1994, June). Not f-f-f-fade away. *Guitar World*, pp. 40-54.

DiPerna, A. (1996, August). Iron man. *Guitar World*, pp. 88-98, 192-194.

Dove, I. (1973, December 7). The Who plays in smashing form. *New York Times*, p. 37.

Duffy, T. (1993a, April 17). Townshend's "Tommy" encore: "PsychoDerelict" expands rock. *Billboard*, pp. 1, 81.

Duffy, T. (1993b, July). Pete Townshend: The punk meets the phantom. *Musician*, pp. 34-37, 39-40, 42-45.

Edwards, H. (1974, June 9). Musical punkism, or, the what, where and why of the Who. *New York Times*, pp. 3, 5.

Empty Glass. (1989, November). Review of *Empty Glass*. *Rolling Stone*, p. 11.

Evans, P. (1993, August). Review of *PsychoDerelict*. *Rolling Stone*, p. 76.

Farber, J. (1993, April 23). "Tommy" scores. *New York Daily News*, pp. 49, 53.

Farber, J. (1994, February 25). Boo Who: Daltrey bash peters out. *New York Post*, p. 45.

Farber, J. (1996a, May 6). Townshend triumphant. *New York Daily News*, p. 29.

Farber, J. (1996b, July 18). Rock like it oughtta be. *New York Daily News*, p. 45.

Fink, M. (1982a, October 29). Rough sailing with Townshend and Daltrey. *Los Angeles Herald Examiner* (NEWSBANK).

Fink, M. (1982b, October 30). 93,000 fans pack Coliseum for Who show. *Los Angeles Herald Examiner* (NEWSBANK).

Finney, T. M. (1935). *A history of music*. New York: Harcourt, Brace and World.

Flanagan, B. (1993, July). Tommy comes to Broadway. *Musician*, p. 38.

Flippo, C. (1974, December). Entwistle: Not so silent after all. *Rolling Stone*.

Flippo, C. (1991). *Everybody was kung-fu dancing: Chronicles of the lionized and the notorious*. New York: St. Martin's Press.

Foege, A. (1993, July). Review of *PsychoDerelict*. *Spin*, pp. 78-79.

Fricke, D. (1982, November). Review of *Music and Rhythm*. *Rolling Stone*, p. 80.

Fricke, D. (1983, April). Review of *Scoop*. *Rolling Stone*, pp. 66-67.

Fricke, D. (1987a, April). Review of *Another Scoop*. *Rolling Stone*, pp. 146, 148.

Fricke, D. (1987b, December). Pete Townshend. *Rolling Stone*, pp. 179-183.

Fricke, D. (1989, August). Review of *The Iron Man*. *Rolling Stone*, p. 91.

Frith, S. (1978). *The sociology of rock*. London: Constable.

Galvin, P. (1994, February 20). Behind the scenes with a rock impresario. *New York Times*, pp. 1, 25.

Gambaccini, P. (1975, December). Quadromania: The Who fuss, fight and hit the road. *Rolling Stone*, p. 12.

Garbarini, V. (1982a, August). Peter Townshend: The Who and beyond. *Musician*, pp. 48-60.

Garbarini, V. (1982b, September). The rat, the river and the hotline to God. *Musician*, pp. 46-54.

Gardner, E. (1993, September). Pete Townshend: New York City. *Rolling Stone*, p. 29.

Gill, C. (1993a, September). Pete Townshend stages his return. *Guitar Player*, pp. 98-110.

Gill, C. (1993b, September). Tommy on Broadway: A view from the pit. *Guitar Player*, p. 102.

Gillen, M. (1993, July 17). In the studio with The Who's "Tommy." *Billboard*, pp. 103-104.

Gilmore, M. (1982, October 29). The Who's last tour comes just in time. *Los Angeles Herald Examiner* (NEWSBANK).

Goldman, J. (1993, June 7). "Angels," "Spider Woman" take top billing for Tonys. *Los Angeles Times*, pp. A1, 15.

Goldstein, R. (1967, April 6). Rock 'n' wreck. *Village Voice*, pp. 23-24.

Good Morning America. (1993, July 27). ABC.

Graf, G. (1993, July 14). The story from Pete Townshend, storyteller. *Philadelphia Inquirer*, pp. E1, E6.

Green, J. (1992, July 14). See it, hear it, feel it. *San Jose Mercury News* (NEWSBANK).

Grieve, T. (1989, August 30). The Who: Who are you? *Sacramento Bee* (NEWS-BANK).

Grout, D. J. (1960). *A history of western music.* New York: W. W. Norton.

Gundersen, E. (1996, June 10). "Quadrophenia" concert to reunite Who mates. *USA Today*, p. D1.

Harrington, R. (1989, July 2). Who's laughing now. *Washington Post* (NEWSBANK).

Hauptfuhrer, F. (1980, May). The Who and Pete Townshend face a tour and their fears after Cincinnati. *People*, pp. 97-102.

Havilah, J., and J. O'Mahony. (1994, February 25). Sinead tried to kill self after her rip on the Pope. *New York Post*, p. 29.

Hebdige, D. (1979). *Subculture: The meaning of style.* London: Methuen.

Heilpern, J. (1993, May). *Tommy*'s next stage. *Vogue.* pp. 132, 136, 138.

Henahan, D. (1970, June 8). "Tommy" is poignantly sentimental. *New York Times*, p. 42.

Hilburn, R. (1972a, December 3). Review of *Who Came First. Los Angeles Times*, pp. 58, 60.

Hilburn, R. (1972b, December 10). A special *Tommy* for the masses. *Los Angeles Times*, p. 66.

Hilburn, R. (1973, October 27). Review of *Quadrophenia. Los Angeles Times*, p. 5.

Hilburn. R. (1974, August 22). Review of *Who's Next. Los Angeles Times*, p. 70.

Hilburn, R. (1975, October 21). Transition time for the Who. *Los Angeles Times*, p. 9.

Hilburn, R. (1977, October 30). Pete 'n' Ronnie's mellow "Rough Mix." *Los Angeles Times*, p. 68.

Hilburn, R. (1978, August 20). Pete Townshend juggles his rock 'n' roll future. *Los Angeles Times*, pp. 70, 74.

Hilburn, R. (1982a, August 20). The last Who rah: Band sets "farewell" tour. *Los Angeles Times* (NEWSBANK).

Hilburn, R. (1982b, October 29). The Who takes final bow with dignity and punch. *Los Angeles Times* (NEWSBANK).

Hilburn, R. (1992, July 11). They've taken a generation's magic away. *Los Angeles Times* (NEWSBANK).

Hinckley, D. (1985, November 19). Won't get fooled again. *New York Daily News* (NEWSBANK).

Hinckley, D. (1993, April 18). Will "Tommy" tilt or triumph? *New York Daily News*, p. 16.

Hochman, S. (1989, June 25). Review of *The Iron Man. Los Angeles Times*, p. 58.

Holland, B. (1994, February 26). Mozart and Daltry [*sic*] as 2 kinds of religion. *New York Times*, p. 13.

Holden, S. (1985, November 24). Film review: *White City. New York Times*, p. 30.

Hughes, D. (1954). *Oxford history of music: Early medieval music up to 1300.* London: Oxford University Press.

Hull, R. (1981, April 8). The Who, dancing to an erratic drummer. *Washington Post*, p. B4.

In the Studio. (1993). The Who's Tommy. The Album Network.

In the Studio. (1994). Thirty years of maximum R & B. The Album Network.

Infusino, D. (1982, November 28). Who hoopla! How Milwaukee got 'em. *Milwaukee Journal* (NEWSBANK).

Interview With A PsychoDerelict. (1993). Eel Pie Recording Productions.

It's Hard. (1982a, September 19). Review of *It's Hard. Minneapolis Tribune* (NEWS-BANK).

It's Hard. (1982b, December). Review of *It's Hard. Rolling Stone,* p. 107.

Jahn, M. (1969, June 8). Britain's high-decibel group, The Who, is still thundering. *New York Times,* p. 79.

Jahn, M. (1971, July 31). The Who play first program of '71 here despite downpour. *New York Times,* p. 13.

Jelcich, S. (1986, Spring). "Horse's Neck." *San Francisco Review of Books,* p. 14.

Johnson, M. (1993, May 2). "Tommy" splendid yet preposterous; Brothers' drags. *Hartford Courant* (NEWSBANK).

Jones, J. (1994, August 18). Channeling choices in music video. *USA Today,* pp. D1-2.

Jones, N. (1965a, January 9). Caught in the act. *Melody Maker.*

Jones, N. (1965b, July 3). Well, what is pop art: Who guitarist Pete Townshend has a go at a definition. *Melody Maker,* p. 11.

Jones, N. (1965c, August 28). The price of pop art: The Who count the cost. *Melody Maker,* p. 9.

Jones, N. (1967a, April 29). Pictures of the Who: We've forgotten immature feelings like – Who's getting all the limelight. *Melody Maker,* p. 9.

Jones, N. (1967b, October 14). I became a hero—smashing guitars. *Melody Maker,* p. 7.

Joyce, M. (1982, September 21). The Who gets harder. *Washington Post,* p. B8.

Kakutani, M. (1985, August 17). His generation. *New York Times,* p. 33.

Kaleina, G. (1983, August 25). Lawyer applauds latest decision in Who litigation. *Cincinnati Enquirer* (NEWSBANK).

Kalogerakis, G. (1994, March 27). Endpaper: Deja Who. *New York Times Magazine,* p. 96.

Kaye, L. (1973, December). Quadrophenia: Who's essay on Mod era. *Rolling Stone,* pp. 72-73.

Kelp, L. (1989, June 28). Who's Townshend keeps tight focus on "Iron Man." *Oakland Tribune* (NEWSBANK).

The Kids Are Alright. (1979). Produced by Bill Curbishley and Tony Klinger, BMG Video.

King, P. (1989, July 17). The Who rekindles band's glory days. *Pittsburgh Press* (NEWSBANK).

Kissel, H. (1993, April 23). We've got a "Tommy"-ache: Stage wizardry ain't theater. *New York Daily News,* p. 53.

Kolson, A. (1985a, November 19). A rock-and-roll giant grows up. *Philadelphia Inquirer* (NEWSBANK).

Kolson, A. (1985b, December 22). Pete Townshend has learned how to let his demons go. *Chicago Tribune* (NEWSBANK).

Kolson, A. (1993, April 22). See it, feel it, hear it. *Philadelphia Inquirer* (NEWS-BANK).

Korte, S. (1993, August). Live from New York: *Tommy* rocks Broadway. *CD Review,* pp. 52-54.

Kot, G. (1993, July 19). Townshend's "Derelict" seems autobiographical. *Chicago Tribune,* p. 12.

Kuchwara, M. (1993a, April 24). A Who-less "Tommy" falters. *San Jose Mecury News* (NEWSBANK).

Kuchwara, M. (1993b, June 7). "Kiss of the Spider Woman" among Broadway's best. *Lafayette Journal and Courier,* p. B1.

Landau, J. (1967, August). Happy Jack. *Crawdaddy,* pp. 43-47.

Larkin, K. (1993, April 27). It's a box-office wizard—"Tommy" sets record. *New York Post* (NEWSBANK).

Late Night with David Letterman. (1993, June 17). NBC.

Late Show with David Letterman. (1993, November 11). CBS.

Leydon, J. (1982, September 27). Film: "Secret Policeman's Other Ball." *Houston Post* (NEWSBANK).

Loder, K. (1982a, June). Pete Townshend: The guitarist faces up to alcoholism and the final days of the Who. *Rolling Stone*, pp. 18-20, 53-54.

Loder, K. (1982b, November). Last time around: The Who say goodbye before they get old, and hello to a very uncertain future. *Rolling Stone*, pp. 25-28.

Loder, K. (1985, February). Review of *Who's Last. Rolling Stone*, p. 60.

MacDonald, P. (1982, October 19). Legendary rock band bowing out while still at the top. *Seattle Times* (NEWSBANK).

Malamut, B. (1976, March). Capsule review: *My Generation. Crawdaddy*, p. 76.

Marcus, G. (1968, November). Review of *The Who On Tour/Magic Bus. Rolling Stone*, p. 21.

Marcus, G. (1970, July). P-P-P-People try to put us down. *Rolling Stone*, p. 40.

Marcus, G. (1978, October). The Who find some answers. *Rolling Stone*, pp. 81, 85-86.

Marcus, G. (1979, August). Marking time with the Who. *Rolling Stone*, pp. 57-58.

Marcus, G. (1981). Pete Townshend. In P. Herbst (ed.), *The Rolling Stone interviews: Talking with the legends of rock & roll* (pp. 404-413). New York: St. Martin's Press/Rolling Stone Press.

Marcus, G. (1990). *Mystery train: Images of America in rock 'n' roll music* (third ed.). New York: Plume.

Marsh, D. (1971, October). Review of *Who's Next. Creem*, pp. 68-69.

Marsh, D. (1973, January). Review of *Who Came First. Creem*, pp. 68-69.

Marsh, D. (1974, October). Ten years on with The Who. *Creem*, pp. 47-48, 72-73.

Marsh, D. (1975, November). Who's ongoing saga of stardom & failure. *Rolling Stone*, pp. 63-65.

Marsh, D. (1977, October). Rock & roll from the soul. *Rolling Stone*, pp. 81-82.

Marsh, D. (1980, June). Rock & roll religion the hard way. *Rolling Stone*, pp. 71-72.

Marsh, D. (1980). The Who. In J. Miller (ed.), *The Rolling Stone illustrated history of rock & roll* (pp. 285-292). New York: Random House/Rolling Stone Press.

Marsh, D. (1983). *Before I get old: The story of the Who.* New York: St. Martin's Press.

Marsh. D. (1995). The Who Sell Out. *The Who Sell Out* (liner notes).

Martin, G. (1993, July 31). Gaga! . . . Oh really? *New Musical Express*, pp. 17, 41.

Maslin, J. (1979a, June 15). Film: Documentary on the Who. *New York Times*, p. 16.

Maslin, J. (1979b, November 2). Film: Quadrophenia. *New York Times*, p. 6.

Maslin, J. (1979c, November 13). The Who look proudly on budding film careers. *New York Times*, p. 8.

Maslin, J. (1993, May 9). The man who reinvented the Who's "Tommy." *New York Times*, pp. E1, 27.

Mayer, I. (1982, October 12). Who-dunit: The band's going out with a bang. *New York Post* (NEWSBANK).

McAuliffe, K. (1983, August). Pete Townshend. *Penthouse*, pp. 115-116, 129, 168-170.

McKenna, K. (1982, July 10). Townshend back with new LP. *Los Angeles Times* (NEWSBANK).

McKenna, K. (1986, March). Free drinking and heavy thinking. *Spin*, pp. 48-50, 65.

McNicoll, D. (1978, September 8). Associated Press release. *New York Times*, p. 17.

Meaty Beaty Big and Bouncy. (1987, August). Review of *Meaty Beaty Big and Bouncy. Rolling Stone*, p. 170.

Mendelsohn, J. (1970, April). Review of "The Seeker." *Rolling Stone*, p. 58.

Mendelsohn, J. (1971, August). Review of *Who's Next. Rolling Stone*, p. 42.

Miller, J. (1974, December). The Who: Talkin' about a generation. *Rolling Stone*, p. 73.

Mills, B. (1977, October 30). Townshend to punk rockers: Welcome to the club. *Los Angeles Times*, pp. 68, 70.

Mills, B. (1978, February 5). Peter Townshend: The "Godfather" of rock 'n' roll. *San Francisco Chronicle*, p. 28.

Milward, J. (1990, May). Review of *Join Together*. *Rolling Stone*, p. 143.

Moon, K. (1966, December 31). Pop think in: Keith Moon. *Melody Maker*, p. 7.

Morison, B. (1993, October). Review of *PsychoDerelict*. *Guitar*, pp. 170, 172.

Moritz, C. (ed.) (1983). *Current biography yearbook 1983*. New York: H. H. Wilson.

Morse, S. (1993, August 11). Townshend's anger ignites explosive rock. *Boston Globe*.

Morton, B. (1985, November 8). Out of the ordinary. *Times Educational Supplement*, p. 31.

Murray, C. S. (1980, July). Love, death and the whole damn thing: Pete Townshend on the record. *Trouser Press*, pp. 16-21.

Nelson, P. (1968, June 2). "Rock is too serious," say The Who. *New York Times*, p. 20.

Nelson, P. (1981, December). The year in records: *Face Dances*. *Rolling Stone*, p. 91.

Newquist, H. P. (1996, August). Pete Townshend: The chronicles of an angry guitarist. *Guitar*, pp. 56-65.

Niesel, J. (1992, July 12). Kinder, gentler "Tommy" lacks fire. *Orange County Register* (NEWSBANK).

A night at the (rock) opera. (1993, May). *Entertainment Weekly*, p. 58.

The One That Got Away. (1996, February 11). BBC documentary on *LifeHouse*.

Pacheco, P. (1993, April 18). Will New York embrace the pinball wizard of La Jolla? *Los Angeles Times* (NEWSBANK).

Palmer, R. (1979, September 16). Pop: The Who's balance. *New York Times*, p. 71.

Palmer, R. (1982a, October 9). The Who's "final" tour arrives in New York. *New York Times*, p. 12.

Palmer, R. (1982b, October 12). Pop: The Who, British rockers on farewell tour. *New York Times*, p. 10.

Pareles, J. (1982, August). Review of *All the Best Cowboys Have Chinese Eyes*. *Rolling Stone*, p. 48.

Pareles, J. (1989a, June 29). The Who, reunited, performs "Tommy." *New York Times*, p. 17.

Pareles, J. (1989b, July 1). A united Who's surprises. *New York Times*, p. 15.

Pareles, J. (1993a, March 28). "Tommy" and his father reach Broadway. *New York Times*, pp. H5, 18, 19.

Pareles, J. (1993b, July 14). Who's still rocking? "Tommy's" father. *New York Times*.

Pareles, J. (1994, February 25). The Who, regrouped and reinterpreted. *New York Times*, p. C3.

Pareles, J. (1995, August 12). New tricks introduced for a cause. *New York Times*, p. C13.

Pareles, J. (1996, July 18). A durable fable of youth revived as an extravaganza. *New York Times*, pp. C13-14.

Perry, C., and A. Bailey. (1974, January 3). Who's spooky tour: Awe and hassles. *Rolling Stone*, pp. 13, 16.

Pete Townshend, Van Morrison, Waterboys and Robert Plant due. (1993, May). *Ice: The Monthly CD Newsletter*, pp. 1, 10.

Pete Townshend's Psychoderelict. (1993, August 7). Produced by VH-1.

Phillips, M. (1970, June 8). The Who and "Tommy" rock the Met. *New York Times*, p. 42.

Phillips, M. (1992a, July 5). "Tommy" for a new generation. *San Diego Union* (NEWSBANK).

Phillips, M. (1992b, July 24). "Tommy" plays his pinball again. *Washington Times* (NEWSBANK).

Piccoli, S. (1989, July 10). The Who's wizardry snares 'em: Rock's daddy pours it on. *Washington Times* (NEWSBANK).

Pollock, B. (1975). *In their own words.* New York: Collier Books.

Pond, S. (1983, April 3). Rummaging through the Townshend attic. *Los Angeles Times* (NEWSBANK).

Pond, S. (1989, July). The Who. *Rolling Stone,* pp. 86-103.

Pratt, W. (1907). *The history of music.* New York: G. Schirmer.

Puckett, J. L. (1993, November 25). Theater review: The Who's Tommy. [Louisville] *Courier-Journal,* p. C3.

Quinlan, M. (1982, October 9). There's no f-f-f-fading away by polished, energetic Who. [Louisville] *Courier-Journal* (NEWSBANK).

Rassenfoss, J. (1982, September 19). The Who continues to mature. *Kansas City Star* (NEWSBANK).

Raynor, H. (1978). *A social history of music: From the middle ages to Beethoven.* New York: Taplinger.

Resnicoff, M. (1989a, September). The second coming of Pete Townshend. *Guitar Player,* pp. 67-84.

Resnicoff, M. (1989b, October). Flailing your way to God: The Pete Townshend interview, part 2. *Guitar Player,* pp. 67-82, 131.

Resnicoff, M. (1993, July). Music must change. *Musician,* p. 41.

Resnicoff, M. (1996). Who Are You. *Who Are You* (liner notes).

Rich, F. (1993, April 23). Capturing rock-and-roll and the passions of 1969. *New York Times,* pp. C1, C23.

Richards, I. A. (1924). *Principles of literary criticism.* New York: Harcourt, Brace.

Ridley, C. (1993, April 25). Rock opera "Tommy" explodes on Broadway. *Philadelphia Inquirer* (NEWSBANK).

Robbins, I. (1978, October). Who knows where the time goes? *Crawdaddy,* p. 69.

Robbins, I. (1994, February 25). Celebrating Pete Townshend, sort of. *Newsday,* p. 79.

Robinson, L. (1982a, October 7). The Who. *New York Post* (NEWSBANK).

Robinson, L. (1982b, October 17). Who: Will the band play on? *San Francisco Examiner* (NEWSBANK).

Robinson, L. (1982c, December 22). Who's live finale showed that video not ready to replace the real thing. [Newark] *Star-Ledger* (NEWSBANK).

Robinson, L. (1993, February 15). "Tommy" tunes up for B'way. *New York Post* (NEWSBANK).

Rockwell, J. (1974a, June 12). Who's basics overpower some snags. *New York Times,* p. 38.

Rockwell, J. (1974b, June 13). Townshend, one of the Who, faces a creative how. *New York Times,* p. 53.

Rockwell, J. (1975, December 17). To faithful, Who is what rock's about. *New York Times,* p. 40.

Rockwell, J. (1976, March 13). Who's sick? Not the Who in the eyes of rock fans. *New York Times,* p. 14.

Rockwell, J. (1979a, June 29). The pop life: The Who is back on the scene. *New York Times,* p. 24.

Rockwell, J. (1979b, September 12). Rock: The Who returns. *New York Times,* p. 22.

Rockwell, J. (1979c, November 2). The pop life: New and old cross tracks on Who album. *New York Times,* p. 14.

Rohter, L. (1975, November 9). Old band, new band. *Washington Post,* p. E16.

Rolling Stone's One on One. (1993). Produced by Global Satellite Network.

Rolling Stone's 1993 Year in Review. (1993, December 14). Fox Network.

Rothman, D. (1979). A conversation with Pete Townshend. *Oui*, pp. 71-73, 118-120.

Rowbotham, J. F. (1895). *The troubadours and courts of love.* London: Swan Sonnenschein.

Sachs, L. (1993, July 19). Rock: Guitar-smashing Townshend turns superficial. *Chicago Sun-Times*, p. 19.

Salewicz, C. (1982, November). Pete Townshend stops hurting people; stops hurting himself: Action for the '80s. *Creem*, pp. 26-31.

Sanders, R., and D. Dalton. (1969, July). Pete and Tommy, among others. *Rolling Stone*, pp. 16-18.

Santiago, R. (1993, August). In the news: Hall of Fame groundbreaking. *Rolling Stone*, p. 18.

Schaffner, N. (1983). *The British invasion: From the first wave to the new wave.* New York: McGraw-Hill.

Scheirman, D. (1992, December). Tommy again. *Live Sound! and Touring Technology*, pp. 8, 10, 38.

Schulps, D. (1977, October). Return of the mod squad. *Crawdaddy*, p. 76.

Schulps, D. (1978, April). Pete. *Trouser Press*, pp. 15-18, 20, 35.

Scoppa, B. (1973, October). Review of *Eric Clapton's Rainbow Concert. Rolling Stone*, p. 61.

Selvin, J. (1978, September 24). "Who" makes you ask why? *San Francisco Chronicle*, p. 49.

Selvin, J. (1981, April 5). Gliding with the Who. *San Francisco Chronicle*, p. 19.

Sheff, D. (1994, February). *Playboy* interview: Pete Townshend. *Playboy*, pp. 51-60, 148-151.

Sherbert, L. (1986, July). "Tommy" plot takes pounding in local show. *Atlanta Journal* (NEWSBANK).

Show Biz Today. (1993a, March 20). CNN.

Show Biz Today. (1993b, June 21). CNN.

Silver, D. (1972, December). Townshend's Meher Baba LP: Mellower vibrations. *Rolling Stone*, pp. 60-61.

Simpson, J. (1993, July 12). Pete, we can hear you. *Time*, p. 55.

Smelt, P. (1985, June 28). Lucky but not special. *Times Literary Supplement*, p. 733.

St. John, M. (1989, July 23). They're back!: Who pound out classics, new singles. *Wisconsin State Journal* (NEWSBANK).

Stamp, C. (1995). A Quick One. *A Quick One* (liner notes).

Staples, B. (1993, July 5). Deconstructing "Tommy": Watch for the Reagan touches. *New York Times.*

Stasi, L. (1994, February 25). Pete's old number too close for comfort. *New York Daily News*, p. 17.

Stearns, D. (1993a, April 23). "Tommy" rocks onto Broadway at full tilt. *USA Today*, p. D1.

Stearns, D. (1993b, April 27). "Tommy" box-office wizard. *USA Today*, p. D1.

Stearns, D. (1993c, May 13). Seeing and feeling "Tommy." *USA Today*, p. D4.

Stearns, D. (1994, February 25). The Who holds out at celebration. *USA Today*, p. D1.

Stearns, D. (1996, July 18). Danger crowded out of Who's "Quadrophenia." *USA Today*, p. D1.

Stock, J. (1993, October). Eminence front. *Pulse!*, pp. 29-31.

Stokes, G. (1974, June 20). A fusion of rage and boogie. *Village Voice*, p. 62.

Strauss, B. (1996, Spring). Deaf, dumb, and blind king. *Entertainment Weekly*, pp. 76-78.

Strauss, N. (1994, April). Toasting Townshend. *Rolling Stone*, p. 20.

Sumrall, H. (1982, September 26). The Who reaches into its past and pulls out a plum. *San Jose Mercury* (NEWSBANK).

Swenson, J. (1971, December). The Who puts the bomp or they won't get fooled again. *Crawdaddy*, pp. 25-35.

Swenson, J. (1974, January). The Who: After ten years of madness the next stage is "Quadrophenia." *Crawdaddy*, pp. 48-54.

Swenson, J. (1979). *Headliners: The Who*. New York: Grosset and Dunlap.

Swenson, J. (1979, November). Mod "Quad." *Rolling Stone*, p. 70.

Swenson, J. (1983, November). Pete Townshend: The one-time guitar-smasher looks back. *Guitar World*, pp. 36-44, 78-79.

Swenson, J. (1994, September). Who story. *Rolling Stone*, p. 76.

Swenson, J. (1996). The Who By Numbers. *The Who By Numbers* (liner notes).

Tannenbaum, R. (1986, January). Review of *White City: A Novel*. *Rolling Stone*, p. 48.

They know Who they are. (1989, April 28). Concert review. *Boston Globe* (NEWS-BANK).

Thigpen, D. (1993, June). "Tommy" sells out. *Rolling Stone*, p. 22.

Thomas, K. (1989, July 23). Townshend proves mettle with spirited "Iron Man." *Atlanta Journal* (NEWSBANK).

Tingen, P. (1993). The generation game. *Guitar*, 3, no. 5: pp. 22-28.

Today. (1993, November 9). NBC.

Tonight with Jay Leno. (1993, July 30). NBC.

Townshend, P. (1966, March 26). Pop think in: Why should James Brown have all of RSG? *Melody Maker*.

Townshend, P. (1967a, January 14). Pop think in: Pete Townshend. *Melody Maker*, p. 7.

Townshend, P. (1967b, August 12). Dear Melody Maker, (Pete Townshend writes from America). *Melody Maker*.

Townshend, P. (1970a, August 22). The Pete Townshend page. *Melody Maker*, p. 7.

Townshend, P. (1970b, September 19). Another fight in the playground. *Melody Maker*, p. 19.

Townshend, P. (1970c, October 17). On the road again. *Melody Maker*.

Townshend, P. (1970d, November). In love with Meher Baba. *Rolling Stone*, pp. 25-27.

Townshend, P. (1970e, November 14). TV miming: Who is being fooled? *Melody Maker*, p. 18.

Townshend, P. (1971a, January 16). Do you suffer from media frustration? *Melody Maker*, p. 16.

Townshend, P. (1971b, February 13). Change—by taking people UP. *Melody Maker*, p. 14.

Townshend, P. (1971c, March 13). Learning to walk—the second time round. *Melody Maker*, p. 12.

Townshend, P. (1971d, April 17). Things are different across the sea. *Melody Maker*, p. 20.

Townshend, P. (1971e, December). Review of *Meaty, Beaty, Big and Bouncy*. *Rolling Stone*, pp. 37-38.

Townshend, P. (1973, January). Advertisement for *Who Came First*. *Crawdaddy*, p. 17.

Townshend, P. (1977, November). The punk meets the godmother. *Rolling Stone*, pp. 54-59.

Townshend, P. (1983, September). On the nature of aging and rock & roll: A discourse on Mick Jagger's fortieth birthday. *Rolling Stone*, pp. 18-19.

Townshend, P. (1984). *"My Generation": A history in music & photographs*. London: Wise Publications.

Townshend, P. (1993a). Pete Townshend: In concert (concert program).

Townshend, P. (1993b). *The Who's Tommy: The musical.* New York: Pantheon Books.

Townshend, P. (1995). Who's Next. *Who's Next* (liner notes).

Townshend, P. (1997, March 7). Conversation with Pete Townshend, Richmond Gate Hotel, London.

Triplett, G. (1982, July 25). Review of *Chinese Eyes. Daily Oklahoman* (NEWSBANK).

Tucker, K. (1993, July 18). In the 90's, "Tommy" plays a fancier pinball. *New York Times*, p. E1.

2 rock musicians accused in assault. (1969, May 19). *New York Times*, p. 24.

Varga, G. (1989, August 20). Who knows its limits. *San Diego Union* (NEWSBANK).

Varga, G. (1992a, July 5). For pop fans, "Tommy" remains the one and only. *San Diego Union* (NEWSBANK).

Varga, G. (1992b, July 24). No one asks Who is most popular boy of rock opera. *Washington Times* (NEWSBANK).

Vitez, M. (1989, July 10). The Who's here: Two generations of fans see the band at the Vet. *Philadelphia Inquirer* (NEWSBANK).

Walker, M. (1992, July 5). The resurrection of "Tommy." *Los Angeles Times* (NEWSBANK).

Walker, M. (1993, May 16). See me, feel me, touch me, stage me. *Boston Sunday Globe*, pp. 15, 25-28, 31.

Waller, D. (1982, September 12). A "whydoit?" from The Who. *Los Angeles Times*, p. 82.

Walley, D. (1969, October). Review of *Tommy. Jazz & Pop*, p. 44.

Watrous, P. (1996, May 6). Charm and honesty in Townshend's greatest hits. *New York Times*.

Welch, C. (1966, December 10). The Who fulfilled—and a mini-opera, yet! *Melody Maker*.

Wells, D. (1982, December 8). 3 parties cleared in crush. *Cincinnati Enquirer* (NEWSBANK).

Wendeborn, J. (1982, October 15). Who's Who: Aging rockers roll on to the end. [Portland] *Oregonian* (NEWSBANK).

Wenner, J. (1981). The *Rolling Stone* interviews: Pete Townshend. In P. Herbst (ed.), *The Rolling Stone interviews: Talking with the legends of rock & roll, 1967-1980* (pp. 32-43). New York: St. Martin's Press.

WFBQ Indianapolis. (1993, November 8).

The what and why of The Who. (1968, September 20). *Time*, p. 86.

White, T. (1990). *Rock lives: Profiles and interviews.* New York: Henry Holt.

Who Rarities. (1994, October 1). Produced by VH-1.

Wicke, P. (1990). *Rock music: Culture, aesthetics and sociology* (R. Fogg, trans.). Cambridge: Cambridge University Press.

Wild, D. (1993, March). Who's on Broadway? *Rolling Stone*, p. 21.

Williams, S. (1985, November 24). Townshend and Daltrey solo together. *Newsday* (NEWSBANK).

Williams, S. (1989, June 21). Who are they: They're commemorating their 25th anniversary—and, not so incidentally, making a lot of money. *Newsday* (NEWSBANK).

Williams, S. (1996a, May 6). Townshend on his terms. *Newsday*, p. B3.

Williams, S. (1996b, July 18). Time travelers: The Who turns back the clock at the Garden. *Newsday*, p. B3.

Willis, E. (1969, July). Musical events: Rock, etc. *New Yorker*, pp. 62-65.

Winer, L. (1993, April 23). B'way "Tommy": The Who sell out. *Newsday*, pp. 71, 108.

Who's "farewell" tour ends era, saddens promoter. (1982, October 27). *San Diego Union* (NEWSBANK).

Who's Next. (1987, August). Review of *Who's Next. Rolling Stone,* pp. 80, 82.

The Who Sell Out. (1968, February). Review of *Sell Out. Rolling Stone,* p. 20.

The Who: The Metropolitan Opera House, New York City. (1987, June). *Rolling Stone,* pp. 74-75.

The Who: Thirty Years of Maximum R & B Live. (1994). MCA Records, Inc.

The Who's Tommy: The Amazing Journey. (1993). Elegant Films.

WNEW New York. (1993).

WXRT Radio Chicago. (1994, August 4).

Young, C. M. (1989, July). Who's back: After seven years off the road, can last generation's heroes start making cents in a material world? *Musician,* pp. 64-76, 121.

Young, J. (1989, June). Review of *Iron Man. Spin.*

Index

About the Author

LARRY DAVID SMITH is Associate Professor of Communication at Purdue University in West Lafayette, Indiana. He specializes in narrative critiques of popular media and is the author of *Cordial Concurrence: Orchestrating National Party Conventions in the Telepolitical Age* (Praeger, 1991).